Praise for **Life During Wartime**

"[These] writers sound a sobering warning: the American government is an iron fist in a velvet glove whose purpose remains preserving the status quo and enriching the rich.... It's hard to discount the evidence presented here of heavy-handed tactics (injunctions, informants, provocateurs, mass incarceration) that have Democratic and Republican politicians alike up in arms."—*Publishers Weekly*

"The state has waged a conspiracy against political movements to retain its power and its called counterinsurgency. This book not only exposes the methods, but ways we can fight back."—Robert King, former Black Panther, former U.S. political prisoner, and author of *From the Bottom of the Heap: The Autobiography of Robert Hillary King*

"Government repression can mean kicking in doors and knocking out teeth, but the tactics described in *Life During Wartime* are arguably more dangerous and destructive. The authors weave personal experiences with historical analysis to show how the same counterinsurgency models being used in Iraq and Afghanistan have developed at home. Anyone interested in building stronger movements for social justice should turn to Life During Wartime for it documents not only a history of repression, but a future of resistance."—Will Potter, author of *Green Is the New Red: An Insider's Account of a Social Movement Under Siege*

"*Life During Wartime* is a timely collection demonstrating that knowledge, history, theory, and action provide the means of resisting counterinsurgency's current efforts to limit freedom. It offers us hope in dark times. This is a brilliant combination of activist heart and political mind, demonstrating that history and action matter."—David Price, author of *Weaponizing Anthropology: Social Science in the Service of the Militarized State*

"What is counterinsurgency and what effects has it had on political uprisings and movements? In the highly engaging *Life During Wartime*, the assembled authors break down how the modern surveillance state and counterinsurgency is used against growing political dissent, to de-legitimize political uprisings and its long, often hidden history. The diverse essays showcase various methods and approaches used by the state; from prisons, and unfettered surveillance in the farce called 'ror', to community policing and the deep legac understand state repression and engage effective for social justice movements struggling to exerc organizer, FBI target and author of *Black Flags a* Common Ground Collective

LIFE
DURING
WARTIME

RESISTING COUNTERINSURGENCY

LIFE DURING WARTIME

RESISTING COUNTERINSURGENCY

EDITED BY

KRISTIAN WILLIAMS,
WILL MUNGER,
AND **LARA MESSERSMITH-GLAVIN**

Life During Wartime: Resisting Counterinsurgency

Edited by Kristian Williams, Will Munger, and Lara Messersmith-Glavin

All essays © 2013 by the named respective authors.

This edition © 2013 Kristian Williams, Will Munger, and Lara Messersmith-Glavin & AK Press.

ISBN: 978-1-84935-130-0
e-ISBN: 978-1-84935-131-7

Library of Congress Control Number: 2013930242

AK Press
674-A 23rd Street
Oakland, CA 94612
USA
www.akpress.org
akpress@akpress.org

AK Press UK
PO Box 12766
Edinburgh EH8 9YE
Scotland
www.akuk.com
ak@akedin.demon.co.uk

The above addresses would be delighted to provide you with the latest AK Press distribution catalog, which features several thousand books, pamphlets, zines, audio and video recordings, and gear, all published or distributed by AK Press. Alternately, visit our websites to browse the catalog and find out the latest news from the world of anarchist publishing:
www.akpress.org | www.akuk.com
revolutionbythebook.akpress.org

Cover design and interior layout by Margaret Killjoy
birdsbeforethestorm.net

Special thanks to the Institute for Anarchist Studies for their support of this project: www.anarchiststudies.org

Contents

PART ONE

CONCEPTS & CONTEXTS

PREFACE
Life During Wartime

WILL MUNGER

WHEN FACING INCREASING WAVES OF STATE REPRESSION, IT IS DIFFICULT TO take bearings amidst the swells and troughs.

How have the social and political horizons been affected by the domestic application of counterinsurgency? How can rebels and radicals build smarter strategies for resisting state repression?

Life During Wartime is a set of texts emerging from several years of collective research into the history, theory, and practice of counterinsurgency. While counterinsurgency is often associated with low intensity conflicts on the so-called peripheries of empire, this collection critically analyzes how the United States' domestic security apparatuses are adapting the strategies, techniques, and technologies of counterinsurgency.

Because the contemporary move toward counterinsurgency is largely decentralized, this collection approaches its subject from several different angles. Introductory chapters lay out the theory and internal logic of counterinsurgency. Intergenerational dialogs and analyses clarify how domestic repression strategies have changed over the past quarter century. Site-specific research shows the planning and implementation of security operations explicitly drawing from counterinsurgency. Critical analyses from several different active struggles offer insight into the potentials for resistance amidst a shifting social and political terrain.

Many of the contributors first met at the 2011 Counter-Counterinsurgency Convergence in Portland, Oregon. The Convergence wove together three goals. It opened space for a historically grounded encounter between researchers and activists who work on issues of security, repression, and the shifting nature of the state. The Convergence worked "to map the contours of transnational counterinsurgency while designing strategies that contest, confound, and confront both counterinsurgency and empire."[1] Several talks and research presentations from the Convergence appear in following pages.

After assembling Convergence materials, the *Life During Wartime* editorial collective also reached out to social movement participants whose current work involves resisting and subverting counterinsurgent apparatuses. These exchanges resulted in several articles that broaden the range of topics covered in this book to include gang injunctions, ecological movements, border controls, the Occupy movement, and more. Another result was a sustained dialogue about how current movements are learning to fight smarter amidst a shifting terrain of repression.

This collection is intended as a step towards strengthening our movements' collective understanding of repression and not as a definitive encyclopedia of resistance to domestic counterinsurgency. We hope this text contributes to grassroots strategic rethinking and facilitates long overdue debates that can orient us in the face of oncoming storms.

Finally, acknowledgement and gratitude are owed to Walidah Imarisha for helping to spark this endeavor; Sam Law, Holly Mills, Caitlin Arnold, Scott Lewis, Paul Silverstein, Jacqueline Dirks, Charlene Makley, and the Reed College Anthropology Department for their support of the Convergence; and the Institute for Anarchist Studies for supporting field research.

NOTES

1   Text from 2011 announcement for the Counter Counterinsurgency Convergence, http://
     countercoin.wordpress.com.

INTRODUCTION:
Insurgency, Counterinsurgency, and Whatever Comes Next

KRISTIAN WILLIAMS

PART ONE:
REPRESSION, COUNTERINSURGENCY, AND THE STATE[1]

OPPOSITIONAL POLITICAL MOVEMENTS INEVITABLY FACE—AND THEREFORE ought to expect—repression at the hands of the state. But, while quick to condemn the most obvious and violent manifestations of this repression, especially when directed against peaceful groups, the left has been slow to grasp the strategy underlying the state's approach.[2]

We tend to characterize repression as the state's response to crisis, rather than seeing it also as a means to preserving normalcy. Hence, it has been very difficult to recognize it in quiet times, and when it does appear it seems like an exception, an excess, a panicked overreaction.

But repression does not always come dressed up in riot gear, or breaking into offices in the middle of the night. It also comes in the form of the friendly "neighborhood liaison" officer, the advisory boards to local police departments, and the social scientist hired on as a consultant. Repression is, first and foremost, a matter of *politics*: it is the means the state uses to protect itself from political challenges, the methods it employs to preserve its authority and continue its rule. This process does not solely rely on force, but also mobilizes ideology, material incentives, and, in short, all of the tools and techniques of statecraft. We have to understand repression as involving both coercion and concessions, employing violence and building support. That is the basis of the counterinsurgency approach.

SOME DEFINITIONS

One of my objectives in this introduction is to broaden and deepen our understanding of repression. I am not seeking to *redefine* "repression," but simply to apply the standard definitions with greater consistency; so I am employing the term in its usual political sense, referring to the "process by which those in power try to keep themselves in power by consciously attempting to destroy or render harmless organizations and ideologies that threaten their power."[3]

"Counterinsurgency"—"COIN" in the military jargon—is not simply synonymous with "repression," but has a narrow, technical meaning, which of course relies on the definition of "insurgency." U.S. Army Field Manual 3-24, *Counterinsurgency*, explains:

> [An] insurgency [is] an organized movement aimed at the overthrow of a constituted government through the use of subversion and armed conflict....
>
> Stated another way, an insurgency is an organized, protracted politico-military struggle designed to weaken the control and legitimacy of an established government, occupying power, or other political authority while increasing insurgent control.

The definition of counterinsurgency logically follows: "Counterinsurgency is military, paramilitary, political, economic, psychological, and civic actions taken by a government to defeat insurgency."[4]

ENDS AND MEANS: LEGITIMACY AND STATECRAFT

"Counterinsurgency," then, refers to both a type of war and a style of warfare. The term describes a kind of military operation outside of conventional army-vs.-army war-fighting, and is sometimes called "low-intensity" or "asymmetrical" combat. But counterinsurgency also describes a particular perspective on *how* such operations ought to be managed. This style of warfare is characterized by an emphasis on intelligence, security and peacekeeping operations, population control, propaganda, and efforts to gain the trust of the people.

This last point is the crucial one. As FM 3-24 declares: "*Legitimacy is the main objective.*"[5]

The primary aim of counterinsurgency is political.[6] That's why, in the context of the American occupation of Iraq, we heard career officers arguing that "victory in combat is only a penultimate step in the larger task of 'winning the peace'."[7] And it's the need for legitimacy that they're referring to when they say that "Military action is necessary…but it is not sufficient. There needs to be a political aspect."[8]

The political ends rely in large part on political means. As the RAND Corporation's David Gompert and John Gordon explain:

> In COIN, the outcomes are decided mainly in the human dimension, by the contested population, and the capabilities of opposing armed forces are only one factor in determining those outcomes. The people will decide whether the state or the insurgents offer a better future, and to a large extent which of the two will be given the chance.[9]

The RAND report is titled, appropriately, *War by Other Means*. War, as Clausewitz observed, is politics by other means; and politics, as Foucault reasoned, is war by other means.[10] But in counterinsurgency, the means are not so "other." In COIN, war-fighting is characterized by the same elements as state-building—establishing legitimacy, controlling territory, and monopolizing violence.[11]

Consequently, the "newness" of counterinsurgency is in some respects debatable. Clearly there is nothing new about repression. And the combination of force and legitimacy is a lot of what makes a state a state. But, as one participant in a 1962 RAND symposium on counterinsurgency recalled, at that time there was already a distinctive COIN perspective emerging—and it was a minority view:

> Probably all of us had worked out theories of counterinsurgency procedures at one time or another, which we thought were unique and original. But when we came to air them, all our ideas were essentially the same. We had another thing in common. Although we had no difficulty in making our views understood to each other, we had mostly been unable to get our respective armies to hoist in the message.[12]

Clearly, then, *something* was new.

What sets COIN apart from other theories of repression, I believe, is the self-conscious acknowledgement that the state *needs* legitimacy to stabilize its rule, and that under conditions of insurgency its legitimacy is slipping. In other words, from the perspective of counterinsurgency, resistance is not simply a matter of the population (or portions of it) refusing to cooperate with the state's agenda; resistance comes as a consequence of the state failing to meet the needs of the population.

It is possible, therefore, to see COIN as representing a "liberal"[13] or even "radical"[14] politics. Yet such apologetics miss the larger point. As a matter of *realpolitik* the authorities have to respond in some manner to popular demands; however, COIN allows them to do so in a way that at least preserves, and in the best case amplifies, their overall control. The purpose of counterinsurgency is to prevent any real shift in power.

Counterinsurgency is all about preserving (or reclaiming) the state's authority. Violence and territory are inherent to the project, but it is really legitimacy—"the consent of the governed," "societal support"—that separates the winners from the losers.[15] As Gompert and Gordon put it: "The key in COIN is not to monopolize force but to monopolize *legitimate* force."[16]

The strictly military aspects of the counterinsurgency campaign are, of course, necessary; but so are the softer, subtler efforts to bolster public support for the government. Both types of activities have to be understood as elements of political power.

OUTSOURCING COUNTERINSURGENCY

This emphasis on the state may be somewhat misleading, however. Increasingly, the state relies on private entities to do the work of repression.[17] The most controversial aspect of this trend is surely the U.S. government's use of military "contractors"—that is, mercenaries—for security and combat operations.[18] But the government is also, with greater and greater frequency, relying on private companies to collect and store and sometimes analyze vast quantities of data on the individuals in whom it takes an interest—thus handily dodging legal restrictions of government surveillance and any requirements concerning the disclosure of the information it collects.

More subtly, the state has—at least sometimes—advanced its agenda by partnering with nonprofit and non-governmental organizations, even those nominally aligned with its critics. By this process, known as "co-option," the state grants certain types of opponents access, representation, or direct support and, by tacit exchange, gains influence that can help capture, channel, or contain political opposition. The result is that—however imperfectly—the state exercises control not only *over* the institutions of civil society, but *through* them.

The RAND Corporation's Daniel Byman argues:

> The ideal allies for a government implementing control are, in fact, nonviolent members of the community the would-be insurgents seek to mobilize. Strong moderate forces can be interlocutors to the community in general and an alternative for political action that does not involve violence. If moderates side with the government, they can provide superb intelligence on radical activities.... If regimes can infiltrate—or, better yet, cooperate with—mainstream groups they are often able to gain

information on radical activities and turn potential militants away from violence.[19]

These privatized efforts are easy to incorporate into the statist understanding of counterinsurgency if we think of the state as a *network* of institutions, rather than as a single unified organization. Authority may extend outward through this network from some nominal center, but power is, to a very large extent, both constituted by and exercised through the network itself; and the constituent parts in turn make demands and help shape the agenda of the whole.[20]

What's more puzzling, analytically, is the adoption of COIN by private companies pursuing their own autonomous ends. For example: In early 2011, a hacking campaign revealed that a computer security firm, HBGary Federal, along with two other companies, offered to set up a "fusion cell" like those "developed and utilized by Joint Special Operations Command (JSOC)" to help the U.S. Chamber of Commerce collect and analyze information on its critics. At the same time, they began tracking the Twitter accounts of union supporters and mapping the relationships between them using specialized software provided by Palantir[21]—a company that produces a similar program, which (they brag) "is broadly deployed in the intelligence, defense, and law enforcement communities…."[22]

The use of counterinsurgency techniques to advance a corporate agenda is politically troubling, since it involves private firms using surveillance and repression to create a political climate suitable for their narrow economic interests. In other words, it shows yet another way that corporations use their resources to exercise power to limit political freedom and undercut democracy. Analytically, it also points to larger questions about the current relationship between the state and capitalism, and the tensions between broad developments that have emerged simultaneously over the past 40 years.

COUNTERINSURGENCY AND NEOLIBERALISM

In the U.S., during the period of prosperity following World War II, the main means for achieving control over the workforce was *negotiation,* along with the ameliorating influence of the welfare state. These social benefits were not *gifts* offered by a generous ruling class, but were won through years of struggle and instituted as a means of preserving stability. Since the 1970s, however, these sorts of institutional arrangements have been in sharp decline.[23] Christian Parenti has argued forcefully that the late twentieth-century prison boom and the simultaneous militarization of domestic police forces are the result of shifts in the strategy of capitalism.[24]

The question this history presents—and to date it remains an open question—concerns the relationship between counterinsurgency and neoliberalism. Both terms are associated with Latin American "dirty wars." But counterinsurgency is largely about expanding government services and offering concessions, while neoliberalism reduces services and imposes austerity. Famously, in Iraq, this contradiction produced a dispute between the Defense Department and the Coalition Provisional Authority, with the backing of the State Department. Paul Brehmer, with his nearly dictatorial powers, advocated privatizing Iraq's state-owned enterprises; Deputy Undersecretary of Defense Paul Brinkley, on the other hand, wanted the occupying authorities to get the state-owned businesses running again in order to provide goods, services, and jobs to the population.[25]

Is it the role of counterinsurgency to clean up the mess that neoliberalism makes? Or is COIN used to carve out the space in which market conditions can be imposed, to create the requisite stability for neoliberal reforms? And how different are these formulations, either conceptually or practically?

Several hypotheses come to mind: The difference might be ideological, reflecting different assumptions about society, the economy, and the state. Or perhaps neoliberalism is the offensive program, and counterinsurgency the defensive. Or maybe—and this is the account I happen to favor—counterinsurgency prioritizes the state's interest in stability and neoliberalism prioritizes capitalism's interest in maximizing profits, the choice between them being determined by the precise degree to which the state is able to act autonomously.

One rather tantalizing possibility is that the contradiction between neoliberalism and counterinsurgency is less important than the contradictions inherent to each of them. Neoliberalism is premised on a rejection of state intervention, yet it requires a repressive state to overcome popular opposition to its program, especially its austerity measures.[26] Counterinsurgency identifies legitimacy as its main objective, but it is often employed as a means to securing ends that are fundamentally illegitimate—such as maintaining corrupt, exploitative, or oppressive regimes.[27]

Interestingly, whichever mode is dominant at the moment, the ultimate limit they each face remains the same—popular resistance.

PART TWO: NETWORK ANALYSIS, NOT CONSPIRACY THEORIES

POPULAR RESISTANCE CAN be understood as the inverse of state legitimacy: as one increases, the other declines.

Because they see insurgency as primarily a crisis of legitimacy, some COIN theorists argue that, conceptually, the "War on Terror" has been a mistake:

first, because it identified "terror" as the problem; and second, because it proposed "war" as the solution.

> The idea of GWOT [the Global War on Terror] ... has fixed official U.S. attention on terrorists, with insufficient regard for the hostility that exists among vastly larger numbers of Muslims.... The indelible image of jihadists scheming alone in remote mountain caves is less the reality of Islamic insurgency than is far larger numbers of jihadists moving freely among Muslim populations.... [T]error inspired by Islamic extremism is part of a larger pattern of Muslim 'resistance' that has significant popular appeal.... [Therefore,] terrorism cannot be defeated unless the insurgencies in which it is embedded are successfully countered.

Thus, the solution requires not just military might but "intelligence, political action, civil assistance, and other nonmilitary means that might curb Islamic militancy more effectively and at less cost and risk" than simple combat.[28] The proposed solution, in other words, follows logically from the analysis of the problem. Counterinsurgency, therefore, cannot be understood as a rigid formula to be implemented by rote; it must be sensitive to the details of the particular insurgency it is facing. And as important, counterinsurgency operations have to adapt and develop as the insurgency does.

THE COIN CYCLE
According to the RAND Corporation, revolutions (and thus counter-revolutions) go through three stages: a proto-insurgency, a small-scale insurgency, and major insurgency.[29] At first, in the "proto-insurgency stage" the movement is

> small, narrowly based, vulnerable, and incapable of widespread or large-scale violence. Proto-insurgents may be barely noticeable, not seen as having the potential to inspire insurgency, or dismissed as criminals or inconsequential crack-pots. Therefore, during proto-insurgency, the most important aspect of COIN is to understand the group, its goals, its ability to tap popular grievances, and its potential. In turn, shaping the proto-insurgency's environment, especially by improving governance in the eyes of the population, may deny it wider support....

In the second stage, as "a small-scale insurgency" the movement begins "attracting followers beyond its original cadre," and it may "commit more daring and destructive acts against the state, not (yet) with a view toward replacing it, but to demonstrate its capabilities, be taken seriously by the population, and recruit." For the government, therefore, "shaping political and economic conditions to head off popular support for the insurgency is imperative." Direct military intervention is *not* recommended at this stage: "As long as the insurgency is still small, action against it can and should remain a police and intelligence responsibility."

If the movement survives, it may develop into a "major insurgency." While it is still "essential" that the state collect information about the movement and intervene to shape social conditions, at this point, "forceful action against the insurgents by regular military units may be unavoidable."[30] Both the overt use of force and covert surveillance, infiltration, and disruption will increase. Emergency powers may be granted, civil liberties suspended, and the life of the overall population increasingly restricted.[31]

Of course, the aim of any counterinsurgency campaign is a return to normal—that is, to the lowest level of manageable conflict.[32] In effect, this is a return to the proto-insurgency stage: opposition is either channeled into safe, institutional forms, or suppressed through normal police and intelligence activity.[33]

The British strategist Frank Kitson summarizes the overall process:

> In practical terms the most promising line of approach [in COIN] lies in separating the mass of those engaged in the [revolutionary] campaign from the leadership by the judicious promise of concessions, at the same time imposing a period of calm by the use of government forces....
>
> Having once succeeded in providing a breathing space by these means, it is most important to do three further things quickly. The first is to implement the promised concessions.... The second is to discover and neutralize the genuine subversive element. The third is to associate as many prominent members of the population, especially those who have been engaged in nonviolent action, with the government....[34]

No one pretends that victory comes easily, and many critics within the armed forces point to Vietnam and Algeria as proof that it simply cannot work. COIN advocates, then, have been at pains to show that victory is at least possible, and that counterinsurgency represents the government's best hope. One RAND study, headed by Christopher Paul, analyzed 30 recent counterinsurgency operations and found that the government lost in 22 of the conflicts (73%) and prevailed in eight (27%). Furthermore the researchers found that *in every case* the competence of the counterinsurgency effort was the best predictor of success or failure: A predominance of good COIN practices is correlated with victory, and a predominance of bad COIN practices is correlated with defeat. "[W]ithout exception, COIN forces that succeed in implementing more good practices than bad win, and those that do not lose."[35]

A separate RAND study, written by Martin Libicki, examined 89 insurgencies spanning the years 1934–2008. It found that in 28 cases the government was victorious, in 25 the government was defeated, 20 had a mixed result, and 16 were ongoing at the time of the study.[36] Bracketing the current conflicts, we see that the government won about 37% of the time, lost 34%, and met with mixed results in 27% of the cases. In contrast to those of the Paul report, Libicki's conclusions are more tentative and varied, pointing to factors beyond the competence of the state forces, including: the aims, tactics, and organization of insurgent forces; social factors such as democracy, urbanization, and industrialization; international support for each side; and public opinion.[37]

Both of these studies, however, only measure the outcomes of insurgencies that have already escalated beyond a certain threshold. Thus they ignore the much larger number of proto-insurgencies that never reach the second or third stage.[38] One implication is that, as an insurgency proceeds to the later stages, the chances that it will succeed increase markedly.[39]

Reflecting on his efforts in Kenya, Cyprus, and Northern Ireland, Kitson observed:

> Looking in retrospect at any counter-subversion or counter-insurgency campaign, it is easy to see that the first step should have been to prevent the enemy from gaining an ascendancy over the civil population, and in particular to disrupt his efforts at establishing his political organization. In practice this is difficult to achieve because for a long time the government may be unaware that a significant threat exists, and in any case in a so-called free country it is regarded as the opposite of freedom to restrain the spread of a political idea.[40]

Concerns with liberty aside, that is exactly what Kitson recommended: restrict the spread of ideas, prevent radicals from achieving influence, and disrupt their efforts to establish oppositional organizations.

RAND, too, advocates early, preemptive action short of direct military force. The problem remains that at the first stage subversion is not obvious and the state may not know that a threat exists. Worse, the real threat must be understood as extending beyond the insurgents themselves—the militants, radicals, and subversives—to include the population they appeal to, the grievances they seek to address, and the social conditions that produce those grievances.

THE SOCIAL SCIENCE OF REPRESSION

To meet the challenges of counterinsurgency, the security forces have had to shift their understanding of intelligence. Since the cause of the conflict is not just a subversive conspiracy, but necessarily connects to the broader features of society, the state's agents cannot simply ferret out the active cadre, but need to aim at a broad understanding of the social system. The U.S. Army/Marine Corps Field Manual on Counterinsurgency, FM 3-24, incorporates this perspective, arguing that strategists "require insight into cultures, perceptions, values, beliefs, interests and decision-making processes of individuals and groups."[41]

This sort of intelligence work is concerned with questions that are primarily sociological.[42] And so, a great deal of FM 3-24 is concerned with explicating basic social-science terms like "group," "coercive force," and "social capital." In fact, the entirety of Appendix B is devoted to explaining "Social Network Analysis and Other Analytic Tools." It offers this picture of how such analysis is practiced:

> [A] social network is not just a description of who is in the insurgent organization; it is a picture of the population, how it is put together and how members interact with one another....
>
> To draw an accurate picture of a network, units need to identify ties among its members. Strong bonds formed over time by family, friendship, or organizational association characterize these ties. Units gather information on these ties by analyzing historical documents and records, interviewing individuals, and studying photos and books.[43]

The security forces can no longer focus narrowly on the hunt for subversives or terrorists, but must also collect information on the population as a whole. This changes, not only the *type* of information they're seeking, but also the *means* they use to collect it. A RAND report on information warfare in counterinsurgency emphasizes:

> Even during a security operation, the information needed for counterinsurgency is as much or more about context, population, and perceptions as it is about the hostile force.... [O]nly a small fraction of the information needed would likely be secret information gathered by secret means from secret sources.[44]

HUNTING THE ELF

John Allison, an anthropologist briefly enrolled in the U.S. Army's "Human Terrain System" program, received a stark education in the military uses of such analyses. Allison resigned in protest amidst war game exercises involving military action in "Lakeland," an imaginary secessionist state to the northeast of Kansas City. In this training scenario, Human Terrain Teams are sent in to Lakeland in response to unrest—specifically, anti-coal actions by the Sierra Club and more radical groups, including the Earth Liberation Front. The Human Terrain Team students were assigned the following tasks:

> 1. 'Find out more details on the criminal activity.'
>
> 2. Find out the best conduits to pass 'information' (PsyOps and InfoOps) to the local population....
>
> [3. P]roduce a 'Research Plan' to understand the situation at the IATAN power plant—people's concerns, desires, etc., and identify those who were 'problem-solvers' and those who were 'problem-causers,' and the rest of the population whom would be the target of the information operations to move their Center of Gravity toward that set of viewpoints and values which was the 'desired end-state' of the military's strategy.[45]

Earth and animal liberationists seem to weigh heavily in the paranoid imaginings of the authorities. A 2009 anti-terror drill at the Cherry Point Air Station in North Carolina centered on a scenario in which environmentalists storm the base, take hostages, and kill Marines. Likewise, a Homeland Security training held on the UC Berkeley campus included an exercise in which animal right activists took hostages and held them at gunpoint.[46]

Meanwhile, in the real world, neither the ELF nor the ALF have ever taken hostages, killed Marines, or formed a breakaway republic. Yet law enforcement agencies have engaged in a decade-long campaign broadly targeting the environmental and animal rights movements. Much of the police action has seemed ham-fisted and ridiculous, as when the FBI sent agents to photograph two people handing out leaflets about vegetarianism.[47]

But the peak of the campaign—thus far—was marked by "Operation Backfire," a set of coordinated arrests launched in December 2005. The Backfire defendants were accused of a series of Earth Liberation Front and Animal Liberation Front arsons from the late 1990s—activities the FBI characterized as "domestic terrorism."[48] Altogether eighteen people were indicted. Two are still at large, fifteen were sent to prison for as long as 13 years, and one—William Rodgers—killed himself soon after his arrest.[49]

The investigation into the ELF started to gain traction in 2001 when a woman in Eugene, Oregon called the police to report her truck stolen. She named her roommate, Jacob Ferguson, as the likely thief, and the police, noticing that the theft coincided with an arson at an SUV dealership, deduced that Ferguson might have started the fire. Both the roommate and the cops were mistaken, but the error proved lucky for law enforcement. Twice Ferguson was called before a grand jury and, in 2004, when the cops finally threatened him with prosecution, he offered them information on more than a dozen Earth Liberation Front and Animal Liberation Front actions, naming the people involved. Ultimately, he would provide details on 22 separate acts of sabotage. Ferguson then spent months traveling the country and wearing a wire to collect evidence for prosecutions. He recorded 88 hours of audio, representing 40 conversations. After each new arrest, the police pressed the suspects for information on others. A few of those arrested fought the charges, or plead guilty without implicating anyone else; most, however, gave evidence against their comrades in exchange for lighter sentencing.[50]

Backfire succeeded largely thanks to a single lucky break, followed by a systematic effort to turn activists into informants. But to be able to take advantage of their good fortunes, the cops needed a substantial amount of more general background information about the community they were investigating. That effort started at least as early as 1999. The anarchist journal *Rolling Thunder* describes the approach:

> What we know of the early Backfire investigation points to a strategy of generalized monitoring and infiltration. While investigators used increasingly focused tools and strategies as the investigation gained steam—for example, sending 'co-operating witnesses' wearing body wires to talk to specific targets—they started out by sifting through a whole demographic of counter-cultural types.... Police accumulated tremendous amounts of background information even while failing to penetrate the circles in which direct action was organized. The approximately 30,000 pages of discovery in the Oregon cases contain a vast amount of gossip and background information on quite a few from the Eugene community.[51]

It's likely that the documents released in preparation for trial are only one small portion of the information actually collected: circumstantial evidence suggests that at least some of the Backfire defendants were subject to warrantless wiretaps managed by the National Security Agency.[52]

INTELLIGENCE AND COERCION
The Eugene investigation was in some respects typical.

As one RAND report explains, counterinsurgency requires that the security forces collect both "information on specific individuals" and "information in which the actions or opinions of thousands, perhaps even millions, of people are highlighted."

"Why collect such information?" the researchers ask.

The answer they provide is quite revealing. Properly analyzed, the information can be used in five types of activity: (1) police and military operations "such as sweeps, roadblocks, or arrests"; (2) assessments of progress in the counterinsurgency campaign ("How many people have been hurt or killed in the war; what kind of crimes are being committed; who is getting employment and where; and who is staying put or leaving the country?"); (3) "the provision of public services, whether security and safety services (e.g., an efficient 911 system) or social services (e.g., health care, education, and public assistance)"; (4) identifying insurgents ("distinguish those willing to help from those eager to hurt"); and, (5) the coercion of individuals for purposes of winning cooperation and recruiting informants: "information about individuals may be necessary to persuade each one to help the government rather than helping the insurgents."

This last point shows something of the recursive relationship between intelligence and coercion. In an insurgency, both sides rely on the cooperation of the populace; therefore they compete for it, in part through coercive means. As RAND researcher Martin Libicki writes: "Those uncommitted to either side should weigh the possibility that the act of informing or even interacting with one side may bring down the wrath of the other side." Whoever is best able to make good on this threat will, Libicki argues, receive the best information: "The balance of coercion dictates the balance of intelligence."[53]

"DISRUPTION MODE"

Of course, the better the intelligence, the more effective the use of force can be. And the purpose of identifying the insurgent network is to disrupt it.

Consider the police efforts to frustrate protests against the 2008 Republican National Convention: A year in advance of the demonstrations, police informants began attending protest planning meetings around the country, while local cops and the FBI kept anti-RNC organizers under intense surveillance—following them, photographing them, going through their garbage.[54] Among the organizations targeted were Code Pink, Students for a Democratic Society, the Campus Anti-War Network, and most famously, "The RNC Welcoming Committee" (which later produced "the RNC 8" defendants).[55]

Simultaneously, the Minnesota Joint Analysis Center invested more than 1,000 hours coordinating with other "fusion centers" around the country to collect, analyze, and disseminate information on suspected anti-RNC activists. The fusion center drew its information from a staggering array of sources, using law enforcement and Defense Department databases, as well as DMV records, court document, and information provided by private businesses.[56]

In the days before the convention, police used this information to mount raids of activists' homes and meeting places, seizing banners, political literature, video equipment, and computers.[57] By the Convention's close, more than 800 people had been arrested, many rounded up *en masse*.[58] The majority—584—were released without charges, or had their cases dismissed. Only ten arrests resulted in felony convictions.[59]

But the conviction rate may be beside the point. One commander stated frankly that the police weren't building prosecutable cases, but were instead acting in "disruption mode."[60] The law, in other words, was a secondary concern; politics was primary.

PART THREE:
THE COMING COUNTER-COUNTERINSURGENCY

I BEGAN THIS essay by suggesting that a great deal of political repression goes unrecognized, and that the left needs to revise its understanding of repression if it is to resist it effectively. This need has developed alongside—in some respects it is a reflection of—similar changes in the thinking of our adversaries.

With the emergence of the counterinsurgency model, the state has ceased to view subversives in isolation from their surrounding society. Increasingly, it has directed its attention—its intelligence gathering, its coercive force, and its alliance building—toward the population as a whole. Repression, in other words, is not something that happens solely, or even mainly, to activists. And it is not something that occurs only in times of crisis, or in response to a direct threat.

Also, it is not something that necessarily happens in secret. It is worth pausing here to note that, while both sides may use clandestine or illegal methods, there is nothing inherently conspiratorial in either insurgency or counterinsurgency. One of the breakthroughs in the counterinsurgency approach was its shift away from J. Edgar Hoover–style conspiracy theories;[61] our understanding of counterinsurgency, likewise, cannot be rooted in conspiracy thinking. Insurgency and counterinsurgency are not the result of invisible actors and secret plots; they are the predictable result of broad and observable social forces, especially those related to inequality. The secret or conspiratorial aspects are operational decisions made pursuant to a broader strategy, not the strategy itself. One of the remarkable things about COIN is how much it occurs in public view—in fact, how much it relies on the public's cooperation.

Repression comprises all those methods—routine and extraordinary, coercive and collaborative, covert and spectacular—used to regulate the conflict inherent in a stratified society. Our task is to decipher the politics implicit in these efforts, to discern the ways that they preserve state power, neutralize resistance, and maintain social inequality.

Our further task is to respond. As repression is primarily a political process, any adequate response must take—at least in part—a *political form*. It will not be enough, as is usual, to put the case before a jury, or adopt strict secrecy in the name of some cloak-and-dagger notion of "security culture." Such things must be done at times, but both these responses, though in very different ways, treat repression chiefly as a legal, and thus technical, problem. They are also entirely defensive. While such devices may protect the individual or small group with greater or lesser efficacy, they do not generally touch—or even attempt to touch—the overall *system* of repression, to say nothing of the social iniquities that system maintains.

Whatever defensive measures may be necessary, an effective response to repression must also involve an *offensive* component—an attack against the apparatus of repression, which will (if successful) leave the state weaker and the social movement stronger. This outcome, of course, should be the aim from the start.

CHALLENGES TO COIN

It is, in a sense, misleading to speak solely in terms of *responding* to repression. Repression exists already. It intervenes preemptively. It forms part of the context in which we act. Oppositional movements cannot avoid repression; the challenge, instead, must be to overcome it.

We cannot afford to underestimate our adversaries, but it is just as mistaken to think them omnipotent. There's a debate within military circles as to how often counterinsurgency works, and some argue that it *cannot* work—but nobody suggests that it *always* works. Sometimes governments fall.

The difficulties inherent to counterinsurgency are numerous: it's labor-intensive and resource-intensive, requires vast amounts of localized intelligence, demands both overwhelming force and careful negotiation, and calls for painstaking analysis, strategy, and planning. That's a pretty tall order even for the most competent organizations. And there are also features of our adversaries' institutions and ideologies that add to their troubles.[62] However good their strategy, in terms of implementation they are constrained by budget difficulties, personnel issues, office politics, inter-agency rivalries, and pure bureaucratic indifference.[63] Any organization can suffer from these faults, but authoritarian institutions seem to especially prone to them. Moreover, these agencies tend to foster a particular outlook among their members, which makes it very hard for them to understand the social movements they confront.[64] Almost as a matter of course, government agents have tended to misunderstand and misinterpret the aims, plans, organizational structures, ideas, and motivations of liberatory movements. Counterinsurgency emphasizes their need to understand these things, but that doesn't mean that they do.

Furthermore, so long as our society remains so starkly unequal, so long as it continues along a suicidal course toward environmental catastrophe, and so long as people lack the control over the conditions of their immediate lives—there will be *cause* for unrest. Even working together in perfect coordination, the cops, military, and intelligence agencies combined cannot change that fundamental fact, without also changing the entire structure of our society—that is to say, without giving up the one thing, above all others, that they are meant to defend.

INSURGENT THINKING

When facing counterinsurgency, we need to learn to think like insurgents. We have to recognize, and even embrace, political and strategic complexity. Every insurgency is different, and a single insurgency may take very different forms from one year to the next, or one street to the next. There are no set paths or ready formulas, which is not the same thing as saying there are no strategies. But our strategies have to correspond with the reality we face, not with an idealized version of some past revolution or some future utopia. And we cannot elevate our own favorite tactics—whether pacifist or insurrectionist—into articles of faith.

The antidote to repression is, simply put, *more resistance*. But this cannot just be a matter of escalating militancy. Crucially, it has to involve broadening the movement's base of support. We have to remember that an insurgency is not just a series of tactical exchanges with the state. It is, instead, a contest for the allegiance of the population. For the rebels, no less than for the authorities, *"Legitimacy is the main objective."*

NOTES

1   Parts of this essay appeared previously in Kristian Williams, "The Other Side of the COIN: Counterinsurgency and Community Policing," *Interface: A Journal for and about Social Movements,* May, 2011, http://interfacejournal.net.

2   When I speak of "the left," I am speaking broadly of all those forces, from lukewarm liberals to insurrectionary anarchists, seeking to push society in the direction of greater equality.

3   Alan Wolfe, *The Seamy Side of Democracy: Repression in America* (Reading, Massachusetts: Longman, 1978), 6.

4   United States Army, FM 3-24, *Counterinsurgency* (December 2006), 1-2.

5   U.S. Army, FM 3-24, 1-113.

6   U.S. Army, FM 3-24, 1-123.

7   Justin Gage, et al., "Winning the Peace in Iraq: Confronting America's Informational and Doctrinal Handicaps" (Norfolk, Virginia: Joint Forces Staff College, Joint Combined Warfighting School, September 5, 2003), 1.

8   General David Petreaus, quoted in "General Says Iraq Talks Critical," *BBC News*, March 8, 2007, http://news.bbc.co.uk/2/hi/6429519.stm.

9   David C. Gompert and John Gordon IV, et al., *War by Other Means: Building Complete and Balanced Capabilities for Counterinsurgency* (Santa Monica: RAND, 2008), 76.

10   Michel Foucault, *"Society Must Be Defended": Lectures at the Collège de France, 1975–76,"* eds. Mauro Bertani and Alessandro Fontana, trans. David Macey (New York: Picador, 2003), 15–6.

11   Max Weber, "Politics as a Vocation," in *The Vocation Lectures*, ed. David Owen and Tracy B. Strong, trans. Rodney Livingstone (Indianapolis: Hackett Publishing Company, 2004), 33.

12   Frank Kitson, quoted in Stephen T. Hosmer, "Foreword to the New Edition," in *Counterinsurgency: A Symposium, April 16–20, 1962*, by Stephen T. Hosmer and Sibylle O. Crane (Santa Monica: RAND, 2006), iv.

The strategy of counterinsurgency has its critics, highlighting its clash with the existing military culture. Military traditionalists see the world, so to speak, through a gun scope—clearly, but narrowly. They want wars, not "nation-building." And they worry that COIN will make the army soft and its soldiers will forget how to fight. See, for instance: Gian P. Gentile, "Eating Soup With a Spoon," *Armed Forces Journal*, September 2007; or Edward Luttwak, "Dead End: Counterinsurgency as Military Malpractice," *Harper's Magazine*, February 2007.

One thing for certain, though: those who write COIN's obituaries do so prematurely.

The trajectory of David Petraeus' career—until it was destroyed by a stupid sex scandal—suggests that COIN is in the ascendancy, and will remain influential for some time to come: Petraeus came to public attention in 2003, when he used counterinsurgency techniques to successfully stabilize Mosul while the rest of Iraq was in upheaval. In 2006, he oversaw the writing of FM 3-24. In 2007, he was appointed head of all combat troops in Iraq. In 2008, he took over Central Command—giving him authority over all U.S. forces from Egypt to Pakistan. In 2010 he took a small step down in the hierarchy to directly manage the war in Afghanistan. And in 2011 he was put in charge of the CIA. John Barry, "Petraeus's Next Battle," *Newsweek*, July 25, 2011.

In 2012, however, Petraeus' career was abruptly derailed by revelations that he had carried on an extra-marital affair with his biographer, Paula Broadwell. The affair was uncovered in the course of an FBI investigation in which, as Glenn Greenwald put it, "based on a handful of rather unremarkable emails sent to a woman fortunate enough to have a friend at the FBI, the FBI traced all of Broadwell's physical locations, learned of all the accounts she uses, ended up reading all of her emails, investigated the identity of her anonymous lover (who turned out to be Petraeus), and then possibly read his emails as well." Glenn Greenwald, "FBI's Abuse of the Surveillance State is the Real Scandal Needing Investigation," http://www.guardian.co.uk, November 13, 2012.

It's not clear what Petraeus' downfall will mean for the counterinsurgency approach with which he has become so strongly identified. But even were the military to abandon COIN, it is likely that such a departure will be short-lived. The military swore off COIN after failing in Vietnam, only to pick it up again, in desperation, thanks to Iraq.

13 Hugo Slim, *With or Against? Humanitarian Agencies and Coalition Counter-Insurgency* (Centre for Humanitarian Dialogue, July 2004), 3.

14 Sarah Sewall, "Introduction to the University of Chicago Press Edition: A Radical Field Manual," in United States, Department of the Army, *The U.S. Army/Marine Corps Counterinsurgency Field Manual: U.S. Army Field Manual No. 3-24; Marine Corps Warfighting Publication No. 3-33.5* (Chicago: University of Chicago Press, 2007), xxi.

15 U.S. Army, FM 3-24, 1-113 and 1-115.

16 Gompert and Gordon, *War by Other Means*, xxxvii.

17 Of the 854,000 Americans with "Top Secret" clearance, 265,000 work for private companies. The number of private contractors working for Homeland Security equals the number of government workers the department employs directly; in its intelligence division, 60% of its workforce are private contractors. Dana Priest and William M. Arkin, *Top Secret America: The Rise of the New American Security State* (New York: Little, Brown, and Company, 2011), 179 and 182.

18 For example: Jeremy Scahill, *Blackwater: The Rise of the World's Most Powerful Mercenary Army* (New York: Nation Books, 2008). However, Scahill quotes prominent military officers complaining that "Armed contractors do harm COIN" (23). See also, pages 35 and 135.

19 Daniel Byman, *Understanding Proto-Insurgencies* (Santa Monica: RAND, 2007), 24.

20 This analysis may sound very postmodern, but it is in fact the way states were formed historically. See: Charles Tilly, *Coercion, Capital, and European States, AD 990–1990* (Cambridge: Basil Blackwell, 1990), 104 and 117.

21 Nate Anderson, "Spy Games: Inside the Convoluted Plot to Bring Down WikiLeaks," *Ars Technica.* February 2011, http://arstechnica.com, (accessed February 2, 2012). For More on HBGary Federal, see: Evan Tucker, "Who Needs the NSA When We Have Facebook?" in this volume.

22 Palantir, "About Palantir." http://www.palantirtech.com/about, (accessed February 2, 2012).

23 David Harvey, *A Brief History of Neoliberalism* (Oxford: Oxford University Press, 2007).

24 Christian Parenti, Lockdown America: Police and Prisons in the Age of Crisis (London: Verso, 1999).

25 Frank R. Gunter, "Economic Development During Conflict," *Strategic Insights*, December 2007.

26 Harvey, *Brief History of Neoliberalism*, 21, 69, and 77.

27 David Price observes, "The *Manual* [FM 3-24] admits that in order for counterinsurgency to succeed, an open acknowledgement of, and corrective action towards fundamental problems must occur … , but the *manual* does not say what is to be done if the fundamental causes to be addressed are neo-colonialism, the installation of illegitimate governments, and illegal invasions." David H. Price, *Weaponizing Anthropology: Social Science in Service of the Militarized State* (Petrolia: Counterpunch, 2011), 185.

28 Gompert and Gordon, *War by Other Means*, 6–8.

29 The report also considers a final possibility—*foreign military intervention.*

30 Gompert and Gordon, *War by Other Means*, 36–37.

31 United States Army, FM 31-20-3, *Foreign Internal Defense Tactics, Techniques, and Procedures for Special Forces* (Washington, D.C., September 20, 1994), 3-23.

32 David Galula, *Counter-Insurgency Warfare: Theory and Practice* (New York: Frederick A. Praeger, 1965).

33 Joseph D. Celeski, *Policing and Law Enforcement in COIN: Thick Blue Line* (Hulbert Field: The JSOU Press, 2009).

34 Frank Kitson, *Low Intensity Operations: Subversion, Insurgency, Peace-Keeping* (Hamden: Archon Books,1971), 87.

35 Christopher Paul et al., *Victory Has a Thousand Fathers: Sources of Success in Counterinsurgency* (Santa Monica: RAND, 2010), 94.

36 Martin C. Libicki, "Eighty-Nine Insurgencies: Outcomes and Endings," in Gompert and Gordon, *War by Other Means*, 377.

37 Libicki, "Eighty-Nine Insurgencies," 395–96.

38 Libicki, "Eighty-Nine Insurgencies," 394.

39 Gompert and Gordon, *War by Other Means*, 39. It is for this reason that David Price wryly remarks, "once a nation finds itself relying on counterinsurgency for military success in a foreign setting it has already lost." Price, *Weaponizing Anthropology*, 190.

40 Kitson, *Low Intensity Operations*, 67.

41 U.S. Army, FM 3-24, 3-2.

42 To help answer these questions, the Pentagon has invested $50 million to recruit social scientists to serve as analysts in its "Minerva Program." Hugh Gusterson, "Militarizing Knowledge" in *The Counter-Counterinsurgency Manual: Or, Notes on Demilitarizing American Society*, ed. Network of Concerned Anthropologists Steering Committee (Chicago: Prickly Paradigm Press, 2009), 51.

The military prefers anthropologists as its in-house advisors, perhaps for historical reasons. But owing to that same deeply problematic history, it has had difficulty finding enough anthropologists to fill its positions.

For a good overview covering the history of militarized anthropology, see Montgomery McFate, "Anthropology and Counterinsurgency: The Strange Story of their Curious Relationship," *Military Review*, March–April 2005. (McFate is a military apologist, and her analysis is almost wholly reactionary. But I believe it is possible to use all of her evidence, and even some of her arguments, to reach exactly the opposite conclusions.)

For an insider's view on the military's training programs for the Human Terrain Teams, with a critical assessment of the program's potential, and an accounting of its failure to draw actual anthropologists, see: Price, *Weaponizing Anthropology*, Chapter 9: "Human Terrain Dissenter: Inside Human Terrain Team Training's Heart of Darkness." In that article, John Allison details the make up of his HTS class: "Though they want to have an anthropologist be the HTT Social Scientist, they are happy to get anyone with what could be remotely considered an 'advanced' degree in a social science. So, although we have five anthropologists, we also have several historians, an economist, an industrial psychologist, etc; and only one for the Iraq group and one (me) for the Afghanistan group has any previous experience in the region of their destination" (Quoted on 160).

43   U.S. Army, FM 3-24, B-47 and B-49.

44   Martin C. Libicki, et al., *Byting Back: Regaining Information Superiority Against 21st-Century Insurgents.* (Santa Monica: RAND, 2007), 133.

45   Quoted in Price, *Weaponizing Anthropology*, 167.

46   Will Potter, *Green is the New Red: An Insider's Account of a Social Movement Under Siege* (San Francisco: City Lights Books, 2011), 235.

47   Potter, *Green is the New Red*, 74.

48   United States Department of Justice, "Eleven Defendants Indicted on Domestic Terrorism Charges [press release]," January 20, 2006. http://www.justice.gov/opa/pr/2006/January/06_crm_030.html, (accessed July 29, 2012).

49   Mike Carter, "Woman Found Guilty of Arson in 2001 University of Washington Fire," *Seattle Times*, March 6, 2008; Mike Carter, "Sentencing Friday for Firebomb Maker in 2001 UW Arson," *Seattle Times*, March 14, 2012.

50   Potter, *Green is the New Red*, 67–8.

51   "Green Scared? Preliminary Lessons of the Green Scare," *Rolling Thunder* 5 (Spring 2008), 30.

52   Potter, *Green is the New Red*, 69–79.

53   Libicki *Byting Back*, 21–23.

54   G.W. Shulz, "Assessing RNC Police Tactics, Part 2 of 2," *Center for Investigative Reporting*, September 2, 2009, http://centerforinvestigativereporting.org/articles/assessingrncpolicetacticspart2of2.

55   Heidi Boghosian, *The Policing of Political Speech: Constraints on Mass Dissent in the U.S.* (New York: National Lawyers Guild, 2010).

     For more on the RNC 8 case, see: Layne Mullett, Luce Guillén-Givins and Sarah Small "From Repression to Resistance" in this volume.

56   G.W. Shulz, "Assessing RNC Police Tactics, Part 1 of 2," *Center for Investigative Reporting*, September 1, 2009, http://centerforinvestigativereporting.org/articles/assessingrncpolicetacticspart1of2; and Shulz, "Assessing RNC Police Tactics, Part 2 of 2"; and G.W. Shulz, "What's the Minnesota Joint Analysis Center?" *MinnPost.com,* September 1, 2009.

     Fusion Centers are multi-agency bureaus that compile, analyze, and redistribute information. The ACLU warns that the arrangement can sidestep legal restrictions on data collection and that it monitors the everyday behavior of large numbers of innocent people. Mike German and Jay Stanley, "Fusion Center Update" (New York: American Civil Liberties Union, July 2008); and, Michael German and Jay Stanley, "What's Wrong with Fusion Centers?" (New York: American Civil Liberties Union, December 2007).

57   Boghosian, *The Policing of Political Speech.*

58   Shulz, "Assessing RNC Police Tactics, Part 1."

59   Emily Gornun, "Last RNC 8 Protestors Plead Guilty—But Remain Defiant," *St. Paul Pioneer Press*, October 20, 2010.

60   Shulz, "Assessing RNC Police Tactics, Part 2."

61   Ken Lawrence, *The New State Repression*, (Portland, Oregon: Tarantula, 2006) 6.

For an example of the "Communist conspiracy" model in action, see: Ben Jacklet, "'It Should Be Noted'," *Portland Tribune*, September 17, 2002.

62 David Price observes, concerning FM 3-24: "The *Counterinsurgency Field Manual's* approach to anthropological theory was not selected because it 'works' or is intellectually cohesive: it was selected because it offers an engineering-friendly, false promise of 'managing' the complexities of culture as if increased sensitivities, greater knowledge, [and] panoptical legibility could be used in a linear fashion to engineer domination. It fits the military's structural view of the world." Price, *Weaponizing Anthropology* 190.

63 Dana Priest and William Arkin offer a stark picture of the bureaucratic woes affecting American intelligence agencies, including: opacity (even to themselves), floods of redundant and useless information, interagency feuds, ignorance of foreign cultures, mission creep, a loss of focus, poor coordination, and a lack of accountability. See: Priest and Arkin, *Top Secret America*, especially Chapter 5, "Supersize.gov," pages 79–103.

64 George Orwell, the former imperial policeman (and then, revolutionary socialist), commented on this fact long ago: "The policeman who arrests the 'red' does not understand the theories the 'red' is preaching; if he did, his own position as bodyguard of the moneyed class might seem less pleasant to him." George Orwell, "The Lion and the Unicorn," in *The Collected Essays, Journalism and Letters of George Orwell, Volume II: My Country Right or Left, 1940–1943*, eds. Sonia Orwell and Ian Angus (New York: Harcourt Brace Jovanovich, 1968), 72.

COINTELPRO TO COIN:
Claude Marks Interviewed

WALIDAH IMARISHA AND KRISTIAN WILLIAMS
APRIL 16, 2011

CLAUDE MARKS'S FILM *COINTELPRO 101* SERVES AS BOTH AN INTRODUCtion to and a retrospective on the FBI's campaign of repression against the movements of the '60s.

Claude Marks screened the film at the Counter-Counterinsurgency Convergence, and spent an hour or so answering audience questions afterward, about the movie, about his own life, and about his work with the Freedom Archives.

Walidah Imarisha and Kristian Williams met up with Marks the following week at the "Law and Disorder" conference at Portland State University. He was generous enough to grant us an extensive interview.

POLITICAL IMPRISONMENT AND FREEDOM ARCHIVES

Kristian Williams: *Can we start by having you tell us a little bit about yourself and your history?*

Claude Marks: At a pretty young age, through peers whose families were very politicized, I was able to start informing myself about things like the Cuban revolution, the backstory to Vietnam—even during the Kennedy presidency—so that it led me to understand something about global politics at a pretty young age, and something of the role the U.S. played in the world.

So then, fast forward to a general inclination to understand the civil rights struggle. I was living in L.A., so during the Watts rebellion, I had more of an open thought process to what was going on beyond the most racist stereo-typed thing about "black people out of control." That led me to some very significant conflict with my father, who felt like we should arm ourselves against the "oncoming black hordes"—which was so clearly a racist thing. Even though I couldn't articulate it at such a young age, I felt very viscerally about taking it on. In a similar period I remember getting punished for going to an anti-war demonstration that was attacked by the cops. Rather than being supported for that I was being punished at home.

By the latter part of the '60s, as the Panthers in L.A. started to mobilize broader community support for their struggle, I was willing to sneak out and go to some of their stuff. Once I left high school and moved to Northern California, and was intentionally cut off by my family, I was able to more freely make my way into the political arena, and through circumstance ended up becoming a journalist with the Pacifica station in Berkeley. Because of their poor staffing, I was thrust into this role of covering a lot of stuff—the Third World strike at Berkeley, the Black Panther Party, the anti-war movement.

It was somewhat later that I felt that I had reached the point in my life that it made sense to more formally be an activist in addition to being a journalist. I reached a point where I felt like I had to make some stronger commitments politically. So that work in conjunction with the work of the black movement and indigenous land occupation, which I participated in, as well as the Puerto Rican independence movement led me to a more committed and radical place—to the point where I chose to do clandestine work.

Ultimately that meant participating in a conspiracy to break a Puerto Rican political prisoner out. It was, unfortunately, infiltrated from within the prison. But we discovered that we were under surveillance and, upon discovering that, our grouping of people managed to elude the FBI for a significant period of time—close to 9 years. At the conclusion, we felt our own isolation was such that, in the long run, it would make more sense to negotiate some sort of surrender. That way the majority of the group could reengage in public work.

We understood that it would mean prison time. But because there was a finite period of time put in front of us, it would be worth it, so that in the long run we could reengage in radical political work. So that was how we came to that conclusion as a collective. We made the decision and placed ourselves in the hands of the state, making it clear that we weren't going to collaborate or debrief at all. So that's what we did.

I did prison time, and in the course of that re-networked myself to open the possibility of doing media work again. The whole conception of what now becomes the Freedom Archives becomes a reality at the point where I get out of prison.

Williams: *Can you say more about the Freedom Archives?*

Marks: A number of different collectives were working at a radio station in Berkeley, many of us had started working together in the early '70s. A lot of the programmers at the station really had roots in various oppressed communities, reflecting the interest of those communities and the politics of the struggles that connected with them. That was a pretty radical concept; it was in contention with the radio station and ultimately was somewhat ghettoized. But because we felt strongly about our work we retained copies of that material ourselves. At least we had some foresight in stuffing it in boxes and hanging on to it.

So some pretty incredible material was at our disposal. And, through happenstance, in January of 2000 we found a small space. By pooling our money we could afford to bring the material together, collectively build shelving, and start to get it out of boxes—start this whole process of seeing what's there.

As we were doing that we also put together our first project—a sampler of the material, which we envisioned would be the basis for telling people about the collection and trying to raise some more serious money to preserve the material. That sampler was our first kind of reassertion of a radical collectivity among independent producers and collectives. And that becomes the genesis of what we are now—having done a series of audio and video documentaries, reasserting a commitment to issues around imprisonment and political prisoners, a sense of internationalism, a sense of the importance of radical culture, and trying to figure out ways to connect with newer generations.

Our intent from the very beginning was to create something that was really grassroots. Every time we tried to get any NGO funding, we realized that this was way too radical to stay on the map of any nonprofit corporate funding stream. That was really fortunate, because it meant a slow and steady growth as a project without any kind of ties to a more conservative political agenda.

In the last eleven plus years, it's actually grown as a resource. The knowledge of it has increased. And our focus on subjugated history, a history that isn't accessible through other means—the heartbeat of the collection—has proven to be something that other people would want to support and utilize. So we continue to try to aspire to meet that kind of expectation.

Williams: *And the films grew out of that effort?*

Marks: Yes, we started doing audio initially. Our first project beyond the sampler, which was called *Roots of Resistance*, was an audio CD called *Prisons on*

Fire. It was a tribute to George Jackson, remembering his murder, and a tribute to the Attica Rebellion. Both happened in 1971.

That was an audio piece, and that led us to do a number of other pieces over time, some shorter edited video pieces about three political prisoners. We thought that it was important to start to give voice to folks who were locked up for some really serious amounts of time. We did a video on women in prison called *Charisse Shumate: Fighting for Our Lives*, which utilized some actual hearings that took place in women's prisons in California—about conditions, about abuse, about the struggle for health rights. It was really an amazing project to work on.

We've done other stuff—a program about the anniversary of the coup in Chile, which was structured around some material from one of our collective members who happened to be working at Radio Havana during the coup in 1973. The Cubans were the only people bringing audio material out of Chile during the coup that didn't fit into the U.S. propaganda machine. So because of his work at Radio Havana we were able to broadcast news from Chile, and some thirty years later we were able to draw on that material and talk about the significance of the coup in Chile in the context of the current U.S. offensives around the world.

Things of that nature—trying to understand the U.S. empire as a global thing, and see how it is responsible for oppression of people within the U.S. as well. We make the connection through both a political vision of the world, or our understanding of the continuity of different facets, and also by acquiring the material to historically draw on it for people who weren't alive or didn't experience it in the same kind of way.

LEGACY OF TORTURE AND COINTELPRO 101

Williams: *So, the most recent film is COINTELPRO 101.*

Marks: I think it's helpful to talk about the genesis of that project.

In December of 1973 I interviewed Herman Bell after he was arrested in New Orleans and transported to New York State for trial. It was at first the New York Five case, and after a hung jury, charges were dropped against two men so it became the New York Three case. In interviewing him, he started talking about how a number of Panthers were arrested in New Orleans; how people were tortured and forced to sign statements implicating themselves and others in a police murder that took place in San Francisco in 1971. In doing a number of programs, including interviewing one the of the torture victims, we were able to support a campaign to expose the torture leading to the dropping of charges in 1975.

Well, fast forward to 2003. We started hearing about an investigation about that same San Francisco case. Having saved the original interviews we were compelled to anticipate, in terms of the state strategy, an attempt to recriminalize the Panthers, to create another "terrorism" case in the wake of 9/11.

In 2005, a number of people, all former Panthers, were called before a grand jury. They all resisted. At the point when they're released, when the grand jury expired, we all met together, and thought: Well, let's get busy doing interviews and discuss the repression in the context of what happened in 1973. So we worked on this film called *Legacy of Torture*, a relatively short documentary that historically contextualized the COINTELPRO attacks against the Panthers and more specifically the torture of Panthers in New Orleans In 1973.

The week of the premiere, charges were filed. Eight people were arrested. Six former Panthers are swept up in early morning raids of their homes. Two others are still in prison—two of the New York Three.

We realized that this film could actually be used to mobilize a broader movement in support of the eight. *Legacy of Torture* did in fact mobilize people, as a piece of independent media. The press conference that we held at the premier of the film in San Francisco—which turned out to be the week of the busts—was totally mobbed by the media, because it was front page stuff. So we were able to hand them copies of this video that talked about torture, COINTELPRO, and attacks on the Black Panther Party. And the news broadcasts that night had to address these issues in a way that preempted the government strategy to totally control the messaging, to vilify these men, and to put them away quickly and quietly. The opposite happened.

After a prolonged struggle of many years, for the most part they were forced to back down and drop charges on six people, and a couple of the folks who were doing time copped to reduced charges that didn't add to the sentences that they were serving. (Update: In August 2011, after over 4½ years, the judge dismissed the final charges for insufficient evidence.)

In doing *Legacy of Torture*, we felt that the broader question of how COINTELPRO functioned, this war against radical movements in the U.S., had to be told in more depth somehow. Not only because it was an important part of the history, but because it also frames and contextualizes both current repression and the reality for political prisoners now in their third or fourth decade of imprisonment. That's what we undertook to do, and *COINTELPRO 101* is a result of that.

Because of the impact of *Legacy of Torture*, we're hopeful that people can embrace *COINTELPRO 101* as a useful tool for talking about the Patriot Act, post-9/11 repression, Islamophobia, the criminalization of immigration, mass imprisonment, and political prisoner issues—all to help us understand the continuity of state repression, the government violence against popular movements, against radical resistance, against groups that assert their rights to self-determination.

THEN AND NOW: ESCALATION

Walidah Imarisha: *How was COINTELPRO different from some of the earlier repression, like McCarthyism, or the more current incarnations like the Green Scare and the War on Terror?*

Marks: Well, I think that the way it breaks from McCarthyism is in the sense of its unrestrained violence and its willingness to actually assassinate people—whether it's the death squads at Wounded Knee, whether it's the murder of Panthers like Fred Hampton and Mark Clark in 1969, or the militarization of police violence towards the Panthers more generally.

In most of these cases the various movements in the U.S. took very clear positions against the war in Vietnam, against the participation by their communities in the war effort. And people were also looking at other successful revolutionary struggles in the world, as colonialism was challenged and overthrown, people identified this to be a viable model for how to transform relationships in the U.S. This represents a crisis for U.S. imperialism. And one of the ways that the state apparatus comes to terms with crisis is by using counterinsurgency to put down the rebellion, irrespective of the cause.

They came to power as a result of being armed and waging genocidal warfare, and they choose to maintain power through the same means. They don't want to push overt violence beyond a certain point if they don't have to; but if they have to, they will. Whether it's an urban rebellion, or whether it's an organization, they're going to put it down, and they'll use any means at their disposal to do it. That's what COINTELPRO is evidence of.

And so, in that period since, they do affect change in the inability of those organizations to grow, and as they put people away, or literally remove them from the face of the earth, they have a tremendous impact on the ability for that radical momentum, on the ability for that sort of liberatory politics, to grow. So that becomes effective. And they use other means that are equally violent and harmful, like the infusion of drugs into communities, done on a massive basis—people who are drugged aren't going to rebel in the same kind of way as people who are angry and have conscious leadership—and the massive, exponential growth of imprisonment. The way they exert social control is by caging people. So we're seeing that. And then criminalization, and the level of fear-mongering that goes with anti-terrorist language—and the leading response is a military response, an imprisonment response, deportation. At its most extreme, you end up with the rendition program, you end up with secret prisons, you end up with torture, whether its Abu Ghraib or Guantánamo. You legitimize Control Unit prisons, try to literally destroy people for what they believe in, what they think, what their politics are, their potential to influence other prisoners even at a social level.

They're trying to destroy any kind of resistance activity and thought in people. The terror of police occupation, the impunity of police murder, in particular in black and brown communities or on the reservation, becomes the model for how you exert military control over people for whom capitalism has no use. There is no valuable use for these people any longer. We're exploiting the world more, we're manufacturing elsewhere. So what do you do with all of these people who don't fit? It gives new meaning to the name "surplus labor"; it means surplus communities. We can't figure out what to do with them, so let's put them in cages, let's destroy their will to resist, let's take them out by any means that we have, neutralize them all, really. That's genocidal.

So I would say that things have escalated. As the agenda for capitalism and imperialism has changed, so has their willingness to unleash an unlimited amount of violence—not just by creating this crazy military machine that's functioning on a global basis, but within our own communities.

PSYCHOLOGICAL WARFARE

Imarisha: *You've talked about both the short-term, direct strategies, like "we're going to attack these organizations in specific ways," and also the long-term, like "we're going to flood these communities with drugs, and we're going to imprison these folks." Can you describe more the relationship, as you see it, between COINTELPRO and counterinsurgency? Are there other differences or similarities? Was there any component in COINTELPRO of the "hearts and minds" strategy?*

Marks: The psychological component of COINTELPRO was very strong, and in the film a number of people speak to it: Geronimo Ji Jaga Pratt talks about the ways in which COINTELPRO both makes the costs of stepping up very high to discourage people from taking a more prominent and active role in fighting for change, and also by the criminalization of, say, the Black Panther Party. By criminalizing it through the mass media particularly, it becomes very challenging to maintain a level of community support for an organization whose reputation is being turned into its opposite. It's part of the political isolation of radical groups. Through the use of mass media, the state gets to define the terms. So that becomes a form of, not only psychological warfare within the movements—by creating contradictions and playing upon contradictions that already exist and utilizing them to create a lot of dissension and conflict internally—but also, to convince the public that these organizations are to be feared and really don't have their interests at heart. Anything is fair when discouraging people from supporting resistance.

I think that skill was being refined under COINTELPRO and becomes even more refined now. The state control over the messaging, the corporatization of the mass media, makes it more difficult for the articulation of other politics, for the fair representation of those who are struggling for justice. If you can cut them off by making it difficult to communicate, you can therefore control the terms of the people's thinking about what's actually going on. And not only do you create a mass culture that supports the militarization and the use of violence at the behest of the U.S., both internally and externally, but you also discredit anything that challenges that.

Not that it's impossible to get other points of view from some research, but as a mass phenomenon it becomes very challenging with this omnipresent set of doctrines that are being perpetuated constantly and in a very subtle form: you love the cops; you love the military; you love the flag. Everybody else is a criminal or a terrorist, a miscreant of some sort or another. The networks and the cable stations are all outdoing one another to be more American and more patriotic and more anti-terrorist. And if you challenge it, you don't get to go on that plane, or you lose your job, or something else that's a major problem for you. You end up on the list.

"POST-RACE" RACISM AND BIPARTISAN REPRESSION

Imarisha: *How was race involved in the counterinsurgency of the '60s and '70s, and what does that look like now when we're being told that we're "post-race"?*

Marks: I think you have to look at the settler-colonial nation-state in the context of white supremacy and Eurocentrism—because that is what the U.S. is from its inception—and to recognize that it is willing to be genocidal in pursuit of its goals. It is true in terms of the genocide unleashed on indigenous people who populated the Americas before the Europeans, and it's certainly clear when you look at the enslavement of Africans, and all the wars fought for the expansion of territory—a soft term for stealing people's land. The supremacy of white people, of Europeans—this is the premise and at the heart of the construct. I think that's why COINTELPRO unleashed itself in its most violent forms against non-white people.

So now post-racialism is being fed to people. I don't know that this lie works very well, because it's so obviously *not* that to anyone who experiences racial oppression. The role of the police in the community is so obvious; whether they're black or not, or brown or not, isn't the point. You know, the goon squads at Wounded Knee were Native Americans who were willing to be part of death squads in the counterinsurgency against the American Indian Movement. Who they are is less important that whose interests they serve.

The mythology of a post-racial America is predicated on the acceptance of a black president, or black cops, or Chicanos on the school board, or the many faces of neo-colonialism. Of course this conceit is ridiculous, because when you look at who feels the impact of racial oppression, it ain't white folks. That's not who is predominately being imprisoned; that's not what all the statistics about the economy say. And yet the post-racial argument becomes the language and logic of why people should accept the oppressive relationship to the state. Whether you're black or brown, Asian or white, you can feel better about oppression if you don't believe it's an expression of white supremacy and racism, despite the reality that the state is carrying out a very white-supremacist and racist agenda.

This is part of the mythology of repression and how it functions, and it's part of reinforcing its acceptability that it puts forward a democratic mythology that is liberating and post-racial. The purpose of creating a black figurehead and electing somebody like an Obama is that, under that political leadership, they can actually accelerate a level of repression beyond what preceded him under Bush.

Williams: *Where do you see repression accelerating under Obama?*

Marks: Let's look at Guantánamo, for example. Obama ran on this campaign that he was going to close Guantánamo. You've got people in there who have been imprisoned without charges for close to a decade. Now they're no longer going to be tried in civilian courts. Let's put them under the jurisdiction of a military tribunal, so that we can have secret evidence that they don't have access to, so that they can't challenge the accusations being put forward.

Many things that Obama campaigned on are being reversed. He pretends that he's more about civil rights, but the reality is the opposite. A renditions case has been brought against a private contractor, a subsidiary of Boeing in California. The suit was an attempt prosecute the organization responsible for the planning and logistics of rendition flights, which has people kidnapped and either put in a secret prison or tortured by a third party nation. The U.S. retains plausible deniability. The logistics are done by this identifiable corporate entity within the boundaries of the United States. But when they were sued in court, that whole process was ended by the Obama administration, claiming the suit violates the national security interests of the United States. The justification for short-circuiting any kind of judicial process is building upon similar moves that happened under Bush—rather than retreating from that as an approach, Obama is maintaining or even accelerating the national security interest justification.

If you've got the power, you use the power. That's how it works.

I guess what I'm saying is, the culpability of both political parties makes them in many situations indistinguishable from one another. Look at the Patriot Act—which is a pretty complex set of legal doctrines that were somehow voted into law almost immediately after 9/11. That's a set of legal constructs that was being worked on for a long time. It has its origins in a bill written and passed under Clinton, the Anti-Terrorism and Effective Death Penalty Act of 1996. That act is a significant first step in ending *habeas corpus* rights, among other things. In practice it also had a huge impact on prisoners by eliminating their rights to education, recreational programs, art programs, music programs, all that stuff. Now the State is going to hard-line the people in cages. Take away any kind of civility to the process of doing time; and their rights to challenge their imprisonment; and increase the sentences; and codify the right of the federal government to invoke the death penalty. And all that happens under Clinton, a Democrat. I'm convinced that they started the process of writing the next iteration of repressive laws, the Patriot Act, after the passage of the 1996 law.

This is a huge, strategic implementation of repressive mechanisms; it is green-lighted by a government bipartisanship that constitutes this great democracy of ours.

CONTINUITIES OF STRUGGLE AND REPRESSION

Williams: *During the question and answer at Reed, after the film, you outlined a trajectory of struggle and repression that went from the Black Panthers to George Jackson to Attica to Marion to Control Units and Communication Management Units. Could you say more about that, and what it signifies?*

Marks: Let's isolate the question of prisons within that, just to limit the scope.

You have a movement within the prisons that reflects mass forms of the assertion of human rights in various oppressed communities. There's the emergence of radical political thinking inside the prisons at the heart of these demands—in some cases leading the politics in the communities, and certainly influenced by the liberation politics of public organizations, whether it's the Panthers, or the Brown Berets, the Puerto Rican Independence movement, or the American Indian Movement. Much of the political thinking both inside and out reflects the rising international situation—national liberation, anticolonialism, certainly the values of socialism.

Obviously in a very oppressed and repressed confined situation like a prison, people are looking for answers to explain their world and their existence as caged human beings; they are often times open to looking at a more worldly political analysis. And they see themselves as playing a role in their people's liberation—to help resolve some of the social contradictions in their own communities. As prisoners, they experience the most refined, most microcosmic version of oppressive conditions: the expression of State violence is much more intense, the expression of racism is much more intense—all that taking place within the prisons. It's not hard to imagine which people would want to organize themselves and do something about it. So you get the Folsom Manifesto, so you get the Attica Manifesto, and you have the emergence of leading political thinkers and actors within prison movements.

People like George Jackson develop their politics within the black population in prison influenced by radical politics outside and by politically radical Islam being practiced in the prisons. That's a fairly suppressed part of that historical memory that Malcolm X talks about—and people like W. L. Nolen, who was a Muslim who played a significant role in the politicization of George Jackson. And that political form of Islam is also responsible for the growth of Eldridge Cleaver, who then becomes part of the Panthers. George Jackson, of course, never leaves prison alive. But radical politics inside become significant, and the level, intensity and profusion of rebellions represented by Attica, Folsom, these different major state prisons, also starts to take place on a much broader scale and is identified as part of liberation struggles.

Putting the rebellions down is a central structural response of the state. There was a necessity to destroy the potential of an unmanageable set of social contradictions within the caged population of the United States in the same way that the growth and expansion of the prisons is part of managing rebellion in the community. It's also the lesson that the state integrates into its racist strategy by preventing the emergence of conscious Third World leadership, making it clear that the cost of rebellion is high.

So you have, in the '80s, the emergence of Control Unit prisons that are designed to physically and socially isolate people, either because of their overt political commitment or because of their potential to influence other people. The state constructs institutions where it can relegate those potential or real leaders to a physical existence in which they no longer can socialize, in which it tries to destroy them, and in which the only means of leaving that totally isolated environment are by rejecting or repudiating a radical politics. The prisons justify this by claiming that people are part of gangs, or gang leaders and the only way back to general population is to become a snitch, to cooperate with the government's agenda.[1]

In the case of the women's Control Unit prison in Lexington, a successful campaign is mounted to close down that experiment. The prototypical prisoners put in there are very conscious women who have very strong roots in various radical movements, and the campaign is successful there. It's not a successful campaign in the case of Marion.

Ultimately Control Unit prisons proliferate, so that many states also have them. Now someone they decide to define as a gang leader or a member of a gang goes to a control unit prison, where they experience sensory deprivation and isolation and restrictions of access to reading material, to phone calls, to other prisoners, to contact visits, to their families and communities. And under the strictures of international law, those conditions are forms of torture. Because isolation over a prolonged period of time does result in the breakdown of the human psyche. And those prisons are proliferating. Today, the new Communications Management Units are simply a form of Control Unit prison that target mainly Muslim prisoners—along with a small number of Green Scare prisoners as well.

The intent of harsh prison conditions, and of mass prison construction, is to keep a lid on growing discontent. I mean, it doesn't always succeed: you still have things like the Georgia prison strike, where people declare that they're not going to work, they're not going to leave their cells, until certain human rights demands are met to improve their conditions. But it's also true that 75 prisoners that participated in that struggle were disappeared within the Georgia state prisons for a time. What happened to these people? No one knows. And the movement on the outside wasn't capable of amassing enough pressure to demand any accountability on the part of the Georgia state prison system. So prisons punish calls for human rights—at least they will until they're stopped.

It's no different than the taking back of Attica by military means. And what happened? 43 people are murdered by the cops, and the prisoner leadership that survives the attack is tortured. That's documented. And it takes 30 years for there to be any level of accountability. By which time, a lot of the victims have died, and some few people are remunerated some pittance that can't possibly reconstruct their lives. Thirty years later, that's what happens.

In the first reports out of Attica, the *New York Times*—the media of truth in this country—was full of bullshit and propaganda about what was going on in there: "The guards had their throats slit by the animals that took over"—none of which happened, *none* of which happened. Almost all of the trials in the wake of the Attica rebellion, the trials of the prisoners, ended in acquittal. Because what was being said by the authorities wasn't factually true. They couldn't prove their charges, and people were acquitted. Just like under COINTELPRO, the entire Black Panther Party leadership in New York was arrested and held in prison for two years—they were ultimately acquitted of all charges after the jury deliberated for only 45 minutes. But the impact of the repression succeeds by dismembering the leadership of the organization, and dealing a severe blow to the organization as a whole.

GREEN AND RED, IN BLACK AND WHITE

Imarisha: *Some of the rhetoric around the Green Scare is that it is the new COINTELPRO, that in the '60s it was the Black Panthers, and now it's the green movement. It is interesting for me, hearing people say the words "political prisoners" and feeling like we mean something completely different in terms of who we mean and the struggles and support work. At the Counter-Counterinsurgency Convergence there were conversations about political prisoners that never touched on race or colonialism. Can you address some of those tensions? What are the paths forward to build a stronger movement?*

Marks: "Green Scare" is a recent term, but the roots of the attack on radical environmentalism—you don't have to go that far back to look at the bombing of Judi Bari. Earth First!, at that point in history, is much more sophisticated politically, not because of its choice of tactics *per se*, but because of its understanding and because it is still attached to its origins with other liberatory struggles. I mean, Judi Bari was unique in the sense of actually having a consciousness about COINTELPRO, and a consciousness about the role of labor, and the destruction of the planet, and an analysis of the corporate infrastructure that drives it, benefits from it, and the ways it is tied into the state. That's why they tried to bomb Judi Bari, because the danger that she represents. In that same period of time, the state also plans what a counterattack means. Because it's the most developed politics that are targeted first.

I think it's interesting and unfortunate that more radical environmentalists don't look to Judi Bari as a model for political leadership. Because she's emblematic of a very holistic part of radical environmentalism that is clear about its anti-corporate nature, that's much more sophisticated in its analysis of the state and its relationship to corporate interests. More recently we have an environmental politics committed to some similar views, but one that I think is a little bit less sophisticated because it doesn't have the same intentional relationship to other movements and is somewhat more isolated. That's unfortunate.

The state is going to go after these politics in very much the same way— maybe not the same level of violence that they directed against Judi Bari and Darryl Cherney and Redwood Summer—but clearly criminalizing environmental and animal rights activity. As in the case of the SHAC folks, prosecuted for running a successful website and an effective anti-corporate campaign. Arson also becomes terrorism. The Animal Enterprise Terrorism Act criminalizes chalking in front of a researcher's home, with potentially huge sentences simply because this form of activity is also now considered a form of terrorism.

Looking at it from the point of view of repression, when they come out and they say that the Animal Liberation Front and the Earth Liberation Front are major targets, it's literally true in some ways, but also they are not the only targets. The state also campaigns to increase the levels of Islamophobia and focuses on the criminalization of immigration.

Now unfortunately, the people who embrace the politics of radical environmentalism and animal rights aren't making these connections politically. And so you end up with a slogan that says "green is the new red." That's an unfortunate slogan, because—not only implicit—but as an explicit part of that, there is an omission of anything that would care to look at the racial politics of the United States. It says: you have the repression against Sacco and Vanzetti and the anarchists; you have the repression that ends up in the execution of the Rosenbergs; leap forward to now, these white kids are being targeted. While true, what does it omit? It omits COINTELPRO. And the racist politics of COINTELPRO have to be at the center of any analysis of fighting against the same empire that's willing to destroy the planet, or that is willing to accept the way animals are dealt with. Regardless of what you think about these issues, they can't be dealt with in isolation.

It's certainly my view that it's worth making a struggle with the activists who identify with those movements, pushing them to have a more far-reaching analysis of empire—both because they will be more effective, but also because I think it's important for them to be committed to an anti-racist politics when they're carrying out their organizing work, and also to take on the issues of male supremacy and homophobia. I mean, that is a holistic picture.

For my work, I've tried to pursue constructive engagement with the activists and supporting the political prisoners in those movements, while at the same time challenging them to develop a more anti-imperialist and anti-racist worldview. I'm opposed to an exceptionalization of white prisoners that doesn't see their imprisonment in the context of people who are in their third or fourth decade inside, who are also fighting for a better world and a more humane kind of society, who represent liberation struggles and the fight for self-determination. The danger is the creation of a mainly white movement that separates its concerns from the reality of imperialist wars and of unrestrained police violence in communities of color.

There are other political problems within the environmental and animal rights movements as well. There have been some attempts by activists emerging from those movements, and people emerging from political imprisonment, to take a more candid and careful look at the kind of situation that has led to such a high percentage of people cooperating with state repression once they were arrested. You have to look at the high degree of collaboration with government investigations if you want to look honestly at the structural problems of the movements, particularly at the embracing of individualized political action. Even though there *are* small groups involved, they've essentially fallen apart at the point at which repression has hit the hardest—not that you don't have examples of that in other movements, but not in terms of the number of people who tried to deal out of their imprisonment once it became clear that the costs were much greater than they anticipated. Without totally overstepping my bounds as a commentator, I think that they, those hoping to rebuild these movements, have a responsibility to take a better look and to challenge some of their assumptions in order to build stronger and more effective movements in the future, movements that can also take on the global empires and how they impact the planet.

You know, the planet will survive—but maybe not without huge sacrifices of human and other animal life. We all have an interest in preventing that. The question is, where do these issues of human rights and planetary survival actually converge? Where can mobilized struggles have the greatest impact? Where is the critique of environmental racism in the politics of environmentalism? I'm not saying nobody discusses these types of issues, but they are not that centrally embraced. Only a more holistic analysis can build some unity with other kinds of communities so that this isn't a white-only issue.

The challenging of narrower ideas can be a way to build the viability of more radical politics, speaking to a more complex understanding of the world and a clearer vision of what a just planet can be. I would also encourage people to build organizations that aren't solely reliant on small groups of unaffiliated people to accomplish tactical results. This challenge will require a commitment to engaging with people with other kinds of politics. This engagement is healthier for everybody. A more holistic and organized movement has the potential for actually succeeding, and not just being an expression of individualized anger.

I think there are examples of positive practice along these lines: as the grand juries hit in the Bay Area in 2005, they targeted former Panthers and they also targeted people in the radical environmental and animal rights circles. Our goal at that time was to bring those folks together to mount a more unified resistance to the grand juries and make an argument for non-cooperation. In the course of a more unitary campaign, real human relations were built for fighting against the repression. I don't want to blow it out of proportion, but there were real relationships that developed, there was joint work, and it was healthy politically.

I point to my friendship with Jeff Luers. I corresponded with him when he was in prison. We didn't agree about everything politically, but I felt it to be my responsibility as an activist coming out of a different set of movements, to recognize the legitimacy of his politics and the need to support him when repression hit. That relationship grew into something where, in the course of time, we learn from one another and our mutual experience.

As a matter of principle, we can't allow political prisoners to become isolated by limiting their support only to the movements that they are part of. That's a mistake. And I think those prisoners also have a responsibility of seeing themselves in a broader, more historical, context in relation to state repression; so they, too—even though they have just embarked upon political imprisonment and may be getting less time—have a responsibility to recognize the people who have preceded them, many of whom have already been locked for three and four decades. To me, building that unity is important.

THE PAST AND THE FUTURE

Imarisha: *You've talked about the control of the message, and history as a way of countering that. Do you see the work of the Freedom Archives in the spectrum of counter-counterinsurgency? And what are other ways that people can protect themselves from state repression?*

Marks: Not to be dismissive, but I don't think movements *can* protect themselves against counterinsurgency. I think they can become more healthy as movements so that they're not so easily impacted by counterinsurgency when it rears up its head. But there are no guarantees.

This is a fundamentally antagonistic relationship between movements and a state. We're relatively weak; they're very strong. It's not going to change very rapidly. So we shouldn't be shocked if they are unfair in their application of the rules that they themselves have made. That's the nature of it, and power is totally skewed in their favor for the time being.

Fundamental change requires a protracted struggle and that's how we need to look at it. That means we need to figure out ways of dealing with repression, and infiltration, and to be prepared for all the tactics that they're willing to use. We need to respond in ways that allow us to succeed despite the repression, to continue to build and to fight for much more human values and a different, more humane kind of world.

I think the answer is global, and not just about our own communities. We do need to organize our own communities, though, and figure out a way to do that that's principled, so that we can overcome tendencies toward sectarianism or subjugation in our relationships to one another. That's particularly important, because we've learned that the state can play upon our internal contradictions very effectively to diminish our capacity. We can be more transparent in our work together, we can root out racism and sexism within our movements. That's in our power to do.

To avoid the repression, to avoid the infiltration—well, that's not in our power at this point. We can't really avoid it. The question is: what isolates the repression, or minimizes its impact? We can succeed, but we really have to live by the values that we claim to be committed to in the ways we build relationships among ourselves and with our communities.

We need to be prepared to challenge oppression and unprincipled behavior in an honest way when we see it take place among us. That's not a process of tearing people down, rather it's an attempt to improve our health as individuals, communities and cultures. We need to respect the fact that there are differences among us, and people experience the impact of capitalism in different ways depending on who they are and what community they're a part of. The key intersections, the principled points of unity that we can arrive at remain to be seen, but we should try lots of different approaches, and must encourage our imaginations in the course of trying to figure out better and better ways of working.

It is with that self-conscious awareness that we [at the Freedom Archives] do our work—which is a very, very, very small slice of trying to contribute to holding on to a more truthful history: not just of the repression, but of the resistance—not to deify people, but to help us remember that what seems like a pretty awful situation today is preceded by a long history of resistance and resistors. We are responsible for holding onto a set of values, politics and culture that have enriched that resistance over time. We can be part of creating a level of healthy oppositional politics that creates healthier interactions and healthier lives and communities.

We do our little piece by trying to keep us honest to our historical antecedents, both understanding the role of the state and understanding the role of the righteous peoples' struggles. We should feel good about carrying on our struggles, not feel bad about how impossible it seems. Understanding radical history can help us interpret and reinterpret the lessons of the past, and eventually we'll build something more profound, and strong, and just.

NOTES

1   Editors' note: This dynamic is reflected in the five core demands of the 2011 Pelican Bay Hunger Strike, which spread to a number of California prisons. http://prisonerhunger-strikesolidarity.wordpress.com/the-prisoners-demands-2/ (accessed Dec 17, 2012).

REPRESSION, CIVIL LIBERTIES, RIGHT-WINGERS, AND LIBERALS:
Resisting Counterinsurgency and Subversion Panics

CHIP BERLET[1]

José Palafox was waiting at the BART Station at 19th and Broadway in Oakland, California on May 9, 2012 when two people approached him. They "identified themselves as Carrie and Matt from the FBI, and served me a subpoena to testify before a federal Grand Jury." Palafox immediately posted a statement online warning other activists that more subpoenas would be issued as part of a "government attempt to gather information on" people who the government suspected were "involved in the animal rights movement."[2]

Another incident in September 2010 involved FBI raids on the homes of activists in Minneapolis and Chicago. Over a dozen subpoenas to appear before a grand jury investigating terrorism were handed out. This grand jury was trying to unravel a network of people organizing against U.S. policies in the Middle East and South America.[3]

Increased government surveillance and repression against anti-war, Muslim, and ecology activists—among others—has given increased urgency to educating activists about state repression and its relationship to right-wing organizing and liberal concepts of civil liberties. Understanding the history, strategies, and tactics of political repression helps us build movements than can resist. At times this leads to some tactics that may seem counterintuitive.

Back in 1970, author James Baldwin concluded in a public letter to radical activist Angela Y. Davis after her arrest, "if they take you in the morning, they will be coming for us that night."[4] That highlights the need for progressive activists to protect each other. Government repression and unnecessary violence can lead to physical assaults against and the murder of targets, especially people of color and armed dissidents.

It is easy for those of us on the left to see the need to defend activists who are our political allies. What about legal government repression using the legal system? Should leftists have defended the group of white supremacists indicted by a grand jury and put on trial in Ft. Smith, Arkansas in 1987? Should the left celebrate when the government shovels up racist trash? What if the right-wingers were charged with supporting terrorism? What if they were eventually charged with "criminal sedition"—defined as a conspiracy to overthrow the U.S. government? What if those charges seemed exaggerated or trumped up? Should we speak up?

DO RIGHTISTS HAVE "RIGHTS"?

WHY SHOULD LEFTISTS defend the Constitutional rights of rightists? "At first it might seem reasonable to be supporting the FBI against the neonazis" or other rightist groups who may even be "physically attacking us or our progressive allies," advises Sheila O'Donnell. "That might seem like one arena where those of us on the left might seem to have common cause with the Feds. But it is always a bad idea." That's the position of a number of experienced progressive activists, both young and old, including some who have faced down government repression targeting the left. O'Donnell is a co-founder of the original Public Eye network, established in the mid-1970s to investigate and expose the relationship between government repression and right-wing attacks on the left.

For those who are card-carrying members of the American Civil Liberties Union (ACLU), the premise is that the First Amendment protections that undergird our civil liberties are for everyone—no exceptions. For civil libertarians, this is a matter of political principle. For leftists, there are strategic and tactical reasons as well. Every time liberals, progressives, or radicals on the left cheer on government repression of right-wing dissidents, the government turns around and uses the same techniques against the most vulnerable activists on the left.

"I like the pure ACLU analysis for both reasons," says O'Donnell, a licensed private investigator who has worked for the ACLU and National

Lawyers Guild on lawsuits against government spying and other forms of political repression.

This chapter will explain the thinking behind these claims, and put them in contemporary and historic context. My conclusion is that it is appropriate to oppose illicit government repression targeting right-wing groups; at times, to temporarily work with right-wing groups to roll back repressive government legislation and policies—and even publicly denounce specific abusive incidents. I know I have a lot of explaining to do.

GOVERNMENT CHARGES OF SUBVERSION AND TERRORISM HAVE A HISTORY OF ABUSES

GOVERNMENT PROSECUTORS USE scary language about subversion, terrorism, and sedition to justify their politicized use of grand juries to probe dissident political activism such as in the incidents described above. Criminal sedition, for example, is a charge used in the past by prosecutors to silence dissent and break up organizing efforts that challenge U.S. domestic and foreign policies. Sedition in this context is a serious criminal charge of advocating the immediate or imminent overthrow of the United States government by force. Conviction carries steep prison sentences.

Arthur Kinoy already knew all about government "criminal sedition" when he heard about the Ft. Smith trial of right-wing white supremacists mentioned above. Kinoy, now deceased, was a famous radical left civil liberties attorney who represented communists and alleged communists charged with criminal sedition in the late 1940s and 1950s. Interviewed in 1998, Kinoy agreed the white supremacists in the Ft. Smith case were "disgusting," but he said, "I'm worried about the charge of sedition against anyone." Kinoy expressed concern with the legal charge of sedition, noting its historical use by the government to attack all dissent, especially on the left.[5] Civil liberties attorney Harvey Silverglate agreed. "I know it is a tricky and emotional issue, but sedition is a very serious charge."

According to Silverglate, the charges in the Ft. Smith case were "patently absurd."[6] Fourteen white supremacists were indicted in the highly-publicized case, including ten charged with criminal seditious conspiracy. Much of the case was based on the testimony of a former associate of those charged: James Ellison of the Covenant, the Sword and the Arm of the Lord. Ellison told the jury he received direct guidance from God, and was a descendent of the biblical King David. The jury deadlocked and the judged ordered the defendants acquitted.[7] The important lesson, suggested Silverglate, was that "You can't be cheering when the government brings a charge of sedition against the Aryan Nations crowd and then be complaining when they bring it against your friends."[8]

In 2012, members of the right-wing Michigan Hutaree Militia went on trial charged with seditious conspiracy, which carries a maximum penalty of life imprisonment. The Hutaree Militia saw themselves as Christian warriors in an underground movement to oppose the federal government and its alleged plans for tyranny.[9] The FBI had planted an informer inside the group, paying him more than $30,000 over a two-year period.[10] Then a New Jersey FBI agent moved to Michigan and entered the group undercover. The District Judge, Victoria Roberts, recognized that Hutaree Militia leader David Stone hated the federal government, but said Stone's "statements and exercises do not evince a concrete agreement to forcibly resist the authority of the United States government," and that while his "diatribes" may have even indicated a "desire to fight or kill" law enforcement personnel, this was "not the same as seditious conspiracy."[11]

COINTELPRO

OBSESSIVE FEAR OF subversion and revolutionary conspiracies motivated the FBI to create the Counterintelligence Program (COINTELPRO), the name given to a specific series of illegal covert projects to crush dissent through surveillance and disruption; it ran from 1956 to 1971. We can learn a lot about how government repression functions by briefly reviewing some features of the program. While some analysts use the term "COINTELPRO" in a generic sense, it is important to understand that specific techniques and tactics of counterinsurgency and repression vary over time.[12]

The original COINTELPRO project was aimed at the Communist Party USA and the Socialist Workers Party, which the FBI could claim included some aspect of foreign involvement. In 1964, however, the Bureau expanded the program to include a domestic organization: the Ku Klux Klan and other "White Hate" groups.

In *The War at Home*, National Lawyers Guild attorney Brian Glick outlined four main operational forms of repression in the United States under COINTELPRO.[13] They are:

Infiltration: Agents and informers did not merely spy on political activists. Their main purpose was to discredit and disrupt. Their very presence served to undermine trust and scare off potential supporters. The FBI and police exploited this fear to smear genuine activists as agents.

Psychological Warfare From the Outside: The FBI and police used myriad other "dirty tricks" to undermine progressive movements.

They planted false media stories and published bogus leaflets and other publications in the name of targeted groups. They forged correspondence, sent anonymous letters, and made anonymous telephone calls. They spread misinformation about meetings and events, set up pseudo-movement groups run by government agents, and manipulated or strong-armed parents, employers, landlords, school officials, and others to cause trouble for activists.

Harassment Through the Legal System: The FBI and police abused the legal system to harass dissidents and make them appear to be criminals. Officers of the law gave perjured testimony and presented fabricated evidence as a pretext for false arrests and wrongful imprisonment. They discriminatorily enforced tax laws and other government regulations and used conspicuous surveillance, "investigative" interviews, and grand jury subpoenas in an effort to intimidate activists and silence their supporters.

Extra-Legal Force and Violence: The FBI and police threatened, instigated, and themselves conducted break-ins, vandalism, assaults, and beatings. The object was to frighten dissidents and disrupt their movements. In the case of radical black and Puerto Rican activists (and later Native Americans), these attacks—including political assassinations—were so extensive, vicious, and calculated that they can accurately be termed a form of official "terrorism."[14]

CONTEMPORARY TECHNIQUES AND TOOLS OF REPRESSION

THERE ARE A variety of mechanisms to chill dissent and undermine movements for progressive or radical change and labor union organizing. *What Everyone Should Know About State Repression* by revolutionary strategist Victor Serge covers the type of government action about which many on the political left already are at least partly aware.[15] Repression, however, is a lot more complicated than what might appear at first glance.

Sometimes repression is carried out by non-government agents. Political repression can involve right-wing paramilitary groups (such as the Ku Klux Klan), private security forces hired by corporate interests, or even hirelings of foreign governments sent to the United States—such as agents of the Iranian SAVAK under the Shah, or informers and disrupters from El Salvador who disrupted the Central America solidarity groups in the 1980s.[16] In 1937 Leo Huberman wrote about *The Labor Spy Racket*, describing how company thugs broke up union organizing, while in the 1970s George O'Toole wrote about *The Private Sector: Private Spies, Rent-A-Cops, and the Police-Industrial Complex.*[17]

Repression can be overt. That is often the case when the target groups are immigrants or people of color. Writing about the Palmer Raids, Louis F. Post describes the year-long campaign as *The Deportations Delirium.* Thousands of swarthy immigrants were deported as dangerous radicals: Italians were deported as suspected anarchists and Russians were deported as suspected Bolsheviks—no matter that there was seldom a shred of evidence of political activity (or even inclination) on the part of the deportees.[18] Today Muslims, Arabs, Mexicans, and Chinese in the United States face similar suspicions of potential subversion.

Repression, however, can also be covert. The FBI COINTELPRO program was secret until it was exposed in 1971 by anti-war activists who raided an FBI office in Pennsylvania and mailed the files to reporters.[19]

Sometimes repression is lethal. Ward Churchill and Jim Vander Wall traced how COINTELPRO operations used the most lethal techniques against people of color, especially the American Indian Movement and the Black Panther Party.[20] Jeffrey Haas documents this in chilling detail in his book on the murders of Chicago Black Panthers Fred Hampton and Mark Clark, shot dead in a raid set up by an FBI informant, who had provided fraudulent information about illegal weapons.[21]

Some of the major forms of repression progressive activists in the United States face today are: grand jury abuse; the use of informers and entrapment; indictments under the Racketeer Influenced and Corrupt Organizations Act (RICO); new laws concerning incitement to violence, actual planning for armed revolution, material support for terrorism, and participation in terrorist plots; and societal witch hunts and subversion panics promoted by right-wing ideologues and hardliners in government law enforcement agencies.

GRAND JURY ABUSE

Joe Iosbaker and Stephanie Weiner of Chicago endured a hard lesson about government repression when some two dozen agents spent ten hours prowling through their house in 2010. The Feds were looking for evidence of "material support" of terrorist organizations.[22] Both Iosbaker and Weiner are active in opposing U.S. foreign policy in South America and the Middle East, but scoff at the idea that they support terrorism. "It was truly to intimidate, to divide, to silence and separate the movement," Weiner told NPR News.[23]

Attorney Michael Deutsch of the People's Law Office in Chicago agrees, charging that the Feds are "using the grand jury as a witch hunt to investigate political activists."[24] Deutsch is coordinating the legal defense of the activists searched and subpoenaed to appear before a grand jury seated in Chicago. The wording of the subpoenas and search warrants handed out in Chicago and Minneapolis made it clear the grand jury was investigating "material support of terrorism" specifically linked to the "Popular Front for the Liberation of Palestine and the Revolutionary Armed Forces of Colombia, or FARC." The Feds were authorized to retrieve "records of travel by the activists in the Middle East and South America."[25]

The way the grand jury process has been manipulated allows the Feds to punish resisters and those who invoke Constitutional safeguards such as the Fifth Amendment protection against self-incrimination. Those subpoenaed resisted testifying before the grand jury. It's a risky tactic, since a judge could sentence them, without a trial, to up to 18 months for contempt of court. The judge can extend that another 18 months.

The news of the raids in Chicago and Minneapolis left Fred Solowey, a long-time labor activist and writer, shaking his head. Back in the 1970s Solowey, now in his '60s, ran the Coalition to End Grand Jury Abuse. The project emerged from the work of National Lawyers Guild attorneys defending progressive, left, and labor activists called before grand juries and asked to testify under oath against their friends, political colleagues, and organizations with which they were active. The Coalition was set up to educate people about how the grand jury process, originally established to protect people from abusive government indictments, had over time turned into a government fishing expedition looking for evidence, or a hammer to beat down dissent and break up movements.

The grand jury "became a political witch hunting institution," says Solowey. "Over time, the process became tremendously perverted because there was no right to counsel" when witnesses were called inside the room where the secret deliberations of the grand jury took place. Solowey explains the idea of changing the rules of how a grand jury worked was "pitched to the public as a way to investigate organized crime." The Coalition to End Grand Jury Abuse was established to move beyond the legal defense of those subpoenaed or indicted, and start a "broader political fight" against the abuses through "political education and legislative action," explains Solowey.[26]

It was the Nixon administration that really refined the idea of using the grand jury process "for intelligence gathering and political disruption," says Solowey. It was not only used to "disrupt the work of political organization that opposed Nixon's policies," but also "it was a way to jail people who were not being linked to actual crimes." Then Solowey nails the underlying issue on the head: "Look, *any* person and *any* criminal defendant should have more rights before the grand jury. There is a potential [for] abuse if it is used against *anyone*." What if next week the right-wing militia activists or some other right-wing group are called before a grand jury? "Learn from it," Solowey advises. "Understand what the government is up to. And to the degree it is relevant, and doesn't disrupt your political work, it is worth people on the left saying something like, 'We think what these right-wingers are doing is un-American, but the attack on them by the government is even more un-American.'"

INFORMERS AND ENTRAPMENT

DAVID McKAY AND Brad Crowder, political activists from Austin, Texas, had years of freedom carved out of their lives in 2009. McKay and Crowder, both in their early 20s, were sentenced to four and two years of prison, respectively, after being set up for arrest by an FBI informer at the 2008 Republican National Convention in St. Paul, Minnesota. They were convicted on charges of making, possessing, and planning to use Molotov cocktail firebombs. The paid informer who nailed them, Brandon Michael Darby, was for a number of years prior to the arrests a well-known and controversial left-leaning political activist based in Austin.

Progressive reporter James Retherford, himself a longstanding political activist, wrote that there were warning signs. "Given his history of bizarre and provocative behavior in Austin and New Orleans, many local activists immediately suspected Darby of manipulating the younger men into a criminal adventure and then busting them."[27]

Government agencies and private intelligence regularly place spies and informers inside dissident groups. They are notoriously difficult to expose with certainty. The standard advice for movement activists is not to try to attribute bad behavior to government spies or mental illness. That reinforces making snap judgments without the needed information. It is also a waste of time. Hold people accountable for their disruptive behavior.[28]

Veteran organizer Victoria Welle was concerned when she saw Darby engage in egotistical, macho, sexist behavior and making dangerous adventurist suggestions: "Some of the lessons I have learned are that if someone is continually engaging in a pattern of disruptive behavior ... that people must make clear agreements about what kind of behavior is OK and not OK and then collectively hold each other to those agreements."[29]

An *agent provocateur* is a particular type of an "informant or undercover operative who incites a target to take unlawful action." *Agents provocateurs*, especially those hired by private companies to break up labor union organizing, were especially prevalent in the late 1800s and early 1900s.[30] The role of *agents provocateurs* is fictionalized in dramatic films such as *The Molly Maguires* and *Burn!* During the Cold War Red Scare (1947–1957), the COINTELRPO Period (1956–1974), and in the years since the 9/11 terror attacks in 2001, real-life informers and *agents provocateurs* have played major roles in producing national headlines about terrorist plots that seldom had any substance in terms of independent capability to engage in violence. These waves of histrionic hyperbole, however, can and do lead to convictions in court, often based more on fear than concrete evidence.

Entrapment is when an *agent provocateur* coaxes a target into discussing plans for an illegal action, and then arrests the hapless target before or after the act is carried out.[31]

RICO ROULETTE

IN 2009, TWO environmental activists in Indiana were arrested under the RICO Act. The pair was "allegedly 'conspiring' to engage in tree sits, participate in non-violent civil disobedience, and make an inflammatory blog post."[32]

The Racketeer Influenced and Corrupt Organizations Act (RICO) was originally justified by its proponents as the only way to break up organized crime networks. When that was normalized in the minds of the public, major liberal feminist organizations organized a campaign to support using RICO to target anti-abortion activists. Clearly there was some sort of organized underground national campaign to target reproductive health clinics and abortion providers with disruption, violent attacks, and assassinations.[33]

In the mid-1980s, "the National Organization for Women (NOW) and National Women's Health Organization clinics in Delaware and Milwaukee filed suit against" leading anti-abortion activist Joseph Scheidler and the others. Author Frederick Clarkson explained the "women's organizations sought a nationwide injunction to stop the clinic invasions and also asked the courts to make those responsible for the attacks pay for the damage they caused." Clarkson wrote that using "laws created as tools against organized crime, NOW and the two clinics set out to prove a nationwide conspiracy of violence and terror against women's health care clinics."

At the time, civil libertarians across the political spectrum warned that extending the reach of RICO was a bad idea. Twenty years later, that warning was shown to be true by Xavier Beltran in a law review article where he noted:

> After the extension of RICO to anti-abortionist protesters in *Scheidler*, it did not take long for private organizations and companies to employ RICO as a legal and financial weapon against other types of non-profit political advocacy and protest groups. Within two years of the *Scheidler* decision, RICO was turned upon animal rights activists in *Huntingdon Life Sciences v. Rokke*.[34]

INCITEMENT, REVOLUTION, MATERIAL SUPPORT, AND TERRORISM

ON PAPER AT least, it is technically legal protected speech in the United States to call for the armed overthrow of the United States.[35] This protection under the First Amendment is derived from a 1969 Supreme Court decision: *Brandenburg v. Ohio*.[36] The actual test language is whether or not the attack calls for "imminent lawless action." On a theoretical basis, this generally means you or your group can urge the overthrow of the United States Government—unless you or your group engage in one or more of the following ill-advised acts of incitement:

- Sets a time in the near future

- Sets a specific place

- Offers specific instructions

- Has the material resources, or can acquire them in the foreseeable future, to launch an attack or engage in violence.[37]

As a result of several Supreme Court decisions, including *Brandenberg*, the Smith Act, used to prosecute Communist Party leaders in the 1950s, is currently considered "unenforceable" by most legal scholars.

The Patriot Act and other legislation, however, along with broad claims by the executive branch under both Presidents George W. Bush and Barack Obama, are used to sidestep the incitement test when it comes to "Material support or resources" given to a group listed by the government as a *foreign* terrorist organization.

According to one legal resource, material support or resources is broadly "defined to mean any tangible or intangible service, training, expert advice, financial services, communications equipment, personnel, transportation, financial services—essentially any kind of help except for providing medicine or religious materials."[38]

The transition from anti-communist scares to anti-terrorist scares was predictable. As early as 1978, civil liberties attorney Frank Donner warned that the term "terrorist" was destined to replace the term "communist" as the scapegoat for countersubversive witch hunts. Donner went on to write two classic books on the subject of spying and repression.[39]

WITCH HUNTS AND SUBVERSION PANICS

IN FEBRUARY 2011, Representative Peter T. King (R-NY), Chairman of the House Committee on Homeland Security, announced hearings on what he called the "radicalization of the American Muslim community and home-grown terrorism." A coalition of over 100 civil and human rights organizations protested the hearing, stating that, as described in the press, "these hearings will single out American Muslims for public scrutiny. By doing so, the hearings will place an entire community under suspicion."[40] The hearings were a farce scripted as part of a right-wing countersubversion effort.

Congressional witch hunts are a mainstay linking state repression and right-wing "subversion panics." They were not only the form used by the Cold War Witch Hunts in the Red Scare of the late 1940s and 1950s. When Ronald Reagan was elected president in 1980, right-wing senators attempted to revive the congressional witch hunt against the left with the Senate Subcommittee on Security and Terrorism (SSST). Initial targets included alternative media such as *Mother Jones* magazine and the Pacifica Radio network.[41] One flyer warned that red-baiting ideologues were "promoting a theory of a domestic 'terrorist' threat which is linked to 'international terrorism.'" This rhetoric should sound familiar because it is identical to the justifications today for the Patriot Act and other erosions of our collective civil liberties.

The Reagan-era SSST committee was blocked by "No More Witch Hunts," a national organizing campaign that produced an educational pamphlet and held rallies in several major cities. In Chicago an audience of over 1,000 heard speeches by Victor Navasky of *The Nation* magazine, and Harold Washington (then an Illinois congressman, later the mayor of Chicago).[42] This is an example of liberals and radicals working in an effective and principled tactical coalition to defend civil liberties from right-wing and state attacks. Debra Chaplan, who helped organize the national campaign while at the Center for Constitutional Rights, says that such broad coalitions are important to build public support, and that progressives need to consider carefully reaching across political boundaries to extend these coalitions.[43]

A national network of liberals and radicals—and a few conservatives and libertarians—have been working collaboratively to develop tactics to roll back the Patriot Act and other attacks on civil liberties for all. This broad network blocked the passage of the "Violent Radicalization and Homegrown Terrorism Prevention Act" in 2008.

In late 2011, this task took on renewed urgency when a coalition of countersubversive liberals and conservatives in Congress revealed plans to stigmatize dissent and target Muslims. In the Senate, a provision in the Department of Homeland Security authorization bill created a coordinator "to counter violent extremism in the U.S., particularly the ideology that gives rise to

Islamist terrorism." In the House, the Wolf Amendment to the intelligence bill would create a commission on "terrorism and domestic radicalization." This shifts attention from criminal acts to "radical" ideas and "extreme" views on politics and religion. This attempt to demonize radical thought and dissent and target Muslims is led by Democratic Senator Joseph Lieberman, a Cold War liberal hawk turned neoconservative bigot.[44]

COUNTERSUBVERSION "EXPERTS"

SUBVERSIVE PANICS AND right-wing witch hunts rely on countersubversion "experts" who tell scare stories often built around pre-existing ethnic, racial, political, or religious bigotry. These experts roll in and out of favor.[45]

In August 2007, the New York City Police Department (NYPD) released a 96-page document entitled "Radicalization in the West: The Homegrown Threat." The study misrepresented sociological theories about mass movements and was laced with bigoted assertions about the nature of Islam. A coalition of groups representing both Muslim communities and civil liberties activists joined to criticize the report, which relied on bogus "expertise."[46] By 2011, several media reports and studies had demonstrated that right-wing Islamophobic "experts" were training federal, state, and local law enforcement and anti-terrorism agents using shockingly biased and inaccurate claims.[47] One such pseudo-expert is Republican Party icon and former U.S. Representative Newt Gingrich; another is terrorism pundit Frank Gaffney, a favorite of the Christian Right. One progressive media group issued a study calling these and others the "Smearcasters."[48] Attorney Thomas Cincotta, active with the National Lawyers Guild, produced a major study on Islamophobic speakers who train law enforcement.[49] Cincotta warns, "we keep exposing these so-called 'experts' as bigots who spread false and inflammatory information about Islam and terrorism, but they keep getting booked to conduct trainings for law enforcement, keep getting invited as guests on TV and radio, and are cited approvingly across the Internet."[50]

Discredited "experts" get recycled as the nation's fear of subversion grows. Various times in his remarkable career, right-wing spymaster John Rees has been condemned or congratulated by the FBI and local police intelligence units for his knowledge of left-wing political movements and groups. In the 1960s, one FBI memo described Rees as "an unscrupulous unethical individual and an opportunist who operates with a self-serving interest. Information he has provided has been exaggerated and in generalities. Information from him cannot be considered reliable." A few years later Rees was again supplying information to the FBI and local Red Squads.[51]

CYCLES OF REPRESSION

REPRESSION BY THE colonial settlers against the original population moved from displacement, to genocide, to counterinsurgency, to a normalized structure of institutional oppression.[52] Andrea Smith extends this model from the Colonial period to the current wars in Afghanistan and Iraq.[53] Historic episodes of repression tied to subversion panics include the passage of the Alien and Sedition Acts; Chinese Exclusion legislation; the Palmer Raids; the antifascist "Brown Scare"; internment of Japanese citizens and residents during World War II; McCarthyism; the FBI's illegal COINTELPRO operations; and the campaign against Muslims and Arabs following the terror attacks on September 11, 2001.

At various times the state moves from containment, to countersubversion, to counterinsurgency as part of the primary goal of defending and extending existing hierarchies of power and wealth. Scholars of repression have noted that state agencies and their privatized proxies are engaged in an endless system of moves and countermoves in which dissidents, radicals, and insurgents develop new ways to organize and government agents and their informers and vigilantes develop new ways to clamp down on that organizing. Sociologist Gary Alan Fine puts it this way:

> The question is how to define troubling actions as illegal subversion. At each point the strategy of the government is to target those who have not committed a crime but who have sympathies that stand against state power. Yet, at each historical moment, agents of social control must work around those constraints that resulted from the past excesses of regime power. Each episode provides the conditions for addressing future troubles. Put another way, government response is culturally path dependent. As Charles Tilly (1996) reminds us, we improvise until we are, for the moment, satisfied with the outcomes.[54]

FEDS AND RIGHT-WING GROUPS

WHY IS IT that the U.S. government seems so ready to make use of the right to violently attack the left, but not the other way around? The history of the United States demonstrates there are complex relationships and dynamics involving consistent state political repression against left-wing dissidents, periodic crackdowns on right-wing dissidents, and occasional state tolerance and even alliances with right-wing vigilantism.[55]

This latter situation was made abundantly clear when in the 1960s an arrow streaked into a Chicago-area anti-war coffeehouse, terrorizing the patrons. The bowman was with the Legion of Justice, a right-wing vigilante group working with the Chicago Police "Red Squad" in a collaborative effort providing information on the left to the FBI.[56] During the COINTELPRO period there was active collaboration between government agencies, private right-wing spies, corporate security, and right-wing vigilante groups. In addition to the Legion of Justice in Chicago, there was Operation Breakthrough in Detroit, and the Secret Army Organization in San Diego.[57]

According to David Cunningham, "The Klan was embraced as a target by a liberal constituency," although not the targets of later operations such as Black Nationalists and the New Left. Cunningham, however, concludes that "largely through the liberal support received for COINTELPRO—White Hate Groups, Hoover and the FBI achieved sufficient insularity and autonomy to establish counterintelligence programs against domestic targets without the approval of Congress or other actors outside the FBI."[58]

Cunningham found that under COINTELPRO the FBI generally sought to "control" the activities of the Klan and reduce its use of violence and other illegal means of political dissent. On the other hand, the FBI sought to "eliminate" the New Left and others deemed to be subversive[59].

The consequences are real. Veteran investigative reporter Ross Gelbspan covered the attacks on the Committee in Solidarity with the People of El Salvador (CISPES) in the 1980s. He reported that hundreds of offices, homes, and cars were broken into, files were ransacked or stolen, but valuable equipment was left untouched. Several years, hundreds of interviews and many thousands of pages of FBI files later, Gelbspan documented how the FBI forged back-channel ties to far-right anti-communist groups in the U.S. and a shadowy network of government agencies and death squads in El Salvador, and how the press was used in the campaign. Gelbspan concluded the perpetrators of the robberies will probably remain a mystery, but reveals the FBI repeatedly lied to Congress about the extent and purpose of its investigations into the same network of Central America activists victimized by the robberies.[60]

LIBERAL SWITCH HITTING

According to sociologist Wojtek Sokolowski, "The state by definition is an oppressive apparatus, and if it is not oppressive it is not a state." He observes, however that since "it is clear, from historical record, that the state sometimes is controlled by the propertied class and sometimes it is not or even acts against the propertied class.... [A] far more interesting approach... is to investigate the conditions facilitating each of the outcomes."[61]

One factor is that centrist political liberals sometimes defend dissent against government repression and sometimes look the other way as the state crushes dissent using legal and extra-legal means. Why does this happen?

In *The Liberals and J. Edgar Hoover*, William W. Keller suggested that liberal legislators are generally uncomfortable having oversight over agencies of police power, and by default, they allow their more reactionary colleagues to craft agencies such as the FBI into tools of repression. That is especially true when liberal elites and elected Democratic Party politicians fear the threat of violence and terrorism more than the threat to civil liberties. In these periods, liberals tend to retreat even more from their normal oversight duties, allowing more repressive actions by the federal government.[62]

My colleague Matthew N. Lyons and I wrote a study of "Repression and Ideology," originally to assist attorneys litigating against intelligence abuse.[63] We theorized that:

- When right-wing groups become system-oppositional or insurgent, they are no longer allies of the state but enemies of the state. Liberals then rally behind the state and tolerate (or openly support) repressive measures to limit the system-oppositional activity of the rightists.

- During periods when liberals and radicals share a criticism of the state that is not shared by rightists, law enforcement agencies often forge ties with system-supportive right-wing groups (even clandestine paramilitary units) in extralegal campaigns against progressive and radical movements that shift the momentum of the criticism toward liberal reforms or simply crush dissent to buttress the status quo.[64]

- When progressive or radical left forces gain a mass following for demands that would radically transform the existing economic or political system, liberals often rally behind the state and tolerate (or openly support) repressive measures to limit the system-oppositional activity of the leftists. The same is true when left and right both raise criticisms of the state.[65]

Liberals often embrace a Centrist-Extremist Theory—the idea that a "Vital Center" protects democracy from "extremists" of the left and right. When leftists use the term "extremist" they are unwittingly assisting right-wing ideologues in marginalizing the left.

DYNAMICS OF COUNTERINSURGENCY & COUNTERSUBVERSION

THE STATE'S REPRESSIVE force matches their often-false assumptions of the threat posed by dissident insurgents. This reflects the sociological maxim: "Situations defined as real are real in their consequences."[66] The level of government repression is based on their *perception* of threat, not the reality of a threat.

Over time, histrionic fear of subversion and revolution has prompted three theories for justifying political repression in the United States:

THE SLIPPERY SLOPE THEORY OF SUBVERSION

- Global liberation movements are not prompted by a genuine response to social conditions but by outside intervention, most often by communists or their proxies.

- Domestic social change movements are not fueled by a genuine response to social conditions but by outside agitators, most often revolutionaries or those under the control of revolutionaries.

- Liberalism is the crest of a slippery slope which leads downhill to the Welfare State, then Socialism, and inevitably to Communism or Totalitarianism.

- Dissent is provoked by subversion. Subversion is a terrorist movement. Terrorism is criminal.

THE ONION RING THEORY OF SUBVERSION

- Subversive cadre bore into the core of all social change movements both at home and abroad.

- To uncover the cadre who are engaged in subversive criminal activity, an informant must work step-by-step from the outside onion ring of non-criminal free-speech activity through several rings of hierarchy toward the center core where the criminal activity lurks.

- Honest-though-naïve activists are often unaware they are being manipulated, and therefore should welcome attempts to expose the core of crafty covert criminal cadre.

THE COUNTERINSURGENCY (COIN) THEORY OF SUBVERSION

- Subversive organizing and insurgent movements are spawned by the government's failure to meet the real and perceived needs of a large segment of the population. Repression is necessary to prevent discontent from being mobilized into lawlessness or even revolution.

The COIN theory of subversion recognizes contemporary sociological theories of how social movements are built and sometimes become insurgent and challenge the government for control. These social movement theories gained strength beginning in the mid-1970s. Up until that time the predominant sociological explanation for social unrest was that people who joined dissident social movements were ignorant, incompetent, politically dysfunctional, mentally unstable, or all of the above.

In an essay on "Counterinsurgency Warfare: The Use & Abuse of Military Force," in *South Asia Intelligence Review*, Vijendra Singh Jafa observes that Lt. Col. Frank Kitson "is the best known exponent of the new ideas on special operations (counter-terrorism, raids, rescue and commando operations etc.) which form much of the basis of the British army's training in counterinsurgency warfare." Kitson is praised as having "had counterinsurgency experience in Malay, Kenya and Cyprus, as well as having commanded the 19th Airportable Brigade in Northern Ireland during the 1970s" and therefore Kitson's "qualifications are beyond question."[67]

Anti-repression researcher Kristian Williams explains that in Kitson's view of counterinsurgency:

- The main battle in revolutionary warfare is political rather than military;

- The left challenges the state's legitimacy before it challenges its military.

- If the state can prevent the challenge to its legitimacy, it can easily handle any armed challenge.[68]

This can be construed by the most zealous ideologues in government law enforcement and intelligence agencies that civil disobedience may be the prelude to armed struggle—so best nip it in the bud. The consequences of the widespread adoption of Kitson's model are significant. Kitson's "well-known book," *Low Intensity Operations* "is considered to be an outstanding professional manual on the subject" according to the Jafa essay.[69] Cynical anti-repression activists quip that in this scenario "Low Intensity" means that while the bullets from state agents are still high velocity ... the corporate media coverage is of low intensity. The Jafa essay continues:

> The only problem with [Kitson's] views, however, is that they are based on the assumption that the enemy is the 'Left', the pro-testers, organisers of strikes and demonstrations in Third World countries, and maker[s] of movements for national liberation—in short, a colonial orientation. He sees all types of political protest by the Left, the 'subversives', as a preparation for armed action. This plants the idea in the minds of the soldiers that the radical elements in the society or the exercise of the democratic rights by the people must be dealt with by military methods.[70]

Well... that's hardly the "only problem" with Kitson's theories... but it is an accurate appraisal nonetheless.

International solidarity work is frequently framed by law enforcement as subversion or treason. This accusation is extended to any person or group that is seen as adopting any form of Marxism, anarchism, or collectivism. The overlap between right-wing ideology, countersubversion, and counterin-surgency in this regard is very clear. It can lead to violence by state actors and individual right-wing terrorists.

For example, Christian Right ideologue William S. Lind has not only propounded a theory that "Cultural Marxism" is a subversive conspiracy to destroy Western Culture, he is also considered a leading theorist on "Fourth Generation" warfare, a form of counterinsurgency analysis discussed and used by U.S. military strategists.[71] Lind's essay should be mandatory read-ing for any student of repression and counterinsurgency. One reader was Norway terrorist Anders Behring Breivik, a right-wing Christian who based his murderous actions in part on reading the conspiracist Islamophobic work of Lind.[72]

RESISTANCE IS NOT FUTILE

PROGRESSIVE ACTIVISTS HAVE always been aided by small groups of experi-enced leaders, skillful strategists, and anti-repression researchers; over time a series of lessons have been learned about how repression is deployed and how to resist it. One of the best contemporary manuals for resistance is *The War at Home* by Brian Glick, available from South End Press or online.[73] In her classic guide to "Common Sense Security," Sheila O'Donnell writes:

As our movements have become stronger and more sophisticated, the techniques of the state, corporations, and right-wing groups have also become more sophisticated. We have seen government agents, corporate security, and right-wing intelligence networks share information as well as an ideology. Caution and common sense security measures in the face of the concerted efforts to stop us are therefore both prudent and necessary.

Spend a few minutes to assess your work from a security point of view: understand your vulnerabilities; assess your allies and your adversaries as objectively as possible; do not underestimate the opposition. Try to assess your organizational and personal strengths and weaknesses. Do not take chances. Plan for the worst; work and hope for the best.[74]

CONCLUSIONS

IN THE UNITED States, the political game is rigged against the left like in a crooked gambling house. The odds are with the government to begin with, and the political right is allowed to win more than it loses. The left has to struggle to win anything; and both the government and the right agree to try to fleece the left of any winnings it might pick up. Liberals sometimes complain about the cheating, and sometimes look the other way.

This reality explains why we use the slogan "Don't Talk to the Feds."[75] Most agents don't understand the left. The goal of some of the people who hire them is to crush the left. Catching criminals is often not their actual main mission. An open mouth shuts down progressive social change. You have a right to keep silent until you consult an attorney. Don't be a macho fool. Zip it.

As a range of leftist strategists have pointed out for decades, we face a three-way fight to defend and extend liberty and equality. Those of us on the political left need to resist government repression as well as challenge right-wing initiatives. Anti-fascist muckraker George Seldes observed in 1938, "Fascism and Reaction inevitably attack. They have won against disunion. They will fail if we unite."[76]

At the same time, there are two important reasons folks on the left should avoid being cheerleaders for state action targeting our opponents on the political right.

- Defending civil liberties across the board for everyone is a bedrock foundation of theories of democracy and open societies, especially in a global scene facing economic instability and rapidly changing demographics. We should push for the state to be neutral with regard to ideology.

- Encouraging the state to use a repressive hammer on your political opponents—even when they are on the political right—is short-sighted and counter-productive. History demonstrates that once a government uses a repressive technique with popular support from any political sector, the government adopts it as a tool of repression used against all political dissidents.

That means we on the political left may sometimes need to defend the rightists against the state. It does not prevent us from challenging and confronting the right ourselves. And we must always be alert to attempts by the right to work with the state (and liberals) to smash us and our allies.

If I can't convince you of the moral or theoretical issues, please recognize the pragmatic concerns. Government repression to crush political dissent is a constant threat. As J. Edgar Hoover explained in an FBI memo, COINTELPRO was just the name given to a specific set of operations, but when "given another name" only encompassed "everything that has been done in the past or will be done in the future." That's why the civil rights movement taught us that "freedom is a constant struggle."[77]

NOTES

1   Some of the research in this chapter was originally conducted for and used in Chip Berlet and Matthew N. Lyons, "One Key to Litigating Against Government Prosecution of Dissidents: Understanding the Underlying Assumptions." In *Police Misconduct and Civil Rights Law Report*, in two parts, Vol. 5, No. 13, January–February Vol. 5, No. 14, March–April, West Group: 1998. A few sentences are borrowed with permission.

2   Personal correspondence between author and José Palafox. The exchange resulted in the posting of a public statement: José Palafox, "Grand Juries as a Political Weapon: From José Palafox in California," http://www.buildingliberty.us/grand-juries/palafox/, May 9, 2012.

3   Andy Grimm, "More anti-war activists subpoenaed, attorney says: Action apparently part of federal terror-funding inquiry," *Chicago Tribune*, http://articles.chicagotribune.com/2010-12-23/news/ct-met-anti-war-subpoenas-20101223_1_grand-jury-anti-war-activists-subpoenas, December 23, 2010; David Schaper, "FBI Targets Peace Activists For Alleged Terrorism Support," *NPR News*, http://m.npr.org/news/front/130274688, Oct. 2, 2010.

4   James Baldwin, "An Open Letter to My Sister, Miss Angela Davis," *New York Review of Books*, http://www.nybooks.com/articles/archives/1971/jan/07/an-open-letter-to-my-sister-miss-angela-davis/, November 19, 1970.

5   Interview by author with Arthur Kinoy, 1997.

6   Interview by author with Harvey Silverglate, 1997. Conducted for and used in Berlet and Lyons, "One Key to Litigating Against Government Prosecution of Dissidents."

7   Chip Berlet, "Inside a Fright-Wing Cell," *Boston Phoenix*, August 19, 1988. The author, while undercover as an investigative journalist, attended a dinner featuring one of the defendants, Robert Miles, and heard the case discussed in detail by Miles.

8   Interview by author with Harvey Silverglate.

9   Chip Berlet, "'Christian Warriors': Who Are the Hutaree Militia and Where Did They Come From?" *Religion Dispatches*, http://www.religiondispatches.org/archive/politics/2413, March 31, 2010.

10   Emma Reynolds, "Michigan militia are CLEARED of plotting to overthrow government - despite massive undercover FBI operation," *Mail Online*, March 28, 2012, http://www.dailymail.co.uk/news/article-2121490.

11   Ibid.

12   Gary Alan Fine, "The Chaining of Social Problems: Solutions and unintended consequences in the age of betrayal," *Social Problems*, 53, no. 1 (Feb. 2006), 3–17.

13   Brian Glick, *War at Home: Covert Action Against U. S. Activists and What We Can Do About It.* (Boston: South End Press: 1989). Glick has authorized the full text of his book to be placed online at http://www.buildingliberty.us/war-at-home/glick_overview.html.

14   Glick, *War at Home.*

15   Victor Serge, *What Everyone Should Know About State Repression*, (London: New Park Publications, 1979).

16   On the Iranian SAVAK, see Library of Congress, *Iran: A Country Study*, http://lcweb2.loc.gov/frd/cs/pdf/CS_Iran.pdf, (2008). On El Salvador secret police operations, see Ross Gelbspan, *Break-Ins, Death Threats, and the FBI: The Covert War Against the Central America Movement.* (Boston: South End Press, 1991).

17   Leo Huberman, *The Labor Spy Racket*, (New York: Modern Age Books, 1937); George. J. A. O'Toole, *The Private Sector: Private Spies, Rent-A-Cops, and the Police-Industrial Complex*, (New York: Norton, 1978). See also Frank Donner, *The Age of Surveillance: The aims and methods of America's political intelligence system* (New York: Knopf, 1980); and *Protectors of Privilege: Red squads and political repression in urban America* (Berkeley: University of California Press,1992).

18   Louis F. Post, *The Deportations Delerium of Nineteen-Twenty*, (Chicago: Charles H. Kerr, 1923). It would have been nicer if Post had mentioned this assessment while signing the deportation orders for Attorney General Palmer.

19   Allan M. Jalon, "A Break-In to End All Break-Ins," *Los Angeles Times*, March 8, 2006, http://articles.latimes.com/2006/mar/08/opinion/oe-jalon8.

20   Ward Churchill and Jim Vander Wall, *Agents of Repression: The FBI's Secret Wars Against the Black Panther Party and the American Indian Movement*, (Boston: South End Press, 1988); and *The COINTELPRO Papers: Documents from the FBI's Secret Wars Against Domestic Dissent*, (Boston: South End Press, 1989).

21   Jeffrey Haas, *The Assassination of Fred Hampton: How the FBI and the Chicago Police Murdered a Black Panther*, (Chicago: Chicago Review / Lawrence Hill, 2010).

22   David Schaper, "FBI Targets Peace Activists for Alleged Terrorism Support," National Public Radio, October 10, 2010, http://www.npr.org/2010/10/02/130274688/

fbi-targets-peace-activists-for-alleged-terrorism-support.

23   Schaper, "FBI Targets Peace Activists For Alleged Terrorism Support."

24   Grimm, "More anti-war activists subpoenaed."

25   Grimm, "More anti-war activists subpoenaed."

26   Interview by author with Fred Solowey, 2011.

27   James Retherford, "Brandon Darby, The Texas 2, and the FBI's Runaway Informants," *The Rag Blog*, May 26, 2009, http://theragblog.blogspot.com/2009/05/james-retherford-brandon-darby-texas-2.html.

28   Victoria Welle, "Brandon Darby in New Orleans: FBI Informant Was Egotistical Sexist," *The Rag Blog*, May 26, 2009, http://theragblog.blogspot.com/2009/05/brandon-darby-in-new-orleans-fbi.html; Kristian Williams, "Profiles of Provocateurs," *Portland Indymedia*, June 9, 2011, http://portland.indymedia.org/en/2011/06/408869.shtml.

29   Welle, "Brandon Darby in New Orleans"; Williams, "Profiles of Provocateurs."

30   Huberman, *The Labor Spy Racket*.

31   Trevor Aaronson, "Terms of Entrapment: A Guide to Counterterrorism Jargon," *Mother Jones*, September/October 2011, http://www.motherjones.com/politics/2011/08/counterterrorism-glossary.

32   Will Potter, "Mafia Law Used Against Environmentalists for Tree Sits, Civil Disobedience," *Green is the New Red*, April 29, 2009, http://www.greenisthenewred.com/blog/mob-law-i-69-environmental-activists/1804/.

33   Frederick Clarkson, "Terror in the Name of the Lord," *Ms Magazine*, Winter, 2002, http://www.msmagazine.com/dec02/clarkson.asp; Political Research Associates, "What is the Army of God?" http://www.publiceye.org/reproductive_rights/violence/aog.htm.

34   Xavier Beltran, "Applying RICO to eco-activism: Fanning the Radical Flames of Eco-Terror," *Boston College Environmental Affairs Law Review* 29, No. 2 (2002).

35   The author is not an attorney; this text should not be considered competent legal advice. Always consult an attorney on questions of law. Please do not test the limits of repression to prove a political point without first speaking with an attorney about your risks.

36   Brandenburg v. Ohio, 395 U.S. 444 (1969). See resource pages at IIT Chicago-Kent College of Law, http://www.oyez.org/cases/1960-1969/1968/1968_492; and Boston College, http://www.bc.edu/bc_org/avp/cas/comm/free_speech/brandenburg.html.

37   The test is discussed here: Doug Linder, "Advocacy of Unlawful Action and the 'Incitement Test': The Issue: When does the First Amendment allow the government to punish individuals for expression that may lead to unlawful conduct?" *Exploring Constitutional Conflicts*, http://law2.umkc.edu/faculty/projects/ftrials/conlaw/incitement.htm.

38   Linder, "Advocacy of Unlawful Action and the 'Incitement Test.'"

39   Donner, *The Age of* Surveillance (1980); *Protectors of Privilege* (1992). See also: Chip Berlet, "Government Intelligence Abuse: The Theories of Frank Donner," Political Research Associates, (2008), http://www.buildingliberty.us/repression/#donner

40   "Coalition Letter to Chairman Peter King," Addressed to "The Honorable Peter T. King, Chairman, House Committee on Homeland Security," February 23, 2011, http://www.buildingliberty.us/repression/dox/Coalition-Letter_Peter-King.pdf.

41 Chip Berlet, [1987] 1993, *Hunt for Red Menace: How Government Intelligence Agencies and Private Right-wing Countersubversion Groups Forge Ad Hoc Covert Spy Networks that Target Dissidents as Outlaws*, monograph, Somerville, MA: Political Research Associates, http://www.buildingliberty.us/repression/#hunt.

42 Personal observation; the author helped organize the Chicago event. Personal collection of flyers and programs for the event.

43 Interview by author with Debra Chaplan, 2011.

44 Chip Berlet, "Chairman Lieberman's 'War on Terror,'" *Right Web*, September 16, 2008, http://www.rightweb.irc-online.org/articles/display/Chairman_Liebermans_War_on_Terror.

45 Chip Berlet, "Violence and Public Policy," *Criminology and Public Policy*, special issue on terrorism, Vol. 8, Issue 3, (October, 2009): 623–31.

46 Muslim American Civil Liberties Coalition (MACLC), "Counterterrorism policy: MACLC's Critique of the NYPD's Report on Homegrown Radicalism," *MACLC website*, http://maclcnypdcritique.files.wordpress.com/2008/11/counterterrorism-policy-final-paper3.pdf.

47 Tim Murphy, "Meet the White Supremacist Leading the GOP's Anti-Sharia Crusade," *Mother Jones*, March 1, 2011, http://www.motherjones.com/politics/2011/02/david-yerushalmi-sharia-ban-tennessee; Salim Muwakkil, "The Muslims Are Coming!" *In These Times*, April 7, 2011, http://www.inthesetimes.com/article/7156/; Tanya Somanader, "Asked About AZ Shootings, Gingrich Pivots To Slamming Liberals For Ignoring Threat Of 'American Islamists'," January 11, 2012, http://thinkprogress.org/politics/2011/01/11/138222/gingrich-islamophobia-az-shooting; Chip Berlet, "Islamophobia, Antisemitism and the Demonized 'Other',"*Extra!*, Fairness and Accuracy in Reporting (FAIR), August 14, 2012, http://fair.org/extra-online-articles/islamophobia-antisemitism-and-the-demonized-other/.

48 Fairness and Accuracy in Reporting (FAIR), "Smearcasting," 2008, http://www.smearcasting.us/.

49 Thomas Cincotta, *Manufacturing the Muslim Menace: Private Firms, Public Servants, & the Threat to Rights and Security*, Political Research Associates, (2011), http://www.buildingliberty.us/repression/#muslim.

50 Interview by author with Thomas Cincotta, 2012.

51 Berlet, *Hunt for Red Menace*. See a special page devoted to the escapades of Rees and his network, http://www.buildingliberty.us/repression/informers/rees-escapades.html.

52 Richard Drinnon, *Facing West: The Metaphysics of Indian-Hating and Empire-Building*. (New York: Schocken Books, 1990).

53 Andrea Smith, *Conquest: Sexual Violence and American Indian Genocide*, (Cambridge: South End Press, 2005).

54 Gary Alan Fine, "The Chaining of Social Problems: Solutions and Unintended Consequences in the Age of Betrayal," *Social Problems*, Vol. 53, 1, 3–17.

55 Robert Justin Goldstein, *Political Repression in Modern America, From 1870 to Present*, (Cambridge, Schenkman, 1978).

56 Frank Donner, "The Terrorist as Scapegoat," *The Nation*, 20, May 2 (1978), 590–94; Donner, *The Age of Surveillance* (1980); Berlet, *The Hunt for Red Menace* (1993).

57 Donner, "The Terrorist as Scapegoat." The "Secret Army Organization" in the United States should not be confused with the French nationalist "Secret Army Organization," also known as the "Organization of the Secret Army," which in French is "*Organisation de l'Armée Secrete*" or "*Organisation Armée Secrète*" (OAS).

58 David Cunningham, *There's Something Happening Here: The New Left, the Klan, and FBI Counterintelligence*, Berkeley: University of California Press, (2004), 32, 111–12.

59 Cunningham, *There's Something Happening Here*, 145.

60 Ross Gelbspan, *Break-Ins, Death Threats, and the FBI: The Covert War Against the Central America Movement*, (Boston: South End Press, 1991).

61 Wojtek Sokolowski, "The State," *Left Business Observer* Listserv, (LBO-Talk Archives), September 25, 2009, http://mailman.lbo-talk.org/2009/2009-September/013295.html.

62 William W. Keller, *The Liberals and J. Edgar Hoover*, (Princeton: Princeton University Press, 1989).

63 Chip Berlet and Matthew N. Lyons, "Repression and Ideology," (1998), http://www.buildingliberty.us/repression/#ideology.

64 See Donner, *The Age of Surveillance*, 414–51; Gelbspan, *Break-Ins, Death Threats, and the FBI*, 73–84, 169–73, 183–95; Berlet, [1987] 1993.

65 Berlet and Lyons, 1998.

66 William I. Thomas and Dorothy Swaine Thomas, "Situations defined as real are real in their consequences" (1970): 154–55, in Gregory P. Stone and Harvey A. Faberman, *Social Psychology Through Symbolic Interaction*, (Waltham: Xerox College Publishing, 1970).

67 Vijendra Singh Jafa, "Counterinsurgency Warfare: The Use & Abuse of Military Force," *South Asia Intelligence Review*, http://www.satp.org/satporgtp/publication/faultlines/volume3/Fault3-JafaF.htm.

68 Personal correspondence between author and Kristian Williams, 2012.

69 Singh Jafa, "Counterinsurgency Warfare: The Use & Abuse of Military Force."

70 Ibid.

71 William S. Lind, "Understanding Fourth Generation War," Lew Rockwell website, January 6, 2004, http://www.lewrockwell.com/lind/lind3b.html. The website is a clearinghouse for White Nationalist Paleocons. Note that LewRockwell.com has a slogan "anti-state, anti-war, pro-market." For a principled anti-racist critique by a conservative economic libertarian, see Tom Palmer, "From Lew Rockwell to Racist Collectivism," March 2, 2005, http://tomgpalmer.com/2005/03/02/from-lew-rockwell-to-racist-collectivism/.

72 Chip Berlet, "Breivik's Core Thesis is White Christian Nationalism v. Multiculturalism," *Talk to Action*, (2011), http://www.talk2action.org/story/2011/7/25/73510/6015.

73 Glick, *War at Home*; Chip Berlet, "Encountering and Countering Political Repression" in *The Global Activists Manual*, eds., Mike Prokosch and Laura Raymond, (New York: Thunder's Mouth Press/Nation Books, 2002), http://www.buildingliberty.us/security/countering_repression.html; See also Sheila O'Donnell, "Common Sense Security," Public Eye Network, (2012), http://www.buildingliberty.us/security/common-sense-security.html.

74   Sheila O'Donnell "Common Sense Security."

75   New York City Chapter of the National Lawyers Guild, "You Have the Right to Remain Silent: A Know Your Rights Guide for Law Enforcement Encounters," NLGNYC website, http://www.nlgnyc.org/pdf/publications/kyr-righttoremainsilent.pdf.

76   George Seldes and Clarice A. Rosenthal, *You Can't Do That: a survey of the forces attempting, in the name of patriotism, to make a desert of the Bill of Rights*, (New York: Modern Age Books, 1938).

77   "Freedom is a Constant Struggle," lyrics to the song as used in the play, "McComb, U.S.A.," written by students of the McComb, Mississippi, Freedom School in 1964, and archived by the Department of Curriculum & Instruction at the University of Illinois at Champaign-Urbana, http://courses.education.illinois.edu/ci407ss/freedomconstant-struggle.html.

A webpage consisting of additional resources, updates, and active links (when available) for changed URLs in these notes is available at http://www.buildingliberty.us/repression/coin/.

A COLD WIND BLOWING

RICARDO LEVINS MORALES[1]

The cold winds of political repression have begun to blow a little colder. The widening FBI probe into the anti-war and solidarity movements—launched with coordinated raids in Minneapolis and Chicago in September, 2010—attests to the expanding reach of Washington's repressive apparatus. The new face of domestic repression is characterized by rapidly developing technical capacity for surveillance and data sharing, the integration of local policing into the national security system, and a blurring of boundaries between private and government police functions and goals.

Repression—the use of state power to limit political action and discourse—doesn't develop in isolation. It compensates for the weakening of other, less intrusive methods for ensuring social stability. Today it corresponds to growing economic inequality driven by the flight of manufacturing, the demolition of public sector services, the decline of union power and the ascension of a ravenous financial sector. These changes severely strain the mechanisms that maintain popular consensus.

Our task in the following pages will be to note current trends in political and social police repression, identify some of the systemic vulnerabilities they betray and to find points of leverage from which to launch a pro-democracy counter-offensive. We are experiencing a system-wide assault on the democratic public space, encompassing attacks on academic expression, criminalization of whistle-blowing, corporatization of elections and hobbling the open internet. Piecemeal, defensive strategies will not be adequate. We will need to mount a challenge to the repressive enterprise as a whole. In particular I would assert that our strategy should promote solidarity and cooperation among the sectors that bear the brunt of repression but have historically remained separate in their responses.

Within days of the September, 2010 raids several hundred people turned out at a south side community church in Minneapolis to begin organizing a defense campaign. Several days later, a similar-sized crowd gathered on the city's north side to support the family of Fong Lee, a Hmong teenager killed by police in 2006, at that time appealing his case to the U.S. Supreme Court. Between them, these cases embody the two levels of a police-repressive system that has operated in the United States since its earliest days.

The September raids marked a shift in the "anti-terror" narrative. Until then the domestic front of the "war on terror" had targeted dark people with foreign names and accents. Most of the over five hundred terrorism cases pursued since 9/11 have involved informants, provocateurs, or undercover agents as participants or instigators of the plots. They have often targeted financially desperate, mentally unstable, or otherwise vulnerable men in Muslim communities. These hapless individuals have been cajoled, threatened and even bribed into conspiratorial activities conceived, financed, and equipped by the FBI. These prosecutions have not foiled real threats to public safety, but they do "send a message" that the nation is under attack from Islam at home and abroad and must "circle the wagons" in defense.[2]

This time the targets are U.S. citizens, predominantly of European descent and with respectable, mostly white-collar jobs; well-known in their communities for public protest and educational activities. Repression usually targets those who can easily be isolated and moves up the social ladder as it builds the case that enemies are all around us. This is the principle famously summed up by Pastor Martin Niemöller in his 1946 statement, "First they came for the Communists…" The September raids represent a rather abrupt leap up that ladder, risking an outpouring of support for their targets that has, indeed, materialized.

It has been widely noted that the raids came on the heels of a Justice Department report critical of the FBI for spying on peaceful activism. Their timing suggests a defensive move on the part of the Bureau, saying, in effect, "See, peace activists really *are* in league with terror!"

The report was released by the Department of Justice's Inspector General under pressure from senators, following a Pittsburgh newspaper exposé. A revealing incident in its pages involves an agent sent to observe a protest organized by the pacifist Thomas Merton Center. When pressed by investigators to justify the spying, Bureau officials quickly created a false back story (complete with paper trail) to pretend that their intent was to keep tabs on Farooq Hussaini, the director of the local Islamic Center. The problem is that they had no legitimate reason to spy on Hussaini either! The officials seemed to assume that by linking the protest to a prominent member of an Ethnically

Targeted Community (an ETC), they would escape criticism. A similar ploy may be discerned in the September raids; the inclusion of a single Palestinian, Hatem Abudayeh (the respected director of Chicago's Arab American Action Network), to provide the necessary intimation of guilt. (More Palestinians were targeted in a subsequent round of subpoenas.)[3]

While the DoJ report may explain the timing of the raids, their pretext flags them as a test of new police powers stemming from the Supreme Court ruling in *Holder v. Humanitarian Law*. This ruling criminalizes interaction with groups deemed "terrorist" by the Feds, even for the purpose of conflict resolution, investigation, or humanitarian aid. This new instrument is, logically, being tested on leftist activists rather than mainstream institutions like the Carter Center, which has expressed alarm over its draconian reach.[4]

COLONIAL LEGACY

Today's police system has its roots in the colonial past. Control over Ethnically Targeted Communities was the operative principle of the early slave patrols and, later, of the urban militias who monitored a growing number of free Black workers and Native people (whose movements were subject to a pass book system). As these organizations morphed into police departments, their mandate would evolve to include maintaining order among immigrant factory workers, keeping wages down by suppressing union agitation and, eventually, becoming the enforcement arm for corrupt political machines.[5]

In a racially stratified country, compliance with the social order is based on a two-tiered modality: collective management of ETCs and other low social strata, but individual treatment for offenders from the privileged classes. Charges might be pursued against a white person who disturbed the public order whereas an entire Black community would be punished if one of their own stepped out of line.

This pattern is familiar to U.S. communities of color. It plays out in the indiscriminate rage directed at local communities when a member of the force has been shot by an unknown assailant; in post-Katrina New Orleans, where the police acted as enforcers to assist white communities and suppress dark ones; in the contrasting responses to the Oklahoma City Federal Building bombing and the 9/11 attacks. The first, perpetrated by white Christian racists was treated as individual criminal pathology whereas the latter unleashed a full-bodied assault on Muslim and immigrant communities which has yet to end.[6]

A shift in police philosophy, beginning in the 1970s, places domestic policing into a frame of counterinsurgency. Rather than seeking out the perpetrators when crimes have been committed, counterinsurgency emphasizes widespread surveillance and infiltration to identify and neutralize threats before they materialize. Based as it is on a war paradigm, counterinsurgency ("COIN," in the professional jargon) justifies police action on the basis of intent, suspicion, and association rather than the higher standards of evidence associated with a crime-fighting model. Within the logic of COIN, civil society is a breeding ground for subversion, crime, and terror and must be closely monitored to guard against outbreaks. There is a presumed natural progression from truancy, petty theft and political discontent to protest, organized crime, and terrorism. The more effectively you disrupt these threats to stability when they are seeds, the more you will succeed in preventing their becoming thistles. Spying on and disrupting pacifist groups, mine protestors, death penalty opponents, and civil libertarians, therefore, are not instances of careless overreach or poor supervision but, rather, are the purest application of counterinsurgency logic. In communities of color—where preventive disruption has long been the norm—the introduction of COIN has, through "community policing," increased police reliance on informants to trigger reckless paramilitary home raids.[7]

These developments fit within a broader cultural offensive aimed at dividing and disrupting civil society. Thus we see the imposition of racist immigration laws in Arizona (to keep down labor costs and redirect white economic fears) linked to the banning of Ethnic Studies instruction (to undermine the cultural foundations of resistance).

The racialized dual structure of U.S. policing finds expression in the deepest racial/cultural divide in our society: the chasm that cuts across public perceptions of the police. The admiration and trust for police with which white, middle class children are inculcated stands in irreconcilable contrast to the hatred and fear with which they are viewed by the young of the ETCs. These sets of perceptions are rooted in real disparities in treatment experienced in these communities. The fact that cases like Fong Lee's (or the better-known Oscar Grant case) are commonplace is not known to white America, where conflict with the police is seen as evidence of criminality. Poet Bao Phi distills it clearly:

> Put a blindfold on me
> Tell me who you fear
> And I will tell you
> Your skin.[8]

When Fong Lee and his friends were confronted by the police, it's not surprising that his impulse would be to get away. Officer Jason Anderson, an officer with a brutal history, chased Lee around a school building, shooting him eight times. A handgun that materialized later turned out to have come from storage in a Police Department evidence room. As a young member of an ETC, it would be assumed by the white public that he must have done something pretty bad to attract police bullets. The attorneys for the city exploited this bias by repeating the word "gang" as many times as possible in connection with Fong's name while excluding evidence of the officer's anti-Asian racism and penchant for brutality.[9]

AN EXPANDING WEB

RACIAL AND POLITICAL repression is systematized through vast databases that have morphed into virtual maps of their respective social sectors. State-level gang databases are, like lobster traps, easy to get into but difficult to leave. In some states saggy pants and hip-hop sensibilities are enough to flag you as gang-connected and that, in turn, implicates your friends. For young people in trouble with the legal system, a gang "association" can bring enhanced penalties.

Anti-dissident databases are equally sweeping in scope. Data collected from direct surveillance and infiltration, commercial sources, phone, car rental and travel records, public sources (such as Facebook) and past investigations are amalgamated through over 70 regional, state, and city "fusion centers." These are staffed by police and agents from multiple agencies alongside private security contractors (who are conveniently exempt from oversight laws). The resulting map of personal connections and associations identifies key hubs of activism for closer inspection.

Revelations involving fusion centers in Missouri, Virginia, Pennsylvania, Maryland, Illinois, California, and Texas, among others, expose a systematic pattern of spying on legal activity.[10] In some cases the data is collected with the assistance of corporations who are the targets of protests and who, in turn, receive intelligence reports about their critics. An inadvertently posted memo from the director of Homeland Security in Pennsylvania highlights this cozy relationship: "We want to continue providing this support to the Marcellus Shale Formation natural gas stakeholders while not feeding those groups fomenting dissent against those same companies."[11]

Driving the expansion of police powers is a decline in the global position of the U.S., shifts in its racial makeup, and growing inequality globally and locally. The accelerated integration of private and public police functions reflects a parallel integration of corporations and government at all levels, from the federal cabinet (composed increasingly of executives from the most powerful corporate sectors); to legislatures selected with unlimited private contributions; to the leadership and staff of regulatory agencies. This merger has given rise to a brazen kleptocracy in which corporate criminality carries little risk of punishment while those who expose or protest it are treated as insurgents.

Growing inequality and impoverishment produce three predictable responses from the base of the social pyramid: protest, crime, and psychological/emotional breakdown. These expressions of social distress—not the systemic exploitation that engenders them—are the problems which an expanded police universe is assigned to contain. All of these challenges will increase as a returning stream of psychologically and physically wounded war veterans collides with a drastically downsized social safety net.

Into this volatile mix, corporations have poured hundreds of millions of dollars to sponsor a resurgence of right-wing political action. The agenda of the new rightist groups is to support corporate-friendly measures (dressed up as defenses of personal liberty) and to pin the blame for societal collapse on vulnerable populations. Counterinsurgency policing exactly complements this conservative agenda by disrupting the opponents of corporate power and suppressing the responses (organized or random) of the hardest-hit communities. There is a high degree of overlap between the targets of hate radio and its vigilante followers and those of Homeland Security and the repression-technology complex.

Stripped of its ideological baggage, the grievances of the Tea Party rank and file can be summarized as: "things are getting worse and I'm being treated unfairly." The right-wing sound machine directs these sentiments into resentment toward "elites" who conspire with brown people, foreigners, queers, and the parasitic poor to deprive white citizens of all they have worked so hard for. The same frustrations (albeit with a different narrative) are experienced in the marginalized communities that came out of the shadows to elect Obama only to find him expanding the policies they had rejected. Whatever the actual reality, the idea of fair play is deeply engrained in U.S. culture. Painful as financial hardship is in its own right, the perception that there are privileged people who rate special treatment is what turns frustration into rage.

Evidence of impunity stares us in the face every day, although different expressions of it are visible to us depending on where we stand: Wall Street gamblers unleash massive social destruction and are rewarded with the keys to the treasury; BP destroys the Gulf ecology and is protected by the government and is punished with a fine which, while the largest ever imposed by the United States, amounts to less than half of one quarter's profit;[12] police kill unarmed youth, falsify the evidence, and face no punishment; Blackwater mercenaries massacre civilians and are spared prosecution; an investment banker crashes his car into a cyclist and faces reduced charges because the prosecutor feels that a felony record could have "serious job implications for someone in (his) profession"; simple consumer purchases and services come wrapped in complex agreements that allow companies to change the rules at will; wars are unleashed on the basis of faked evidence, and kidnapping and torture are routinized with no consequences to the perpetrators; Dick Cheney and Halliburton slip free of criminal bribery charges in Nigeria by paying a fine smaller than the original bribes; retirement benefits guaranteed in union contracts are gutted with court approval to protect shareholder investments; police beat, raid, frame, and harass on the street with little concern for fallout even when caught on video; insurance executives who deny needed treatment to the ill and injured remain free and powerful. Those who protest or resist these injustices are the ones that face investigation and harassment at the hands of the criminal justice system.

TURNING THE TABLES

THE REPRESSIVE UNIVERSE has grown quickly and haphazardly, post-9/11, creating a profusion of organizations and a confusion of interests. Such uncontrolled growth creates its own contradictions and vulnerabilities. Foremost among these is the size and technological prowess of the system itself. Unassailable superiority easily leads to "power blindness"—an over-reliance on a few blunt tools to control a complex and changing cultural reality. This has proven the downfall of U.S. ambitions in Iraq and Afghanistan; its lopsided advantage led planners to assume they could roll a massive military machine across these societies without regard to their cultures, traditions, and history. As I observed in a 2003 piece,[13] this weakness would doom the occupation virtually from the start. What an opponent considers its great strength may be its Achilles heel.

The full-spectrum nature of the repressive assault produces another unintended consequence. It largely removes the option of seeking personal safety by staying below the government radar. Even seemingly inoffensive activity falls within the purview of the national security state now under construction. That construction must be blocked and reversed or it will continue to besiege the shrinking democratic space.

This sets the stage for exactly the kind of political challenge that repression is meant to prevent: the building of broad alliances among segments of society that are traditionally fragmented but who can perceive an increasing danger to their own interests. As a practical matter, repression depends on fomenting division, fear, confusion, and isolation among marginalized communities and political movements. It only works when we obligingly become divided, fearful, confused and isolated. Repressive agencies do not aim to imprison everyone who harbors dissenting thoughts. Instead they target the few so as to frighten the many. In fact, repression is never completely effective because the very conditions that make it necessary will continually generate new resistance. Their hope is to disable democratic protections sufficiently that whatever opposition emerges can be prevented from becoming a political force.

Three levels of response are called for:

1. Prevention: preparing activists and communities to identify and re-sist divisive tactics, intimidation, and entrapment;

2. Defense: supporting and defending those singled out for persecu-tion; and

3. Counter-offense: building a movement across traditional social bar-riers that targets the sources of repressive power and legitimacy.

It is a useful exercise, from time to time, to try and see ourselves as our opponents see us. The resources that the government is devoting to the repres-sive endeavor make clear that it sees in our nascent movements and battered communities a serious threat to be contained. Our custom on the U.S. left of seeing only our own weaknesses and our opponents' strength does not serve us well. The advantage in political conflict does not accrue to the side with the greatest technological and financial might, but to the side that can seize and re-tain the initiative. This fact is clearly understood by the right, which is setting the national political agenda by defining and fighting for a set of values. The left, in contrast, fights mostly defensive battles, hoping against the evidence that the liberal wing of the establishment will provide the leadership that we ourselves have abdicated. This is of particular importance in relation to repres-sion, where a liberal White House is simultaneously pursuing the protection of state secrecy and the eradication of personal privacy (to the extreme of claim-ing a right to order extrajudicial assassinations of enemies foreign or domestic).

A reckless corporate feeding frenzy has thrown families out of their homes, workers out of their jobs, and students into debt. The current trajectory is aimed at evicting all but a small, bloated elite from the governance of society, a course that will lead to still greater inequality. The national security-police-prison complex has been assigned the impossible task of ensuring that this process goes smoothly. Its primary mission is to prevent the emergence of effective solidarity within and between domestic communities and with the international victims of the same exploitative policies. Challenging repres-sion, however, can open new avenues for building that very solidarity. Just as President Nixon demonstrated that the cover-up can be more damning than the original crime, so repression can magnify the vulnerabilities in a regime that comes to rely on it. Mistreatment at the hands of the police has more than once sparked youth-led movements, organizations, and uprisings that quickly draw attention to the injustices it was intended to defend. How we rise to the challenge will determine, more than any other factor, whether today's chill wind will usher in a new ice age.

NOTES

1   An earlier version of this essay appeared as Ricardo Levins Morales, "Big Brother and the Holding Company: Turning Repression into Resistance," http://www.rlmartstudio.com, February (2011).

2   Naomi Wolf, "How many more fake terror plots will a gullible media swallow?" *The Guardian*, May 9 (2012); Trevor Aaronson, "The Informants," *Mother Jones*, Sept./Oct. (2011).

3   U.S. Department of Justice, Office of the Inspector General, *A Review of the FBI's Investigations of Certain Advocacy Groups*, Sept. (2010).

4   David Cole, "Advocacy is not a Gun," *NY Times*, June 21, 2010.

5   Kristian Williams, *Our Enemies in Blue: Police and Power in America*, (Cambridge: South End Press, 2007). Re. slave patrols, p. 36; urban patrols, p. 41; urban machine politics, p. 39; workers and unions, p. 105.

6   Trymaine Lee, "Rumors to Fact in Tales of Post-Katrina Violence," *NY Times*, Aug 26, 2010; Jordan Flaherty, "From Heroes to Villains: NOPD Verdict Reveals Post-Katrina History," *AlterNet* Aug. 8, 2010 (from Colorlines); Tim Wise, "Rationalizing Racism: Panic and Profiling after 9/11," *AlterNet*, Dec. 10, 2001.

7   Christian Parenti, *Lockdown America: Police and Prisons in the Age of Crisis*. (London: Verso, 1999). Shift to COIN, p. 17–18; paramilitary raids, p. 123; Williams, *Our Enemies in Blue*, p. 218.

8   Bao Phi, *Song I Sing*. (Minneapolis: Coffee House Press, 2011).

9   Juliana Hu Pegues, "The Case of Fong Lee: Racial Profiling, Police Brutality, and Asian American Movement Organizing," Conference Paper, "Out of the Margins: Asian American Movement Building," (Ann Arbor: University of Michigan, March, 2011).

10   The Constitution Project, "Recommendations for Fusion Centers," The Constitution Project, http://www.constitutionproject.org/pdf/fusioncenterreport.pdf, (2012). Mike German and Jay Stanley, "ACLU Fusion Center Update," American Civil Liberties Union website, http://www.aclu.org/pdfs/privacy/fusion_update_20080729.pdf, (July, 2008); Marc Levy, "'Appalled' Pa. gov. shuts down reports on protests," *Nation and World*, (AP), Sept. 14, 2010; Anthony Newkirk, "Fusion Centers and the Maryland Spying Scandal," *Z Magazine*, October (2010); Kaley Fowler, "Senate Investigation finds anti-terrorism hubs fail to protect privacy," *The Colombia Chronicle*, Oct. 15, 2012.

11   Mathew Harwood, "James Powers and the murky world of 'Top Secret America,'" *The Guardian UK*, http://www.guardian.co.uk/commentisfree/cifamerica/2010/sep/28/private-surveillance-pennsylvania-scandal, (accessed Sept. 28, 2010).

12   Richard Schiffman, "How BP's historic Deepwater Horizon fine will be paid by the US military," *The Guardian*, Nov. 16, 2012; Rebecca Leber, "BP to Pay Largest Criminal Fine in US History for Deepwater Horizon Disaster," *ThinkProgress*, Nov. 15, 2012.

13   Ricardo Levins Morales, "The Return of History: Mirage of Conquest, Oasis of Resistance." www.rlmartstudio.com. November, 2003.

PART TWO

POLICE & PRISONS

THE OTHER SIDE OF THE COIN:
Counterinsurgency and Community Policing[1]

KRISTIAN WILLIAMS

IN AUGUST 2011, BRITISH PRIME MINISTER DAVID CAMERON CALLED William Bratton to ask his advice concerning the riots sweeping the UK following a police shooting.

That is a curious and revealing fact, especially as Bratton's reputation—as Police Chief in New York, then in Los Angeles—was not built on his handling of riots or his response to controversial police shootings. He is known, instead, for declaring war on panhandlers and gangs. Given Bratton's heavy-handed "zero tolerance" approach and tough-guy reputation, his advice was also notable: "Community policing is the philosophy that saved America in the 1990s," he told the BBC. "It's about partnership, the police working with the community...."[2]

To understand what these things have to do with one another—riots, gangs, "zero tolerance" and "community policing"—it is important to understand the nature of counterinsurgency warfare.

This essay argues that, despite the term's association with colonialism and Latin American "dirty wars," many contemporary counterinsurgency practices were developed by police agencies inside the United States and continue to be used against the domestic population.

PART ONE:
MILITARY/POLICING EXCHANGES

In my book *Our Enemies in Blue*, one chapter, entitled "Your Friendly Neighborhood Police State," is devoted to the argument that the two major developments in American policing since the 1960s—militarization and community policing—are actually two aspects of a domestic counterinsurgency program. I summed up the idea with a simple equation: "Community Policing + Militarization = Counterinsurgency."[3]

In the years since then, the counterinsurgency literature has made this point explicit. For example, the RAND Corporation's report *War by Other Means* lists, among the law enforcement "capabilities ... considered to be high priority" in COIN: "well-trained and well-led community police and quick-response, light-combat-capable (constabulary) police."[4] Similarly, a Joint Special Operations University report, *Policing and Law Enforcement in COIN: The Thick Blue Line*, purports:

> The predominant ways of utilizing police and law enforcement within a COIN strategy ... consist of the adoption of the community-policing approach supported by offensive policing actions such as paramilitary operations, counterguerrilla patrolling, pseudo operations [in which state forces pose as insurgent groups], and raids.[5]

The advantages the state receives from each aspect are fairly clear: militarization increases available force, but as important, it also provides increased discipline and command and control. It re-orders the police agency to allow for better coordination and teamwork, while also opening space for local initiative and officer discretion.

Community policing, meanwhile, helps to legitimize police efforts by presenting cops as problem-solvers. It forms police-driven partnerships that put additional resources at their disposal and win the cooperation of community leaders. And, by increasing daily, friendly contacts with people in the neighborhood, community policing provides a direct supply of low-level information.[6] These are not incidental features of community policing; these aspects speak to the real purpose.

In fact, one RAND Corporation study goes so far as to present community policing as its *paradigm* for counterinsurgency:

> [P]acification is best thought of as a massively enhanced version of the 'community policing' technique that emerged in the 1970s.... Community policing is centered on a broad concept of problem solving by law enforcement officers working in an

area that is well-defined and limited in scale, with sensitivity to geographic, ethnic, and other boundaries. Patrol officers form a bond of trust with local residents, who get to know them as more than a uniform. The police work with local groups, businesses, churches, and the like to address the concerns and problems of the neighborhood. Pacification is simply an expansion of this concept to include greater development and security assistance.[7]

The military's use of police theory—in particular the adoption of a "community policing" perspective—shows a cyclical exchange between the various parts of the national security apparatus.

THE CYCLE OF VIOLENCE: IMPORTS AND EXPORTS

Domestically, the unrest of the 1960s left the police in a difficult position. The cops' response to the social movements of the day—the civil rights and anti-war movements especially—had cost them dearly in terms of public credibility, elite support, and officer morale. Frequent and overt recourse to violence, combined with covert (often illegal) surveillance, infiltration, and disruption, had not only failed to squelch the popular movements, it had also diminished trust in law enforcement.

The police needed to reinvent themselves, and the first place they looked for models was the military. The birth of the paramilitary unit—the SWAT team—was one result.[8] A new, more restrained, crowd control strategy was another.[9] Military training, tactics, equipment, and weaponry, made their way into domestic police departments—as did veterans returning from Vietnam, and, more subtly, military approaches to organization, deployment, and command and control. Police strategists specifically began studying counterinsurgency and counterguerilla warfare.[10]

At the same time, and seemingly incongruously, police were also beginning to experiment with a "softer," more friendly type of law enforcement— foot patrols, neighborhood meetings, police-sponsored youth activities, and attention to quality-of-life issues quite apart from crime. A few radical criminologists saw this for what it was—a domestic "hearts and minds" campaign. As *The Iron Fist and the Velvet Glove* pointed out:

> Like the similar techniques developed in the sixties to maintain the overseas empire (on which many of the new police techniques were patterned), these new police strategies represent an attempt to streamline and mystify the repressive power of the state, not to minimize it or change its direction. The forms of repression may change, but their functions remain the same.[11]

Both militarization and community policing arose at the same time, and in response to the same social pressures. And, whereas the military largely neglected COIN in the period following defeat in Vietnam, the police kept practicing, and developing, its techniques. Decades later, facing insurgencies in Iraq and Afghanistan, the military turned to police for ideas.[12]

The lines of influence move in both directions.

STATISTICAL CONTROL

Among the police innovations that COIN theorists recommend for military use are: the Neighborhood Watch, embedded video, computerized intelligence files, and statistical analysis.[13] The last pair are particularly interesting.

In *Byting Back*, Martin Libicki explains the utility of statistical analysis programs, pointing to New York's Compstat (computerized statistics) system as an example.[14] Instituted under Chief William Bratton, Compstat worked by compiling crime reports, analyzing the emerging statistics, and presenting the information on precinct-level maps, thus enabling commanders to identify high-crime areas, deploy their officers strategically, and measure the progress of their efforts. Though its effect on actual *crime* is debatable, Compstat certainly served as the organizational keystone for the NYPD's city-wide crackdown during the Giuliani years.[15] Since that time, other departments around the country have adopted similar systems.[16]

The Los Angeles Police Department's system was proposed by Shannon Paulson, a police sergeant and a Navy intelligence reservist; it, too, was implemented under the leadership of William Bratton, who had since become the LAPD Chief. In Los Angeles, street cops carry a checklist of 65 "suspicious activities"—behaviors such as taking measurements, using binoculars, drawing diagrams, making notes, or expressing extremist views. Officers are required to file reports whenever they see such things, even if no crime has been committed. The "Suspicious Activity Reports" are then routed through the nearest fusion center, the Joint Regional Intelligence Center, where they are compiled, analyzed, and shared with other agencies—including local and national law enforcement agencies, the military, and private corporations. The LAPD, along with the U.S. Directorate of National Intelligence, are hoping to replicate this system in 62 other cities around the country, beginning with Boston, Chicago, and Miami.[17]

Meanwhile, in New Jersey, Charles McKenna, the head of the state's Office of Homeland Security and Preparedness, is enthusiastic about what new computer technologies might contribute to his department's efforts: "We are particularly interested in computer profiling, which is much more sophisticated, and quicker, than traditional racial profiling."[18]

MAPPING MUSLIMS

The U.S. government's mapping of the American Muslim population should be viewed in this light. In 2002 and 2003, the Department of Homeland Security requested—and received—statistical data, sorted by zip code and nationality, on people who identified themselves as "Arab" in the 2000 census.[19] And in February 2003, FBI director Robert Mueller ordered all 56 Bureau field offices to create "demographic" profiles of their areas of operation, specifically including the number of mosques. One Justice Department official explained that the demographics would be used "to set performance goals and objectives" for anti-terror efforts and electronic surveillance.[20]

Civil liberties groups compared the program to the first steps in the internment of Japanese Americans during World War II[21]—a notion that seems less than hyperbolic if we recall that, during this same period, 700 Middle Eastern immigrants were arrested as they complied with new registration rules. More than 1200 were detained without explanation or trial following the September 11 attacks, and thousands more were "interviewed" under FBI orders.[22] At the same time, the FBI has sent infiltrators into mosques throughout the country to root out—or sometimes, to set up—terror cells.[23]

In 2007, the LAPD began planning its own mapping program, dressed in the rhetoric of community policing. As the *L.A. Times* reported, the "Los Angeles Police Department's counter-terrorism bureau proposed using U.S. census data and other demographic information to pinpoint various Muslim communities and then reach out to them through social service agencies."[24]

Deputy Police Chief Michael P. Downing, head of the Counter-Terrorism Unit, explained:

> While this project will lay out geographic locations of many different Muslim populations around Los Angeles, we also intend to take a deeper look at their history, demographics, language, culture, ethnic breakdown, socioeconomic status and social interactions…. It is also our hope to identify communities, within the larger Muslim community which may be susceptible to violent ideologically based extremism and then use a full spectrum approach guided by intelligence-led strategy.[25]

After widespread public outcry, the LAPD publicly repudiated the plan.

Based on the Los Angeles controversy, the New York Police Department decided to keep its surveillance secret. Developed with CIA assistance—advice, training, and embedded staff—the NYPD's program was modeled on Israeli intelligence operations in the West Bank. The department's Demographic Unit uses census data to identify Muslim neighborhoods and sends undercover officers to monitor the conversations at hookah bars, cafés, and restaurants, as well as the literature at bookstores. At the same time, the Terrorism Interdiction Unit recruits informants to report on neighborhood activities and monitor the sermons delivered at the mosques. When young men of Middle Eastern descent are arrested—regardless of the nature of the charge—they are commonly interrogated by intelligence officers as part of the department's "debriefing program." Muslim prisoners are promised better conditions if they provide information. And the department has used minor licensing problems or traffic violations to pressure Pakistani taxi drivers to become informants.

Based on the resultant information, police analysts have produced a report assessing every mosque in the city for its possible terrorist ties. One NYPD official justified the program using a term that originated with the House Un-American Activities Committee (in a report on the Black Panthers) and that has since been carried forward into the counterinsurgency literature: the point, he said, is to "map the city's human terrain."[26]

ZERO TOLERANCE IN THE WAR ON TERROR

None of the NYPD's spy games should have been particularly surprising. It was, with some variation, more or less in line with what some top police theorists were publicly recommending.

In 2006, the criminologist George L. Kelling and L.A. Police Chief William Bratton wrote an article titled "Policing Terrorism" for the Manhattan Institute's *Civic Bulletin*.[27] Kelling was one of the authors of the "Broken Windows" theory underlying police zero-tolerance campaigns;[28] Bratton was one of the theory's most famous adherents. In their article, they explain that the cops' "everyday presence" in a designated area—the basis of community policing—means that patrol officers are well-placed to "notice even subtle changes in the neighborhoods they patrol." And: "They are in a better position to know responsible leaders in the Islamic and Arabic communities and can reach out to them for information and for help in developing informants."[29] At the same time, cops can ask "Business owners ... [as well as] doormen, private security guards, and transit workers,"—ultimately, "general public"—to "remain vigilant, to report any suspicious activity to police, and to 'ask the next question'"—that is, to stay "alert to preventive and investigatory possibilities" (or, less politely, to snoop).[30]

Once collected, the information provided by these various sources can be entered into a Compstat-type system for analysis, and "to share data ... across jurisdictions and levels of government."[31] It's for these reasons that Fusion Centers and Joint Terrorism Task Forces are important. The Fusion Centers "pool information from multiple jurisdictions," making it possible to share information "horizontally," while the JTTF's help it to flow "vertically," between the locals and the feds.[32]

At the same time, Kelling and Bratton advocate "creating a hostile environment for terrorists" by focusing on "illegal border crossings, forged documents, and other relatively minor precursor crimes," by increasing police visibility to "create a sense of omnipresence," and by "using cameras, random screenings, and sophisticated sensors" to pull in information. (They point admiringly to London's 40,000 security cameras.)[33] By taking this "Broken Windows" approach to counter-terrorism, the police can leverage minor infractions, vague suspicions, and even just routine contact into useful intelligence: "When it comes to recognizing suspicious behavior, U.S. law enforcement can learn much from the Israeli police. When the Israelis come into contact with criminal suspects, they ask such questions as: Why are you in Israel? How long have you been here? Where are you staying?—and then watch for behavioral responses."[34]

But this approach may require a shift in police priorities: "Prosecution of the case is less important than gathering intelligence and putting it into a database. No incident should be considered too minor for interaction with potential terrorists and for the collection of intelligence."[35]

PART TWO: GANG WARS

THE DOMESTIC ASPECTS of COIN are not limited to the widespread surveillance of Muslims rationalized by official fears of terrorism. The model is meant to be generalizable, and its techniques can be broadly applied. As New Jersey's Homeland Security Director Charles McKenna so frankly explained: "Jihad, Crips, extreme animal-rights activists, it's all the same: people trying damage the system."[36]

FROM CALIFORNIA TO AFGHANISTAN

The use of counterinsurgency in the "War on Terror"—both in the U.S. and abroad—builds directly on strategies and practices that police have tested and refined in their campaigns against gangs.

In the summer of 2010, 70 marines from Camp Pendleton spent a week accompanying Los Angeles police in preparation for deployment to Afghanistan. The marines wanted to learn the basics of anti-gang investigations, standards of police professionalism, and techniques for building rapport with the community.[37]

A *New York Times* profile of Marine Captain Scott Cuomo gives some idea of what he learned in L.A., and how he applied it in the combat zone:

> The same Marines patrolled in the same villages each day, getting to recognize the residents. They awarded the elders construction

projects and over hours of tea drinking showed them photographs they had taken of virtually every grown male in their battle space. "Is this guy Taliban?" the Marines asked repeatedly, then poured what they learned into a computer database.[38]

After a couple months, their efforts paid off. A villager identified a suspect, and the marines raided his house, arresting him and seizing weapons and opium. They placed the man, Juma Khan, in "a holding pen the size of a large dog cage" and interrogated him for two days. The marines then tried him, and found him guilty of working with the Taliban. But under an agreement with local elders, once Khan swore allegiance to the new Afghan government, he was released as a free man—or not quite.

In exchange for his freedom, and a job cleaning a nearby canal, Khan will be supervised by a group of elders, who in turn report to the American military. And he will himself become an informer, meeting regularly with the marines and answering their questions about his neighbors and friends.[39]

FROM AFGHANISTAN TO CALIFORNIA

Again, we see the lines of influence moving in both directions: Marines train with cops to prepare themselves for the work of managing a military occupation; and at the same time, military lessons are battle tested overseas and cycled back into the homeland.

Since February 2009, combat veterans from Iraq and Afghanistan have been serving as advisors to police in Salinas, California, with the stated aim of applying counterinsurgency tools to local anti-gang efforts.[40] Along with their expertise, the military advisors also arrive with software, including a computer program that maps the connections between gang activity, individual suspects, and their social circles, family ties, and neighborhood connections.[41]

This police-military partnership is occurring simultaneously with a renewal and expansion of the SPD's community policing philosophy.[42] The new community focus (encouraged by the Naval advisors) includes Spanish language training, a "Gifts for Guns" trade-in event, an anonymous tip hotline, senior citizen volunteer programs, a larger role for the Police Community Advisory Council, and programs that provide "more youth in the community alternatives to gang lifestyles and in the process develop a growing pool of home-grown, future police officers."[43]

Salinas police have also initiated partnerships with other local, state, and federal law enforcement agencies, including the Marshals, the ATF (Alcohol, Tobacco, and Firearms), the FBI, and Immigration and Customs Enforcement.[44] The most spectacular product of these partnerships, so far, was a set of coordinated raids on April 22, 2010, codenamed "Operation Knockout." The raids—coming after months of investigation—mobilized more than 200 law enforcement agents and resulted in 100 arrests, as well as the confiscation of 40 pounds of cocaine, fourteen pounds of marijuana, and a dozen guns.[45]

Operation Knockout was intended, not only to disrupt the targeted gangs, but to serve as a warning to others. Deputy Police Chief Kelly McMillin said: "We're going to follow quickly with call-ins of specific groups that we know are very active…. We are going to tell them that what happened on the 22nd could very well happen to them."[46]

The SPD's agenda for the future remains ambitious, illustrating an emerging, multi-faceted intelligence-sharing network. It includes plans to expand the city's video surveillance and gunfire-triangulation system, to adopt Compstat, to connect to the regional law-enforcement database COPLINK, and to create "a centralized information center (Fusion Center) in Salinas for the purpose of gathering and sharing information from Federal, State and local sources."[47]

Leonard A. Ferrari, provost of the Naval Postgraduate School, is enthusiastic about the program's potential. "The $1 trillion invested so far in Iraq and Afghanistan could pay a dividend in American streets," he told the *Washington Post*. The Salinas approach, he suggested, could become "a national model."[48]

CEASEFIRE, COMPSTAT, COIN

In fact, the Salinas collaboration, "Operation Ceasefire," is *already* part of national model, following a strategy developed in Boston under the same name.

In 1996, Boston's Ceasefire began with a focus on illegal handguns, but soon broadened its attention to include the gangs that used them. In response to ongoing gang conflict, the Boston Police Department convened a working group consisting of law enforcement officers, social workers, academics, and members of the Black clergy.[49]

Researchers working with police created a list of 155 murders, mapping the crimes geographically and demographically. They examined the criminal records of both the victims and (where known) the assailants. Using this information, they created a map of various gangs, their territory, and conflict points.[50]

Prioritizing the likely trouble-spots, police officers then sat down with gang members and gave them a clear choice: if there was gang violence in their area, both the cops and the district attorney were going to hit with everything they had.

> They could disrupt street drug activity, focus police attention on low-level street crimes such as trespassing and public drinking, serve outstanding warrants, cultivate confidential informants for medium- and long-term investigations of gang activities, deliver

strict probation and parole enforcement, seize drug proceeds and other assets, ensure stiffer plea bargains and sterner prosecutorial attention, request stronger bail terms (and enforce them), and even focus potentially severe Federal investigative and prosecutorial attention on, for example, gang-related drug activity.[51]

On the other hand, if the gang members wanted to clean up their act, the police would help them do so. Because of their coalition work, the cops came with offers of job training, drug counseling, and other services.[52] In this respect, Operation Ceasefire grew directly from the Boston Police Department's pre-existing community policing programs.

The strategy worked through direct deterrence, denying the benefits of violence and raising the costs. As importantly, "those costs were borne by the whole gang, not just the shooter."[53] So the cops could begin applying meaningful pressure before identifying a suspect, and the gang had an incentive to keep their members under control and maintain the peace.

The key elements of Operation Ceasefire—social network analysis, community partnerships, inter-agency cooperation, and a direct approach to deterrence—were quickly replicated and taken further in other cities, intersecting trends like zero-tolerance policing and the Compstat program. A report from the Justice Department's Office of Community Oriented Policing Service, *Street Gangs and Interventions: Innovative Problem Solving with Network Analysis*, provides a case study illustrating the result:

In the mid-1990s Newark's police were being remolded according to the pattern set by Giuliani's New York. The director of the Newark Police Department, Joe Santiago, introduced a Compstat system and, in 1996, proposed a partnership with Rutgers University professor George Kelling. Slowly, Santiago built a working group including cops, scholars, social workers, the clergy, and even public defense attorneys. This partnership, the Greater Newark Safer Cities Initiative (GNSCI), began by focusing on a small number of repeat offenders, using the same deterrence model developed in Ceasefire. Then, in 2003, GNSCI turned its attention to gangs, leading it to look beyond the city limits. The North Jersey Gang Task Force was born.[54]

Coordinating with law enforcement agencies statewide, the Rutgers researchers began to collect a wide array of data on gang membership, recent crimes, recruitment practices, family ties, and so on—as well as "information on the criminal histories of all identified gang members." Once the data was assembled, the researchers, following Boston's example, used it to map gang territory and perform a social network analysis, illustrating rivalries and alliances, and identifying likely sites for conflict. They then took the analysis to the individual level, charting the connections between gang members and others who associate with them. By diagramming these relationships, researchers were able to distinguish between core members and those only marginally involved.[55]

Such information was crucial for making both tactical and strategic decisions. Police could approach particular members differently, based on their role in the gang and their level of commitment. And they could identify the pressure points and know where to strike for maximum effect.

> Network analysis also allows one to identify people who hold structurally important positions within the gang networks. Cut points, people who are the only connection among people or groups of people, may be ideal selections for spreading a deterrence message or for affecting the structure and organization of the street gangs.[56]

Unlike Boston, where the focus was strictly on stopping gang *violence*, in New Jersey the aim was to disrupt the gangs themselves.

CARROTS AND STICKS, HEARTS AND MINDS

Operation Ceasefire and its progeny work chiefly through a "Cost/Benefit" approach to counterinsurgency: the government provides an admixture of incentives and deterrents to shape the choices of the rebels, their supporters, and the population as a whole. Simply put, the state creates a strategy to raise the costs associated with continued resistance and to reward cooperation. If the government can bring more force to bear and offer better rewards than the insurgents, rational self-interest should (in theory) lead people to side with the state rather than the rebels.[57] Ceasefire applied this same thinking to gangs.

At the same time, in developing Ceasefire, the police made sure to align other sources of legitimacy—social services, community organizations, the clergy—with its efforts, thus simultaneously increasing its leverage and heading off potential resistance. For example, in Boston, the Ceasefire coalition included Black ministers who had been vocal critics of the police. These men of the cloth began advising the cops in their anti-gang work, and eventually "sheltered the police from broad public criticism."[58]

The other major approach to COIN—the older and more famous "hearts and minds" strategy—operates by a somewhat different logic, focusing on "the problems of modernization and the insurgent need for popular support." As RAND explains, the aim was to rebuild public confidence in the government by instituting reforms, reducing corruption, and improving the population's standard of living.[59]

We can see the "Hearts and Minds" approach employed in a separate domestic experiment—the federally-funded "Weed and Seed" program.

WEED AND SEED: CLEAR-HOLD-BUILD

Weed and Seed was conceived in 1991, and gained prominence a year later as part of the federal response to widespread rioting after the acquittal of four Los Angeles cops who had been videotaped beating Black motorist Rodney King. Since that time, it has been implemented in over 300 neighborhoods nationwide.

The Department of Justice describes the project:

> The Weed and Seed strategy is based on a twopronged approach:
>
> 1. Law enforcement agencies and criminal justice officials co-operate with local residents to 'weed out' criminal activity in the designated area.
>
> 2. Social service providers and economic revitalization efforts are introduced to 'seed' the area, ensuring long-term positive change and a higher quality of life for residents.[60]

In terms of strategy, Weed and Seed closely resembles the military's "Clear-Hold-Build." As the U.S. Army's *Counterinsurgency Field Manual*, FM 3-24, elaborates: "Create a secure physical and psychological environment. Establish firm government control of the populace and area. Gain the populace's support."[61]

Clearing and *holding* refer to the removal and exclusion of hostile elements. *Building*, on the other hand, means both, literally, repairing infrastructure and, more metaphorically, gaining trust and winning support. However, even *building* includes an element of force:

> Progress in building support for the HN [Host Nation] government requires protecting the local populace.... To protect the populace, HN security forces continuously conduct patrols and use measured force against insurgent targets of opportunity.... Actions to eliminate the remaining covert insurgent political infrastructure must be continued....[62]

The domestic analogy is pretty straightforward. One police chief described the role of paramilitary units in his community policing strategy:

> [The] only people that are going to be able to deal with these problems are highly trained tactical teams with proper equipment to go into a neighborhood and clear the neighborhood and hold it; allowing community policing officers to come in and start turning the neighborhood around.[63]

In such campaigns, the relationship between community policing and militarization is especially clear. They're not competing or contradictory approaches. They work together, simultaneously or in series. One does the weeding; the other, the seeding.

The implications are not lost on those subject to this sort of campaign. "They're gunning for us," Omari Salisbury, a Seattle teenager, said when he heard about Weed and Seed. "They're gunning for Black youth."[64]

GANG POLITICS

Gang suppression has to be viewed, not only in terms of crime, but also in terms of politics.

This is true in two respects. First, police are not only (or even mainly) fighting crime, enforcing the law, or preventing violence—they are also disrupting and dis-organizing an incipient political force, striking against it before it can become a real nexus of resistance. A growing body of literature now specifically argues that gang violence should be treated as a type of insurgency.[65] And, by applying the techniques and analysis of counterinsurgency to counter-gang campaigns, the state tacitly admits that there is a political dimension to what is ordinarily presented as pure criminality. Insurgency and counterinsurgency are, together, a struggle over legitimacy. By applying the COIN framework domestically, the government concedes that its legitimacy is being challenged and that the challengers (however localized and weak) are rivals, or potential rivals, with independent claims to legitimacy and distinct spheres of influence.

Second, the gangs are sometimes self-consciously engaged in political action. As John Sullivan, an L.A. County Sheriffs Deputy, writes in one RAND report:

> [S]ome [gangs] have begun to adopt varying degrees of political activity. At the low end, this activity may include dominating neighborhood life and creating virtual "lawless zones," application of street taxes, or taxes on other criminal actors. Gangs with more sophisticated political attributes typically co-opt police and government officials to limit interference with their activities. At the high end, some gangs have active political agendas, using the political process to further their ends and destabilize governments.[66]

Among the examples Sullivan cites are the Gangster Disciples, a gang with 30,000 members in 35 states. In addition to employing themselves in the drug trade, "GD members infiltrate police and private security agencies, sponsor political candidates, register voters, and sponsor protest marches."[67] Other gangs have been active in resistance against gentrification, loan sharks, slum lords, price gouging, and police brutality.[68]

Historically, the Black Panther Party recognized the political potential of gangs. In Philadelphia, in the late 60s, the Panthers organized a series of gang conferences and tried to use negotiations to quell neighborhood violence. The Panthers also directed some of their public education and recruitment efforts toward gang members. Some gangsters did enlist to help in the Panthers' free breakfast program, and a few went on to become full Party members.[69] Most strikingly, the Los Angeles chapter was formed by a former gang leader, Alprentice "Bunchy" Carter of the Slauson Renegades.[70]

ANTI-GANG POLITICS

Facing these challenges, police anti-gang campaigns typically combine a variety of elements analogous to those in counterinsurgency: the creation of databases listing suspected gang members; the mapping of the social environment, illustrating connections between gang members, associates, families, etc.; the development of community contacts, especially with local leaders. These intelligence efforts are then paired with a campaign of persistent low-level harassment—stops, searches, petty citations, and the like. Each instance of harassment offers police the opportunity to collect additional information on the gang network while at the same time creating an inhospitable environment for those associated with gang activity.

For example, the main group responsible for such work in Salinas is the Monterey County Gang Task Force, called "The Black Snake" by youths in the community. The Task Force has 17 members, drawn from local police and sheriffs departments, the California Highway Patrol, and the state Department of Corrections. Wearing distinctive black uniforms and driving black cars, Task Force members conduct mass-arrest "round-ups,"[71] make random traffic stops, and regularly search the homes of gang members on parole or probation.[72] The sheer volume of such activity is astonishing: in its first five years of operation, the Task Force was responsible for 21,000 vehicle or pedestrian stops, 5,000 parole and probation "compliance" searches, and 2,800 arrests.[73]

Such anti-gang efforts are always implicitly political, especially as they become permanent features of life in poor Black and Latino communities. Though ostensibly aimed at preventing gang violence, counter-gang campaigns inevitably lead police to monitor the community as a whole. A Fresno cop explains the intended scope of his department's gang files: "If you're twenty-one, male, living in one of these neighborhoods, been in Fresno for ten years and you're *not* in our computer—then there's definitely a problem."[74] Disproportionate attention, especially when paired with lower—or "zero"—tolerance for disorder, then contributes to higher rates of arrest and incarceration.[75]

Sometimes officials extend enforcement by securing gang injunctions, special court orders prohibiting activities that would otherwise be legal—barring alleged gang members from appearing together in public, restricting the clothing they can wear, and subjecting them to a nighttime curfew.[76] At a broader level, the police will often engage in efforts disruptive of ordinary social life in gang-affected areas, such as cordoning, saturating, or sweeping select locations (e.g., parks, streets, or bars) or targeted events (ballgames, parties, car shows).[77]

In the most advanced campaigns, police sometimes take the further step of strategically *causing* gang conflict. Following the 1992 Los Angeles riots, for example, police did what they could to wreck a city-wide truce between the Bloods and the Crips. The cops attacked negotiating meetings and inter-gang social events, and also engaged in some underhanded tactics to create friction: covering one gang's graffiti with another's, or arresting a Blood only to release him deep in Crip territory. This occurred, not only in a context of widespread anger and recent unrest, but also at a point at which the gangs themselves were becoming increasingly politicized.[78]

Mike Davis described the government's response to the riots in military terms: "In Los Angeles I think we are beginning to see a repressive context that is literally comparable to Belfast or the West Bank, where policing has been transformed into full-scale counterinsurgency ... against an entire social stratum or ethnic group."[79]

PART THREE:
PRESERVING ORDER, PREVENTING CHANGE

THUS FAR, I have focused chiefly on the "hard" side of repression—the direct coercion, the forceful disruptions, the criminalization and incarceration, the violence. Now we need to look at the "soft" side—the strategic use of concessions, the promise of representation and access, the co-optation of leadership, and, comprising all of these, the *institutionalization* of dissent.[80] These elements represent, at this point, the state's most typical response to opposition from the left. And, by these means, the state does not only achieve control and exercise power *over* the organizations of the left, but *through* them.

One RAND researcher argues:

> The ideal allies for a government implementing control are, in fact, nonviolent members of the community the would-be insurgents seek to mobilize.... If regimes can infiltrate—or, better yet, cooperate with—mainstream groups they are often able to gain information on radical activities and turn potential militants away from violence.[81]

Broadly speaking, counterinsurgency offers two approaches to dealing with opposition, and they must be used selectively. Some adversaries, especially moderates, may be co-opted, bought off, and appeased. Others, the more recalcitrant portion, must be forcefully dis-organized, disrupted, deterred, or destroyed. The balance of concessions and coercion will be apportioned accordingly.

Some adversaries win new posts—offices in a "reformed" administration, or jobs in "responsible" nonprofits, labor unions, or progressive think tanks. They gain access, inclusion, or representation in exchange for working within the existing institutional framework. The others will face harsher outcomes—including, for example, imprisonment, exile, or assassination. Whatever the approach in a particular case, the important thing is that the opposition is neutralized—rendered harmless, made controllable, and exploited as either the object or the tool of state power.

"FORCE MULTIPLIERS": THE MILITARY-NGO COMPLEX

Counterinsurgency theory places a heavy emphasis on shaping the social environment in which the population lives and resistance develops. One way governments exercise this influence is with their money. As FM 3-24 explains:

> *Some of the Best Weapons for Counterinsurgents Do Not Shoot....* Counterinsurgents often achieve the most meaningful success in garnering public support and legitimacy for the HN government with activities that do not involve killing insurgents.... [L]asting victory comes from a vibrant economy, political participation, and restored hope. Particularly after security has been achieved, dollars and ballots will have more important effects than bombs and bullets.... 'money is ammunition.'[82]

Foreign aid has thus often been criticized as an instrument of imperialism, even when the funds are distributed indirectly through nongovernmental organizations or nongovernmental humanitarian organizations (NGOs or NGHOs).[83]

As the U.S. began its war against Afghanistan in October 2001, Colin Powell—the former general, the founding chairman of the nonprofit America's Promise Alliance, and, at the time, the Secretary of State—managed to embarrass NGO leaders with his praise for their work. Speaking at the National Foreign Policy Conference for Leaders of Nongovernmental Organizations, he said: "just as surely as our diplomats and military, American NGOs are out there serving and sacrificing on the front lines of freedom.... [NGOs] are such a force multiplier for us, such an important part of our combat team."[84]

Later, guidelines negotiated by representatives of the military and the major humanitarian groups discouraged any repetition of Powell's gaffe, specifying that "U.S. Armed Forces should not describe NGHOs as 'force multipliers' or 'partners' of the military."[85] FM 3-24 managed to retain Powell's meaning while avoiding the offensive language: "Many such agencies resist being overtly involved with military forces," it cautions; but then: "some kind of liaison [is] needed... to ensure that, as much as possible, objectives are shared and actions and messages synchronized."[86]

The RAND study *Networks and Netwars* outlines "a range of possibilities" for the military's use of international nonprofits:

> from encouraging the early involvement of appropriate NGO networks in helping to detect and head off a looming crisis, to working closely with them in the aftermath of conflicts to improve the effectiveness of U.S. forces still deployed, to reduce the residual hazards they face, and to strengthen the often fragile peace.[87]

One result of this perspective is that aid money, and thus NGO attention, increasingly follows the state's priorities—and its military's priorities in particular.[88]

For instance, in 2010 the U.S. awarded $114 million to aid groups working in Yemen, with the stated goal of "improving the livelihood of citizens in targeted communities and improving governance capabilities."[89] This supposedly humanitarian assistance came alongside $1.2 billion in military aid, clandestine military and intelligence activity, and a CIA assessment that the Al Qaeda affiliate in Yemen represented the largest threat to the United States' global security.[90] General David Petraeus was frank in referring the U.S. involvement in the country as "Preventive Counterinsurgency Operations."[91]

But of course, the United States has not restricted itself to preventive action. The following year, the U.S. continued to provide military aid and development assistance, and escalated its covert military actions—including the controversial assassination of the cleric Anwar al Awlaki (an American citizen)—even as the State Department expressed concern over the Yemeni government's brutal repression of a popular "Arab Spring" uprising.[92]

As the military invests more deeply in "nation-building" projects, and as humanitarian assistance finds itself militarized, the distinctions between military and development aid are becoming increasingly irrelevant.[93] Writing in *The New Republic*, David Rieff concludes: "development is a continuation of war by other means."[94]

THE MARSHAL PLAN

The domestic counterpart to the nongovernmental "force multiplier" is the community policing "partnership." We've seen nonprofit funding tied to the criminal justice agenda in the Weed and Seed program; the use of social services and Black churches to create "the 'network of capacity' necessary to legitimize, fund, equip, and carry out" Boston's Operation Ceasefire;[95] the collaboration of social workers, the clergy, and public defense attorneys for similar ends in Newark; police-sponsored youth and elders programs in Salinas; and, in Los Angeles, a plan to use social service agencies to gain access to Muslim communities suspected of breeding terrorists.

But sometimes police-led partnerships go further, using progressive nonprofits to channel and control political opposition, moving it in safe, institutional, and reformist directions, rather than toward more radical or militant action. For example, consider the efforts of liberal nonprofits to contain community anger after transit police shot and killed an unarmed Black man in Oakland, California:

Oscar Grant was killed on January 1, 2009. A week later, on January 7, a protest against the police turned into a small riot.[96] Organizers with the Coalition Against Police Executions (CAPE)—a group largely composed of progressive nonprofits and Black churches—denounced the crowd's violence. One CAPE leader said that he wept watching the riots on television, feeling that years of hard work were being "destroyed by anarchists."[97]

But—likely because of the revolt—the cop in the case, Johannes Mehserle, was arrested and charged with murder. Before the riots there had been no statement of concern from the mayor's office, no Justice Department investigation, and no arrests. In fact, Mehserle's employers had not even interviewed him about the incident. "The rebellion was really about the fact that nothing was being done," George Ciccariello-Maher explains. "If there's one lesson to take from this, it's that the only reason Mehserle was arrested is because people tore up the city. It was the riot—and the threat of future riots."[98]

In an effort to reassert its leadership, CAPE organized another demonstration for January 14. Speakers included Mayor Ron Dellums, the rapper Too $hort, and representatives of various nonprofits—all of whom urged the crowd to remain peaceful. Furthermore, CAPE's designated marshals, operating under the supervision of a private security guard, surrounded the demonstration while unidentified informants mingled in the crowd to look for troublemakers.[99]

Despite the tight control, things did not go as planned. When the speeches were over, much of the crowd refused to leave. Organizers announced that police would intervene if the group would not disperse; but rather than wait, CAPE's own marshals formed a line and began pushing people off the streets. The crowd—now very angry—started breaking windows. The security team, after consulting with police, withdrew from the area and left it to the cops to handle the crowd. The police fired teargas and made arrests.[100]

Future demonstrations, beginning on January 30, were likewise handled with threats, arrests, and violence.[101] At the same time, and in keeping with the COIN model, local, state, and federal agencies all undertook extensive intelligence operations targeting protest organizers—monitoring websites, videotaping crowds, sending plainclothes officers into the demonstrations, and infiltrating planning meetings.[102]

"If we learned on January seventh that our power was in the streets," Ciccariello-Maher concludes, "what we learned on the fourteenth is that the state was going to counter-attack…. The state didn't counterattack by force at first; the state counter-attacked through these institutions, the nonprofits."[103]

NO JUSTICE, URBAN PEACE

A year later, the process repeated itself. As Johannes Mehserle's trial approached, Nicole Lee, director of the nonprofit "Urban Peace Movement," circulated an email focused not on winning justice, but on preventing violence should justice be denied. Titled "Bracing for Mehserle Verdict: Community Engagement Plan," the June 23, 2010 memo offered two sets of instructions:

1   Organizations, CBOs [Community-Based Organizations], and Public Agencies should be thinking of ways to *create organized events or avenues for young people and community members to express their frustrations with the system* in constructive and peaceful ways. If people have no outlets then it may be easier for folks to be pulled toward more destructive impulses.

2   We need to *begin "inoculating" our bases and the community at-large so that when the verdict comes down, people are prepared* for it, and so that the "outside agitators" who were active during the initial Oscar Grant protests are not able to incite the crowd so easily.[104]

The memo listed several talking points, which served the state's interests so well that the City of Oakland ran an edited version on its webpage.[105]

Around the same time, another organization, ironically named "Youth Uprising," sponsored a public service announcement centered on the slogan, "Violence is Not Justice." The video includes local rappers, civil rights attorneys, school administrators, representatives from nonprofits, a police captain, and the District Attorney of San Francisco—all urging a peaceful response to the verdict.[106]

Religious leaders also got into the act, using the pulpit to ask people to remain safely at home when the verdict was announced.[107]

The pacifying efforts, though broadly distributed, were centrally coordinated. Shortly before the trial, the mayor and police held a meeting with several Bay Area nonprofits. The topic, of course, was the prevention of riots.[108]

In practice, avoiding unrest became the primary focus of the institutionalized left; CAPE's stated goal, the prevention of police brutality, receded into the background. If anything, by condemning the rioters and cooperating with the cops, liberal leaders helped to legitimize the police counter-attack and made further brutality more, not less, likely.

In the end, Officer Mehserle was convicted, but of a lesser charge—manslaughter, rather than murder. And, when the verdict was announced, rioting did ensue.[109] Hundreds of people, mostly young people of color, braved not only the clubs and the tear gas of the police, but also the condemnation of their purported community leaders.[110]

ADVANCE THE STRUGGLE

In their published analysis of the Oscar Grant crisis, the revolutionary group Advance the Struggle argued that, by trying to defuse popular anger, "Bay Area nonprofits effectively acted as an extension of the state."[111]

Had the rage over Grant's murder not been channeled into ritualized protest, had the leaders not been more concerned with controlling the community response than in confronting injustice, had the organizing not been, in a word, institutionalized—it is hard to know what might have been possible.

Advance the Struggle contrasted the trajectory of events in Oakland with those of Greece, just a few weeks before the Grant killing:

> There, the police murder of a 15-year-old Alexandros Grigoropoulos triggered reactions which, very quickly, evolved from protests to riots to a general strike in which 2.5 million workers were on strike in December 2008. Within days the killer cop and police accomplices were arrested, but even this concession didn't trick the movement into subsiding. The police murder set off the uprising, but the participants connected the murder with the issues of unemployment, neo-liberal economic measures, political corruption, and a failing education system. Aren't we facing similar problems in Oakland…?[112]

Of course there are differences between Oakland and Athens—differences of geography, history, and political culture. The type of insurrection unleashed in Greece may not have been possible in California. But that is not an *objection* to the radical analysis; it is, instead, *the premise*. The political environment in Oakland has been shaped in such a way so as to sharply limit the potential for struggle. And the institutionalization of conflict in professionalized nonprofits is an important part of that restrictive context. There is no guarantee that things would have gone further had the nonprofits not intervened, or that greater conflict would have won greater gains. But their intervention certainly helped to contain the rebellion, and closed off untold possibilities for further action. That is, quite clearly, what it was intended to do.

CONCLUSION: WARTIME

IN THIS ESSAY, I have tried to illustrate something of the transfer of counter-insurgency theory, strategy, technique, and personnel from the military to the police, and *vice versa*. I've shown how COIN has informed the government's wholesale surveillance of the American Muslim population, how anti-gang campaigns are both shaping and being shaped by military operations abroad, and how the state uses non-governmental and nonprofit agencies, alongside military and police action, to channel and control opposition.

In this context, the chapter's title—"The Other Side of the COIN"—has three distinct meanings, which correspond to the main themes of my argument. First, it refers to the strategic pairing of direct coercion and subtle legitimacy-building activities. Second, it points to the joint development of military operations overseas and police control domestically. And third, it reminds us that when the authorities turn to counterinsurgency it is because they fear that insurgency is brewing. Wars—especially revolutionary wars—have two sides.

The state understands that there is a war underway. It is time that the left learns to see it.

NOTES

1   This paper was published, in a different form as Kristian Williams, "The Other Side of the COIN: Counterinsurgency and Community Policing," *Interface: A Journal for and about Social Movements.* Interfacejournal.net. May, 2011.

   I am grateful to the numerous people who offered detailed comments on earlier drafts, in particular: Jules Boykoff, George Ciccariello-Maher, Emily-Jane Dawson, Colette G., Don H., Chris Knudtsen, Peter Little, Geoff McNamara, Will Munger, Steve Niva, Janeen P., Josef Schneider, M. Treloar, Kevin Van Meter, and Lesley Wood.

2   Quoted in Laura Trevelyan, "Bill Bratton to Advise at UK Gang Conference," *BBC News*, October 9, 2011. http://www.bbc.co.uk/news/uk-15229199.

3   Kristian Williams, *Our Enemies in Blue: Police and Power in America* (Brooklyn: Soft Skull Press, 2004), 255. I would refer readers to the ninth chapter, "Your Friendly

Neighborhood Police State," for my full account of the relationship between militarization and community policing.

4   David C. Gompert and John Gordon IV et al. *War by Other Means: Building Complete and Balanced Capabilities for Counterinsurgency.* (Santa Monica: RAND, 2008), xlv.

5   Joseph D. Celeski, *Policing and Law Enforcement in COIN: Thick Blue Line* (Hulbert Field, Florida: The JSOU Press, 2009), 40.

6   William Rosenau, *Subversion and Insurgency* (Santa Monica: RAND, 2007), 15.

7   Austin Long, *On Other War: Lessons from Five Decades of RAND Counterinsurgency Research* (Santa Monica: RAND, 2006), 53.

8   Center for Research on Criminal Justice, *The Iron Fist and the Velvet Glove: An Analysis of the U.S. Police* (Berkeley, California: Center for Research on Criminal Justice, 1975), 48–50.

9   Clark McPhail et al., "Policing Protest in the United States: 1960–1995," in *Policing Protest: The Control of Mass Demonstrations in Western Democracies*, eds. Donnatella Della Porta and Herbert Reiter (Minneapolis: University of Minnesota Press, 1998).

10 Daryl F. Gates (with Diane K. Shah), *Chief: My Life in the LAPD* (New York: Bantam Books, 1992), 109; and, Ken Lawrence, *The New State Repression* (Portland, Oregon: Tarantula, 2006), 13–16.

11 Center for Research on Criminal Justice, *The Iron Fist and the Velvet Glove*, 30.

12 Jason H. Beers, *Community-Oriented Policing and Counterinsurgency: A Conceptual Model.* (Fort Leavenworth, Kansas: U.S. Army Command and General Staff College, 2007), 77.

13 Celeski, *Policing and Law Enforcement in COIN*, 43; Martin C. Libicki, et al., *Byting Back: Regaining Information Superiority Against 21st-Century Insurgents* (Santa Monica: RAND, 2007), 79–80; and, Gary D. Calese, *Law Enforcement Methods for Counterinsurgency Operations* (Fort Leavenworth, Kansas: U.S. Army Command and General Staff College, School of Advanced Military Studies, 2004), 41–42.

14 Libicki, *Byting Back*, 25.

15 Sidney L. Harring and Gerda W. Ray, "Policing a Class Society: New York City in the 1990s," *Social Justice*, Summer 1999.

16 Christian Parenti, *Lockdown America: Police and Prisons in the Age of Crisis* (London: Verso, 1999), 75–76 and 83–89.

17 Siobhan Gorman, "LAPD Terror-Tip Plan May Serve as Model," *Wall Street Journal*, April 15, 2008; Josh Meyer, "LAPD Leads the Way in Local Counter-Terrorism," *Los Angeles Times*, April 14, 2008; Michael German and Jay Stanley, *What's Wrong with Fusion Centers?* (New York: American Civil Liberties Union, December 2007); and, Mike German and Jay Stanley, *Fusion Center Update* (New York: American Civil Liberties Union, July 2008).

18 Quoted in Judy Peet, "NJIT Homeland Security Center Studies Groundbreaking Anti-Terrorism Technology," *NJ.com*, June 12, 2010.

19 Lynette Clemetson, "Homeland Security Given Data on Arab-Americans," *New York Times*, July 30, 2004.

20 Michael Isikoff, "Investigator: The FBI Says, Count the Mosques," *Newsweek*, February 3, 2003.

21   American Civil Liberties Union, "ACLU Calls FBI Mosque-Counting Scheme Blatant Ethnic and Religious Profiling [press release]." January 27, 2003.

22   Philip Heymann, "Muslims in America After 9/11: The Legal Situation," in *Muslims in Europe and the United States: A Transatlantic Comparison* (The Minda de Gunzburg Center for European Studies at Harvard University, December 15–16, 2006), http://www.ces.fas.harvard.edu/conferences/muslims/Heymann.pdf.

23   Jerry Markon, "Tension Grows Between Calif. Muslims, FBI After Informant Infiltrates Mosque," *Washington Post*, December 5, 2010.

24   Richard Winton, et al., "LAPD Defends Muslim Mapping Effort," *Los Angeles Times*, November 10, 2007.

25   Quoted in Winton, "LAPD Defends Muslim Mapping Effort."

26   Matt Apuzzo and Adam Goldman, "With CIA Help, NYPD Moves Covertly in Muslim Areas," *Associated Press Archive*, August 25, 2011. [Database: Newsbank-American's News, accessed January 10, 2012.]
      For a short history of the "human terrain" idea, see: Roberto González, *American Counterinsurgency: Human Science and the Human Terrain* (Chicago: Prickly Paradigm, 2009), especially Chapter Two, "The Origins of Human Terrain," 25–44.

27   George L. Kelling and William J. Bratton, "Policing Terrorism," *Civic Bulletin*, September 2006.
      The Manhattan Institute's website proudly describes itself as "an important force in shaping American political culture and developing ideas that foster economic choice and individual responsibility…. Our work has won new respect for market-oriented policies and helped make reform a reality." "About the Manhattan Institute," http://www.manhattan-institute.org/html/about_mi_30.htm, (accessed February 6, 2012).

28   James Q. Wilson and George L. Kelling, "Broken Windows," *Atlantic Monthly*, March 1982.

29   Kelling and Bratton, "Policing Terrorism," 2.

30   Kelling and Bratton, "Policing Terrorism," 4.

31   Kelling and Bratton, "Policing Terrorism," 5. The authors do offer a *pro forma* caution: "We also need to be mindful of the mess that local police departments got themselves into in the 1960s by illegally spying on anti-war and civil rights groups. Uniform training procedures and standards on how intelligence is gathered, stored, and accessed need to be developed and disseminated to local law enforcement in order to safeguard citizens' privacy and civil rights." Kelling and Bratton, "Policing Terrorism," 5.

32   Kelling and Bratton, "Policing Terrorism," 6.

33   Kelling and Bratton, "Policing Terrorism," 3.

34   Kelling and Bratton, "Policing Terrorism," 4.

35   Kelling and Bratton, "Policing Terrorism," 4–5.

36   Quoted in Peet, "NJIT Homeland Security Center."

37   Julie Watson, "Cops Show Marines How to Take On the Taliban," *NBC Los Angeles*, July 12, 2010. http://www.nbclosangeles.com/news/local-beat/Cops-Show-Marines-How-to-Take-on-the-Taliban--98202989.html.

38 Elisabeth Bumiller, "U.S. Tries to Reintegrate Taliban Soldiers," *New York Times*, May 23, 2010.

39 Bumiller, "U.S. Tries to Reintegrate Taliban Soldiers."

40 For a detailed discussion of the Salinas partnership, see: Will Munger, "Social War in the Salad Bowl," in this volume.

41 Karl Vick, "Iraq's Lessons, On the Home Front," *Washington Post*, November 15, 2009.

42 Louis Fetherolf, *90-day Report to the Community* (Salinas, California: Salinas Police Department, July 21, 2009),15–16.

43 Louis Fetherolf, *180-day Report to the Community* (Salinas, California: Salinas Police Department, October 20, 2009), 33–34.

44 Fetherolf, *180-day Report.*

45 Julia Reynolds, "Operation Knockout: Gang Raid Targets Nuestra Familia in Salinas," *The Herald*, April 23, 2010.

46 Quoted in Julia Reynolds, "After Operation Knockout, Salinas Police Focus on Prevention," *The Herald*, April 24, 2010.

47 Fetherolf, *180-day Report to the Community*, 10.

48 Quoted in Vick, "Iraq's Lessons, On the Home Front."

49 David M. Kennedy et al., "Developing and Implementing Operation Ceasefire," in *Reducing Gun Violence: The Boston Gun Project's Operation Ceasefire* (Washington, D.C.: U.S. Department of Justice, National Institute of Justice, September 2001); Anthony A. Braga and Christopher Winship, *Creating an Effective Foundation to Prevent Youth Violence: Lessons from Boston in the 1990s* (Rappaport Institute for Greater Boston Policy Brief: September 26, 2005); and, Anthony A. Braga and David M. Kennedy, "Reducing Gang Violence in Boston," in *Responding to Gangs: Evaluation and Research*, eds. Winifred L. Reed and Scott H. Decker (Washington D.C.: U.S. Department of Justice, Office of Justice Programs, National Institute of Justice, July 2002).

50 Kennedy, "Developing and Implementing Operation Ceasefire"; and, David M. Kennedy, et al., "The (Un)Known Universe: Mapping Gangs and Gang Violence in Boston," in *Crime Mapping and Crime Prevention*, eds. David L. Weisburd and J. Thomas McEwen (New York: Criminal Justice Press, 1997).

51 David Kennedy, "Pulling Levers: Getting Deterrence Right," *National Institute of Justice Journal*, July 1998, 5.

52 Braga and Winship, *Creating an Effective Foundation*; Kennedy, "Developing and Implementing Operation Ceasefire"; and, Braga and Kennedy, "Reducing Gang Violence in Boston."

53 Kennedy, "Pulling Levers," 6.

54 Jean M. McGloin, *Street Gangs and Interventions: Innovative Problem Solving with Network Analysis* (Washington, D.C.: U.S. Department of Justice, Office of Community Oriented Policing Services, September 23, 2005), 9–13.

55 McGloin, *Street Gangs and Interventions*, 14–18.

56 McGloin, *Street Gangs and Interventions*, 18.

57 Gompert and Gordon, *War by Other Means*, 25.

58 Braga and Winship, *Creating an Effective Foundation*, 6.

59 Gompert and Gordon, *War by Other Means*, 25.

60 Community Capacity Development Office, *Weed and Seed Implementation Manual* (Washington, D.C.: U.S. Department of Justice, August 2005), 1.

61 United States Army, FM 3-24, *Counterinsurgency*, December 2006, 5-50 and 5-51.

62 FM 3-24, 5-70.

63 Peter B. Kraska and Victor E. Kappeler, "Militarizing American Police: The Rise and Normalization of Paramilitary Units," in *The Police and Society: Touchstone Readings*, ed. Victor E. Kappeler (Prospect Heights: Waveland Press, 1999), 473.

64 Quoted in Dick Lilly, "City Urged to Bury Weed and Seed Plan," *Seattle Times*, March 27, 1992.

65 Max G. Manwaring, *Street Gangs: The New Urban Insurgency* (Carlisle, Pennsylvania: Strategic Studies Institute, March 2005); and, Joseph E. Long, *A Social Movement Theory Typology of Gang Violence* (Monterey, California: Naval Postgraduate School, June 2010); John P. Sullivan, "Future Conflict: Criminal Insurgencies, Gangs and Intelligence," *Small Wars Journal*, May 31, 2009; and, Joint Chiefs of Staff, "Appendix A: Insurgency and Crime," in Joint Publication 3-24, *Counterinsurgency Operations*, October 5, 2009.

66 John P. Sullivan, "Gangs, Hooligans, and Anarchists: The Vanguard of Netwar in the Streets," in *Networks and Netwars: The Future of Terror, Crime, and Militancy*, eds. John Arquilla and David Ronfeldt (Santa Monica: RAND, 2001), 102.

67 Sullivan, "Gangs, Hooligans, and Anarchists," 113–14.

68 Martín Sánchez Jankowski, *Islands in the Street: Gangs and American Urban Society* (Berkeley: University of California Press, 1991), 11–12 and 179–92.

69 Omari L. Dyson, et al., "'Brotherly Love Can Kill You': The Philadelphia Branch of the Black Panther Party," in *Comrades: A Local History of the Black Panther Party*, ed. Judson L. Jeffries (Bloomington: Indiana University Press, 2007), 228–30.

70 Judson L. Jeffries and Malcolm Foley, "To Live and Die in L.A.," in *Comrades: A Local History of the Black Panther Party*, ed. Judson L. Jeffries (Bloomington: Indiana University Press, 2007), 261.

    Carter was later murdered by members of a rival organization, one casualty of a "vendetta" deliberately created by FBI disinformation tactics in the course of its infamous Counterintelligence Program, COINTELPRO. Ward Churchill and Jim Vanderwall, *The COINTELPRO Papers: Documents from the FBI's Secret Wars Against Domestic Dissent* (Boston: South End Press, 1990), 132–33.

71 Salinas Police Department, "Operation Ceasefire & Operation Knockout," *Report to the Community*, July 2010, 4.

72 Scott Kraft, "Aggressive Crackdown Targets Long-Entrenched Salina Gangs," *Los Angeles Times*, June 16, 2010.

73 Regardless, the rate of violent crime has not appreciably decreased. Long, *Social Movement Theory Typology of Gang Violence*, 35–37.

74 Quoted in Parenti, *Lockdown America*, 111, emphasis added.

75 Judith Greene and Kevin Pranis, *Gang Wars: The Failure of Enforcement Tactics and the*

Need for Effective Public Safety Strategies (Justice Policy Institute, July 2007), 6.

76 Critical Resistance Oakland, *Betraying the Model City: How Gang Injunctions Fail Oakland* ([Oakland], February 2011); and, Frank P. Barajas, "An Invading Army: A Civil Gang Injunction in a Southern California Chicana/o Community," *Latino Studies*, 2007.

    For more on gang injunctions, see: Stop the Injunctions Coalition, "Our Oakland, Our Solutions," in this volume.

77 Felix M. Padilla, *Gangs as an American Enterprise* (New Brunswick, New Jersey: Rutgers University Press, 1992), 85; and Randall G. Sheldon et al., *Youth Gangs in American Society* (Belmont, California: Wandsworth, 2001), 244.

78 Mike Davis, "Understanding L.A.: The New Urban Order [interview with *CovertAction Information Bulletin*]," in *USA: A Look at Reality* (Hyattsville, Maryland: Equal Justice USA/Quixote Center, July 1992); Malcolm W. Klein, *The American Street Gang: Its Nature, Prevalence, and Control* (New York: Oxford University Press, 1995); and, Irving A. Spergel, *The Youth Gang Problem: A Community Approach* (New York: Oxford University Press, 1995), 191.

79 Davis, "Understanding L.A."

80 "Institutionalization ... is composed of three main components: First, the *routinization* of collective action.... Second, *inclusion* and *marginalization*, whereby challengers who are willing to adhere to established routines will be granted access to political exchanges in mainstream institutions, while those who refuse to accept them can be shut out of conversations through either repression or neglect. Third, *co-optation*, which means that challengers alter their claims and tactics to ones that can be pursued without disrupting the normal practice of politics." David S. Meyer and Sidney Tarrow, "A Movement Society: Contentious Politics for a New Century," in *The Social Movement Society: Contentious Politics for a New Century*, ed. David S. Meyer and Sidney Tarrow (Lanham, Maryland: Rowman and Littlefield, 1998), 21.

81 Daniel Byman, *Understanding Proto-Insurgencies* (Santa Monica: RAND, 2007), 24.

82 FM 3-24, 1-153, emphasis in original.

83 For example: Arundhati Roy, "Public Power in the Age of Empire," *Democracy Now*, http://www.democracynow.org/2004/8/23/public_power_in_the_age_of#; Ji Giles Ungpakorn, "NGOs: Enemies or Allies," *International Socialism*, October 2004; Yves Engler, "Occupation by NGO," *CounterPunch*, August 13–15, 2010; and James Petras, "NGOs: In the Service of Imperialism," *Journal of Contemporary Asia*, 29.4, 1999.

84 Colin Powell, "Remarks to the National Foreign Policy Conference for Leaders of Nongovernmental Organizations," October 26, 2001. http://avalon.law.yale.edu/sept11/powell_brief31.asp.

85 United States Institute of Peace, *Guidelines for Relations Between U.S. Armed Forces and Non-Governmental Humanitarian Organizations in Hostile or Potentially Hostile Environments* [No date].

86 FM 3-24, 1-122.

87 John Arquilla and David Ronfeldt, "Summary," in *Networks and Netwars: The Future of Terror, Crime, and Militancy*, ed. John Arquilla and David Ronfeldt (Santa Monica: RAND 2001) x.

88 GRAIN. *The Soils of War: The Real Agenda Behind Agricultural Reconstruction in Afghanistan and Iraq*, March 2009. http://www.grain.org/briefings/?id=217.

89 Quoted in David Rieff, "How NGOs Became Pawns in the War on Terrorism," *The New Republic*, August 3, 2010.

90 Greg Miller and Peter Finn, "CIA Sees Increased Threat from al-Qaeda in Yemen," *Washington Post*, August 24, 2010; and, Andrew Y. Zelin, "What if Obama's Yemen Policy Works?" *Middle East Channel*, September 22, 2010. http://mideast.foreignpolicy.com/posts/2010/09/22/what_if_obama_s_yemen_policy_works.

91 Quoted in Robert E. Mitchell, "Yemen: Testing a New Coordinated Approach to Preventive Counterinsurgency," *Small Wars Journal*, August 1, 2011.

92 Jeremy M. Sharp, *Yemen: Background and U.S. Relations* (Congressional Research Service: CRS Report for Congress, October 6, 2011); Mark Mazzetti, "U.S. is Intensifying a Secret Campaign of Yemen Airstrikes," *New York Times*, June 8, 2011; "Jeremy Scahill: As Mass Uprising Threatens the Saleh Regime, A Look at the Covert U.S. War in Yemen," *Democracy Now*, March 22, 2011. http://www.democracynow.org/2011/3/22/jeremy_scahill_as_mass_uprising_threatens.

93 Mitchell, "Yemen."

94 Rieff, "How NGOs Became Pawns."

95 Braga and Winship, *Creating an Effective Foundation*, 4–5.

96 George Ciccariello-Maher, "Oakland's Not for Burning? Popular Fury at Yet Another Police Murder," *CounterPunch*, January 9–11, 2009.

97 Quoted in George Ciccariello-Maher, "'Oakland is Closed!' Arrest and Containment Fail to Blunt Anger in the Streets," *CounterPunch*, January 16–18, 2009.

98 George Ciccariello-Maher, "From Arizona to Oakland: The Intersections of Mass Work and Revolutionary Politics [Bring the Ruckus panel discussion]" (Portland, Oregon: October 23, 2010).

99 Ciccariello-Maher, "'Oakland is Closed!'"

100 Ciccariello-Maher, "'Oakland is Closed!'; and Advance the Struggle, *Justice for Oscar Grant: A Lost Opportunity?* ([Oakland]: 2009).

101 Raider Nation Collective, "Introduction," in *Raider Nation, Volume 1: From the January Rebellions to Lovelle Mixon and Beyond*, ed. Raider Nation Collective (Oakland, California: May 2010); and, George Ciccariello-Maher, "'Fired Up, Can't Take It No More': From Oakland to Santa Rita, The Struggle Continues," *CounterPunch*, February 3, 2009.

102 Ali Winston, "Anarchists, the FBI and the Aftermath of the Oscar Grant Murder Trial," *The Informant*, January 27, 2011. http://informant.kalwnews.org/2011/01/anarchists-the-fbi-and-the-aftermath-of-the-oscar-grant-murder-trial/#more-5247; Ali Winston, "L.A. Oscar Grant Protests Also Monitored by Law Enforcement," *The Informant*, January 6, 2011. http://informant.kalwnews.org/2011/01/la-oscar-grant-protests-also-monitored-by-law-enforcement/#more-4592; Ali Winston, "Logs Detail Oakland Police Surveillance of Grant Protestors, Concerns About 'Anarchists'," *The Informant*, January 7, 2011. http://informant.kalwnews.org/2011/01/logs-detail-oakland-police-surveillance-of-grant-protesters-concerns-about-anarchists/#more-4643; Ali Winston, "Monitoring

Protests: Normal Policing or Something Deeper?" *The Informant*, December 16, 2010. http://informant.kalwnews.org/2010/12/monitoring-the-oscar-grant-protests-normal-policing-or-something-deeper/#more-4378; and Ali Winston, "Police Files Reveal Interest in Oscar Grant Protests, 'Anarchists'," *The Informant*, December 15, 2010. http://informant.kalwnews.org/2010/12/police-documents-reveal-federal-interest-in-oscar-grant-protests-anarchists/.

103 Ciccariello-Maher, "From Arizona to Oakland."

104 Nicole Lee, "Bracing for Mehserle Verdict: Community Engagement Plan," in *Advance the Struggle*, June 27, 2010, emphasis in original. http://advancethestruggle.wordpress.com/2010/06/27/nonpofits-defend-the-state-need-more-proof /#more-773.

105 Raider Nation Collective, "Lessons Never Learned: Nonprofits and the State, Redux," *Bring the Ruckus*, July 2, 2010. http://bringtheruckus.org/?q=node/112.

106 Youth Uprising, "Violence Is Not Justice," *YouTube.com*, July 6, 2010. http://www.youtube.com/watch?v=XqofgXqteuQ. (Viewed October 14, 2010.) The organization's website, YouthUprising.org, later quoted Attorney General Eric Holder, saying the group is a "perfect example of what we need to be doing around the country." (Viewed October 14, 2010).

107 George Ciccariello-Maher, "Chronicle of a Riot Foretold," *CounterPunch*, June 29, 2010.

108 Ciccariello-Maher, "Chronicle of a Riot Foretold."

109 George Ciccariello-Maher, "Oakland's Verdict," *CounterPunch*, July 12, 2010.

110 A few months later, radicals in Seattle reported a similar dynamic, co-opted community leaders suppressing unrest after police killed a Native American man. Nightwolf and Mamos, "How Can We Advance the Anti-Police Brutality Struggle?" *Gathering Forces*, December 24, 2010. http://gatheringforces.org/2010/12/24/how-can-we-advance-the-anti-police-brutality-struggle/.

111 Advance the Struggle, *Justice for Oscar Grant*, 8–9. For similar critiques of the role nonprofits play in managing political struggle, see: Incite! Women of Color Against Violence (editors), *The Revolution Will Not Be Funded: Beyond the Non-Profit Industrial Complex* (Cambridge, Massachusetts: South End Press, 2007).

112 Advance the Struggle, *Justice for Oscar Grant*, 22. Paragraph break added for emphasis. The cop who shot Grigoropoulos was convicted and sentenced to life in prison. Associated Press, "Greece: Police Officer Convicted in Killing That Led to Riots," *New York Times*, October 11, 2010.

SOCIAL WAR IN THE SALAD BOWL

WILL MUNGER[1]

WELCOME TO THE SALAD BOWL

STEPPING OFF THE TRAIN INTO THE WARM DUSTY AIR OF THE SALINAS DEPOT, you can see the top of the National Steinbeck Center peeking out over the roof of Olivia's Café. Salinas is John Steinbeck's hometown and the valley's fields and farm workers were inspiration for his writing. In his best-known work, *The Grapes of Wrath*, Steinbeck details a family's journey amidst the westward migration that brought thousands of Depression and Dust Bowl refugees to California looking for work.[2] His candor about the hardship and the migrants' resilience dovetails with an unflinching look at the violent inequality of the time. Although much has changed since Steinbeck told the valley's stories, some things remain.

Agribusiness is still boss. Located 106 miles south of San Francisco, the Salinas Valley is one of the most fertile farming regions in California. The $4 billion agricultural industry produces fruits, vegetables, wine, and over 80% of U.S. lettuce, earning the Salinas Valley the nickname "Salad Bowl of the World."[3]

The hands that work this industry are still migrant hands. But instead of Oklahoma, the majority of agricultural workers in the region are from Mexico, principally from the highland states of Guanajuato, Michoacan, Jalisco, and Oaxaca.[4]

A crisis of violence is giving traction to a project of adapting counterinsurgency (COIN) for use in Salinas. Initial media about the COIN project embellished the city's crisis with reports that in California prisons, "Instant respect is accorded any inmate tattooed with the words 'Salad Bowl' or 'Salis'—gang shorthand for a city now defined most of all by ferocious eruptions of violence."[5] After taking over the Salinas Police Department in April of 2009, Chief Louis Fetherolf gave a "90-Day Report to the Community" that defined one part of the problem as,

> An estimated 3,500 gang members or associates in Monterey County, most of them living in Salinas. It is common knowledge most of our violent crime is the work of Latino street gangs. We are not able, though, to quantify the *non*-violent crime attributable to gang members, as the data does not exist in our systems. But, I believe there is a *significant economic loss to our community* due to criminals.[6]

There is no denying the recent spate of violence. In 1994, 24 homicides set a new record for the city. 2008 broke this record with 25 homicides (23 attributed by police to gang violence), and 2009 did it again with 28 homicides (all gang-related).[7] "Monterey County had the highest youth murder rate in the entire state. Higher than Los Angeles, Oakland and Richmond, California."[8] These recent statistics were especially troubling for city and police administrators given that Salinas has tried several approaches to reducing violent crime. These approaches have included: increasing the number of police raids and saturation operations for focused periods of time; establishing an SPD Violence Suppression Unit; requesting money from the federal government to start programs like the Safe Schools/Healthy Students Initiative; and partnering with outside agencies like the Prevention Institute to develop strategies for reducing violence.[9] While some of these initiatives did lower violence levels, their implementation was dependent on federal and foundation grants and the efforts ended when the funding ran out. At a 2009 summit, a U.S. Attorney and the California state gang czar criticized the city for lacking a strategic plan to deal with gangs.[10] Salinas needed something new.

GANGS AND INSURGENTS

THE TRANSLATION OF COIN strategies, techniques, and technologies began in 2009 as a collaborative consultation and planning initiative between the Naval Postgraduate School (NPS), the Salinas Police Department (SPD), and the City of Salinas. This chapter contextualizes and critically analyzes the theoretical architecture of the NPS/SPD collaboration. It tracks how strategies, techniques, and technologies of governance and control flow between different conflict zones as well as within different elements of state security apparatuses. In providing a snapshot of the process of translating COIN for domestic application, it builds a launch pad for future questions needed to understand evolving police operations in Salinas and elsewhere.

The idea for the NPS/SPD collaboration originated in conversations between Salinas Mayor Dennis Donahue, California Democratic representative Sam Farr, and Leonard Ferrari, Provost of the Naval Postgraduate School. Ferrari thought there might be something that NPS could do to apply the institution's knowledge.[11] NPS instructor Hy Rothstein says the provost looked to the faculty at the Department of Defense Analysis because they have focused on the subject of irregular warfare for over 20 years. Rothstein remembers when the collaboration was proposed:

> Initially we didn't know [what to recommend] because we're not experts in gang violence. We suspect there may be overlaps between the way gangs operate and the way insurgents operate. We wanted the folks in Salinas to make that connection, not us. I set up an initial series of meetings; [in] one of which we presented theories of counterinsurgency as well as concepts of insurgency. We asked the folks in Salinas to determine the overlap between what we do and what happens with gangs in the city; they were the ones that determined the overlap was very significant.[12]

NPS instructors like Rothstein are links in the pedagogical process between COIN theory and practice. This pedagogy is usually directed towards members of the U.S. military, though the Salinas collaboration is expanding the audience to include police. Rothstein, a retired Special Forces colonel whose career includes advising COIN operations in El Salvador during the 1980s, now translates theory and practices for irregular conflict zones like as Afghanistan and Salinas.

NPS researchers agree that the COIN model is adaptable for use in Salinas because both insurgents and gangs need the active or tacit support of the population to conduct their activities. Asked what was adaptable to Salinas, Rothstein replied,

> There are several theories of counterinsurgency: when you look at the role of the population—where they sit is in a pivotal position, the role of government, the role of the anti-government, and outside players. That's the COIN model. What folks in Salinas saw was a similar dynamic where you have the population, the government, the anti-government: the gangs, and outside agencies. Agencies supporting gangs like Mexican Mafia, agencies supporting government like county, state, federal law

enforcement agencies or agencies that provide economic aid and so forth. The model looked exactly the same to them.[13]

It is easy to find similarities when the theory's categories are so all-encompassing. For example, the U.S. Army-Marine Corps *Counterinsurgency Field Manual*, FM 3-24, gives the following graphic figure to describe the model.[14]

Support for an insurgency

In any situation, whatever the cause, there will be—
An active minority for the cause.
A neutral or passive majority.
An active minority against the cause.

NPS researchers do make analytical distinctions between insurgents and gangs. On a strategic level, they understand that insurgents work to rupture the existing social and political order and reallocate power. Gangs, on the other hand, are engaged in illegal activity outside the "normal markets established by the state," but only seek to "push the expansion of their illegal markets further into society."[15] While Rothstein agrees that there is a difference between a political insurgency and gang activity, he maintains that there is an overlap that also highlights what is distinct about counterinsurgent policing.

> [Gangs] still have a link to the population, they still have influence. They are still corrosive to the social fabric of a particular society. And the cancer grows. How to do you arrest that cancer and eliminate the conditions that allow that cancer to form and grow? That's where you see some overlapping concerns with insurgencies and gangs.

He explains:

> Why do people join gangs? There are a variety of reasons and that's where you need to start. We need to identify those reasons and try to mitigate those reasons with a combination of carrots and sticks. People need opportunities, and people need to be hit very hard if they don't take advantage of those opportunities.[16]

Translating COIN for anti-gang application means focusing state resources on producing and shaping social activity that prevents and disrupts gang formation. The implication is that a COIN-based approach requires more than just law enforcement activity or investigations designed to take out gang leadership.

NPS researchers argue that the model is adaptable to Salinas because people in the Hispanic community of East Salinas are not actively giving information to the police. SPD commanders agree with the NPS theory that the "passive nature of the relationship" between the government and the Hispanic population allows gangs to hide within the population.[17] Without being able to 'see' the gang networks in the population, the SPD lacks the intelligence to target gang formations and operations.

The problem is understood by NPS as one of *connectivity*—a concept that, in computer science, refers to the capacity to make a connection between two or more points in a network. In Salinas, the gangs have strong connectivity with the Hispanic population: there are numerous points of contact, and information flows freely. The police, in contrast, have weak connectivity: few points of contact, and a thin flow of information. Strategically, this imbalance is crucial. COIN theory recommends that police start a campaign by prompting the population to give information to the police in order to map gang networks.

KNOWLEDGE, POWER, AND POPULATION

THE BULK OF NPS research into Salinas' situation has been publicly published in three Masters theses, some with classified content redacted. This research examines Salinas' environmental conditions,[18] social movement dynamics,[19] and SPD information dominance.[20] The first two NPS theses are concerned with demographic data because they try to identify the forces that enable, shape, and constrain particular modes of sociality among the targeted population.

Between 1980 and 2009, a major demographic shift occurred as Salinas' population went from 80,438 to 152,597. With this growth came a change in the racial composition. In 1980, Salinas was 52% Caucasian, 38% Hispanic, 8.2% other, and 1.7% African American. In 2007, the U.S. Census Bureau estimated the racial demographics as 70% Hispanic, 18.6% Caucasian, 9.6% other, and 1.8% African American.[21] Salinas' agricultural industry requires a significant labor pool, and this demand for seasonal, low-paying work is a significant force that shapes the composition of the local population. This economic dynamic has a long history of encouraging migration to the Salinas Valley and today's migrants come from countries south of the U.S. border, from Mexico in particular. In addition to Salinas's approximately 150,000 residents, there are around 20,000 documented and undocumented migrants who annually circulate through the city.

The demographic composition is important to the NPS calculation because language barriers and different perceptions of police legitimacy affect whether members of the Hispanic population provide information about gang members. COIN theory posits that their recalcitrance is a problem because it inhibits the information flow to the SPD. Police lack connections to the population, but gang networks are able to maintain connectivity to the population. This connectivity is the gang's 'center of gravity' in the COIN model: their information dominance allows them to operate freely. To break this connection, a campaign must start by analyzing *why* the police and government have little legitimacy and low connectivity to the population. The first step in this analysis is to account for the conditions that shape the targeted population's everyday life.

In the late 1990s and early 2000s, a population boom combined with a shortage of low-income housing to create a concentrated pocket of racialized poverty in East Salinas. NPS researchers Clarke and Onufer argue that Salinas' recent population rise occurred partially because of increasing home prices in the nearby Monterey and San Jose areas.[22] An influx of middle-class commuters pushed Salinas' home prices up to some of the most expensive in the U.S. This influx contributed to the spatial concentration of race and class in East Salinas:

> The lower income residents of Salinas were hit extremely hard by the trend, adding to other woes including a high unemployment rate and low-paying jobs. The combination of these factors caused high population density in some areas of Salinas, particularly the eastern portions of the city, and forced extended families to share inadequately small spaces.[23]

The concentrated poverty of East Salinas also exposes stark contrasts of power and wealth. Monterey County is in the most distressed quartile of all counties nationwide, according to the March 2009 Associated Press Economic Stress Index.[24] The spatial concentration of Hispanic populations in East Salinas, high unemployment, and a crumbling public education system all contribute to a context of gang formation. Spatial concentration and material conditions alone, however, do not simply equate to gang violence. We must also take into account the effect of institutions like prisons and the police.

Years of repressive policing by the SPD isolated the Hispanic community. Further, an over-reliance on prisons provided an opportunity for gangs to network in a manner that intensified inter-community violence. NPS researcher Major Joseph Long explains,

[T]he prison system has… created a vicious cycle where the system used to deter and punish gang activity has become a large part of the system that causes it. By keeping prisoners locked up longer, street gangs are afforded greater opportunities for using prognostic frames that drive incarcerated gang members toward pursuing a criminally violent lifestyle…. With all emotional, financial, and pragmatic connections to the outside world severed, street gangs are free to creatively inject strategic framing back into the isolated population.[25]

Additionally, Long suggests that a lack of meaningful political participation and perceptions of inequality alienate Salinas' Hispanic population from the government. "Only 12.5 percent of the Salinas government is of the same ethnicity as 70 percent of the Salinas population. For members of Salinas' majority Hispanic community, such underrepresentation in local government contributes directly to the sense of isolation."[26] He theorizes that this alienation is compounded by negative channeling, which in social movement theory involves controlling behavior by regulating key resources.[27]

[B]oth gang and non-gang members of the community equally observe negative channeling through large discrepancies in funding for federal, state, and local law enforcement when compared to other programs designed to educate, assist, or mentor those 16-22 year-old [*sic*] youth most affected by gang violence. [28]

Amidst the austerity and budget cuts across the state, young people rightly perceive that there is always money for new anti-gang programs.

Research from NPS shows that distrust of the police also stems from a pattern of SPD interactions. Hispanics compose 70% of the population and 86% of the total SPD arrests. Of the 189 violent crimes reported in 2009, 100% of the arrests were against Hispanics. Furthermore, NPS research shows a widespread perception in Salinas that the SPD is illegitimate due to indiscriminate use of coercive repression. When asked if the police department cares about the average citizen, the SPD overwhelmingly believes that it does (73.9%). However, only 44.8% of the general population and 45.2% of other city employees agree that the Salinas police care about them.[29]

Sgt. Rich Rodriguez of the Monterey County Gang Task Force and SPD Chief Fetherolf used stronger language, admitting that many in the Hispanic community viewed the police as an occupying army.[30] The officers suggested that migrants from Latin America distrust police and government because of their experience in their home countries with corrupt, authoritarian, and violent state officials. It is critical to point out that U.S. military intervention in Latin America contributed to this dynamic, especially through advising COIN operations that contributed to extensive civil wars. The fact that Rothstein deployed as a Special Forces adviser to COIN operations in El Salvador is more than ironic. The original members of *Mara Salvatrucha* (MS-13, a commonly-cited example of criminal insurgency or 3rd Generation Gangs[31]) were refugees from the Salvadorian civil war. MS-13 gained size, strength, and reach by networking within the U.S. prison system, and they established transnational networks when key members were deported.[32] Now military and police leaders advocate transnational COIN operations against MS-13. This demand illuminates the claim, "Unlike the modern State, Empire does not deny the existence of Civil War. Instead it *manages* it."[33]

ASSEMBLING NETWORKS FOR INFORMATION DOMINANCE

DECLASSIFIED AND PARTIALLY redacted upon its release in April 2011, the NPS thesis *Small Town Insurgency: The Struggle For Information Dominance to Reduce Gang Violence* argues for a strategy based on the proactive collection of information about gangs and social networks within the targeted population, along with improvements in the SPD's analytic capacity. The NPS researchers contrast a proactive information-centric strategy with a "reactive prosecution-based strategy intended to disable these criminal networks in a more iterative, piecemeal fashion."[34]

A central difference between proactive and reactive policing is the role of information dominance. In theory, information dominance allows the counterinsurgents to better identify the gangs and their support networks among the population. For intelligence to be actionable, it must be delivered to the operational level in time for security forces in the field to act on it. In COIN theory, this dynamic is true for both the insurgent and the counterinsurgent.

> Information dominance allows the insurgent to shape and mold his operating environment. He is more likely to influence the people than the government is, since he can more easily move within the population. Once he has information dominance, he can establish his own "shadow government," thus increasing his legitimacy by becoming the authority....
>
> Conversely, information dominance can aid the counterinsurgent in "seeing" the insurgent's infrastructure and effectively targeting it. By properly collecting and exploiting information, the counterinsurgent can raise the cost to the insurgent of acquiring resources such as new recruits, weapons, and finances.[35]

The two main problems facing the SPD in implementing this strategy are: 1) the lack of information flow; and 2) lack of technical capacity to turn the flow into actionable intelligence. NPS research claims the lack of information flow is due to the compromised police legitimacy within the Hispanic population. The lack of legitimacy makes it difficult for the police to achieve a level of embeddedness and connectivity such that they are receive constant updates on gang activity. Passive measures like tip lines are not doing the job. In addressing the problem of connectivity, the COIN-based anti-gang strategy must affect the targeted population's sensibility to the point that people start informing on gang members. NPS researchers describe this as a "bottom-up" process that actively produces and shapes social life at the neighborhood level:

> [O]ur research showed that if the population was empowered through the formation of, and participation in community organizations, they would be more inclined to share crime information with the police....
>
> The establishment of community groups at the neighborhood level accomplishes several things: (1) increase the unity of effort between the community and the city, (2) allow dialogue to occur among members of the community and city officials on a routine basis, (3) establish a sense of trust between group members, (4) allow police to provide the community with specific information requirements they are seeking, and (5) reassure the community that their input counts.
>
> Building strong community group networks allows the city to build a more personal relationship with the community, and ultimately receive more information about criminal activity through those relationships.[36]

The NPS researchers' claim about the relationship between community policing and COIN is fairly developed within military literature and earlier in this book.[37]

> The community groups described here, in their simplest form, are hubs in the city's information network. When properly manned, resourced, and utilized they have the potential to be a great force multiplier against gang violence. The gangs that thrive in Salinas are also a network. What we are recommending is the City of Salinas fight the gang network with a network of their own.[38]

Community groups make up only part of this distributed network. NPS research recommends building new intergovernmental and multi-jurisdictional operations integrating the information systems used by law enforcement agencies, emergency services, the military, and civilian agencies. "When integrated as a whole, these institutions can effectively retard the levels of gang violence in an area by increasing the volume and analysis of information that is extracted from the population."[39]

PLANNING

IN THE POLITICAL imagination of COIN theory and NPS researchers, human subjects and communities are shaped within a field of conditions defined by interpersonal and informational networks and, in the case of the Salinas Action Plan, by COIN protocol. This political terrain extends from the daily interaction on the street, to the structure of governmental apparatuses, to social networking sites like Facebook.[40]

As these populations, technologies, communities, and institutions all have their own properties and histories, NPS researchers propose a process of *bricolage* to link together distributed networks coordinated through an information-centric counterinsurgency strategy. As Rothstein explains:

> The Action Plan has all the agencies involved and all the re-
> sources they bring to the table. The essence of the plan is co-
> ordinating and synchronizing their activities in a specific loca-
> tion to achieve specific effects. In this workshop we have on
> Monday, we have people from the faith-based community,
> people from all the social service agencies, education institu-
> tions, the library, recreational services, the police, the mayor's
> offices, community organizations, county and state agencies.
> All these people are there in order to make sure that the sum
> of the efforts and resources they provide adds up to something
> greater than their parts. In the past it hasn't been that way,
> everybody has been doing their own thing. What we're find-
> ing out in the workshop is that one organization didn't even
> know another organization had a particular capability. And
> that capability—communications, alert capabilities, or web-
> sites—rather than develop this on our own, we already have a
> network, a system.[41]

The Action Plan begins the work of counterinsurgency in the community center of the Hebron Heights neighborhood. The details of this particular

East Salinas neighborhood, however, were kept under wraps until late April 2011. Rothstein defends the secrecy:

> The essence of the plan we don't want out. It's like giving the enemy the game plan. There are going to be some public affairs aspects. There are some significant strategic communications aspects to this plan. But there are also some security aspects of the plan, just like you have in any plan. So we don't want too much out there so people figure out what the City of Salinas is doing. There are a couple reasons for this. If the gangs know where we are and what we're doing and where the priority is, they may go somewhere else. If the citizens think that this location is getting all the attention and no one else is, they'll get pissed off. So all of this has to be managed in an interesting way. [42]

The Action Plan is concentrated in a particular area and coordinated between police, social services, nonprofit community groups, and other agencies. Rothstein says that once Hebron Heights has been pacified, operations will shift to another area when gang activity increases. Building an expanded SPD intelligence capacity is necessary in order to track gang activity and "keep abreast of this movement so we can do temporary surges in other areas."[43]

This proposed operation has a similar spatial logic to the "Clear, Hold, Build" strategy used in Baghdad during the surge and outlined in FM 3-24.[44] Troop surges and combat operations pushed insurgents out of a particular geographic area. Combat outposts were established in the neighborhood, providing constant surveillance and rapid response times. Development projects and civil service projects were then initiated to prevent insurgents from retaking the territory. But what will the surge of Hebron Heights look like?

FROM COIN TO CASP

ONE RESULT OF the planning process is the "Community Alliance for Safety and Peace (CASP) Initiative," a multi-agency effort focused on a roughly 20-square-block area surrounding North Hebron Avenue in the Alisal District. SPD has taken over part of the Hebbron Family and Community Center and stationed two officers out of it. These "CASP Cops" engage in foot patrols and try to address neighborhood quality of life issues. This basic community policing work is mainly geared towards building trust between the population and the police where everyday "problem solving" policing contributes to a feeling that officers are embedded in and connected to the lives of the population.

The real engine of the CASP initiative is the "cross-functional team" of 34 members from various government agencies and nonprofits. They try to deal with quality of life issues like public drinking, loud house parties, or helping to de-escalate tensions and possible retaliation if a shooting occurs. Media reports focus on how the county Health Department provides a "neighborhood nurse" at the Hebbron Family Center while California Youth Outreach and probation officers help guide young people who want to leave the gang life.[45] From a COIN perspective, the spectrum of agencies is important because they have access and trust with neighborhood families that police do not have. Then, when the cross-functional team meets, information on cases is shared. Rothstein recounted, based on anecdotal evidence, that police have gained important information even if they can't make arrests, for instance when the information has to remain anonymous: "They can do investigations, go into houses looking for weapons, shine a light on someone they know is dirty but they can't prove it. It's like getting a piece of thread from a garment at the meeting, and it's the police's job to pull the threads. Sometimes it's other agencies', too."[46] However, not all relevant agencies are currently involved with the effort. While Rothstein would like to see prison intelligence gathering as part of these cross-functional teams, bureaucratic hurdles remain between different prison agencies and the Salinas cross-functional team.

Strategic Communication is the conceptual key to the action plan. Rothstein draws an analogy to an orchestra: The conductor is the government, the score is the Strategic Communication plan, and the musicians are the various government agencies. The music is the narrative. Depending on the sought-after effect, different sections of the orchestra will be used at different times, or with different emphasis. As a theory, Strategic Communication is a systematic series of sustained and coherent activities, conducted at all socio-economic levels: it develops messaging; identifies effective communications channels; and uses those channels to reach target audiences, promote desirable opinions, and sustain specific types of behavior.[47] In practice, it means trying to maintain a unity of narrative across all of CASP.

Georgina Mendoza does not use COIN theory or military language to describe her work as the city's Community Safety Director. "We don't talk about being at war with gangs. Instead, we talk about building peace and creating safety. Basic needs have to be met. Either gangs do it, or the state does it." When asked about the surveillance that is part of the CASP initiative, she responded, "It's not surveillance, it's a genuine relationship. Without using the word surveillance, we are gathering intelligence."[48] Rothstein's emphasis is different, but only slightly so:

> Hopefully this will in turn let people give information to the Community Policing officer so the SPD can more effectively and

efficiently target gang members based on [a] trusted relationship. So hopefully the shift winds up being the people and the population put more trust in the government to take care of them than they do in the gangs.[49]

Rothstein describes this shift as a magic pivot point that occurs in counterinsurgencies when people start to give up information. It is also the indication that an area has met a desired level of security: reporting from the population increases and people start participating in community watch programs or civic action programs.

> When that happens, it provides additional leverage for the police department. When they know that communities are actively involved and will report outsiders and crime—so the police don't have to be as vigilant in that area because they are now more proactive than reactive. That allows the police to expand their jurisdiction, to expand their control, with fewer numbers of people. The level of involvement of the population is very important, especially in a city like Salinas where the ratio of officers to citizens is very low.[50]

Rothstein recognizes that the magic pivot point in the Action Plan will be a difficult to achieve because the Action Plan targets a densely intertwined population.

> If you look at the demographics of Salinas, its around 65–70% Latino and the two main gangs are almost exclusively Latino. If you look at the population, around 150,000, and do some math looking at the number of family units that exist in the city, probably every family unit has somebody that is in, or knows someone in, a gang. So they're essentially providing information on family members and friends of family members and this is a tough thing to do in a city that's on their third generation of gang members.[51]

HARNESSING COMMUNITY NETWORKS

DEVELOPING THE INTELLIGENCE networks that grow like roots into a population requires subsuming or destroying existing community networks and producing new ones. The actively productive nature of this endeavor blurs the lines between police, social organizations, and community by joining them to a counterinsurgent assemblage. Recognizing the limitations of trust, Rothstein claims,

> The best we can do in Salinas is citizens' watch groups and mo-
> bilizing people to do things that end up creating community.
> Creating a community where people recognize that there is com-
> munity, where there are community leaders, and where these
> leaders and the role of these leaders is recognized by government.
> There happens to be a community organization in Hebron—
> well, one of the things we are going to do is tap into that. The
> leader of this organization is going to start attending some of
> these meetings so that he knows what is going on, and he can
> talk through his own network and they know what is going on,
> so that community members feel that they have a say in what
> happens to their community.[52]

Before leaving the force for health reasons, former SPD Chief Fetherolf was a bit more optimistic about harnessing the targeted population's social life. He suggested going further than leaders of community organizations and trying to marshal the socio-cultural power of the targeted population.

> In the Latino community, who has positive influence on Latino
> youth? *Abuelitas*, grandmas. It's a matriarchal society in terms of
> domination and influence over children. So my idea is to some-
> how harness that, to get *abuelitas* and mothers in a coalition
> working with us to start a counterinsurgency of their own. That's
> an idea I have, it hasn't been implemented.[53]

The desire to harness Hispanic grandmothers and community networks into the state's policing and surveillance apparatus is an example of COIN's weaponizing tendency.[54] As COIN theory increasingly informs domestic policing, we see attempts to reorganize social relationships into weapons and surveillance mechanisms. In the targeted neighborhoods of East Salinas, the police intend to break existing relationships and affinities as they produce a particular type of community. This dynamic adds another layer of analysis to contemporary debates about social war because it is a clear example of how conflict is managed within a stratified society.[55]

Warfare that targets a population's social fabric with a dynamic of simul-taneous targeting/production is also apparent in emerging technologies de-signed for global counterinsurgency.

LIGHTHOUSE

IT IS NO surprise that technology developed for wars in Iraq and Afghanistan is coming home. From drones to biometric scanners, domestic police forces have an array of new equipment for surveillance and control. Another technology being adapted from overseas is Lighthouse, a database analysis platform. Lighthouse emerged from research done in 2009 by NPS information sciences student Marine Corps Captain Carrick Longley. He envisioned a data-collection system that would allow for socio-cultural data to be collected in the field and later analyzed to map targeted social networks. According the NPS,

> The Monterey County Joint Gang Task Force has recently adopted the [Lighthouse] application in tracking and mapping gang activity using mobile devices. Still in its initial phases of implementation, personnel on the task force use their Android- or iOS-based smartphones to input data gathered in their daily interactions with the community.
>
> The app acts much like their traditional paper reports in the field, but enables officers to streamline identifying information—such as tattoos, gang affiliations, and the names of individuals connected to the suspect.[56]

The capabilities of Lighthouse go deeper. The social network mapping capabilities allow COIN operators to visualize community ties in order to engage in social network manipulation.

Longley gives an example from COIN operations in Afghanistan's Khakrez District.[57] After collecting social-cultural data on tribal affiliation networks, Lighthouse was used to produce maps that identified influential individuals. This cartography suggested elder Haji Mohamed Juma as a target.

The U.S. commander in Khakrez was attempting to arm the locals as part of the "Village Stability Platform" and Haji Juma opposed arming villagers. Analysts believed that was because he had a son in the Taliban. Haji Juma had considerable influence over tribal elders and the U.S. needed the elders to legitimize their efforts. Longley says they used their social network analysis to reduce Haji Juma's influence while increasing that of others who were more receptive to the U.S.'s goals. Later, in 2011, the area commander wanted to see what function a targeted individual plays in the overall structure of a community and how removing them could affect the social fabric. "Based on the analysis we did, we determined that this would have an overall positive impact on operations in the area so the commander went ahead with the operation to have the individual removed."[58]

Lighthouse is also being used in other domestic police initiatives that draw on counterinsurgency. The Springfield Police Department is developing what it calls the Counter Criminal Continuum (C^3) Policing methodology, a combination of "community policing, intelligence-led policing, and COIN."[59] The C^3 project is targeting a working-class Puerto Rican neighborhood in the North End section of Springfield, Massachusetts. The police are also getting assistance from Harvard students under the direction of Professor Kevin Kit Parker. Parker, a U.S. Army Major who recently returned from Afghanistan, advises the Pentagon on research projects and has pushed the Defense Department to adopt scientific measures to evaluate the effectiveness of counterinsurgency.

> Parker's students are trying to use this and other crime-related data to help police to improve their methods. They have created a 'war room', where they are working on social-network analysis and computational social science in an effort to predict where crime may happen.
> The students use a variety of methods, including organizing street-level data with Google Maps to plot and photo-document neighbourhoods block by block, and then combining the data with public statistics for crime, demographics and public health. They then use linear-regression techniques to analyze the statistics with the aim of developing computational tools to help police anticipate crime or identify key gang leaders.[60]

In addition to the Harvard students, members of the C^3 project are working with NPS to evaluate their data in hopes that they, too, can expand their model.

LIMITS

C^3 POLICING, LIGHTHOUSE, and the CASP initiative are being developed as models for other police forces. The designers of these models are already forging the technical and political alliances needed to spread these strategies, techniques, and technologies to other security agencies. Yet the proliferation of domestic counterinsurgency is not a seamless or inevitable process.

COIN's theoretical perspectives and technical language seemed removed and irrelevant during a March 2011 ride-along with Sgt. Rodriguez of the Monterey County Gang Task Force.[61] The sergeant had bigger problems than theoretical abstractions.

Sgt. Rodriguez acknowledges that the Gang Task Force will never eliminate gangs or change the root causes of gang violence. As he sees it, his job is to "put a foot on it" and make sure it doesn't affect the lives of the wealthy upper class that live in the foothills around Salinas. Before Rodriguez joined the task force, his job was checking alarms in wealthy neighborhoods in Monterey. He spoke frankly that the Monterey County has distinct classes of people, and that his job was situated in a class and race divide.

> I have to, as a trained professional, if I see Hispanic kids with shaved heads in a white neighborhood, to search for any legitimate reasons to make contact and run their names…. As for gang members, my job is to kick ass, harass, and make their lives as miserable as possible so that kids don't think it's worth it anymore 'cause they can't go outside. If he gets out [of the gang] because he's scared, I did my job.[62]

This sort of candid assessment is noticeably missing from the academic jargon of NPS research.

Like a number of California cities, Salinas is also facing resources limitations. The city has fewer officers per capita than any city of its size.[63] Sitting in his sparsely decorated office, Deputy Chief Kelly McMillin framed gang violence as a public investment issue. "Unless there is public investment in municipal services like schools, recreation facilities, and libraries, gang violence will continue."[64] As if to punctuate his point, McMillin's phone rang during our interview; a sergeant was calling in the shooting of a 16-year-old. "Okay, Sarge," McMillin replied. "Call me if he dies."

Amidst austerity and budget cuts, McMillin is trying to provide municipal services like those offered through CASP. When asked about the repressive potential of services being coupled to surveillance and control mechanisms built on COIN theory, McMillin pointed to a framed copy of the Constitution on his wall. "I take that seriously. My power is limited, and should be." Rothstein also rejects ready comparisons between what is happening in Salinas and other COIN operations. "Some of the techniques are relevant but it's not the same…. It's much easier to conduct COIN operations overseas than it is for police departments to conduct operations against gangs, and that's because in the U.S. there are laws that protect citizens." Of course, we should take these pronouncements with a grain of salt and look at the difference between what the police say they do, and what they do. Although these limits exist as a matter of law, on the streets of East Salinas and other heavily policed neighborhoods, there is a deep working knowledge that theories of equal citizenship do little to stop police violence.

The reality of what Sgt. Rodriguez described is playing out in working class black and brown neighborhoods across California. When 'putting a foot on it' reaches its brutal conclusion, gang policing meets its most significant limit: popular rebellion. Some of the most significant periods of social unrest over the past half-century emerged as conflicts over police violence.[65]

After multiple murders by police, in July 2012 a rebellion erupted in Anaheim, California. The Anaheim Police Department repressed demonstrations with such militarized tactics that some observers compared Disneyland to Afghanistan.[66] Videos showed police dogs attacking Mexican mothers with strollers while police defended Disneyland's gates with digital camouflage, assault rifles, and armored vehicles. After demonstrators were cleared off the streets, an "Incident Action Report" was leaked; its contents identified multiple working-class Mexican neighborhoods in Central Anaheim as "hot zones."

> What's significant about this report is the information it contains suggests the "civil unrest" that recently occurred was not initially confined to one or two working-class Mexican neighborhoods as had been previously reported, but that it spread to different parts of Central Anaheim, including areas quite close to the Disneyland and California Adventure theme parks. In addition, it offers compelling evidence top brass at Anaheim Police knew, despite claims to the contrary by Police Chief John Welter, that "outside agitators" had nothing to do with them; that they were fully aware they were containing a rebellion of and by working-class Mexicans, all residents.[67]

This report shows how the Anaheim Police Department responded to a particular uprising, but more importantly, it demonstrates the cops' understanding that the conflict is rooted in the conditions of Orange County. From Anaheim to Salinas, police are being forced into a role of managing conflict in an increasingly stratified society.[68] This management is best understood as a spectrum of state repression that corresponds with the level of popular rebellion. The Anaheim rebellion emerged because of profound long-simmering rage against anti-gang efforts that rely on racial profiling to maintain a geographic separation of inequality. Although the rebellion demonstrated that police could not murder Latino youth without consequences, ultimately the Anaheim Police did their job: to maintain the overall power (im)balance. Or, as Steinbeck's character John Casey says, "Cops cause more trouble than they stop."[69]

THE TASK AHEAD IS TO REALLY BEGIN: TOWARDS IN-CONCLUSION

BEFORE CLOSING, A bit of humility is in order. This chapter set out to contextualize and critically analyze the theoretical architecture of the NPS/SPD collaboration. It tracked how strategies, techniques, and technologies of governance and control flow between conflict zones as well as within different elements of state security apparatuses.

One limitation of this study is that, in the case of the NPS/SPD collaboration, it is highly one-sided. The research in this chapter "studied up" in order to interrogate the theoretical terrain of domestic COIN. Likewise, it is a snapshot of an incomplete process. Future research is needed to track what happens in Salinas as the Action Plan is implemented. As theory translates into practice, the most interesting questions will appear in the limits.

The (in)conclusions reached in this study should serve as questions, as points of departure to continue researching the blueprints and functions of empire. The research most critical at this junction will not come from the academy. It will come from the prisons, the hotspots, the ICE detention centers,[70] and the streets where the hostile environments of (potentially) endless counterinsurgency are ruptured by rebellions.[71]

The COIN theorists, too, might benefit from some humility. Here is a cautionary tale from a recent experiment with counterinsurgency: *Los Zetas* are one of the most brutal and feared Mexican drug cartels. But where did the *Zetas* come from? A recent report gives evidence that some of the original *Zetas* came from the Airmobile Special Forces Group (GAFE), an elite division of the Mexican military.[72] The report quotes a former U.S. Special Forces commander as saying GAFE was trained by America's 7th Special Forces Group, or "Snake Eaters," at Ft. Bragg, North Carolina. GAFE's U.S. training was designed to prepare them for counterinsurgency—to fight the Zapatista rebels in Chiapas, Mexico.

The Zapatistas, a poorly armed primarily indigenous militia, rose up against the Mexican government on January 1, 1994, the same day the North American Free Trade Agreement (NAFTA) came into effect. The rebels called NAFTA a death sentence, in part because the agreement would allow subsidized U.S. crops to enter the Mexican market, pushing small farmers off the land. The Zapatistas also see themselves in a decentralized and networked relationship to other social movements fighting against what they describe as the empire of money. They call this conflict the Fourth World War.[73]

After battling the Zapatista insurgency, GAFE gained additional training and support from the U.S. to fight the drug trade, the industry that Arsenault argues benefited most from NAFTA.[74] It is probably impossible to measure with accuracy, but certainly NAFTA increased trade flows in many goods, and illegal drugs in particular. It is also undeniable that rural displacement in Mexico (due to neoliberal economic policies) swelled the ranks of unemployed young people eager to make quick cash by any means necessary. While some of these displaced young people joined the Mexican cartels, others crossed the U.S. border to find work in the fields of California. It is not so surprising, then, that they would find counterinsurgency operations occurring simultaneously on both sides of the border. After all, the Fourth World War is, a "total war indeed. Today there is simply no quiet corner to rest and catch one's breath."[75]

While COIN theorists include the Zapatistas in the their categories of "social Netwar,"[76] there are clearly huge difference between the Zapatistas and the *Zetas*. It is an obvious analytic mistake to equate the two groups because of their networked form. It is a bigger mistake to think that more military action can "fix" this problem. As the examples of the Zapatistas/*Zetas* and the Salvadoran Civil War/MS-13 indicate, the perpetual management of conflict through counterinsurgency is exacerbating the very dynamics COIN purports to solve.

Even though COIN theory exhorts its operators to address root causes of conflict, a counterinsurgent police force is antithetical to consequential change of the political, economic, and racial hierarchies that make it necessary. For example, despite clear evidence that Salinas' labor economics, police, and prisons exacerbate gang violence, COIN strategically reinforces the state's security apparatuses. From an ivory tower, this could be called reform. On the streets, it's part of a continual recalibration of repressive forces and institutions that have historically upheld the divisions of race and class. Salinas' own history spirals back and Steinbeck reminds us:

> [R]epression works only to strengthen and knit the repressed. The great owners ignored the three cries of history. The land fell into fewer hands, the number of dispossessed increased, and every effort of the great owners was directed at repression.[77]

NOTES

1   This chapter started as an anthropology thesis.

    William Munger, "Social War in the Salad Bowl: On Gangs and the Domestic Application of Counterinsurgency," Reed College, 2011. Many thanks to Paul Silverstein, Kristian Williams, and Luce for their advice and editing. A grant from the Institute for Anarchist Studies made a second round of field research possible.

2   John Steinbeck, *Grapes of Wrath*, (New York: Penguin, 1939).

3   Jason A. Clarke, and Tracy L. Onufer, "Understanding Environmental Factors That Affect Violence in Salinas, California" Master of Science in Defense Analysis, Naval Postgraduate School, 2009.

4   California Institute for Rural Studies, "The Agricultural Worker Heath Study," Case Study No. 5: Salinas Valley, 2003. The historical dynamics of the north/south migration patterns, particularly the roles of U.S. economic and military policy, are partially covered in Fatima Insolación's essay, "The Insurgent Southwest," in this volume, and

more extensively documented in Juan Gonzales, *Harvest of Empire: A History of Latinos in America,* (New York: Penguin, 2011).

5   Karl Vick, "Iraq's lessons, on the home front," *Washington Post,* November 18, 2009. http://www.informationclearinghouse.info/article24004.htm.

6   Louis Fetherolf, "90-Day Report to the Community," Salinas Police Department, 2009, www.ci.salinas.ca.us/services/finance/pdf/Police_Chief_90-day_Report.pdf. Emphasis in original.

7   Clarke and Onufer, "Understanding Environmental Factors That Affect Violence in Salinas, California," 3.

8   Candice Nguyen, "Salinas: Hundreds Gather To Stop Gang Violence," *Central Coast News KION/KCBA,* April 16, 2011, http://www.kionrightnow.com/story/14460668/salinas-hundreds-gather-to-stop-gang-violence.

9   Ibid.

10 Julia Reynolds, "Salinas Developing own gang strategy. Plan recommends one entity to oversee and evaluate city's anti-violence efforts," *Monterey County Herald,* March 23, 2011.

11 NPS Provost Leonard Ferrari and President Daniel Oliver were recently fired after the Navy Inspector General released an investigative report alleging "waste and misman-agement." Marissa Pendergrass, "Two Top NPS Leaders Fired," *KOIN 13 Central Coast News,* November 28, 2012.

12 Interview with Dr. Hy Rothstein, March 11, 2011.

13 Ibid.

14 United States Army. *FM 3-24, Counterinsurgency,* (2006), 1-20.

15 Laurence H Arnold, Christopher W. O'Gwin, and Jeremy S. Vickers, "Small Town Insurgency: The Struggle for Information Dominance to Reduce Gang Violence," Master of Science in Defense Analysis (Monterey, CA: Naval Postgraduate School, 2010), 3.

16 Rothstein, 2011.

17 Arnold, O'Gwin, and Vickers, "Small Town Insurgency," 158.

18 Clarke and Onufer, "Understanding Environmental Factors That Affect Violence in Salinas, California."

19 Joseph Long, "A Social Movement Theory Typology of Gang Violence," Master of Science in Defense Analysis (Monterey, CA: Naval Postgraduate School, 2010).

20 Arnold, O'Gwin, and Vickers, "Small Town Insurgency."

21 Clarke and Onufer, "Understanding Environmental Factors That Affect Violence in Salinas, California," 2.

22 Ibid.

23 Ibid.

24 Marie Glavin, *Monterey County's Comprehensive Violence Prevention, Intervention, Suppression and Reentry Framework,* (Salinas: Renaissance Resources West, 2009).

25 Joseph Long, "A Social Movement Theory Typology of Gang Violence," 30–31.

26 Ibid, 23.

27 Ibid, 7.

28 Ibid, 25.

29 Arnold, O'Gwin, and Vickers, "Small Town Insurgency," 154.

30 Interview with Louis Fetherolf, March 10, 2011. Interview with Sergeant R. Rodriguez, March 10, 2011.

31 Nicholas I. Huassler, "Third Generation Gangs Revisited: The Iraq Insurgency," Navel Postgraduate School, 2005.

32 MS-13 is not a pseudo-gang in a Kitsonian sense, but it is an example of COIN operations contributing to the formation of violent transnational gang dynamics. Frank Kitson, *Gangs and Countergangs*, (London: Robert Cunningham and Sons Ltd., 1960).

33 Tiqqun, *Introduction to Civil War*, Trans. Alexander Galloway and Jason Smith, (Los Angeles: Semiotext(e), 2010,) 148.

34 Arnold, O'Gwin, and Vickers, "Small Town Insurgency," 17.

35 Arnold, O'Gwin, and Vickers, "Small Town Insurgency," 21.

36 Ibid, 158. Paragraph breaks added for clarity.

37 See, for instance, Kristian Williams' chapter, "The Other Side of the COIN," in this volume.

38 Arnold, O'Gwin, and Vickers, "Small Town Insurgency," 159.

39 Ibid, 36.

40 "Community groups can establish their own accounts on one of these [social networking] websites that would facilitate daily interaction among the group members in between physical meetings. It would also provide a channel for passing information to the police that the group is familiar with." Arnold, O'Gwin, and Vickers, "Small Town Insurgency," 161.

41 Ibid.

42 Ibid.

43 Ibid.

44 United States Army. *FM 3-24, Counterinsurgency*, (2006), 15-16.

45 Julia Reynolds, "Reaching Out: Salinas police establish office, walk the beat in Hebbron area," *Monterey Herald,* Feb. 22, 2012, http://www.montereyherald.com/local/ci_19703669, (accessed Dec. 14, 2012).

46 Interview with Hy Rothstein, April, 2012.

47 Michael Freeman and Hy Rothstein, *Gangs and Guerillas: Ideas from Counterinsurgency and Counterterrorism,* Naval Postgraduate School Technical Report: NPS-06-FY2011-001, 2011.

48 Interview with Georgina Mendoza.

49 Arnold, O'Gwin, and Vickers, "Small Town Insurgency," 33.

50 Rothstein, interview, 2011.

51 Ibid.

52 Rothstein, interview, 2011.

53 Fetherolf, interview, 2011.

54 For more on weaponization, see Vicente Rafael's essay, "Targeting Translation," in this volume.

55 "Social war" also refers to the narrative of "class struggle" developed beyond class to include the complexities and multiplicities of all social relations. Social war is conflict within all hierarchical social relations. Liam Sionnach, "Earth First Means Social War: Becoming an Anti-Capitalist Ecological Social Force," *Earth First! Journal*, http://www.earthfirstjournal.org/article.php?id=388.

56 Amanda Stein, "CORE Lab's Lighthouse Project Casts a Bright Light on IED Networks," April 30, 2012, http://www.nps.edu/About/News/CORE-Labs-Lighthouse-Project-Casts-a-Bright-Light-on-IED-Networks.html, (accessed December 12, 2012).

57 Carrick Longley, "Lighthouse Brief," http://www.youtube.com/watch?v=VTMyxpx1OvM, (accessed December 11, 2012).

58 Ibid.

For a better sense of what it means to "remove" someone, consider: The period between 2010 and 2011 saw an average of 300 Special Forces night raids a month. COIN commanders claim that they are the most effective tools against the insurgents, even as they prompt accusations of abuse and deepening resentment among Afghans. Erica Gaston of the Open Society Institute, who is compiling a new report on night raids, said that while in general night raids had become more accurate, and the conduct of U.S. forces had improved, she still encountered cases of unarmed people being shot when doing things like picking up a cell phone, running away, or rushing to help a wounded relative.

Caroleta Gall, "Night Raids Curbing Taliban, but Afghans Cite Civilian Toll," http://www.nytimes.com/2011/07/09/world/asia/09nightraids.html?pagewanted=all, (accessed December 12, 2012).

59 Bradley G. Hibbard, John Barbieri, Michael Domnarski, and Michael Cutone, "Counter Criminal Continuum (C3) Policing in Springfield, Massachusetts: A Collaborative Effort between City and State Police to Reduce Gang Violence," *The Police Chief* 78 (September 2011): 30–36.

60 Sharon Weinberger, "A data-driven war on crime. Scientific tools inform a unique combination of military tactics and police work," *Nature*, April 4, 2012, http://www.nature.com/news/a-data-driven-war-on-crime-1.10389#auth-1, (accessed Dec 12, 2012).

61 This not to say he and the GTF are not already practicing counterinsurgent policing techniques. But Sgt. Rodriguez did not articulate his activities as a counterinsurgency during a ride-along in March, 2011.

62 Rodriguez, interview, March 10, 2011.

63 Rothstein, interview, 2012

64 Interview with Kelly McMillin, April 23, 2012.

65 It is also important to note that some of the largest gang truces have been negotiated during rebellions, such as the Crips and Blood truce in the midst of the Rodney King Uprisings. See: Davey D, "We Remember the Rodney King Uprisings and the Historic Gang Truce of 1992" April 28, 2012, http://allhiphop.com/2012/04/28/we-remember-the-rodney-king-uprisings-and-the-historic-gang-truce-of-1992/.; Antoine Fuqua and Cle Sloan, producer/director, *Bastards of the Party*, documentary film, 2005; Mike Davis, *City of Quartz: Excavating the Future in Los Angeles*, (New York: Vintage, 1992).

66   "Anaheim: Tale of Two Cities," Al-Jazeera-Frontlines, http://www.aljazeera.com/pro-grammes/faultlines/2012/12/20121211112848544968.html, (accessed December 12, 2012).

67   Duane Roberts, "Containing a Rebellion: Leaked Anaheim PD Report Labels Working-Class Mexican Neighborhoods as "Hot Zones," *The Orange Juice* Blog, August 12, 2012, http://www.orangejuiceblog.com/2012/08/containing-a-rebellion-leaked-anaheim-pd-report-labels-working-class-mexican-neighborhoods-as-hot-zones/, (accessed Dec 12, 2012).

68   The report also contains police maps of the 'hotspots' that invoke the analysis of Ken Lawrence's *New State Repression,* (Portland: Tarantula, 2006), one of the first texts to pro-pose counterinsurgency as a framework for understanding changes in domestic policing.

69   Steinbeck, *Grapes of Wrath,* 80.

70   Immigration and Customs Enforcement (ICE) is the largest investigative agency in the Department of Homeland Security. ICE contracts with private prison companies to run an archipelago of immigrant detention centers across the country. For example, the Northwest Detention Center, one of the three largest detention centers in the U.S., qui-etly lies hidden amongst the warehouses and Superfund sites in the tideflats of Tacoma, Washington. The Northwest Detention Center is run by the Geo Group.

71   One example is the Short Corridor Collective, a group of prisoners involved in organizing prison hunger strikes and gang truces. http://prisonerhungerstrikesolidarity.files.word-press.com/2012/09/agreement-to-end-hostilities.pdf, (accessed Dec 13, 2012).

72   Chris Arsenault, "US-trained cartel terrorizes Mexico," *Al Jazeera English*, November 3, 2010, http://english.aljazeera.net/indepth/features/2010/10/20101019212440609775.html.

73   El Kilombo Intergaláctico, *Beyond Resistance: Everything. An interview with Subcommandante Marcos,* (Durham: Paperboat Press, 2007).

74   Arsenault, "US-trained cartel terrorizes Mexico."

75   El Kilombo Intergalactico, *Beyond Resistance: Everything,* 3.

76   David Ronfeldt, John Arquilla, Graham Fuller, and Melissa Fuller, *The Zapatista "Social Netwar" in Mexico,* (Santa Monica: RAND Corporation, 1998).

77   Steinbeck, *Grapes of Wrath,* 249.

OUR OAKLAND, OUR SOLUTIONS

THE STOP THE INJUNCTIONS COALITION

INTRODUCTION

IN FEBRUARY 2010, CITY ATTORNEY JOHN RUSSO, WITH THE SUPPORT OF THE Police Department, publicly announced plans to institute gang injunctions in the city of Oakland, California. The first of these injunctions delineated a 100-block "safety zone" in North Oakland, a historically Black community bordering a wealthy shopping district. The injunction named 14 Black men, one Vietnamese man, and 70 "John Does"—people who could be added at a later date—and the entire "North Side Oakland" gang. Approved in October 2010, the North Oakland injunction remains in temporary status.[1]

In October 2010, the Oakland City Attorney's office announced a second injunction in the Fruitvale/San Antonio district—a predominately Latina/o neighborhood with a large immigrant population. This injunction sought to greatly expand the reach of this policing tool, both geographically and numerically, as it delineated a 400-block "safety zone" and named 42 individual men and the Norteños street gang as an unincorporated association. A preliminary injunction was filed against five of the named individuals in September 2011, followed by a preliminary injunction against the remaining 37 named individuals in February of 2012. The preliminary injunction also sues the Norteños street gang as an unincorporated association.[2]

All told, the City Attorney planned to implement at least 11 injunctions across the city before the end of 2010. However, when the first injunction was announced, political organizations, community members, lawyers, and some of the defendants immediately organized against it. Understanding that policing is never a viable remedy to neighborhood problems, community members began educating themselves about the history of gang injunctions and what they might look like in Oakland. With this knowledge they started educating the public via street outreach and use of the media, and began discussing non-police alternatives to addressing violence and harm that support strong, healthy communities. In this piece we will first lay out what gang injunctions are and detail the historical background of this type of policing, followed by an analysis of the fight against injunctions in Oakland.

PART ONE:
GANG INJUNCTIONS COME TO OAKLAND

WHAT ARE GANG INJUNCTIONS?

A GANG INJUNCTION is a civil suit filed against a group of people the authorities deem a public nuisance. It prohibits them from participating in certain activities in a defined "safety zone."[3] Barred activities usually include a combination of previously legal and already-illegal actions, such as: being outside during court-determined curfew hours; loitering; appearing in public with anyone police have labeled a gang member (including people not named in the injunction); possessing drugs; and wearing colors that law enforcement associates with the gang in question. In some cases, exceptions are made for attending church, school, and work, but these exceptions may not always include travel to and from these destinations, or, if they do, the individual is still subject to harassment until their destination is confirmed by a police officer. Individuals who violate the injunction can face up to six months in jail and/ or a fine of $1000—without a trial.

Gang injunctions are tools of suppression policing and are rapidly proliferating across California and the U.S. Suppression policing is the practice of aggressively delimiting activities that cops determine to be disorderly (such as loitering, vandalism, or congregating in groups) with the idea that suppressing these activities will prevent "serious crime." Suppression tactics include stop and frisk, cuffing or detaining people without arresting them, pressuring people to consent to police searches, or establishing curfews or restrictions on where people can travel or congregate. Suppression policing is sometimes also referred to as "order maintenance policing" or "quality of life policing." It has the effect of increasing police contact with and control over communities of color, often leading to imprisonment.

The classification of gang injunctions as civil suits creates difficult conditions both for the named individuals and their communities. Because they are not criminal proceedings, the defendants are not entitled to free, court-appointed attorneys, or to jury trials. Further, the burden of proof is lower than in a criminal trial: "clear and convincing" rather than "beyond a reasonable doubt."[4]

Most gang injunctions include an "opt-out" clause. Opt-out provisions ostensibly allow those named on gang injunctions to demonstrate that they have severed ties with the gang. The supposed benefits of opting out include decreased stops and/or searches by police, the ability to have stronger ties to family and friends when not confined by the stipulations of the injunction zone and more options in terms of employment or education and housing. However, opt-out criteria, which are subject to corroboration by police and the District Attorney's office, require that defendants prove that they have not had any contact with law enforcement for two full years after the injunction was filed (even if they had no contact with law enforcement before) and that they are not gang members.[5] Additionally, defendants must pay a filing fee of some hundreds of dollars to participate. The opt-out process puts both the evidentiary and the financial burden onto the named individual. Additionally, the opt-out process can include informing on the activities and associations of other people, and ignores the complexities of involvement with gangs and of negotiating an exit from these organizations. Further, the public naming of people as gang members poses a number of problems: future harassment by law enforcement, exposure to retaliation from rival gangs, and barriers to employment and similar forms of social exclusion.

Ultimately, gang injunctions subject entire neighborhoods to increased surveillance and harassment as police are granted extensive discretion to stop, interrogate, and gather information on people in the injunction zone. The information they collect goes into classified databases such as CAL/GANG, which the American Civil Liberties Union (ACLU) characterizes as a "secret blacklist."[6] Police do not have to receive the approval of a judge or a magistrate to add someone to the database, nor do they have to notify the individual that they have been listed in one. These databases can have terrible consequences for people if they interact with police at a future date, even if they have no prior arrest record, and even if they are not suspected of a crime.

The Los Angeles City Attorney's office filed the first gang injunction in 1987, and there have been over 150 filed in California since. They have been legally challenged on numerous occasions by defense attorneys and third-party litigators like the ACLU. In 1994 Oakland sought an injunction against the "B Street Boys" gang, and the ACLU contested it, saying that injunctions "flagrantly violate the rights of groups targeted specifically because of their age, ethnicity and relationships."[7] The court sided with the ACLU and declined to grant the order, concluding that such an injunction would be "overbroad, vague, and therefore unconstitutional."[8] The 1997 case of *People ex rel Gallo v. Carlos Acuna* challenged the constitutionality of gang injunctions, arguing that injunctions violate defendants' First Amendment right to free assembly. In this case, however, the California Supreme Court upheld the injunctions, finding that gang activity falls under the definition of a public nuisance. This ruling set a green-light legal precedent for future injunctions.

Despite numerous studies on injunctions, there is no conclusive evidence to demonstrate that they significantly decrease violence.[9] Police and media reports of injunctions improving safety are seldom backed by significant or convincing evidence.[10] Cheryl Maxson has written that stories of reductions in crime through the use of injunctions "are often compelling, but are never buttressed with supporting evidence that meets minimal scientific standards of evaluation."[11] Maxson's research team found little support for a positive effect when they researched patterns of violence before and after an injunction was implemented in San Bernadino, California. In fact, negative effects were observed in areas adjoining the safety zone.[12] Other studies highlight the fundamental contradiction that gang injunctions not only fail to reduce violence in the safety zones but also force the activities they are designed to control into the immediately surrounding neighborhoods, as had occurred with the North Oakland injunction by 2011.[13]

The ACLU similarly found that after an injunction was introduced in the San Fernando Valley, crime decreased temporarily, but then rose again.[14] In addition, gang suppression models have been criticized because findings show that in areas where suppression is used, diversion programs fall by the wayside.[15]

Most telling, an investigation by the *Long Beach Press-Telegram* found the city's gang injunctions had not reduced violence in targeted neighborhoods. However, Oakland Police Chief Anthony Batts—who had introduced the injunctions when working as chief in Long Beach—pointed to the Long Beach injunctions as successes.[16] Likewise, the Oakland City Council was twice presented with dismal statistics revealing that violent crime had increased in North Oakland since the temporary injunction had been in place, neither politicians nor police made any move to deauthorize the injunctions.[17]

Clearly perception often trumps reality: in response to the statistics showing violent crime had gone *up* in the North Oakland safety zone since the injunction went into effect, one Oakland City Council member said that she would vote to continue the injunctions because her constituents and outside corporate interests interested in settling in Oakland *perceived* that crime had decreased.[18] In our experience during City Council meetings, these constituents were usually members of the Chamber of Commerce, members of Neighborhood Crime Prevention Councils (NCPCs; organizations with pre-existing information-sharing relationships with the OPD), homeowners, and even people who do not live in the injunction zones. By contrast, during the same period, we heard story after story of young people of color terrorized by the police. As municipal governments continue to adopt gang injunctions instead of investing in effective safety programs planned and implemented by communities themselves, it becomes clearer and clearer that reducing violence isn't their actual goal.

THE HISTORICAL SIGNIFICANCE OF INJUNCTIONS AND SUPPRESSION-STYLE POLICING

Gang injunctions are part of a long history of racialized police suppression in low-income communities of color. Racist attacks against Black residents in Los Angeles, California in the 1950s set the scene for what we now relate to as street gangs. White young men were known to cruise Black neighborhoods in the city, harassing and beating up the Black residents. The white police force had no interest in addressing this racist violence, so Black residents organized their own groups for self-protection.[19]

By the 1960s, the aggressive and repressive presence of the police in Black communities was foundational to the formation of the Black Panther Party. Self-defense had long been a primary issue of concern in Black urban (and rural) areas and police repression as well as white supremacist terrorism escalated community violence. According to historians Charles E. Jones and Judson L. Jeffries, "The National Advisory Commission on Civil Disorders reported that forty-three race-related uprisings occurred in the United States during 1966…only 15 were reported in 1964."[20] According to author Jeffrey O.G. Ogbar in *Black Power*, most of these rebellions were sparked by cases of police violence.[21]

After years of patient, nonviolent tactics winning only limited state reforms, many Black activists concluded that the government of the U.S. and its constitution were, to paraphrase Huey Newton, unwilling and unable to incorporate racial minorities.[22] "All of these efforts," he wrote in *In Defense of Self-Defense: Executive Mandate Number One*, "have been answered by more repression, deceit, and hypocrisy."[23] While resistance has always been a feature of Black history in the United States, the urban rebellions of 1960s indicated a new level of confrontation with systematic exertions of white supremacy and the violence that persisted throughout, and in spite of, the Civil Rights Movement.

The Black Panther Party was one of many organizations that were openly critical of the established order and voiced dissension towards the government's domestic and foreign policies. The Third World Left, as the social movements for self-determination led by people of color identified themselves at the time, saw U.S. police forces and the FBI as the repressive enemy that reinforced/enforced structural inequality and daily racism. The Black Panther Party identified with revolutionary struggles globally and allied itself with other radical organizations such as the Brown Berets, the Young Lords

Party, the Young Patriots, and the American Indian Movement, which were all challenging the systemic oppression of people of color in the United States and worldwide. Communities of color organized together to provide for the needs that the state had historically, repeatedly, and systematically failed to meet. This approach attracted aggressive attention from the repressive apparatus of the U.S. government—most famously, the FBI's Counterintelligence Program (COINTELPRO). COINTELPRO consolidated federal, state, and local police efforts to infiltrate, watch, imprison, provoke, create conflict between, and assassinate leaders and activists in attempts to neutralize progressive and radical organizations, with a particular focus on Black radical organization.[24] The state through its federal and local policing agencies, sought to suppress these movements with aggressive and decisive actions that would splinter, weaken, and ultimately destroy them. The ability of the state to determine what did and did not constitute criminal behavior was crucial to its ability to maintain political power.[25]

As citizens of the United States, Civil Rights Movement participants demanded equal access to the institutions regulated by the state. In contrast, revolutionary Black Nationalism and the Third World Left recognized that structural oppression was fundamental to the system and demanded a *transformation* of the state and social institutions. Federal, state, and local police had differing responses to these movements. Yet, street-level, highly public violence and orchestrated, federally sponsored disruption served to illustrate the militarized tactical foundation for the suppression model of policing. These models were often intimately connected to the suppression models employed by the U.S. military in places like Vietnam—wherein populations would be strategically pushed into cordoned off areas, their movements restricted and highly surveilled so as to both pacify their ability to resist military occupation while also attempting to sever their contact with organized insurgents (this methodology—also used by the apartheid regime in South Africa, by Israel in the occupied territories, and presently by the U.S. in Iraq—has often been characterized by its abject failure to address its intended effect, and its actual stoking of insurgency.)

In the 1980s, unemployment and poverty rates across the United States remained high throughout as the federal government slashed social spending, seriously depleting housing subsidies, training and employment service, as well as Medicare, Medicaid and Social Security. With industries closing factories and moving labor overseas, manufacturing was no longer an employment sector that could provide working class and union jobs to the urban people of color in California. The simultaneous state repression of Third World Left movements for self-determination created a climate in which poor communities of color were being decimated both politically and economically.

The systematic movement of drugs into these areas, in some cases directly related to U.S. foreign policy (most famously, the emergence of crack cocaine in Los Angeles being a result of U.S. aid to right wing death squads in Central America[26]) spurred an informal economy that promised economic opportunity, in spite of its illegality and potentially lethal danger. In *City of Quartz*, Los Angeles historian Mike Davis writes, "The Crips and the Bloods are the bastard offspring of the political parties of the 1960s. Most of the gangs were born out of the demise of those parties. Out of the ashes of the Black Panther Party came the Crips and the Bloods and the other gangs."[27] As a result, the local and federal criminalization of explicitly Third World Left formations shifted to target street organizations, ushering in a war on gangs.

A series of laws in the 1980s and '90s funneled additional funding to local police agencies, making it possible for them to become increasingly militarized. More and more, they incorporated SWAT teams and military equipment into routine policing and sought out training from military units worldwide. These policy investments paved the way for the proliferation of gang injunctions. In 1988, the Street Terrorism Enforcement and Protection (STEP) Act instituted felony prosecution of active gang members, felony penalties against adults who coerce youth into joining a gang, and possible life terms in prison for murder convictions involving drive-by shootings.[28] The law also outlined penalties for graffiti and the sale of illegal weapons. Then the Violent Crime Control and Law Enforcement Act of 1994 formed the Office of Community Oriented Policing Services (COPS) and implemented the devastating Three Strikes law and the Federal Assault Weapons Ban, which amplified the crackdown on gang activity and provided increased funds for local gang enforcement.[29]

Today, nearly every police department in California has an anti-gang unit, many funded and supported through the 1992 FBI Safe Streets Violent Crime initiative. Following September 11, 2001, the federal government has additionally offered specific funding streams for gang enforcement and incentives for local police collaboration with the Department of Homeland Security and Immigration and Customs Enforcement (ICE). This collaboration exposes defendants to "terror enhancement" penalties for a varied number of charges, including some gang-related offenses.[30] Culturally and politically the lines between "terrorist," "insurgent," "immigrant," and "gang member" have been aggressively blurred. Communities, particularly poor communities of color, find their neighborhoods being viewed by police as warzones, replete with military hardware and technology, as well as theories and strategies of containment, neutralization, and restriction of movement.

WHY WE OPPOSE INJUNCTIONS

While law enforcement, city governments, and the media tout the supposed benefits of gang injunctions, they rarely mention the devastating negative effects. Injunctions lead to increased police harassment and brutality, decreased community unity, family separation, racial profiling, and gentrification. Individuals named in the injunction often find it impossible to get a job, especially since the injunctions appear on background checks.

Injunction enforcement relies on visual identification of alleged gang members and gives law enforcement an incredible amount of discretion. Gang injunctions lead to the increased harassment of people who fit the description of anyone on the list, in effect amounting to racial profiling.[31] They sustain white supremacy by stigmatizing entire groups of people as probable criminals. Young men of color are disproportionately labeled as gang members, and the consequences are felt by family, friends, and community members. While whites make up a significant share of actual gang membership, they are rarely identified as gang members by police. No gang injunction in California's history has ever targeted a white gang or person.[32]

In the long term, gang injunctions frequently usher in a wave of gentrification. The first injunction in North Oakland specifically cited that as an intended outcome. A joint report by the Oakland City Attorney's Office and the OPD, delivered to the Public Safety Committee of the Oakland City Council on February 11, 2010, stated that "providing additional law enforcement tools and resources at the local level to improve public safety and eradicate criminal street gangs will help create a better environment for economic growth and development."[33] Redevelopment, also sometimes called "urban renewal," historically has forcibly displaced poor and working-class populations, turning over their land to wealthy redevelopers for free or a below-market-value price. Even though levels of violence may increase or stay the same with a gang injunction in place, white and middle- to upper-class people perceive that the police are "doing something about crime," so they feel safer and move in.

Proponents of the injunctions explicitly support "blight" policing in North Oakland. Some praise the economic changes that accompany expulsion of poorer people from foreclosed properties and gladly to welcome in "professionals…those who have steady employment, income and reserves in the bank."[34] Meanwhile, people of color are pushed out of neighborhoods as they feel more threatened due to intensified surveillance and increased police presence. Anecdotal evidence suggests that similar push-outs have occurred in those neighborhoods where injunctions were imposed in San Francisco—in the Mission, Western Addition, and Hunter's Point.

Finally, gang injunctions consume a tremendous amount of resources from city budgets that could build strong, stable and healthy communities.[35] In fact, the actual amount of money spent on injunctions is often hard to quantify when considering the multiple pots (City Attorney and police department staff time, costs of patrols, litigation costs, etc.) from which the funding is allocated. City officials, we have found, are resistant to push for disclosure of these various amounts, obscuring the real costs of injunctions and avoiding any accountability. Despite the fact that injunctions have not been proven to be an effective violence prevention tool, municipalities often choose to implement injunctions at the expense of violence prevention programs or community-based programs such as youth centers.[36] Oakland continues to experience a serious budget shortfall, and yet, the city favors investing more money in the police department, rather than supporting the library, education systems, or Parks and Recreation.

The civic participation of named individuals as well as that of their families is invalidated by the criminalizing effects of injunction. As such, their experiences of police harassment, raids, and imprisonment fail to be taken into account as evidence of the negative effects of injunctions. This type of social and economic isolation, which also undermines community cohesion and stability, is more likely to cause, rather than reduce violence. The growing tensions of isolation, disunity, instability, and violence have an extremely corrosive effect on the ground from which individuals and neighborhoods could organize toward changing their conditions in the short, medium, and long term. When viewed in this way, it can be argued that injunctions are not actually intended to reduce violence, but rather are specifically designed to target communities of color for economic and social dissolution.

PART TWO: RESISTING INJUNCTIONS

THE FIGHT BEGINS

In August 2009, the City of Oakland appointed Anthony Batts as the Chief of Police. As Police Chief in Long Beach, CA, Batts had implemented gang injunctions. Working in concert with Oakland City Attorney John Russo, Batts attempted to use injunctions in Oakland as part of his strategic plan to target "gangs, drugs and guns." Batts embarked on an extensive public relations campaign, speaking publicly to neighborhood associations and holding press conferences to support this initiative, while labeling Oakland one of the most dangerous cities in the United States.

In February 2010, John Russo began his own public relations campaign to push gang injunctions, meeting with police-aligned groups like the Neighborhood Crime Prevention Councils (NCPCs) and members of the Oakland Neighborhood Watch Steering Committee. Russo filed both injunctions on behalf of the People of California, allowing him to pursue the suits without having the approval of City Council or the Mayor, while drawing down scarce city funds to litigate and enforce the injunctions. As of June 2011, the litigation cost of the injunctions has topped $2 million.

In addition to naming entire gangs, Oakland's gang injunctions name specific individuals who are allegedly affiliated with "North Side Oakland" and the Norteños. Initially, both injunctions named an additional 60–70 John Does, allowing individuals to be added on a rolling and indefinite basis. The City Attorney's office repeatedly claimed that the injunctions only named adults and would only target adults, yet as of June 2011, youth in North Oakland had reported being stopped by the police and asked if they were named in the injunction.[37]

Police intervention into the East Oakland injunction began early in the process. In an atypical move, the City Attorney used the OPD to deliver documents notifying defendants that they were being named in the injunction. The result was that the OPD began "multitasking": they would stop by an individual's home to deliver the legal papers, and then proceed to search the residence with as many as eight cops at a time. Stop the Injunction Coalition's legal team began receiving calls from unrepresented defendants, and heard stories about how the police had interrogated their younger siblings, terrified their families, and ransacked their homes.

Those defendants who were bold enough to contest the gang injunctions were met with the force of multiple sectors of the prison industrial complex. For example, a parole officer learned that a defendant targeted by the Fruitvale injunction and a co-defendant had been stopped by police on their way to a meeting with their defense attorney. When the defendant next appeared in court to fight against being named on the injunction, the parole officer claimed he had violated his parole by associating with a "known gang member" and was arrested. The co-defendant in question had never been convicted of a gang crime and did not have any "gang conditions" in his probation agreement. The logic here was that because these men were both defendants in the gang injunction case, one could be arrested for "associating" with the other. The assumption is that both defendants are guilty until proven innocent. The defendant that was arrested had been working with the coalition and had just previously given several interviews to media. Upon his arrest, the City Attorney used his Twitter account during working hours to mock the defendant. The defendant spent several months in jail and prison before being cleared of the parole violation.

ORGANIZING OPPOSITION

Almost as soon City Attorney Russo announced his plan to unleash injunctions across Oakland, community members and organizations began to speak out and organize, forming the Stop the Injunctions Coalition (STIC). This broad coalition—composed of organizations, youth, lawyers, named defendants, and other community members—mounted a three-pronged campaign against the injunctions. To date, this is the only campaign to challenge injunctions collectively (rather than each defendant hiring a private attorney) and has informed similar struggles from Santa Barbara to Los Angeles and Sacramento.

STIC understood that increasing police discretion would negatively affect entire communities through the act of policing itself, would drain funds from social services, and facilitate gentrification.[38] With that understanding in mind, we took up both informing our neighbors about the impacts of the injunctions to bolster support for our campaign and to reduce the isolation people named on the list and their families faced as a result of being targeted by the injunctions.

Very early in the process we reached a crucial consensus that we would struggle to defeat the injunctions themselves, and not just try to remove individual people from the list. While the fight in the court forced us to defend individuals, as a coalition we never argued on the basis of innocence or guilt. Instead, we held firm that people who had caused harm to others were still a part of our communities and needed strong support and resources rather than policing and imprisonment. In this vein, advocating for concrete alternatives to reduce violence was always a central part of our strategy, and we looked to coalition members who had been imprisoned, as well as youth who were targeted by policing, to provide this expertise in what strategies could have helped them avoid police violence or imprisonment, had they been available.

We used grassroots organizing and legal strategies that worked in communication with and in support of each other, though not always explicitly. Sometimes this meant that the organizing contingent had to push the public dialogue in ways that the limitations of legal discourse and procedure would not allow. Sometimes the legal team had to prioritize serving the immediate, representational needs of their clients—the named individuals—in ways that further entrenched the discourse in legal bureaucracy, which the grassroots movement could not publicly valorize. Consistent media work supported all of these approaches as we aimed to defeat the injunctions—in the courthouse, with the City Council, and in the public discourse.

MOUNTING RESISTANCE

Gang injunctions were introduced in Oakland just as a large, vibrant grassroots movement against police brutality had been reawakened after the murder of Oscar Grant III—execution style, as he lay face down, handcuffed and restrained on a subway platform—by a public transit cop. His murder was witnessed and recorded by hundreds of people, who disseminated images and video widely. Longstanding distrust of police coupled with the overwhelming attention to Oscar Grant's death put state efforts to immobilize and displace communities of color in sharp relief and provided the context for the struggle against gang injunctions.

While the groups organizing in response to the Grant killing and those against gang injunctions maintained separate identities and courses of action, the Black-led "Justice for Oscar Grant" movement regularly turned out to STIC meetings, town halls, City Council meetings, and other actions to offer support. Likewise, from the beginning STIC's struggle was against the use of policing to address social, economic, and political problems, not just against the use of gang injunctions. While the injunctions provided a worthy target, organizing against the injunctions was also consistently a way to generate opposition to the police state and to develop meaningful community-based solutions to violence.

An organization of formerly imprisoned people, many of whom had personal experience with gangs, called the first meetings of what would become Stop the Injunctions Coalition. The coalition drew from several community organizations' membership bases in Oakland in collaboration with interested individuals from the North Oakland area. STIC was also in contact with organizers who had fought against gang injunctions in neighboring San Francisco. A woman who ran a community center within the injunction zone and had personal connections with the families of many of the young men named in the injunction provided meeting space. While she wasn't a formal member of the coalition, she consistently connected us with people who would be directly affected by the injunction, informed us about community events that we should attend, provided neighborhood history, and gave us tips for building trust in the neighborhood. With a regular meeting place established, we quickly formed media, legal, and outreach teams, and began creating flyers, information packets, talking points, and a petition against the injunctions.

Coalition members developed a set of demands to frame the campaign in North Oakland. The demands included: an end to the use of gang injunctions and removal of people from the gang database; community participation in decision-making affecting Oakland residents; increased support for community programs; an end to gentrification and an increase in safe, affordable housing; police accountability; and enforcement of Oakland's status as a sanctuary city, including non-cooperation with ICE. Having unified demands that were determined collectively by the coalition was crucial to ensuring that we could focus our messaging and campaign strategy.

We developed messages stemming from the demands and used them to inform language for flyers and outreach efforts. Because the coalition emerged from people representing a variety of politics and perspectives, the work to develop coherent messages that all coalition members could get behind was difficult. We wrestled with tensions between what we thought could be winning messages and articulations of what the coalition actually wanted. We struggled to achieve a balance between concrete details and rhetoric. And we debated as to what kind of language would resonate most strongly with the neighbors.

We divided our media effort into two streams: working with the press and developing propaganda. We pursued traditional tactics such as sending press releases, holding press conferences, speaking on radio shows, and writing letters to the editor and op-eds. We also developed fact sheets, rebuttal statements to the City Attorney, a Know Your Rights pocket guide addressing issues related to the injunctions, and outreach flyers. We created a blog (stoptheinjunction.wordpress.com) that served as a repository for all the tools we were developing, and which we also used to publish our own statements about the injunctions, to announce upcoming mobilizations, and to launch the campaign's audio and video media. Working with a local radio personality, STIC also held a "people's town hall" broadcast from the Oakland City Council chamber. During the meeting community members testified about the effects of policing on their communities and offered ideas about what alternatives to policing would make their neighborhoods safer.

Strong messages are only as powerful as their messengers, however. The coalition developed a group of key spokespeople who could offer statements and quotes, speak at press conferences, give interviews, and act as the faces of the movement. STIC's spokespeople included neighbors living in the injunction zone, a parent of one of the named defendants, lawyers, and formerly imprisoned people. We trained them on speaking to media outlets and practiced using the messages in response to a variety of situations. These trainings were good opportunities to prepare coalition members for interviews; they also helped us hone our messaging and tailor our talking points.

Early on, our media strategy focused primarily on community education. Since the City Attorney snuck the temporary North Oakland injunction through with minimal public input, many neighbors did not know that an injunction was to be put in place, or what it would do. In the press we focused on highlighting the anti-democratic nature of the process of implementing the injunctions. As we became more cohesive as a coalition, our press work and propaganda became less about merely sharing information and more about proactively offering analysis and suggesting alternatives to the injunctions. The coalition took up the slogan, "Our Oakland, Our Solutions," as a way to express the centrality of our struggle for self-determination within the fight to eliminate injunctions.

In our early street outreach efforts, we began door-knocking, talking to small business owners and people on the street, going into corner stores and barber shops and cafes, and regularly visiting a flea market that was close to the injunction zone. We also spoke at every community forum we could and presented workshops for organizations and classrooms. We passed out flyers, talked to people about the injunction, invited them to events, and collected petition signatures. Sometimes we had posters to pass out or hang up in businesses. Later on, our outreach teams would each stick to a specific few-block area to build relationships and familiarity with the neighbors.

COMPETING NARRATIVES

People in North Oakland were eager to share their views on policing and its impacts when we did door-to-door canvassing and general outreach at local shops and flea markets. Listening to their stories strengthened our resolve and our ability to talk confidently to a variety of audiences. Documenting individual accounts of police violence was a key strategy to move community members, the City Council, and the media to envision what gang injunction enforcement would look like in North Oakland. It also helped us counter the biggest lie that gang injunction proponents were telling: that the injunction would only affect the individuals who were named by it. The effort to counter that particular misinformation campaign was present in everything we did. Luckily, many North Oakland residents, especially youth of color, were clear that they would be the targets of any increased policing in their neighborhoods whether or not they had been named in the injunction.

Stop the Injunctions Coalition's role was also to help shift the debate so that the terrain on which the grassroots organizing took place was one that we were shaping, rather than the Oakland Police Department and the City Attorney's office. In order to do this, we listened closely to how different sets of people talked about policing, gang injunctions, violence, and interventions so we could be flexible and targeted with our messaging as we moved from audience to audience. Youth groups and local artists made beautiful posters and banners, community members were trained as spokespeople, hundreds of people were mobilized, and we started to help shape the story the media was telling about the injunctions.

The City Attorney's office was caught off guard by STIC's large and loud presence against the North Oakland injunction and immediately tried to discredit us by saying that we didn't care about gang violence. While we had been talking with neighbors, allies, and the media about gang injunctions being a waste of resources, we began to see that we needed stronger language about alternative solutions to gang violence. We fortified our arguments by presenting examples of local organizations working with gang-affected youth—without involving cops. These included a community center bringing youth from different neighborhoods together for a weekly dinner and political education, and an arts center providing after-school programming. We offered these organizations and others as strong community and youth empowerment resources and collaborated with them in our organizing efforts. City officials were not receptive to these ideas, but the public often was. By highlighting local groups' programs, we forged key alliances that were crucial in building a broad-based movement.

IN AND OUT OF COURT

Alongside these community efforts, STIC's legal strategy always played a defined role in the campaign, developing from a relationship between organizers from targeted communities and legal advocates. At its core, the approach was based on the shared assumption that litigation could not be the primary path to eliminating the injunctions, and that building power and unity at the community level is the only way to make lasting change. At the same time, since courts are where the gang injunctions are prosecuted, we had little choice but to fight there as well and to work with attorneys to bring community voices into that forum.

From the beginning of the struggle we used the court dates as opportunities to rally against the proposed injunctions, build momentum, and gather media attention. Community mobilizations to court and rallies outside the courthouse were important parts of an integrated legal and organizing strategy during the North Oakland hearing and continue to be part of STIC's strategy. A consistent and strong community presence offered support to the defendants, let the judge know his decisions were being monitored, and also gave the coalition opportunities to voice our side of the story, developing rally speakers and media spokespeople in the process.

As we grew, our coalition began to shape the terms of the debate. We produced educational flyers and videos, screened movies on the policing of youth and street organizations, held Know Your Rights events, and created police complaint reporting forms and an anonymous police abuse hotline for Oakland residents. The cumulative effect led to clear calls for neighborhood self-determination being heard in City Hall, in the press, and beyond.

MOVING EAST

The lessons we learned organizing against the North Oakland injunction left us well positioned to fight when the City Attorney announced plans for a second injunction, this time in the Fruitvale/San Antonio neighborhoods of East Oakland.

Fruitvale already had established networks that were tapped by organizers from the neighborhood to spread information and mobilize people. These networks were based on long-standing relationships with community-based organizations in the injunction zone, including some that had direct connections to many of the defendants. Although the Fruitvale neighborhood has experienced some development, it had not experience the decades of destabilizing, fragmenting, and disenfranchising gentrification that the North Oakland neighborhood had.

When the second injunction was announced, Fruitvale organizers and residents had already seen the results of the North Oakland injunction and understood what it would mean to give police even more authority. Fruitvale is a predominantly Latina/o community that is heavily impacted by the collaboration between local cops and ICE agents. In relationship to recent city-sponsored economic redevelopment projects in the area, Fruitvale residents saw a heightened police presence—and with it increased racial profiling, harassment, checkpoints, raids, imprisonment, and deportations, and police killings.[39]

Years earlier, in 2007, several organizations with broad working-class, Third World constituencies—many of them based in the Fruitvale—joined to form the Oakland Sin Fronteras Coalition. The focus of the alliance was to bring attention to the attacks on migrants and show their relationship to militarization, imprisonment, and police violence. When the injunctions hit, many of these organizations understood the importance of stopping yet another attempt to augment policing powers. Member groups of the Sin Fronteras Coalition took the lead in gathering together educators, community members and youth groups, including those working with gang-impacted and gang-affiliated youth, to discuss strategies and community solutions. They came to a North Oakland STIC screening of *Bastards of the Party*, a film STIC had been showing with ally organizations to deepen a shared historical analysis of injunctions. After the film, the group from the Fruitvale continued to visit North Oakland STIC meetings to learn what strategies had been successful in the North and to initiate collaboration and tool sharing. The groups ultimately joined forces and STIC expanded our focus to include East Oakland.

Several lawyers took the Fruitvale/San Antonio cases on a *pro bono* basis, offering substantially more legal support than defendants had when fighting the North Oakland injunction. The attorneys met with gang outreach workers to learn more about the individuals named on the list. The legal team began by representing a single defendant, hoping to get his name removed from the injunction, but soon realized that they couldn't effectively litigate the case that way. They realized the only way to challenge the scope of the injunction and the various restrictive terms was to represent as many of the defendants as possible.

The court system inherently individualizes social and economic problems, so the legal team had no choice but to try to prove that their individual clients were no longer gang members, were innocent of their charges, or had been rehabilitated—or else, to highlight school- or job-related reasons the injunction shouldn't be applied. At the community level, organizing and messaging were shaped to make sure that this individualization did not leave anyone behind; we fought for more community resources and argued that the injunctions were illegitimate. This combined pressure forced the judge to waive the $945 court fees.

By the time the City Attorney pushed for the East Oakland injunction, we had already learned some important lessons for our media and public education work. We knew that consistent core messages and reliable, articulate spokespeople were our strongest assets. As the organizing began to incorporate the struggle in East Oakland, we worked with community organizers in the Fruitvale to modify STIC's messages to integrate their language and priorities. We expanded our pool of spokespeople to include defendants in the new injunction, as well as young people, youth advocates, and others from East Oakland. We also consolidated demands from the two neighborhoods:

1. Stop the injunctions and all police violence.

2. Community self-determination: We know what our communities need; we have our own solutions.

3. Defend immigrant communities. No deportations or collaboration with ICE.

4. Stop gentrification.

5. Accountability from city government and increased decision-making power for all Oakland residents.

SHAPING PUBLIC DISCOURSE

Fighting the injunctions in the press could only work as one means of drawing attention to the issue. Drawing on the long, vibrant history of cultural resistance in Oakland, art, music, and performance have become crucial pieces of STIC's media work. Creating a visual language for the campaign was as important as solid talking points. We joined forces with an artists' collective to create campaign posters, and coalition members in both neighborhoods held banner-making parties to ensure that our public presence was as dynamic and colorful as the coalition itself. Local musicians wrote songs and shot videos specifically for the anti-injunction effort. Youth organizers created chants based on popular songs, including a coalition favorite based on Cali Swag District's "Teach Me How to Dougie." Members of a local cultural center helped coordinate street theater performances for our rallies and incorporated an anti-injunction storyline into their youth theater group's year-end performance. Artists from that same cultural center have also collaborated with defendants named in the East Oakland injunction to design murals in the injunction zone.

As we refined our demands, talking points, and strategy, we knew that we had to educate and include the community that would be impacted by the injunctions. We began by conducting town halls where we disseminated information, developed strategy and demands, and collected ideas about ways to mitigate violence in the neighborhoods without increased policing. To organize the town halls we began by outreaching to the defendants, their families and friends, community elders, and gang-affected and gang-affiliated youth. Through this process we were able to get a number of defendants to lead pieces of the organizing work, tell their stories in community settings, become media spokespeople, and educate young people about the affect the gang injunctions had on their lives, their families, and on the broader community.

We all agreed on the need for activities during which we could shape the public discourse, rather than just showing up whenever the City Attorney or police chief spoke about the injunctions. Youth took the lead in creating spaces where young people could develop ideas for actions and led the planning and training for them. Some actions followed those tested in North Oakland, including press conferences, marches, City Hall and court mobilizations, as well as street theater, educational workshops, banner drops, wheat pasting, and community bike rides through the injunction zones.

A WEEK OF ACTION

Because City Council is supposed to direct the City Attorney's office, we knew that it was important to get Council members to take a public stance on the injunctions. We began driving a wedge between the unpopular City Attorney and the City Council. The City Council and the newly-elected mayor initially dodged the issue by saying that they hadn't been briefed on the injunctions, and therefore could not speak about it. We began mobilizing hundreds of community members once or twice a month to attend the City Council Public Safety Committee meetings and to speak against the injunctions.

During this period, our messaging gelled among our supporters, and a large and very diverse crowd seemed to speak with a single voice. After several months, we were able to pressure the Public Safety Committee, and later the entire City Council, to request further information about the injunctions from the City Attorney's office and the Oakland Police Department. When the report was released, it showed that after one year the injunctions had cost $760,000. We gained substantial ground on our argument that injunctions are a waste of resources in a cash-strapped city, and we used the informational hearing to offer our own report on the financial and social costs, as well as our suggested alternatives.

Meanwhile, the youth organizers suggested a "Week of Action" to educate and stir up energy among community members and to put pressure on city officials. That week in March 2011 became one of the most memorable moments in the campaign and generated energy not only among Oaklanders, but also among people fighting injunctions in neighboring cities.

The week was designed to build community support and culminated in a mass rally. We opened the week with a press conference highlighting the voices of teachers and emphasizing the trade-offs between education spending and the money spent on the injunctions. We also took the opportunity to reiterate that injunctions were not driven, recommended, or desired by the neighbors who would be most impacted by them. The next day we held bike rides in the North and East Oakland injunction zones to continue informing community members about this issue. The cyclists made stops at schools and other key community institutions in the zones. On Wednesday, we conducted more than 35 workshops throughout the Oakland school system, reaching at least 500 youth, during which STIC discussed the injunctions and collected suggestions for addressing violence in our neighborhoods. These responses were turned into a report that was submitted by STIC youth members to the city later that month. Wednesday ended with a youth concert to create a safe and fun place for young people to enjoy themselves as a means of highlighting how rare such events are for the youth in Oakland.

Thursday we held a vigil for people affected by violence. It was attended by residents who had been hurt by all forms of violence, including families of those who have died at the hands of the Oakland police. The vigil demonstrated a key part of our strategy—showing that we, too, have been impacted by violence and care deeply about the solutions to it. Rejecting policing as a response to violence is foundational to our rejection of the gang injunction strategy. The vigil helped us reiterate that policing causes harm; that policing will only augment violence, not quell it.

The Week of Action culminated with a youth-led action in which young people walked out of school and marched through the East Oakland injunction zone, taking over nine major intersections, before arriving at the STIC demonstration. Over 500 people gathered in a main city plaza to rally against gang injunctions. The rally featured street theater, hip-hop acts, and speakers.

MARKING PROGRESS

In spring 2011, after more than a year of controversy, City Council succumbed to pressure to bring the issue to a full vote, with the potential of defunding injunctions entirely. With only two weeks notice, we seriously stepped up our outreach. STIC and our allies made hundreds of calls and sent hundreds of emails to the City Council members and the mayor opposing the injunctions—and policing more broadly. We asked our allies to reach out to their members and to commit to speaking out against the injunctions.

The night of the vote, 30 community organizations sent representatives to testify against the injunctions, and 300 community members turned out, with more than 150 staying until midnight to speak to the City Council. While we lost the vote 4–3, the City Council also voted that no more injunctions could go forward without an independent review of the proposed East

Oakland and temporary North Oakland injunctions. They also ordered that all John Does must be removed from both injunctions.

While these may seem small steps, they represent the most effective challenge to gang injunctions to date. Striking the John Does from the injunction limits the discretion police may apply in targeting potential defendants and thus limits the formal means through which police may exert their power. Instating a check system—"no more gang injunctions without an independent review"—actually halted hasty implementation of additional injunctions later that summer, thus representing a real strategic win; we curbed the ability of politicians to deploy injunctions at will.

In the course of the campaign, we faced many challenges, not the least of which was deeply ingrained support for policing among city officials. Additionally, the City Attorney's office was equipped with substantial resources for a propaganda offensive against us. The fight has been constant, with various battlegrounds, and there have been months during which we would ask people to turn out once a week to court hearings, City Council meetings and even committee meetings within City Council. Maintaining energy and momentum and making sure that we were consistently reflecting on strategy and not just jumping from action to action were serious concerns that we struggled with. Another large challenge was making sure that as we fought this policing strategy, we also continued providing support to the defendants and their families, especially those who were becoming primary targets due to their involvement in resistance work.

In North Oakland specifically, we had large challenges to overcome. We were unable to create sustained relationships with defendants named on the list for several reasons: *Pro bono* legal representation had not been available in that case and many of the people named were already imprisoned. We had a largely white outreach team trying to make meaningful, yet quick, connections in a working and middle class Black neighborhood experiencing gentrification. That this particular North Oakland community had been worn down from decades of trauma, including the deadly police repression of the Black Panthers, also had an effect on organizing. Moreover, after the City Council decision, many people were deeply discouraged. Because so much of our base is made up of people who are generally excluded from decision-making, this disappointment had a serious impact on momentum. Yet the gains Oaklanders have made in our struggle against gang injunctions put us in a strong position for the next phase of our ongoing fight.

In August 2011, two City Council members proposed amending the May 17 vote and introducing two new injunctions. They also simultaneously proposed a day and night youth curfew and anti-loitering legislation. Calling upon our allies again and reminding them of our show of power just months earlier, we mobilized hundreds of concerned Oaklanders to City Hall in early October to speak out against all the proposals. We stayed at the microphone until midnight, challenging the racist nature of the policies and showing them to be exclusionary tools that would inflict more violence on communities already feeling the burden of policing. We also stressed how irresponsible it would be to funnel more funding toward new injunctions without having done the review of the existing ones. The City Council voted to send all three measures back to the Public Safety Committee for further review. As of June 2012, they have not pursued these proposals any further.

By uniting courtroom and grassroots organizing strategies under core demands linking gang injunctions to the systemic violence of policing, gentrification, the criminalization of immigrants, and lack of access to decision-making, the Stop the Injunctions Coalition sustained and grew itself and generated new possibilities for future struggles against state violence in Oakland and elsewhere.

PART THREE: LESSONS LEARNED

As of this writing STIC's campaign against gang injunctions is ongoing.

When we look ahead at what is next, we draw on some important lessons. Strong, clear, consistent messages are our most effective tools in making our case. When we speak in our own words using our own language, rather than that of the state, we are able to establish the terms of the fight and put ourselves in the position to take the offense rather than continually responding to our adversaries. Using the media, we have been able to help keep the political priorities of the campaign focused and clearly articulated across neighborhoods, organizations, and events, helping provide a picture of the coalition as unified. We kept opposition to the injunctions at the forefront of public discussion for over a year. We garnered attention and solidarity from communities across California, the U.S., and the world.

Our messages are only as strong as our messengers. Our effectiveness has come from our spokespeople remembering that they are delivering the messages of the coalition and not promoting themselves. Our coalition members did not lose sight of this. And we do not need to rely on corporate media outlets to engage local communities. We successfully combined self-made media with corporate media to provide a wide range of pieces in a variety of formats to communicate why injunctions are such a violent, dangerous policing tool. Creative use of self-made media can be powerful in subverting dominant messages. Most of all, our campaign is best served when media tactics follow the organizing strategy rather than trying to lead it.

In the courtroom, we were able to learn lessons from other legal fights and to wage the first "people's" legal struggle against gang injunctions. By staying connected with the grassroots organizing, going over language and possible legal strategies, and taking much direction from the community, the legal team was able to bring the politics into and out of the courtroom—bringing defendants into the organizing, exposing the injustice of injunctions themselves, and creating time and space for the rest of us to move strongly in City Hall and in the media. We have to remember: most gang injunctions are implemented in a matter of weeks, with hearings often lasting only minutes. The Fruitvale courtroom struggle lasted many, many months and is far from over. While we have not been able to defeat the injunctions in court, we have scaled them back; the Fruitvale injunction is perhaps the weakest ever to be imposed.

When the City Attorney announced his gang injunction plans, he did so with a puffed-out chest and expecting no resistance. Because of the community's organizing efforts, things have changed. Oakland has only two temporary injunctions, instead of the ten proposed. The once-arrogant City Attorney, John Russo, left town to take a job in a neighboring city, and Anthony Batts, the police chief who brought gang injunctions with him from Long Beach, resigned soon after. In the media, injunctions are almost always preceded by the adjective "controversial" and followed by comments about their costliness and unpopularity. Most Oaklanders now know what a gang injunction is, and more and more people are against them. Future injunctions seem unlikely.

FIGHTING HARD, FIGHTING SMART

Anti-injunction organizing has required a systemic analysis of policing and power that is challenging but that also creates many opportunities. By working to understand the systems that gang injunctions are a part of, as well as the histories of those systems, we were able to keep an eye on a bigger picture even as we were required to take specific actions in the here and now. In order to fight against the injunctions, we had to think and plan and act strategically. We had to ask: Why gang injunctions? Why now? Where do these things come from? Where are they going? We had to learn some history. We had to educate ourselves politically. We had to figure out ways to respectfully navigate cultural and linguistic barriers.

For many of us, hanging around City Hall wasn't how we necessarily wanted to spend our Tuesday evenings and the courtroom was one of the last places we would go willingly. Many of us had never talked to the press before. Many of us had never sat through hours of planning meetings or done much organizing at all. But by building an organizing framework that valued collectivity, leadership development, accountability, and discipline we were able to engage with these challenges and weaknesses and to turn that engagement into strength. One of the tests of that strength will be our ability to learn further lessons and apply them in the future. Another test will be our ability to communicate these lessons and have them applied by others in different locations.

In our grassroots organizing work, we learned how to make decisions as a coalition, build the leadership of a variety of people, and ignite the participation of other organizations for mobilizations. We learned that the city government, specifically the OPD and the City Attorney, were very well resourced, but were often lumbering and clumsy. While we know they are able to smash you hard if you're under their boot, we also learned that we could beat them in creativity, predict their moves, get out ahead, and out-flank and out-sprint them. This knowledge was inspiring and we gained a lot of support and momentum in that process. But morale and momentum are hard to sustain, especially in the face of defeats—however technical and short-term.

THE FUTURE IS UNWRITTEN

The history of the Stop the Injunctions Coalition in Oakland is still being written. We have been around for less than two years. And we have much fighting ahead of us.

The immediate future of STIC will be to monitor, delegitimize, and smash the existing injunctions; defend against the slim possibility of future injunctions; and continue to build and highlight all the community-based work happening to fight violence and harm in Oakland. Just as we learned a great deal from other cities' struggles, STIC has been contacted by organizers in cities throughout California beginning or continuing to fight injunctions in their communities. While much of the organizing in Oakland has been within the starkly delineated zones where the injunctions have been imposed, the ideas and strategies developed here could be useful elsewhere.

We hope that just as we learned from others, we will be able to share what we have learned. We hope that others will be able to improve on those lessons and strike decisive victories against gang injunctions all over the country. We hope that those victories will act as a basis for further gains against the violence of policing and toward fundamental shifts in power.

The idea of self-determination remains at the heart of how we understand and articulate our fight against gang injunctions. It helps us to remember that this fight is as much about building what we want as it is about tearing down what we do not want. Self-determination by definition is a long-haul proposition, but it is surely attainable and definitely worth the struggle.

NOTES

1   Oakland City Attorney, "The People ex rel. John A. Russo, as City Attorney, etc., Plaintiff and Respondent, v. North Side Oakland et al., Defendants and Respondents; Yancie Young, Defendant and Appellant," *Oakland City Attorney*, October 31, 2011, http://www.oaklandcityattorney.org/notable/gang%20injunction.html, (accessed March 21, 2012).

2   Oakland City Attorney, "The People of the State of California ex rel John A. Russo, City Attorney for the City of Oakland, Plaintiff, v. Norteños," *Oakland City Attorney*, February 22, 2011, <http://www.oaklandcityattorney.org/PDFS/Norte%C3%B1os%20 Injunction/Norte%C3%B1os%20Order%20Phase%20II.pdf> (March 25, 2012).

3   Note on language: To be accessible to readers who have not been involved in anti-injunction struggles, we will use certain terms like "gang" and "safety zone," which are used by legal and law enforcement systems (courts and cops). Although we don't endorse these terms, nor desire to validate their relevance beyond courts and cops, we will employ them here for clarity and consistency.

4   Oakland City Attorney and Oakland Police Department, "City of Oakland Agenda Report: Joint Informational Report from the City Attorney's Office and the Oakland Police Department on the City's Civil Injunction Cases against the North Side Oakland Gang and the Nortenos Gang," *Oakland City Attorney*, February 10, 2011, <http://www. oaklandcityattorney.org/PDFS/Report%20to%20Public%20Safety%20Targeted%20 Injunctions%202.22.11.pdf> (accessed April 4, 2012).

5   Or are "no longer gang members" since the civil court order classified them as such.

6   Linda S. Beres and Thomas D. Griffith, "Demonizing Youth," *Loyola of Los Angeles Law Review* 34, no. 2 (2001): 760.

7   Youth Justice Coalition, "Campaign Goals Gang Injunctions and Gang Databases NO WAR ON YOUTH," *Stop the Injunctions in Oakland*, May 31, 2006, <http://stopthein-junction.files.wordpress.com/2010/03/ganginjunctionplatformcc06.doc> (accessed April 4, 2012).

8   Kate Moser, "Oakland Revisits Gang Injunction Strategy," *The Recorder: Essential California Law Content*, February 19, 2001: 1.

9   Cheryl Maxson, Karen M. Hennigan, and David C. Sloane, "'It's Getting Crazy Out There': Can a Civil Gang Injunction Change a Community?" *Criminology and Public Policy* V4I3 (August 2005): 577–605.

10 Two contradictory articles illustrate the police/media reports of conflicting realities of safety: Ali Winston, "Crime rises in area covered by North Oakland injunction," *The Informant*, November 7, 2011, http://informant.kalwnews.org/2011/11/crime-rises-in-area-covered-by-north-oakland-injunction/; and Mattahi Kuruvila, "Oakland reports crime drop in gang-injunction zone," *San Francisco Chronicle*, November 8, 2011, http://www.sfgate.com/cgi-bin/article.cgi?f=/c/a/2011/11/07/BANA1LRPBS.DTL.

11 Cheryl Maxson, Karen M. Hennigan, David C. Sloane, "For the Sake of the Neighborhood?: Civil Gang Injunctions as a Gang Intervention Tool in Southern California," in *Policing Gangs and Youth Violence*, ed S. Decker, (Belmont: Wadswort, 2003).

12   Cheryl Maxson, Karen M. Hennigan, David C. Sloane, and K Kolnick, *Can Civil Gang Injunctions Change Communities? A Community Assessment of the Impact of Civil Gang Injunctions.* Report submitted to the National Institute of Justice, U.S. Department of Justice (2005).

13   Winston, "Crime."

14   The American Civil Liberties Union of Southern California, *False Premise, False Promise: The Blythe Street gang injuction and its aftermath: A Report.* (The Foundation, 1997).

15   Judith Greene, Kevin Pranis. "Gang Wars: The Failure of Enforcement Tactics and the Need for Effective Public Safety Strategies," (Justice Policty Institute, 2007), 71.

16   Russell, Wendy Thomas. "Do gang injunctions work?" *Long Beach Press Telegram,* November 15, 2003, http://sfpublicdefender.org/wp-content/uploads/2007/08/study-on-long-beach-gang-injunction.pdf, (accessed March 25, 2012).

17   Desley Brooks, Oakland City Hall, May 17, 2011, City Council Meeting, http://oakland.granicus.com/MediaPlayer.php?view_id=2&clip_id=861 (accessed April 4, 2012).

18   Pat Kernighan, Oakland City Hall, May 17, 2011, City Council Meeting, http://oakland.granicus.com/MediaPlayer.php?view_id=2&clip_id=861 (accessed April 4, 2012).

19   *Bastards of the Party.* Directed by Cle Sloan, 95 min., Fuqua Films, 2005, DVD. 2005.

20   Charles Jones E., ed., *The Black Panther Party Reconsidered* (New York: Black Classic Press, 1998), 25.

21   Jeffrey O. G. Ogbar, *Black Power: Radical Politics and African American Identity,* (Baltimore: Johns Hopkins University Press, 2005), 86.

22   G. Louis Heath, ed., *OFF THE PIGS! the History and Literature of the Black Panther Party* (Metuchen, N.J.: The Scarecrow Press, Inc., 1976), 378.

23   Philip S. Foner, ed., *The Black Panthers Speak* (New York: Da Capo Press, 1995), 40.

24   Paul Wolf, "Director to 23 Field Offices, Aug. 26, 1967," in "Black Nationalist Hate· Groups" ("FBI COINTELPRO Documents") from *COINTELPRO* (1996–2004), http://www.icdc.com/%7Epaulwolf/cointelpro/hoover26aug1967.htm.

25   Nancy Armstrong and Leonard Tennenhouse, eds., *The Violence of Representation: Literature and the history of violence,* (London: Routledge Kegan & Paul, 1989), 17.

26   Gary Webb, *Dark Alliance: The CIA, the Contras, and the Crack Cocaine Explosion,* (New York: Seven Stories Press, 1998).

27   *Bastards of the Party.*

28   California State Legislature, *California Street Terrorism and Enforcement and Prevention Act, CA Penal Code 186.20,* (California State Legislature: 1988), http://www.leginfo.ca.gov/cgi-bin/displaycode?section=pen&group=00001-01000&file=186.20-186.33 (accessed March 25, 2012).

29   U.S. Department of Justice, *Violent Crime and Law Enforcement Act of 1994,* October 24, 1994, (National Criminal Justice Reference Services), https://www.ncjrs.gov/txtfiles/billfs.txt, (accessed March 25, 2012).

30   Lois M Davis and Michael Pollar et al. "Long-Term Effects of Law Enforcement's Post-9/11 Focus on Counterterroism and Homeland Security," Report to the U.S. Department of Justice, (RAND Corporation: December 2010).

31 Victor Rios, *Punished: Policing the Lives of Black and Latino Boys*, (New York: New York University Press, 2011), 39.

32 Judith Greene, Kevin Pranis. "Gang Wars: The Failure of Enforcement Tactics and the Need for Effective Public Safety Strategies," (Justice Policy Institute, 2007), http://www.aclunc.org/issues/criminal_justice/gang_injunctions_fact_sheet.shtml (accessed March 25, 2012).

33 Oakland City Attorney and Oakland Police Department, 8.

34 Fight Blight, "North Oakland and South Berkeley Continue to Be Hot Real Estate Markets" *We Fight Blight in South Berkeley–North Oakland*, January 18, 2010, http://wefightblight.blogspot.com/2011/01/north-oakland-and-south-berkeley.html (accessed March 25, 2012).

35 Eric K. Arnold, "Public Safety Committee Report Reveals Cost of Injunctions—But Is It Worth It," *Oakland Local*, February 15, 2011.

36 Oakland City Attorney and Oakland Police Department, 7–8.

37 Bushrod Recreation Center Staff, conversation, Spring 2011.

38 Byron Williams, "Must be careful with Oakland's injunction," *The Oakland Tribune*, CA, April 25, 2010.

39 Paul Flores, Cause Data Collective, and Unity Council of Oakland, "Latino Men and Boys Oakland Project Final Report," (The Unity Council of Oakland, 2010).

ON MEMORY AND RESISTANCE:
Excerpt from the Keynote Address, Counter-Counterinsurgency Convergence

ELAINE BROWN
APRIL 8, 2011; REED COLLEGE, PORTLAND, OREGON[1]

I'M GOING TO FOCUS MY REMARKS ON THE RECENT GEORGIA PRISONER UPRISING.
And, I'm going to talk tonight about why it is that over 50% of the prisoners in America are black. And the reason I'm going to do that is because black people represent only 13% of the population. This is a reflection, a very clear reflection of exactly what is going on and what is wrong in this society. I'm going to talk about why this is and how it happened.

There are over two million people in prison in America today. That is the highest number of people in prison in any country in the world, and it represents the highest ratio of prisoners to population of any country in the world.

Among those two million people in prison is a young man whom everybody in the Georgia prison system knows as "Little B." His name is Michael Lewis, and I wrote a book about this boy called *The Condemnation of Little B.* In 1997 in Atlanta, Little B was 13 years old, and he was arrested for a murder—which, parenthetically, he did not commit. I only say "parenthetically" because I don't know how relevant it is to discuss the question of the guilt or innocence of a young boy, a 13-year-old who was arrested and tried as an adult for murder and sentenced as an adult to life in prison, which is what happened to Little B. This is the only country in the world that puts children on trial as adults. At 13 years old in America, you can't buy cigarettes, you can't buy liquor, you can't drive a car, you can't vote, you really can't do anything independently. You have to go to school. You have all kinds of rules and restrictions. You're actually not considered a full citizen. Everybody understands that a 13-year-old can't make decisions based on understanding the consequences of an act, so we don't hold children to the standard of an adult, children being people under 18 years old. But when it comes to so-called crime, we change our minds, and we hold children to an adult standard and put them in prison.

When I saw the headlines in the *Atlanta Journal-Constitution*, I was simply shocked to see the face of this little boy, and to read that he was being deemed a "thug," charged with the killing of an innocent black father. That's how it was characterized. It all took place in an area of Atlanta called the Bluff. The Bluff is where poor black people live, which used to be called the ghetto, the inner city, whatever you want to call it. And, it's a place where you have no real commerce other than drugs. You can buy crack cocaine, powder cocaine, you can buy "purple," you can buy Ecstasy, you can buy whatever illegal drug you want in the Bluff. And you can drive by and buy it. You can order your drugs by telephone from Georgia Tech, which is nearby, or Spelman or Morehouse Colleges, which are also nearby, and you can roll through the Bluff and get whatever you want. It's one of the roughest neighborhoods in Atlanta, but people generally don't get killed there buying drugs, because drug dealers are not trying to kill their customers.

So that's where Little B grew up. By the time he was eight years old, his mother had become a crack head, and his house was a crack house. The Bluff was a hotbed of all of this, so when a guy got killed on one of its corners, it wasn't particularly newsworthy. Indeed, the case was absurd because nobody's goes there to buy a soda, as the wife claimed as to why she and her husband ended up on that corner where he was killed. You only go to the Bluff to buy one thing, and that's dope. But, in any case, this guy gets killed and he's cast as this good guy, a good husband and father; and in the meantime there's Little B, who, arrested for the murder of this good husband and father, is cast as this thug. Early on, the black mayor of Atlanta referred to Little B as an "evil in the city."

But he didn't talk about how it is that a kid like Little B could grow up without any support, so that by the time he was 11, the juvenile court had to rule that he was not being taken care of by his mother, declaring him a deprived child and removing him from the home—though it really didn't make any difference because there wasn't really a home there. By the time Michael was eight, he'd become responsible for taking care of himself and his little sister, five years old, getting her dressed, combing her hair, taking her to school because that was the only way they could get any food, free breakfast and lunch. Later, he would say his mother smoked up every dime.

If he were an aberration, or if he were just one kid in one neighborhood, we could say, well, this is a sad little story. But, unfortunately, there are very many Little Bs in Atlanta, and in Chicago, Philadelphia, Detroit, Boston, L.A., what have you. There are, indeed, millions of children in America living without any support, millions of black children.

When he was 11, Michael ran away from the foster home where he had been placed because he was being abused there. He ran away back to the Bluff, where he sold dope for his brother and a lot of other older guys. And those are the same people who testified against him at trial, using him, a boy, to take the weight for their murder. In any case, Michael was convicted of murder in November of 1997.

Now around the same time as Michael's case, there was a kid right here in Oregon named Kip Kinkle, who lived in or near Eugene. He was a 14-year-old kid, a white kid. Kip got up one morning and killed Mom and Dad, and put a backpack full of guns on his back, an assault rifle in his hand, taped a hunting knife to his chest, and went off to middle school. He shot up 25 people, killing three, before they took him down, and

INTERVIEW WITH A STRIKING PRISONER

At one point during her talk, Elaine Brown called one of the prisoners involved in the Georgia prisoner strike.

I'm going to talk to one of the brothers that was one of the leaders, who is a Muslim.

Q: *You want to tell us about why you organized this strike, and who was involved, and how you did it?*

A: We had to get together. You know, try to lay down, no working, you know what I'm saying? See if we could get some kind of attention, you know. Right now, all across Georgia, they're treating us bad, with the working for free and getting no proper education. A lot of things that we don't have down here that we trying to get. With the help that Elaine gave us, a lot of us got together, and we sat down and talked.

Q: *What about the question of the different sets of blacks, the whites, Mexicans, what have you? You got together with all of them, right?*

A: Oh yeah, everyone who'd talk—the Mexicans, the whites, the Brothers, you know. We sat down and huddled, had a conversation about what we needed to do, and brought this thing together. Everybody agreed on it. We're trying to get some sort of progress, freedom, right? Everybody got together and said let's do it. When we laid down, it should have gotten their attention.

Q: *Why did you get together with some of the people who were enemies before? How did you decide not to be against each other, and join together?*

A: First of all, our enemy is not each other. You know, we are together behind these doors. So we got together because we knew that as one we can make it happen. If we were separate—blacks, whites, Mexicans—we can't get nowhere like that. So we had to sit down together and get some understanding. And once everybody got together and came to that agreement, we went on and sat down inside our cells.

Q: *How many prisons were involved, as far as you know?*

A: How many prisons? Well, it was like six, seven.

Q: *And in the prison where you are, everybody there laid down. How many people there?*

A: Down here, we got around sixteen hundred, somewhere around there.

Q: *Listen, I just wanted everyone to know that one of the leaders of the strike was here, and that you are still struggling. Can you just say one thing about what you were fighting for? What were the issues that you wanted to bring up?*

A: What we were fighting for was, like, the amount of time they were giving us, the way they were treating us, making us labor for free, no education, no health care, a lot of things on

arrested him. Kip killed five people that day, and tried to kill the police who arrested him. We all know that if Kip had been a black kid, he would have been dead, killed by the police.

The next day after Kip's arrest, there was a big banner in front of his middle school that said, "Why Kip?" *Looking at too many violent videos? Feeling isolated in exurbia?* Was he one of those kids who was being taunted, bullied? What was Kip's problem? Everybody started examining this, throughout America, why these young people, young white people, so many of them, in Columbine and elsewhere, why were they killing people. And there was a national debate around the question of what was going on with "our youth."

Not one person called Kip Kinkle a thug, though. Even today, we don't think of Kip as a thug. But my boy is a thug, a boy *charged* with the killing of one person, not a boy known to have killed five. Nobody thought of Kip as a thug; he was a good kid who just did a bad thing. *What happened? We need to look at this.* But we don't need to condemn him to life in prison like we did Little B. We make a distinction in America when it's a white kid and a black kid. Crime in America has a black face. Crime is a political question.

So, in November 1997, Michael Lewis, Little B, was convicted of murder and sentenced to prison for life. Life in prison in Georgia at that time carried a mandatory minimum sentence of 14 years. Today, it's a mandatory minimum of 30 years.

Fourteen years have passed now. In March of this year, last month, right after his birthday, his 28th birthday, Michael was denied parole. The basis for the denial was "nature of the crime." "Nature of the crime" means he'll never get out, because if he's going to be denied based on the nature of the crime, obviously the nature of the crime cannot ever change. So he will never be free.

He's still in prison there in Georgia. And he was part of the uprising on December 9 of last year [2010], which involved around 10,000 men. He was at Macon State Prison. The main prisons that were involved were Macon State, and Smith, Telfair, Hayes, Augusta. There are approximately 2,000 men in each prison, and at least five of those prisons were shut down on account of the prisoners' labor strike in December.

The prisoners determined that they were not going to work, as a protest to being forced to work for free. It was just going to be a one-day strike. Then, they said, we're not going to work for free. We're not going to work until we get the things that we want. And we're going to make this a nonviolent protest. These are guys who could have, you know, taken over the prison, like at Attica, Lucasville. But they knew what the results would be so they developed a strategy, one that was very powerful. They just refused to step out of their cells. They agreed, everybody is going to just lay down. That's how they put it. There's something very powerful about that language for me: "We're

the inside that we need that we're not getting.

Q: *What about people being put in the hole and beaten up and everything?*

A: Oh yeah, that's a big one right there. Oh, man. They're really killing guys and getting away with it, you know, like it's legal, right? You know what I'm saying?

Q: *You've been put in the hole yourself a number of times, right?*

A: Yeah, but, you know, you've got to stand up for what's right. Right? And when you rebel against them like that—that's why I said to the other fellas, try not to act out, just sit down. Once you sit down, there ain't nothing they can do. But, they can cover everything up if you try to act out physically. They would try to cover it up by saying, well, he acted out, so we had to, we had to retaliate and try to beat him some kind of way. And, we got a lot of guys that's in here, some of them got jumped on real bad, some got killed by the officers, you know, a lot of things.

Q: *All right, Brother. I'm going to let you go, because I'm going to continue talking to the young people that are here, and hopefully they'll get inspired to get involved in the whole movement trying to get human rights for prisoners.*

A: Okay. Tell the young people I said to stay out of this place right here. 'Cause it's rough in here.

just going to lay down. We're not going to get up. We're not going to work." Like Bob Dylan wrote, "We're not going to work on Maggie's Farm no more."

There were the blacks who were in various sets in the prison, including the Muslims; and you had whites from the Aryan Nation; and you had Mexican Mafia or what have you; and you had Rastafarians—one of whom called me the other day to tell me that they had retaliated by beating him pretty badly and cutting off his locks. You had all of these groups that have been fighting each other, who were pretty tough guys, and they decided that they're not going to fight each other anymore. They've recognized they have a common enemy. They're not going to fall in love with each other or go off together singing Kumbaya, but they all said: "We have conditions here that are so terrible that we're all suffering under so we're going to do this thing this day together. We don't know what's going to happen, and we don't know what the result is going to be, but it's going down, and we're standing together."

You remember when Dr. King was killed during the Memphis garbage strike? And, the striking sanitation workers carried large picket signs that said, "I am a man." That's what these men were saying: "We're still human beings. Despite our condition as prisoners, we're still human beings."

I like to talk about Dr. King, because everyone can relate to Dr. King. At the end of his life, he became a revolutionary, ideologically. In 1967, he said: "We've achieved civil rights, one could say, because of the Voting Rights Act. But when I look out, I have to ask, 'where do we go from here?' And to know where to go, we have to look at where we are. And when I look at the condition of black people I see that when the Constitution was written, we were 60% of a person. But now we are less than that. We are 50%, because we have half of what is good and double of what is bad in America."

Now the reason I'm focusing on blacks is because our condition presents the clearest case of what is going on in this county, in terms of inequalities and injustices. We pretend, now that we have a black president, that everything must be all right. But if we look at where we are today, black people, as I said, represent 50% of the prison population. We have the highest unemployment, lowest education levels, and so on. And so the question is, why? How did we get here?

The present prison situation arose in the Clinton administration. You know, we all like to talk about Bush; it's so easy to talk about Bush. But we act like there's some big difference between Clinton and Bush, or Obama and Bush; like there's some big difference between these different administrations. But, under the Clinton administration, this very interesting thing happened in the so-called criminal justice system. He set forth his position on crime in November of 1993, during the first year after he was elected president.

Clinton got up on the podium where Martin Luther King gave his last speech. You know, that great speech where he said, "I'm not fearing any man tonight." That was the speech he gave at the end of his life: "I've been to the mountaintop. I have seen the other side. I know we as a people will get there. I might not get there with you." That great speech, that last moment of his life. And there was Bill Clinton standing in that same spot, in that same church, a sea of black people there listening to him. He's down there in Memphis to tell black people something special, to deliver a message to black people. He asked the blacks there, "You know, if Martin Luther King were standing here by my side today, what would he say?" And now Bill Clinton is going to tell us what Martin Luther King would say if he were alive today. I mean, this is an incredible leap of faith, not to mention incredibly arrogant. But, Clinton tells all these black people, this is what Martin Luther King would say. Dr. King would say, "I died for your freedom, but look what you've done with it." "We have all this black-on-black crime, all these unwed teen mothers, and the breakdown of the black family." That's what Dr. King would say, Clinton said.

But, we have to examine this. What do you mean, all this black-on-black crime? The majority of crime in America is committed by white people, against white people. Why? Because white people are the majority of the people in America. It's not very complicated. But Clinton convinced black people, *the reason you have all these problems is, something is wrong with you. But I'm going to fix it for you. You've got this crime; you've got these unwed teen mothers. I'm going to do something about your problems.*

Now, let's examine the breakdown of the black family. I would say that happened back in the 1600s when Europeans started snatching people out of Africa and bringing them into Jamestown as slaves. And let's not talk about how the black family was living for 250 years under the institution of slavery. But, according to Clinton, *we* are the problem, unable to maintain our families. There's nothing wrong with America anymore. There's something wrong with black people.

And we have bought into that neoliberal ideology, which I call New Age racism, where you are responsible for your cancer or your poverty. That's the kind of thinking. It's your fault you are poor or sick. And, *you* need to fix it, because there's nothing wrong with the scheme of things. And we've bought into that.

So Bill Clinton says: "I'm going to help you. I'm going to give you a crime bill that's going to be so powerful that all these career criminals and these thugs—like Little B—we're going to get them off your streets." So Clinton gave us the Omnibus Crime Bill of 1994, which Newt Gingrich and the Republicans were promoting; but Clinton pushed it through and took credit for it. And, you have people like the members of the Congressional Black Caucus who supported this thing, who said, yes, this is how we're going to deal with crime in our communities. As a result, you have the three-strikes-and-you're-out laws. The third strike could really be any crime, like the famous California case where a guy stole a piece of pizza, which was deemed his third strike, for which he got life in prison. This is coming out of Clinton's legislation, which all the states adopted. The other part of that legislation was to adjudicate children as adults for certain crimes, the so-called "seven deadly sins." As a result, from 1994 to 2004 the prison system in America doubled, and became the largest prison system in the world. We can thank Bill Clinton for that.

The second failing among blacks according to Clinton was the so-called unwed teen mother. So, Clinton followed up his crime legislation with the 1996 Welfare Reform Bill, criminalizing poor mothers.

The mass incarceration of blacks, however, is not really new. This relates to what the brothers in Georgia were talking about, prisoners working for free. In the prison system of Georgia, you do not get paid one dime for your work. Of course, the larger reality is that people outside prison are working every day for what amounts to little or no money. But, if you've been in prison for 15 years and you come out with only the 25 or 50 dollars the system provides you when you leave, you have to return to society without a dime, and you don't have any backup. Well, what do you figure you're going to be doing in the next day or two? Trying to find some way of surviving, using any means necessary, desperate measures—which is why we have a high recidivism rate. So, common sense would tell you that it might behoove us to pay people for cleaning these prisons. We pay the prison system a lot of tax money, but that doesn't translate to any benefit to the prisoners. But, the reason I said the mass incarceration of blacks is not new has to do with the history and application of the 13th Amendment. While the 13th Amendment calls for the abolition of involuntary servitude, it states that an "exception" is "as a punishment for crime." And, even prisoner advocates have come to accept that this exception means the State is empowered to force prisoners to work for free.

So I'm just going to go back a little through the history of things to discuss why black people have such a great number in the prison system today, so we can see the importance of the prison system as part of the same scheme that was put into place when this country was founded.

Barring the 250 years of slavery before, when the Civil War started, it was because the South seceded over the prospective abolition of slavery. And, people like to say that the war wasn't over slavery but over the expansion of the country. But when you read the secession statements of South Carolina and all the other seceding states, what you realize is that they all said, "Slavery is our economic engine. We cannot live without it. You are cutting us off." You should check those statements out. They have a lot to do with this country, remembering that in 1776, when the country was founded, it was founded as a slave-holding nation.

So, in 1863, the Southern States of the Confederacy were winning the war. And Lincoln had to decide what to do. *We've got to do something to win this war, so I'm going to undercut the labor force in the seceding states by freeing the slaves.* So, he issued the Emancipation Proclamation as "a necessary war measure," which is precisely what it says. And when he did that, a lot of blacks just left the southern plantations and started walking toward the north to find their way away from slavery.

By the time Sherman was about to burn Atlanta, thousands and thousands of blacks were walking behind him. And, when he did the great march to the sea, to Savannah, even more thousands of blacks were marching behind him. This is why, in 1865, when the war was over, Sherman issued Field Order #15, ordering the Union Army to distribute 40 acres of tillable land he had seized in the war to every former slave family so they could start a life in this country as non-slaves. Sherman wasn't an abolitionist but a practical man, who saw how dangerous it would be for all these former slaves to be walking around with nothing to do and nowhere to go. You've got 4 million ex-slaves, what are you going to do with these people? So, he said, we're going to give them all this confiscated coastal land along the southeast corridor of the country, from North Carolina to Florida.

But, of course, once Andrew Johnson took over, after Lincoln was killed, it wasn't but a minute before they removed the blacks from those lands granted under Field Order #15. And that left blacks in a very peculiar position. That left blacks as a people who were not slaves but not citizens, with no land and few options for survival.

At the same time, before the 13th Amendment was ratified, the so-called Black Codes were enacted in the South. These were laws criminalizing certain behaviors of blacks. And, one of the greatest crimes a black could commit at that time was "vagrancy," which meant having no job. Now, there were no prisons like we have today. So what was done when a black man was convicted of the "crime" of vagrancy? He was leased out to a private company and sent to do work on a farm or in a coal mine, put into a chain gang to work for free as punishment for his crime. So, blacks went from being a slave class to a criminal class. We were the only people in either class. We were the only people for whom vagrancy was a crime punishable by being put on the chain gang to work for free. Blacks were effectively re-enslaved.

Now, why is this important? Because under the Black Codes, blacks were in the same position of working for free as under slavery, as before the 13th Amendment—and, as now. The same class of people, the capitalists and profiteers, were doing the same thing for the same reason, before and after and since the enslavement of blacks, exploiting blacks as cheap labor for the production of products and profits, for the development of wealth in America.

So when we talk today about the blacks who are prisoners—and the majority of prisoners in Georgia, almost 80%, are black—when we talk about people going to prison, then we have to connect these dots and have this historical understanding. Now, I just want to go over a little more of this history.

The struggle that blacks then faced was to survive. When we get to the Supreme Court's *Plessy v. Ferguson* decision in 1896, blacks really had nowhere to go. The *Plessy* decision was really just about whether or not there was any possibility that blacks could have any share in this society as citizens.

Homer Plessy was a very light-skinned black man, who, when he got on a train in New Orleans, was told to get off. They told him he could not sit in the white section of the train: *you're black, get back to the back of the train and sit in that back car.* Plessy sued, and took his case all the way to the Supreme Court. And the Supreme Court said: *Look, Plessy, we cannot make you white and we cannot make these white people like you; the only thing we can tell you is that the accommodations can be separate as long as they're equal.* And, that sounds like a good plan, doesn't it? Separate-but-equal sounds all right. But nobody was building an equal train car for black people. So, you could be separate, but there was no equal car for you. So, if you wanted to get on a train, you had to get on at the back, a train or bus, whatever it was. Thus, there was no equal employment opportunity, not even to join a union, and no way to make a claim for equal treatment anywhere. So, after *Plessy*, blacks had no place to go and nothing to be. So, we struggled for food, for clothing, for housing, for education, for everything. The *Plessy* decision had absolutely destroyed the last hope we had because it said that "separate" was all right. With segregation, Jim Crow, "Whites Only" policies, blacks were forced even farther back.

There were no accommodations for blacks. And, we didn't have anything to accommodate ourselves. That's why Booker T. Washington said we needed our own money. The Marcus Garvey movement started out by talking about economic independence. And you had the NAACP and all those various other efforts that tried to find for a way for black people to live in America, all the way to 1954 and the *Brown* decision—which didn't overturn *Plessy*, because nothing has ever overturned *Plessy*. *Brown* said separate is not equal in the public schools, the Supreme Court ruling that schools should be desegregated. And, this country had not seen the level of bloodshed since the Civil War as when one black child tried to go to school and sit in a classroom with some white children. It's amazing when we think about it, because now we act like this stuff never even happened.

Now, we're at 1954, almost a hundred years since the end of slavery, and all we're talking about is where some children go to school. Don't have housing, don't have jobs, don't have our 40 acres, don't have food, don't have medical care. Finally, you get to 1955, that moment when Rosa Parks, like Plessy, said:

"I want a seat on the bus. I paid my money, I just want to sit on the bus." Can you imagine, we're actually arguing for a seat on the bus in 1955?

That's when the big moral questions were raised, when Dr. King got involved in the Montgomery bus boycott. And TV started showing it. Everybody was hearing Dr. King's voice, everybody was seeing those dogs attacking King's nonviolent civil rights protestors. Everybody could see this stuff. And the whole world saw it, and saw the truth of America that called itself the land of the free and the home of the brave. And America was shamed before the eyes of the world. And, so, you had the beginning of this new uprising in this country, the Freedom Movement.

We never called it the Civil Rights Movement—the Freedom Movement. "Before I'll be a slave, I'll be buried in my grave." And there was the rise of organizations like the Student Nonviolent Coordinating Committee, which was headed by people you probably know of, H. Rap Brown and Stokely Carmichael. You had the Congress of Racial Equality. Of course, you had the Urban League and the NAACP. The Mississippi Freedom Democratic Party with Fannie Lou Hamer. All these people trying to find different ways to gain basic rights for blacks.

And then the Black Panther Party came into being. And we talked about revolutionary change. We wanted freedom for black people, but we recognized that our freedom could not come in the existing scheme. In order for us to be free, the whole scheme had to change. We were Marxist-Leninists. And we formed coalitions with the Brown Berets, with the Young Lords, with the Red Guard, with the Young Patriots, out of Chicago, a white organization—which I always say was composed of left-leaning Timothy McVeighs. We formed international coalitions—these were real coalitions—with the PAC in South Africa, with FRELIMO in Mozambique, ZANU in Zimbabwe. We supported the efforts of the Vietnamese people for national liberation. As a matter of fact, we called not for peace in Vietnam but for victory for the Viet Cong. Of course, you can imagine, this didn't endear us to the American government. J. Edgar Hoover referred to us as "the greatest threat to the internal security of the United States," and did everything to try to destroy us, and just about did.

Among the things we did was organize people around the question of food, the human right to have food. We started free breakfast programs to point out this fundamental human right. We started free clinics in the community, to organize people around the right to medical care. We talked about and demonstrated the right of the people to bear arms, saying we had the right of self-defense, especially when the police came into our neighborhoods and attempted to murder our children and our families. And one of the other things we did was become involved in the rising prisoner movement, as led by George Jackson, who, at that time, was the Field Marshal of the Black Panther Party.

When George Jackson talked about the prisoner, he said the prisoner was confined in a prison within a prison, the oppressed on the outside being also in prison. He talked about how we needed to set aside our differences, understand our common threat, and rise up together—and many of the Georgia prisoners quoted him on this. And George Jackson's murder by prison guards in August of 1971 was so momentous that it inspired an uprising in Attica State Prison in New York, in September of 1971. These men took over one wing of Attica, and what did they demand? The same things the guys in Georgia did. They demanded better food, nutritional food, a decent place to sleep, the end of cruel and unusual punishments, an education. This is what these men asked for in Georgia, and also, they wanted to be paid for their labor. That's what they mainly focused on in Georgia. The Governor of New York then, Nelson Rockefeller, sent in troops and, in a couple of minutes, that army mowed down 40 people, ending the one-week uprising. This was why the men in Georgia decided they would do something different.

Now the question is, as we look over all this, where do we go from here? That's the question that Dr. King asked that I'd like to go back to.

Before his assassination—you know, a lot of people think that King was killed because he was against the war, or because he led the garbage strike, or whatever. No, King was organizing something else before he was killed, an effort called the Poor People's Campaign. What was the theme of the Poor People's Campaign? It was to have whosoever will, let him come and join all the other poor people in America to march on Washington to demand a *guaranteed* income for everyone who needed it. *You are putting all these billions of dollars into war, and you can't find us a job. If you can't get me a job, then somebody needs to get me some money to live on. I need a guaranteed income.* That's a pretty radical statement, isn't it? As a matter of fact, it sounded "communistic." Then, King talked about guaranteed health care. Not health insurance, health *care*. And then he talked about the redistribution of the wealth of this nation. This was what he was doing when he was assassinated.

What Dr. King was talking about at that point is what the Black Panther Party was talking about. There had to be some kind of fundamental change. We had to be geared to making change that was fundamental.

Now, I want to close with something Dr. King said in that last period of his life. Of course, being a Christian minister, he talked about the Bible. He said there was a story in the Bible about a man who came to Jesus and said, "Jesus I understand you're in the business of saving people who have sinned. I've committed a lot of sins. Do you think you can save me?" And Jesus said, "No, Nicodemus, I can't save you. You have to be born again. You've committed so many sins, you can't be fixed." So, Dr. King said, "When I look at America today, and I see the poverty, and I see the lack of education, and I see the war, and I see all these things that are terrible things going on, I say, America, you're going to have to be born again."

NOTES

1   Special thanks to Circle A Radio for recording the keynote address.

RAZE THE WALLS

BERIAH EMPIE & LYDIA ANNE M. BARTHOLOW
OF THE COMMITTEE TO CONNECT THE DOTS

> *"These places were built with us in mind."*
> —*George Jackson*[1]

FOR THOSE OF US WHO DESIRE FUNDAMENTAL SOCIAL, ECONOMIC, AND PO-
litical change towards more equitable forms, it is imperative that we understand the forces at work to prevent such transformation. The Prison Industrial
Complex (PIC) serves a counterinsurgent role both defensively and offensively. It retaliates fiercely against political prisoners for the actions they have
taken in the pursuit of liberation struggles, and separates them from the
movements they contribute to, thereby weakening the movement. It also prevents insurgency by controlling the most oppressed members of society, those
with the most to gain from revolutionary change.

This relationship is intimately tied to race in this country. As such, the
PIC is a cornerstone of white supremacy. It creates, and recreates, the social
inequities that we are struggling to change.

PART ONE:
COUNTERINSURGENCY AND CRIMINAL JUSTICE

ON A NATIONAL scale policing and prisons are transitioning, or have transi-
tioned, to operational models based on counterinsurgency. Counterinsurgency
focuses on legitimizing the state, taking subtle and nonviolent forms like

propaganda, psychological operations, information gathering, building community support, and as a result, control of the population.

For example, in 2009 two Massachusetts state troopers applied the counterinsurgency training they received as Green Berets deployed in Iraq to the largely Puerto Rican neighborhood of Brightwood, in Springfield. One of the troopers outlined the dual goal of combating gangs and gaining the trust of the citizens: "Work by, with and through the local population to detect, degrade, disrupt, and dismantle criminal activity," because, "gang members and drug dealers operate very similar to insurgents." Police tactics included town hall meetings, police going door-to-door, and establishing a "hand picked team of street leaders." These people served as an "informal intelligence network." As proof that these tactics worked, the police recount an incident in which they were pursuing a suspect who fled a vehicle stop; they received a "flurry" of calls from citizens describing what the suspect looked like, and where he had been spotted most recently. However, a community member named Wilfredo DeJesus points to another side of these practices. Outside the town hall meetings there is a board with pictures of people who are barred from entering. He states, "People think they are child molesters or something," but they "didn't do bad things."[2]

The Department of Justice calls this approach Community Policing. The model emphasizes the need to gain trust and information by working with stakeholders in the community, such as the media, nonprofits, religious institutions, businesses, parole officers, and even activists. The department has produced an 85 page write-up specifically on increasing attention on prisoner reentry to the community, heightening surveillance and police presence in the neighborhoods that people return to. The report states outright that one of the main challenges in gaining the trust of the citizens in such instances is, "because many reentry initiatives are focused in high crime, minority communities that receive high numbers of returning prisoners, this type of police involvement can give the appearance of racial profiling."[3] The problem, from the state's perspective, is not with racial profiling *per se*, but rather that the perception of unequal treatment undermines public support for policing.

PART TWO:
WHITE SUPREMACY AND COUNTERINSURGENCY

RACE IN THIS country is generally seen in terms of racism, or individual acts of bigotry. This is a piece of the issue, but fails to acknowledge the systemic ghosts that haunt each of us.

The phrase "white supremacy" more fully articulates the magnitude of the societal networks heaping privilege upon white people, and actively keeping whiteness at the pinnacle of the social hierarchy. Elizabeth Martinez describes it as such: "White supremacy is an historically based, institutionally perpetuated system of exploitation and oppression on continents, nations, and peoples of color by white peoples and nations of the European continent, for the purpose of maintaining and defending a system of wealth, power and privilege."[4]

Since white supremacy is the *modus operandi* of the U.S. (and given its influence, the world) using this descriptive phrase shifts the focus from individual acts of bigotry (or racial profiling), toward political, economic, and social institutions. At this level of permeation, the only thing one needs to do to support white supremacy is to do nothing.

The very creation of whiteness can be viewed as counterinsurgency. In the 1600s "white people" did not exist in the way they are conceptualized now. The European indentured servants and African slaves worked and lived in close proximity. Not to falsely insinuate that their situations were comparable, however, it was only a matter of time before they realized they shared an oppressor. Living and working together matured into running away together, stealing together, sleeping together, and eventually rebelling.

The planter elites were outnumbered by their labor force, which was growing increasingly unified and violent. The governor of Virginia described the situation as such, "How miserable that man is that Governes a People where six parts of seven at least are Poor Endebted Discontented and Armed [*sic*]."[5]

The most well-known of these rebellions was Bacon's Rebellion of 1676. Bacon himself should not be romanticized, as he hated the indigenous, and counted among his demands the taking of more land. However, his militia of African slaves and European servants, which marched on Jamestown burning government buildings, caused great fear for demonstrating the revolutionary potential of a unified population. This fear, and the fact they were outnumbered, caused the ruling class to seek a system of social control that did not rely on military might. They took a page from the British playbook: earlier in the 1600s, the British had imported Scottish Protestants into Catholic Ireland to be used as a buffer class; all Scots, no matter how lowly, were granted privileges that the Irish were not.

Following this pattern, a litany of privileges towards Europeans and restrictions towards Africans were put in place to separate and control the population. Africans could not raise their hand against a European, or own a firearm, thereby outlawing self-defense. In 1705 the colony confiscated all property owned by slaves. African people were also banned from holding public office or testifying in court. It is around this time that the word "white" began to appear in legal documents of Virginia and Maryland, referring to all Europeans, both rich and poor. This white race served to re-legitimize the ruling class and control the population. Once it was created, the Southern white worker began venting the frustration of their condition on the slaves, and no longer on the slave system and its white ruling class.[6]

Modern science demonstrates that there is no biological basis for racial classification. Even when using a genetic computer program no distinction great enough to justify a separate category can be found. There are no natural sub-categories within humanity, at least not enough to systematize into species, or even varieties. The conclusion is that race does not exist biologically; it is a scientific fiction.[7]

And yet, human subjectivities can not be reduced to genetics and scientific testing. We exist as narratives, intellects, spiritual beings, histories and so much more. We move through the world in relation to one another, in relation to systems of power, and in relation to one another within systems of power. It is in these interactions that race becomes a truth, creating a complex dialectic in which race is simultaneously a biological fiction and a social reality.[8]

For the state, whiteness is the incentive dangled in front of European immigrants to prevent them from arriving and siding with people of color. Currently it would not be surprising to situate Irish, Italian, and Jewish people in the overarching category of white. However, there have been times when they would have been excluded from accessing the full range of privileges entitled to white people. The first step on the path to whiteness is a step away from people of color.[9]

A contemporary example of whiteness being defined by violence against people of color and access to state power can be seen in the case of George Zimmerman shooting and killing Trayvon Martin. Zimmerman, a community watch volunteer, followed the unarmed 17-year-old Martin claiming he was "suspicious," and ended up murdering him. When the police arrived they identified Zimmerman as white. Zimmerman, whose father is white and mother is originally from Peru, has since been referred to by the media as "Hispanic,"[10] usually to argue that the incident was not about race. However, what truly determined Zimmerman's whiteness is that he shot an unarmed, underage, black male and was not arrested. That access to power is at the center of what it means to be white.

PART THREE:
FROM PLANTATION TO PRISON

WE SEE THE roots of Zimmerman's suspicion and violence in the rise of the modern prison system. The 13th Amendment made slavery and involuntary servitude illegal except in the case of punishment for a crime.

Responding to the advances of Reconstruction, the state, corporations, and landowners made laws that were impossible not to violate. They also instituted a form of punishment that was still very profitable.[11] Succinctly stated, the primary response to the revolutionary advancements made during Reconstruction was mass incarceration.

At the end of the twentieth century, we could see the pattern repeat. When analyzing the incarceration rates, one sees that in 1910, for every 100,000 people in the population, there were 122 incarcerated. By 1980, the rate was at 209 per 100,000. Throughout the decades in between, the rate held steady between 100 and 200. However, between 1980 and 1990, the rate surged from 209 to 461. It continued to rise, reaching 703 in 2000, and 760 in 2010.[12/13]

This spike in incarceration rates was, yet again, a response by the state to the revolutionary upheaval of the previous decades. There were hundreds of violent uprisings between 1965 and 1968. In 1964, presidential candidate Barry Goldwater first raised crime as an issue in his candidacy. Goldwater lost, but his message on crime won big. Journalist Christian Parenti elaborates on this new rhetoric: "At the heart of this new type of politics was a very old political trope: white racism and the self-fueling fear bred by it. Crime meant urban, urban meant black, and war on crime meant a bulwark built against the increasingly political and vocal racial 'other' by the predominantly white state."[14]

When faced with a situation in which it was losing legitimacy and violent repression was not working, the state turned to less overt means to regain its legitimacy. In 1968 after the assassination of Dr. King, when hundreds of cities across the country broke out in revolt, Congress worked to establish the first large federal crime bill—the Omnibus Crime Control and Safe Streets Act of 1968. It was now legal for police to tap phones and plant bugs, and when authorities were faced with an "emergency" they were free to intercept communications without a warrant for 48 hours.

President Nixon pushed things even further. Writing in his diary, Nixon's Chief of Staff, H.R. Haldeman wrote, "[President Nixon] emphasized that you have to face the fact that the whole problem is really the blacks. The key is to devise a system that recognizes this while not appearing to."[15] Parenti asserts, "That 'system' was the war on crime and the criminal justice buildup." Despite the lack of evidence of a national narcotics issue, the war on drugs was the White House's Trojan horse for intensified federal involvement in policing. It allowed Nixon to deliver on his campaign rhetoric of being tough on crime while stifling organized political rebellion.[16]

The PIC was used offensively to remove people from their communities before being able to organize, and defensively to combat existing organizations.

For instance, the Louisiana State Penitentiary, better known as Angola, was a slave plantation in the nineteenth century, and is now the largest maximum security prison in the U.S. Congruent with Convict Lease Labor, in which ex-slaves were imprisoned and then rented out to plantation owners, it is also a working prison.[17] Let us imagine that a photograph was taken of a group of black men working in a cotton field (one of the crops still grown there) when this site was a plantation, and then another picture was snapped today in the same field. There would be very little to distinguish the two images.

At Angola, and across the nation, those incarcerated are vastly disproportionately people of color. Compare the incarceration rates per 100,000 of the population in the year 2000. The rate for white males was 1,000, while the rate for African American males is nearly 7,000. Incarceration rates per 100,000 in 2004 regardless of gender shows the same disparity. White people were at 393, Latinos 957, and blacks 2,531. To get an accurate vision of state repression against Latinos, it would be necessary to factor in detention centers and deportations, which would indeed greatly increase the rate: the daily population in INS detention climbed from 5,532 in 1994 to 13,210 by 2001.[18]

PART FOUR: CRIMINALIZATION AND COUNTERINSURGENCY

ONE BYPRODUCT OF the racially disproportionate incarceration rates is the racialization of crime, which manifests in numerous ways both overt and covert. People of color in general, and black men specifically, are viewed by white society as the perpetual criminal. The mass media perpetuates this racist caricature, police use it to justify racial profiling, and too many innocent black men are murdered in the name of law and order. A tragic example is that of 25-year-old Keaton Otis. In 2010, Otis was stopped by police while wearing a hooded sweatshirt and driving on the streets of Portland, Oregon. Once he was pulled over, the situation rapidly deteriorated. Otis was tasered and then shot 23 times; police claim he also fired at officers, injuring one. Given the severe use of tasers, it is a highly suspicious claim still warranting further independent investigation. Officer Ryan Foote (a member of the gang unit known as the Hot Spot Enforcement Action Team) admits that, while Otis had not done anything wrong, he "kind of looks like he could be a gangster."[19] To even begin to grasp the devastation carried out by the prison industrial complex, we have to see these incidents that we are encouraged to see as isolated, or unfortunate mishaps, as all being interconnected and self-perpetuating. Once again, we think of Trayvon Martin on the other side of the country. The details of the incidents are vastly divergent; however, we keep hearing the use of buzzwords like "hoodie" and "gangster." We hear Nixon's echo in finding ways to signal, without actually saying, *black*.

There also exists the day-to-day element of counterinsurgency that focuses on controlling and intimidating, both physically and psychologically, communities of color. Michelle Alexander goes into detail in her book *The New Jim Crow*. One well-known study will serve to illustrate the point. In the 1990s, a racial profiling study conducted in New Jersey found that "only 15 percent of drivers on the New Jersey Turnpike were racial minorities, yet 42 percent of all stops and 73 percent of all arrests were black motorists—despite the fact that blacks and whites violated traffic laws at almost exactly the same rate."[20]

Speaking about racial profiling in general, Alexander brings to light the Supreme Court case, *United States v. Brignoni-Ponce*. "The Supreme Court has actually granted the police license to discriminate. [...] The Court concluded it was permissible under the equal protection clause of the Fourteenth Amendment for the police to use race as a factor in making decisions about which motorists to stop and search."[21] We can balance the legal precedent with a personal account to illustrate that such practices have always been routine and permissible. Leonard Peltier offers a lucid view that we can learn from:

> Ask any Indian kid: you're out just walking across the street of some little off-reservation town and there's this white cop suddenly comes up to you, grabs you by your long hair, pushes you up against a car, frisks you, gives you a couple good jabs in the ribs with his nightstick, then sends you off with a warning sneer: "Watch yourself, Tonto!" He doesn't do that to white kids, just Indians [...] when you grow up Indian, you don't have to become a criminal, you already *are* a criminal. You never know innocence.[22]

These day-to-day workings of the PIC can be marshaled to respond to revolutionary movements. There are an array of tactics that range from the preventative to locking up movement leaders for life. Often times just the threat of imprisonment is sufficient to deter a great deal of people from joining in a struggle, or taking a stand against oppression. It is no exaggeration to call this psychological warfare.

Furthermore, the bureaucratic elements of the PIC are put to very effective use to siphon resources away from social movements, often resulting in the complete collapse of a project or an organization. David Gilbert describes how the police and FBI would attack underground newspapers that were reporting the truth about the war in Vietnam. He recounts, "In addition to the standard techniques of sowing distrust and divisions among people, they used multiple busts, on any pretext, to bankrupt these shoestring operations with legal costs. At the same time, the FBI systematically worked to scare off advertisers."[23]

Criminal charges did not in any way need to be valid to have the desired effect. The mere process of defending one's self in court can be enough to derail normal operations. For instance, in 1969, 21 leading members of the New York chapter of the Black Panthers were faced with the utterly fallacious charge of conspiring to bomb department stores. Gilbert, who worked diligently to gather support for the defendants, summarizes, "it took a jury just ninety minutes to declare all defendants not guilty on all charges. But the two years of jail time, bail money, trials and legal costs left what had been a very effective Panther chapter completely decimated."[24]

The state was able to neutralize this chapter without firing a shot.

Peltier recalled a similar strategy being used against the American Indian Movement, underscoring the fact that these were national campaigns to erode the progress that such movements were making, and to prevent further advances. "Target us, set us up, arrest us, beat the shit out of us, hang a phony rap on us, drag us off to jail, impoverish us with legal expenses even if we never did a damn thing. That, we later learned, was what the FBI called 'neutralization'...."[25]

PART FIVE: CONCLUSION

THE CASE OF the San Francisco 8 is a harsh reminder of how long the state continues its assault, and how the tactics from the 1970s are still being utilized. In 1973, thirteen members of the Black Panther Party were captured and tortured in New Orleans. The interrogators were trying to gain evidence against them in connection with the killing of a police officer. A court threw out all the "evidence" acquired from these interrogations. But more than thirty years later, the same police officers and FBI agents reappeared to serve the same men with grand jury subpoenas. Instead of cooperating, the men went to jail for contempt of court. One of the men, Richard Brown, states, "I'm a family man. When you take me away from my family my children suffer. And, my community suffers because I'm a community activist, and this was their whole purpose. To just disrupt me from my focus."[26]

That is exactly what the PIC accomplishes: the devastation of families and communities, and the removal of political organizers from those communities. It employs seemingly race-neutral justifications for increased surveillance and policing in neighborhoods of color. It also serves the ultimate counterinsurgency aim of legitimizing the state and its violence. Who would protect us from "criminals," "drug dealers," and "crack heads" were it not the state? We must see the PIC, not as a source of social safety, but as the pillar of white supremacy that it is.

When struggles for liberation have gained ground in this country we have seen incarceration rates increase. When we begin to be aware of the numerous ways in which the PIC infects our lives, our communities, and our struggles for liberation we begin to see our charge: to abolish the offspring of slavery.

For a world without prisons!

NOTES

1   George Jackson, *Soledad Brother: The Prison Letters of George Jackson* (Chicago: Lawrence Hill Books, 1994), 146.

2   Erica Goode, "With Green Beret Tactics, Combating Gang Warfare," The New York Times web site, http://www.nytimes.com/2012/05/01/us/springfield-mass-fights-crime-using-green-beret-tactics.html?pagewanted=1&_r=2 (accessed July 28, 2012).

3   Nancy La Vigne et al., "Prisoner Reentry and Community Policing: Strategies for Enhancing Public Safety," Department of Justice web site, http://www.cops.usdoj.gov/Publications/e12051219.pdf (accessed on July 28, 2012).

4   Elizabeth Martinez, "Race: The U.S. Creation Myth and its Premise Keepers," Challenging White Supremacy web site, http://www.cwsworkshop.org/pdfs/WIWS/1Race_US_Creation_Myth.PDF (accessed December 21, 2012).

5   Chip Smith, *The Cost of Privilege: Taking on the System of White Supremacy and Racism* (North Carolina: Camino Press, 2007), 17.

6   Ibid., 21.

7   Keita, S.O., Kittles, R.A., Royal, C.D.M. et al., "Conceptualizing Human Variation," *Nature Genetics* 36 (11 Suppl. 2004): S17-20.

8   Joel Olson, *The Abolition of White Democracy* (Minneapolis: Minnesota Press, 2004), 111.

9   Noel Ignatiev, *How the Irish Became White* (New York: Routledge, 1995).

10 Suzanne Gamboa, "Trayvon Martin Case: George Zimmerman's Race is a Complicated Matter," The Huffington Post web site, http://www.huffingtonpost.com/2012/03/29/trayvon-martin-case-georg_n_1387711.html (accessed July 28, 2012).

11 Angela Davis, *Are prisons obsolete?* (New York: Seven Stories Press, 2003), 93.

12 Justice Policy Institute, "The Punishing Decade: Prison and Jail Estimates at the Millennium," Justice Policy Institute web site, http://www.justicepolicy.org/images/upload/00-05_rep_punishingdecade_ac.pdf, (accessed July 28, 2012).

13 CPS: School of Law : King's College, "World Prison Brief," *World Prison Brief*, London, http://www.kcl.ac.uk/depsta/law/research/icps/worldbrief/ (accessed July 20, 2012).

14 Christian Parenti, *Lockdown America: Police and Prisons in the Age of Crisis,* (New York: Verso, 1999), 7.

15 Ibid., 3.

16 Ibid., 12.

17 Mary Bosworth, *Encyclopedia of prisons & correctional facilities* (California: Sage Publications, 2005), 8.

18 Victoria Law, *Resistance Behind Bars: The Struggles of Incarcerated Women* (Oakland: PM Press, 2009), 146.

19 Maxine Bernstein, "Portland Police Explain What Led to the Fatal Stop of Keaton Otis," *The Oregonian,* http://www.oregonlive.com/portland/index.ssf/2010/06/post_20.html (accessed July 28, 2012).

20 Michelle Alexander, *The New Jim Crow: Mass Incarceration in the Age of Colorblindness,* (New York: The New Press, 2010), 131.

21 Ibid., 128.

22 Leonard Peltier, *Prison Writings: My Life is My Sundance,* (New York: St. Martin's Press, 1999), 67.

23 David Gilbert, *Love and Struggle: My Life in SDS, The Weather Underground, and Beyond* (Oakland: PM Press, 2012), 81.

24 Ibid., 81.

25 Ibid., 105.

26 Freedom Archives, "Legacy of Torture," Freedom Archives web site, http://www.freedomarchives.org/BPP/torture.html (accessed on July 28, 2012).

PART THREE

TERRITORY/POPULATION

THE INSURGENT SOUTHWEST:
Death, Criminality, and Militarization on the U.S.-Mexican Border

FATIMA INSOLACIÓN

"The prisons and camps don't contain only those inside them but also those outside them. All human beings are transformed into prisoners and prison guards."
—Sophia Nachalo and Yarostan Vocheck, *Letters of Insurgents*

INTRODUCTION

THE SONORAN DESERT HAS BECOME A REMOTE OUTPOINT OF DEATH, A UNIQUE site of resistance, and a study in how military strategies are effectively used to create profit while maintaining social control. The militarization of the U.S.-Mexican border has caused a lot of suffering; thousands of people have died trying to cross since the mid-'90s. The exact number is not known, but according to the *Coalición de Derechos Humanos*, "it is estimated that the remains of more than 6,000 men, women and children have been recovered on the U.S.-México border."[1] Why these people died where they did does not make a lot of sense until one begins to trace the flow of capital.

Many people think the main purpose of border policy is to stop the flow of migration. It is not. The main purpose of border policy, and specifically counterinsurgency on the border, is to manage mixed-status communities both in the border regions and in the interior.[2] Counterinsurgency (COIN) in the Southwest expresses itself through an increase in internal controls: checkpoints, deputized police, and a vigilant citizenry. These controls are justified through the constructed crisis of the "war on drugs," racism, and a myriad of fears about crime.

The inward expansion of the border has been accomplished through a shift from civil to criminal law when dealing with undocumented populations, and a careful balance of hard and soft controls as enacted by police, military, paramilitaries, nonprofits, and civilians. Hard controls include imprisonment, deportation, torture, deprivation, assault, and death. Soft controls include information gathering, reporting to state authorities, psychological operations, and ideological warfare. COIN is present in internal controls, the blurring of police/military functions, and the focus on managing populations as well as territory. COIN seeks to make surveillance and control seem not only normal, but participatory.

Border militarization, and all its internal controls, only function well because so many people accept the discursive parameters and categories they utilize. We have forgotten that the border is a man-made thing. It actually hasn't existed for all that long. Human hands, machinery, and greed put it up, and human hands could take it down. In order to resist it, we must examine the recent militarization, identify the economic forces that profit from it, understand the expansion of internal controls and our part in them, and ultimately deconstruct (and destroy) the ideological and categorical assumptions that allow these systems to function.

NEOLIBERAL POLICY LEADING UP TO NAFTA

IN ORDER TO understand the history of the border and how its populations are now being managed it is essential to understand the economic policies that accelerated northern migration, the militarization of the geographical border itself, and Border Patrol enforcement in the desert. The history of neoliberal economic policy is not a simple one, but to understand the current political situation, it is useful to have a cursory understanding of the global debt-bondage system.

In 1982 Mexico's inability to service its debt sent shock waves through the international financial community.[3] To many observers it was a sign that the international financial system was on the brink of collapse. If Mexico defaulted, could other nations be far behind? Something needed to be done if the global financial system was going to emerge intact.[4]

The U.S. government stepped in to protect the interests of the banks that held most of the Mexican debt. The International Monetary Fund (IMF) and World Bank, along with the U.S. government, bailed out the private banks. The U.S. government then pressured the IMF to extend new loans to Mexico so that it could keep up on its loan payments. Northern donors,[5] primarily the United States, offered to double their funding for the IMF, but only for highly conditional loans.[6] The new conditions came in the form of Structural Adjustment Programs (SAPs).[7] SAPs eliminated price and interest rate controls, privatized state-owned enterprises, reduced tariffs and other restrictions to foreign trade, and reduced regulations for businesses in order to encourage local and foreign investment.[8] The idea was that by implementing these neoliberal economic policies, Southern economies would become more productive and efficient. Opening economies up to the global market would provide growth and offer a way out of poverty.

There were a few problems with this model. Narrowing the size and scope of government meant large-scale downsizing for public sector employees. Local businesses closed because they could not compete with transnational corporations, and new investment did not create jobs at the expected rates.[9] In order to meet targets for reducing fiscal debt, most states greatly reduced their spending on social expenditures in health, education, and welfare. These austerity measures effectively dismantled the social safety net; thus, when the promised economic opportunities did not materialize, there was nothing to fall back on and communities were left to their own devices. In this way, Structural Adjustment was devastating for poor constituents.

During the '90s large numbers of *campesinos* were pushed off their land by changes in collective land holdings imposed by the Salinas government. Article 27 of the Mexican constitution was amended in 1991 in order to make it legal to sell *ejido* (communal) land. It also allowed peasants to use their land as collateral for loans. Many farmers took out loans, which they were unable to service due to currency devaluation, the associated cost of living increases, and an inability to compete in the "free market." Prices for commodities plummeted as local markets were flooded with U.S.-subsidized agriculture. Structural Adjustment initially led to a rural-to-urban migration. There were not enough jobs in the cities to accommodate the influx of the disenfranchised, and so people migrated north to the U.S. Although northern migration has always occurred, neoliberal economic policies created a sizable influx of families fleeing poverty. This generation of economic refugees is now being managed and criminalized for profit by the private prison industry.

MILITARY THEORY AND BORDER MILITARIZATION

NEOLIBERALISM WAS A major contributor to the border crisis, but the crisis wouldn't have occurred without the concurrent process of militarization. To understand the specific tactical and strategic underpinnings of border militarization it is useful to examine the development of the Low-Intensity Conflict doctrine (LIC). In *The Militarization of the US-Mexico Border,* Timothy Dunn meticulously traces the rise of LIC doctrine from 1978–1992. He writes:

> The principle concern of LIC doctrine has been with countering revolution (especially in Central America during the 1980s), followed by a concern for maintaining social control in other unstable settings. Within those areas, there are three general focal points of LIC doctrine: (1) an emphasis on internal (rather than external) defense of a nation, (2) an emphasis on controlling targeted civilian populations rather than territory, and (3) the assumption by the military of police-like and other unconventional, typically non-military roles, along with the adoption by the police of military characteristics.[10]

These principles outline the militarization and control techniques implemented in the borderlands over the last few years. There is an emphasis on internal defence, but it is happening under the rhetoric of an external threat. Distinctions between police, military, and paramilitary are blurring; the police are being militarized, and the military is being given increasing access to civilian populations. Police are partnering with community organizations to create "community policing." The Border Patrol utilizes the legitimizing language of human rights, and large portions of the civilian population are being required to police one another through mandated reporting in the workplace.

Equally important, the border is increasing in its infrastructural reach as it expands ever inwards. Some of this expansion, like the increase in checkpoints, is territorial, but the major force behind border expansion, like police deputization and participatory civilian vigilance, is psychological. This escalation is justified to the public by the "drug war," the "war on terror," and racial hysteria. These tactics were described by Dunn:

> Among the notable features of these efforts were a heavy emphasis on surveillance activities involving the use of advanced military technology; the growing presence of law enforcement and military personnel; the greatly expanded legal authority of the Border Patrol; and the ongoing stops (especially at checkpoints), requests for identification from persons of "foreign appearance," searches, and deportations. These activities all helped to contain the Mexican-origin population in the border region. The cumulative effect of such efforts can be interpreted as "preventive repression," enacted to restrain the principal subordinate groups in a crucial region that was vulnerable to instability.[11]

What has changed with COIN, in contrast to LIC, is the level of nuance in who is defined as an "enemy." In the desert, all migrants are the enemy, and hard controls are common. Meanwhile, in urban spaces, some undocumented people fit into the category of "enemy," and some don't; soft controls become more important. This differentiation doesn't weaken social categories, it refines them.

Counterinsurgency on the border depends on distinguishing between categories of people who are "deserving" of leniency and those who are "criminal." These distinctions, which underlie the liberal idea of "humane border policy," may get some people a reprieve from hard controls like deportation, but they do not challenge the control regime. They are, in fact, an integral part of it. Disguising controls within the fabric of everyday life, and cloaking them in narratives of human rights and liberality, is an important part of social management.

Before we examine how the border has expanded inward, we need to look at the period of militarization that occurred in the '90s, as militarization was a necessary precursor to internal expansion.

EXPANSION OF THE BORDER INFRASTRUCTURE

IN THE PREFACE of *Border Games*, Peter Andreas describes two photos hanging in the Border Patrol headquarters in San Diego:

> The first photograph, taken in the 1990s, shows a mangled chain-link fence and crowds of people milling about, seemingly oblivious that the border even exists. The Border Patrol is nowhere in sight. The image is of a chaotic border that is defied, defeated and undefended. The second photo, taken a number of years later, shows a sturdy ten-foot-high metal wall backed up by lightposts and Border Patrol all-terrain vehicles alertly monitoring the line; no people gather on either side.[12]

This transformation occurred through a series of government operations that sealed the cities and pushed traffic into the geographically remote desert regions: Operation Hold the Line in 1993 in El Paso/Juarez, Operation Gatekeeper in 1994 in Southern California, Operation Safeguard in 1994 in southern Arizona, and Operation Rio Grande in 1997 in southeast Texas.[13]

The border wall expansion came with new strategies for enforcement that focused on sharpening the psychological burden of crossing. Beginning in 1994, Congress and the Border Patrol acted jointly to initiate a policy of "prevention through deterrence," which would "elevate the risk of apprehension to a level so high that prospective illegal entrants would consider it futile to enter the U.S. illegally."[14] This policy changed the journey north. It did not make crossing "futile" exactly—but it did make it more physically taxing, expensive, and dangerous.

The militarization of the border created business opportunities for many players. After the traffic got pushed into the desert, the price of crossing increased considerably. U.S. economic and border policy created something of a captive market and smuggling infrastructures expanded to accommodate the needs of the increasing numbers of crossers. Cartel consolidation brought with it an increase in violence. Stories of rape, assault, blackmail, and abandonment have become painful reminders of what happens when people are commodified.

As a humanitarian aid volunteer, I have witnessed the trek through the desert increase in length and distance year by year as more checkpoints and patrols are put in place. Migrants are allowed to move slowly north through the desert for a few days, only to get picked up miles north, as part of a sadistic game of experiential deterrence. The heat, exhaustion, and delirium of the desert are used as both a geographical and psychological barrier.

Border Patrol officers like to say that they are "out in the desert saving lives." I have had many agents on the ground over the last few years tell me this word for word. "Salvation" from potential death in the desert is being used to justify low-intensity warfare, domination, and repression which are, under liberal democracy, indignities to be suffered always for one's own good. If they are saving people, it is only from a labyrinth of potentially fatal ends that Border Patrol policy itself has created. People have only been dying in high numbers since militarization pushed migration out to the remote Sonoran desert.

Border enforcement is a kind of tactical harassment meant to disorient and scatter groups of migrants. The practice of "dusting" those crossing is a good example. Border Patrol helicopters buzz groups in the desert, hovering close overhead but not actually landing. This practice does not result in the physical custody of migrants, but it does cause people to scatter in all directions. People are separated from their guides, and as a result get lost in a huge geographic no-man's-land.[15] The practice of dusting is intentional tactical warfare meant to make the process of crossing unpleasant. Those who are captured are then subject to dehumanizing abuse while in custody. To quote "Culture of Cruelty," a report written from direct experiences recorded in Naco, Sonora:

> The abuses individuals report have remained alarmingly consistent for years, from interviewer to interviewer and across interview sites: individuals suffering severe dehydration are deprived

of water; people with life-threatening medical conditions are denied treatment; children and adults are beaten during apprehensions and in custody; family members are separated, their belongings confiscated and not returned; many are crammed into cells and subjected to extreme temperatures, deprived of sleep, and threatened with death by Border Patrol agents.[16]

Border policy functions to terrorize migrants; it doesn't actually seal the border.[17] Whether Border Patrol enforcement takes this form because of incompetence or strategic intent is hard to prove one way or the other. It is more useful to talk about the functional realities of enforcement as opposed to what it is "meant" to do. Memories of brutality don't go away; they may recede once people have made it north and settle back into family life, but the ever-present potential violence of state agents is not forgotten. Numerically ineffective but psychologically scarring Border Patrol enforcement operations serve industry's need for undocumented labor and makes the management of those populations easier by instilling fear and forcing people to live hidden lives.

Saying that "the border is everywhere" used to be an emotive way to explain the ways we all internalize our indoctrination as citizens. It was a way to open conversations about the pragmatic advantages that come with citizenship: being able to move relatively freely, being allowed to be legally exploited in the labor market, being able to access what is left of the social welfare net, being able to exist as a recognized entity in this society. These are the privileges of citizenship in the U.S. and they come at a terrible cost. The papers one person holds only have value because someone else is without them. The value of papers is based on created scarcity. Papers hold a manufactured worth and are effective tools of control, because not everyone can obtain the "right" kind of documentation.

Delineations always reinforce something. In this case, citizenship gives people something to spiritually horde and rally around. It provides a false sense of community and security.[18] These processes by which state—and increasingly, corporate—interests are taken on through citizenship as one's own are an essential part of participatory controls. "The border is everywhere" isn't a metaphor anymore. It has become a reality and it functions because so many people accept the idea that the state should be allowed to police our communities through the arbitrary category of citizenship.

THE PRISON INDUSTRY

IN ADDITION TO creating a market for human smuggling and keeping a portion of the workforce frightened and exploitable, militarization has also proved a boon to the private prison industry. The process has been driven by a shift toward the criminalization of status offenses. The move into criminal court can be seen in programs like Streamline. First implemented in Del Rio, Texas, in 2005, Streamline is a "zero-tolerance" enforcement program designed to criminally prosecute unauthorized entrants by charging migrants in federal criminal court.[19] Prior to Streamline, entry through non-official routes was dealt with mostly through civil immigration court, and the U.S. Attorney prioritized repeat crossers and those with criminal records. Now, for all functional purposes, being undocumented is the actual crime. Even more common than prosecution through Streamline is the charge of "illegal re-entry," which now accounts for almost one fourth of all federal prosecutions—making it the most commonly filed federal charge.[20]

While programs like Streamline criminalize border crossers, charges like "illegal reentry" can be utilized anywhere in the country. The burden of proof is on the prosecution to prove that someone has tried to cross before and is once again in the country without "proper" documentation. Better records and database cross-checking has made proving illegal reentry easier. Increased collaboration between different agencies is the main trend behind the expanding internal border. SB 1070 is a perfect example.

SB 1070, the infamous Arizona law deputizing local police for immigration enforcement, has now gotten the court's go-ahead for implementation. The provision requires police to check immigration status while enforcing other laws if they have "reasonable suspicion" that someone is in the country illegally. In a way, SB 1070 is just a codification of business as usual in Arizona. SB 1070 is trying to do at a state level what local governments have been doing at a municipal level through 287(g) for a long time. According to the ICE website,

> The 287(g) program, one of ICE's top partnership initiatives, allows a state and local law enforcement entity to enter into a partnership with ICE, under a joint Memorandum of Agreement (MOA), in order to receive delegated authority for immigration enforcement within their jurisdictions.[21]

In other words, law enforcement is deputized to check immigration status. Many of the 287(g) agreements are actually being phased out in favor of a new program called Secure Communities. Secure Communities runs the names of those booked into jails and prisons through the ICE database. According to ICE,

> Secure Communities is a simple and common sense way to carry out ICE's priorities. It uses an already-existing federal

information-sharing partnership between ICE and the Federal Bureau of Investigation (FBI) that helps to identify criminal aliens without imposing new or additional requirements on state and local law enforcement....

Under Secure Communities, the FBI automatically sends the fingerprints to ICE to check against its immigration databases. If these checks reveal that an individual is unlawfully present in the United States or otherwise removable due to a criminal conviction, ICE takes enforcement action....[22]

Once inmates are identified by Secure Communities, they are held past their sentence and transferred into ICE custody. The Obama Administration would like to see Secure Communities go national by the end of 2013. Like 287(g), Secure Communities funnels people from jails into ICE detention while programs like Operation Streamline funnel people from ICE custody into the prison system.

These agreements between state and municipal agencies ensure that interactions with any level of law enforcement have the potential to lead to ICE detention, and ICE detention can easily parlay into a longer prison term. In this way, optimal use and maximum profit is extracted from each person arrested.

The corporations that run private prisons are not only profiting from these laws, but help to write and pass them. The American Legislative Exchange Council (ALEC) offers a perfect example of how corporate and legislative interests work together to create criminalizing laws for profit. ALEC is a public-private legislative partnership, made up of more than 2,000 state lawmakers (one-third of the nation's total legislators) and more than 200 corporations and special-interest groups. It represents Corrections Corporation of America (the largest private jailer in the U.S.), the Geo Group (the second largest), and Sodexho Marriott (which provides food services in private prisons).[23]

ALEC writes "model legislation" that benefits its corporate members. These model bills are then taken by ALEC's legislative members back to their states where they try to get them passed. ALEC produced a wave of tough sentencing laws in the 1990s, which increased the population of state prisons by half a million and increased the demand for private jails.[24] These laws included mandatory minimum sentences, "Three Strikes" laws, and "truth-in-sentencing" limits on parole.

ALEC also wrote the template for SB 1070. Two-thirds of SB 1070's 36 sponsors were ALEC members, and 30 had received donations from the prison industry.[25] ALEC was also one of the main mechanisms through which SB 1070 "copycat laws" spread throughout the country. ALEC has been an important player in the manufactured crisis of the drug war, the criminalization of undocumented populations, and the expanded control net that feeds this profiteering.

EXPANDING THE NET

WHERE COULD ONE realistically expect to be picked up and deported in Arizona? While crossing the border, during a workplace raid, during a traffic stop—at any time, really. Long before the advent of SB 1070, police have had discretion to enforce immigration and collude with Border Patrol within 100 miles of the border. Because of that discretion, any interaction with police could lead directly to deportation. The Border Patrol also routinely does "police work" and pulls over cars under the guise of enforcing traffic laws.[26] This blurring of the lines between police and Border Patrol is in accordance with COIN and LIC doctrine.

Over the last few years, immigration enforcement has expanded well past this merging of duties to include people, like social workers and hospital workers, who are not traditionally considered to be part of the careful management of civilian populations. Our personal economic survival now depends on our willingness to police each other.[27] HB 2008, which passed in Arizona in 2004, requires government employees to report to immigration authorities any undocumented immigrant who requests public assistance. Those who don't face up to four months in jail.[28] Social workers in this context are no better than Border Patrol agents.[29] People have had ICE called on them at the Department of Economic Security, even when applying for benefits for their documented children. Undocumented patients have been deported from Arizona hospitals after being deemed to be in a "stable" condition.[30]

Border enforcement is becoming a part of everyone's job. How are people convinced to be enforcers? It happens through a series of manipulative narratives that provide alternative stories that people can tell themselves about their participation in controls. It involves convincing people that some kinds of enforcement, like "anti-trafficking" raids, are ethical—even admirable.

CREATING COMPLIANCE

ON APRIL 15TH, 2010, there was a raid in South Tucson. The *Arizona Daily Star* reported:

> Immigration agents raided four shuttle companies on Tucson's south side Thursday morning as part of a major binational operation targeting an illegal-immigrant smuggling network. Officials

mobilized more than 800 federal, state and local law enforcement officers to arrest 68 total people in Tucson, Phoenix, Rio Rico, Nogales, Ariz., and Nogales, Sonora....[31]

The raids were portrayed in the local press as standard "war on drugs" "anti-trafficking" enforcement. Federal, state, and local law enforcement agents wearing balaclavas and carrying semi-automatic weapons, went door-to-door asking for papers. People who were trying to report on and witness the raid were interrogated and put into ICE vehicles. Teenagers were pulled off of city buses, and homes were raided, sometimes without warrants. There was not adequate identification by law enforcement, and many people initially thought they were being robbed by masked gunman. I heard an account of two parents being forced to kneel at gunpoint in their homes as their children were told by a masked agent, "Say goodbye to Mommy and Daddy."[32]

The effect on the community was immediate and chilling. After the raid, people were afraid to pick their kids up from school, shop, and otherwise go about their daily lives. This state of terror was localized to Tucson's undocumented and mixed-status families. In most other parts of the city, life continued as "normal" with little to no understanding of the increasing feelings of siege on the south side.

The night before the raid, ICE went to local organizers looking to create a partnership focusing on human and drug trafficking.[33] In that meeting, the community relations officer Rudy Bustamante attempted to reach out to community leaders, but didn't tell them about the raid planned for the next day. Community leaders received a tip later that evening warning of the raid, but did not put a wider alert out to the community for fear of creating mass panic. ICE's attempt to create "good relations" with community leaders by momentarily playing nice is not a new tactic. Distinctions between the law-abiding "deserving" migrant and the "criminal element" are often used to manufacture support for ICE. When these distinctions are upheld by community organizers, human rights advocates, and other social managers, they become a form of soft control.

Soft and hard controls are not mutually exclusive; they should be viewed on a continuum. Liberal democracy, in the U.S., relies on normalizing policing within certain communities and normalizing mass incarceration in order to maintain control and profit. It need not be a uniform process; in fact, it is better if it is not. Soft controls rely in some ways on keeping hard controls present, but not too visible.

Hard controls, like being murdered by the Border Patrol, are part of the implied threat and power of border enforcement for many communities in the Southwest. Border Patrol agents have murdered 18 people, both U.S. and Mexican nationals, along the border since 2010.[34] In order to assure these deaths are not viewed as cold-blooded murder, there is usually an attempt to associate those killed with the drug war, insinuate that they were putting agents in extreme peril through rock throwing, or otherwise set them up as a criminal elements.[35] Criminality is usually presented as a choice or an innate characteristic. It is not usually considered to be a category imposed by the state, although that is the way it functions. Being undocumented, being in transit, and not being white are enough to get you killed and frequently blamed for your own death in Arizona. If one has the misfortune of being murdered by the Border Patrol, somehow you deserved it, as good citizens never find themselves in the cross hairs of enforcement.

Impunity to kill is in keeping with a military culture in which Border Patrol agents are fighting a dirty war. Guilty verdicts cannot bring "justice" in these cases. The legal system is designed to reify existing divisions and grant legitimacy to the armed wing of the state, not rectify harms done. Mediation within a statist infrastructure cannot hold "accountable" perpetrators of violence, because these same institutions are responsible for the terms of engagement and the delineations that create, feed, and justify that violence. Simply pointing out state terror, however, is not enough. We must have a more nuanced understanding of power. Border enforcement is not simply an externally imposed occupation, it is a participatory process. In order to resist, we must recognize our compliance.

PARTICIPATORY SOFT CONTROLS

Hard controls like imprisonment and abuse in custody may be carried out by a relative few, but soft controls are enacted by pretty much everyone. Every social worker who reports, every nurse who allows the transfer of a patient into Border Patrol custody, each person who drives past a police traffic stop without inquiring complies. So does every activist who reinforces "deserving" and "undeserving" categories, and every community organizer who agrees to work with ICE to fight "trafficking." Inadvertent participation with low-intensity warfare is woven into the fabric of our everyday lives. We have all found ourselves complicit at one point or another—out of ignorance, naïveté, fear, or a sense of futility and despair.[36]

HB 2008 and SB 1070 have provisions that allow for the prosecution of citizens or municipal agents who fail to sufficiently enact them. The infrequency with which these provisions are actually utilized does not make them less effective; the potential consequences of dissent keep most people in line. Those who enact soft controls are themselves subject to hard controls, and rather than deal with the emotive conflict this brings up, many people choose to identify with border enforcement. Compliance and snitching are written into our job descriptions in sanitized ways, and bloody forms of control are hidden away and masked by disingenuous collective values like justice, democracy, and peacekeeping.

Yet the iron fist of repression has become more apparent under the velvet glove of governance. The processes we have been seeing on the border are not exceptions to the rule; they are the rule. When there is wider recognition of the ways these systems of control work, soft controls are no longer so effective, and more explicit methods of social domination must be used. Resistance begins with a questioning of categories.

THE BUSINESS OF DEATH

ONE OF THE major narratives used to militarize the borderlands is that of the "drug war." Jan Brewer, the governor of Arizona, insists:

> Well, we all know that the majority of the people that are coming to Arizona and trespassing are now becoming drug mules.... They're coming across our borders in huge numbers. The drug cartels have taken control of the immigration.... So they are criminals. They're breaking the law when they are trespassing and they're criminals when they pack the marijuana and the drugs on their backs.[37]

It doesn't really matter that this is a total fabrication; it's the emotional appeal that counts. Criminality and the "drug war" are used to justify hard controls and get people to participate in soft controls. A close examination of the history of U.S. drug policy and enforcement on the border shows us that the Border Patrol, *federales*, and cartels should not necessarily be considered mutually exclusive entities. A lot of money is flowing south to shore up government and cartel interests, and these interests are often exquisitely intertwined.[38]

An instructive example of the blurred lines between those on government and cartel payrolls is offered by the case of Border Patrol agent Abel Canales. Canales was involved in the shooting of Jesus Enrique Castro Romo in November of 2010. Castro survived and is now suing over the incident. Canales was indicted in 2011, accused of accepting a bribe—in October of 2008—to allow vehicles with drugs and/or undocumented migrants to pass through the Border Patrol checkpoint on Interstate 19. This agent was in the field with a gun, and all the associated immunity, two years after investigators witnessed him taking bribes.[39]

These kinds of formal charges are only a shadow of the actual level of "corruption" taking place in the border region. "Corruption" itself as a term should be questioned because something can only be a corruption in relation to a code of ethical behavior that is actually upheld. Collaboration between different state/border enforcers and cartel workers, police, and paramilitary happens with such frequency that it can be considered "corruption" only in the eyes of a misinformed public.

In the 2009 book *Drug War Zone: Frontline Dispatches from the Streets of El Paso and Juarez,* Howard Campbell unpacks the term "cartel."

> Transportation routes and territories controlled by specific cartels in collusion with the police, military and government officials are known as plazas. Control of a plaza gives the drug lord and police commander of an area the power to charge less-powerful traffickers tolls, known as pesos. Generally, one main cartel dominates a plaza at any given time, although this control is often contested or subverted by internal conflict, may be disputed among several groups, and is subject to rapid change. Attempts by rival cartels to ship drugs through a plaza or take over a plaza controlled by their enemies [have] led to much of the recent violence in Mexico. The cartel that has the most power in a particular plaza receives police or military protections for its drug shipments. Authorities provide official documentation for loaded airplanes, freight trucks, and cars and allow traffickers to pass freely through airports, and landing strips, freeway toll roads and desert highways, and checkpoints and border crossings.
>
> Typically, a cartel purchases the loyalty of the head of the federal police or the military commander in a particular district. This official provides officers or soldiers to physically protect drug loads in transit or in storage facilities, in some cases to serve as bodyguards to high-level cartel members. Police on the cartel payroll intimidate, kidnap, or murder opponents of the organization, although they may also extort large payments from the cartel with which they are associated. Additionally cartel members establish relationships [or] connections with state governors or mayors of major cities, high-ranking officials in federal law enforcement, military, and naval officers and commanders and other powerful politicians and bureaucrats. These national connections facilitate the use of transportation routes and control of a given plaza.[40]

With this understanding of the ways that government officials and military agents in the U.S. and Mexico can serve double duty and work for the cartels, it becomes clear that the rigid lines drawn for the public are nothing but propagandist illusion, though one that is used to funnel a lot of money into Mexico.

One of the ways that money is flowing into Mexico to "fight the drug war" is through the Merida Initiative. The Merida Initiative is a security agreement between the United States, Mexico, and Central America. The U.S. provides training, equipment, and intelligence to combat drug trafficking. According to the U.S. Department of State website, the four pillars of the Merida Initiative are:

1. Disrupt Organized Criminal Groups

2. Strengthen Institutions

3. Build a 21st Century Border

4. Build Strong and Resilient Communities[41]

These are accomplished to the tune of "$1.6 billion since the Merida Initiative began in Fiscal Year 2008."[42] How are Mexican institutions "strengthened"? According to the U.S. Department of State website, Mexican institutions are strengthened by the following:

> The United States is supporting Mexico's implementation of comprehensive justice sector reforms through the training of justice sector personnel including police, prosecutors, and defenders, correction systems development, judicial exchanges, and partnerships between Mexican and U.S. law schools.
>
> The U.S. Agency for International Development (USAID) is partnering with the Government of Mexico and civil society to promote the rule of law and build strong and resilient communities by supporting the implementation of Mexico's new justice system; increasing knowledge of, and respect for, human rights; strengthening social networks and community cohesion; addressing the needs of vulnerable populations (youth and victims of crime); and increasing community and government cooperation.[43]

This kind of partnering hides hard controls behind nation-building. The U.S. has been widely criticized for training military and paramilitary forces in Mexico in the use of torture. In early July 2008, a video came to light of the city police from Leon, Guanajuato being taught torture techniques by a U.S. security firm instructor.[44] The training took place in April of 2006; after the public outcry over the incident the program was suspended.

Torture tactics taught by U.S. security firms are used by police and military in Mexico and yet more funding, training and strengthening the "rule of law" is supposed to lead to less, not more, state violence. In an attempt to deflect criticisms that the Merida Initiative will necessarily engender more of the same abuse it has a stipulation requiring Mexico to convince the U.S. Congress it is improving human rights standards and using some of the funds to overhaul the judicial system.[45] Once again a narrative of strengthening democracy and rights is being used to whitewash what is simply an outsourced version of the School of the Americas (SOA).[46] Violence is justified just as often through 'anti-corruption,' institution-building, and human rights discourse as through more explicit narratives of war.

How well does U.S.-led counterinsurgency training work and shore up Mexican democracy? The ascension of the Zeta cartel provides a useful historical example. *Los Zetas* were founded in 1999 when commandos of the Mexican Army's elite force, trained by the U.S. Army's 7th Special Forces Group at Fort Bragg, deserted to work for the armed wing of the Gulf Cartel.[47] The *Vancouver Sun* reported that in February of 2010, *Los Zetas* broke away from the Gulf Cartel to form their own organization, "attacking Gulf operatives wherever they found them and claiming the turf for themselves. The Gulf Cartel allied with their old Sinaloan rivals to fight back, engulfing the region in violence."[48] Such shifts in allegiance have to be understood in a context where the "drug war" is a business first and foremost. Commitments follow profit margins more than nation-state interests, and cartels, police, *federales*, military, and paramilitary roles can overlap, shift, and change with frequency.

There is now a paramilitary group called the *mata Zetas* whose only purported objective is the take out the Zeta Cartel.[49] This new development is being used to further support the idea that there is a "narco-insurgency" at hand. The Cato Institute's Ted Carpenter said, "If you look at the tactics cartels are using, they resemble paramilitaries or insurgent groups rather than just criminal gangs."[50] Writing for the *Small Wars Journal,* Robert J. Bunker and John P. Sullivan also see in this growing crisis the beginnings of a war over the socio-political integrity of Mexico:

> Our impression is that what is now taking place in Mexico has for some time gone way beyond secular and criminal (economic) activities as defined by traditional organized crime studies.... Not only have de facto political elements come to the fore— i.e., when a cartel takes over an entire city or town, they have no choice but to take over political functions formerly administered by the local government—but social (narcocultura) and religious/spiritual (narcocultos) characteristics are now making themselves more pronounced. What we are likely witnessing is

Mexican society starting to not only unravel but to go to war with itself.... . Traditional Mexican values and competing criminal value systems are engaged in a brutal contest over the 'hearts, minds, and souls' of its citizens in a street-by-street, block-by-block, and city-by-city war over the future social and political organization of Mexico.[51]

What does this narco-insurgency narrative mean for policy? Narco-violence as a "new" ascending form of terrorism is being used to justify more border infrastructure, more agents on the ground, more internal controls, and more partnering with Mexico to fight against the cartels. Counterinsurgency is needed to fight the narco-insurgency, which threatens the power of the state so skillfully because cartels like the Zetas were trained by the U.S. in counterinsurgency. Fighting the narco-insurgency is the perfect excuse for maintaining the narco-insurgency.

DEATH TO THE BORDER

THE PRODUCTION OF narco-insurgency and counterinsurgency shape daily life in the borderlands. They are used, in subtle and not-so-subtle ways, to make us afraid and/or make us criminals. We should not be surprised that the military shapes border policy through low-intensity warfare, or that the state has identified some of us as enemies to be captured, deported, or killed.

The entire infrastructure of the borderlands is designed to create unforgiving categories. Terms like *documented, undocumented, humane, inhumane, legitimate, illegitimate* and *criminal* hide the functional purpose of the border, which is to divide, repress, and control. Democracies rely on the misrecognition of interest ("citizenship"), cognitive dissonance ("humane enforcement") and collective fiction ("criminal justice") to produce compliance. When it comes to the border, we are so often willing fools.

Those who oppose states, corporations, and the profiteers of human misery should hold a healthy skepticism for all discourses that do not question the legitimacy of the state. Human rights rhetoric still positions nation-states as legitimate entities that must recognize the humanity of their subjects. These narratives reinforce state power! A good example is the call for a "humane border policy." What border policy, given the state of late-stage capitalism, could ever be humane? The very real and meaningful concessions we win when we invoke a human rights narrative come at a cost. When we reinforce these narratives, we lose another opportunity to call the social contract into question. The predominant human rights frameworks do not question the basic assumption that is used to control us—that we have consented to be governed.

Pragmatic coalition work with a wide variety of people, not all of whom are anti-statist, is a necessary part of resistance. That said, we must not confuse tactical coalitions with a passive acceptance of ideological tendencies like the desire for a "humane border." If we are not careful, statist logic can channel our passion and anger into border management instead of resistance. It hurts my heart to go to protests and listen to people plead for an expansion of citizenship. I don't judge anyone's desire for legal status, or question the fear and hardship that comes with not having it, but someone is always going to find herself on the outside of those lines. There are no easy answers to these questions of strategy. They must be approached contextually, community by community. We must not shrink from hard conversations.

Let's learn lessons from the security analysts and military theorists who write about border enforcement. The major issue at hand is that of legitimacy and the battle for legitimacy. History teaches us that nation-states and their boundaries can shatter. Do we believe that this empire, too, is beginning to crumble? Until there is a wider recognition of our own power to dismantle society, everyone bound within this social cage is required, and will continue to be coerced, to police each other. Many will do this willingly; those who refuse will be criminalized.

The borderlands are a vision of the future, and at present it is not a nice vision. It is one of state and paramilitary violence, expanding police power, volatile racial exchanges, and mass incarceration. But there are other options. The border is a contested and ever-changing territory. It isn't under the total jurisdiction of any one group all the time. Military theorists are worried about legitimacy because it is produced through social narratives that are not absolute.

In places like Arizona, the state is losing its mask of humane governance. The more people see methods of social control for what they are, and the more economically and ecologically unstable the world becomes, the more alternative visions of social organization and the struggles that might make them a reality will be given credence. There might not, at present, actually *be* an insurgency in the Southwest—but there are in many other parts of the world, and there could be one here someday. Security is a huge industry because instability and resistance are real and have power.

As the state loses legitimacy, some of its power will fall away. It may then try to hold on by using more extreme methods of control, or at least by using those already employed on a larger percentage of the population.[52] To make it through the period of expanded control and repression we are entering, those of us invested in resistance must build our capacity to survive without the support services the state currently provides.

The social safety net is not apolitical or benevolent; if it did not serve the state as a method of social control it would not exist. As we are trying to resist state control over our lives, it would behoove us to try and limit our dependence on the state, or at least gain skills that will eventually be able to replace those services. We should do this both because participating in them gives the state power, and because we cannot access some state infrastructures—like hospitals and welfare offices—without putting ourselves and our loved ones at risk.

Now that we understand soft controls, we can build and seek out alternatives to those surveillance and control mechanisms. Dealing with hard controls is more difficult, and the consequences are brutal. Let's start by calling dehumanization, repression, murder, and mass imprisonment what they are—the inevitable consequences of border enforcement.

Resistance is happening on the border and I encourage you to come and be a part of it, but the struggle is not just in the borderlands.[53] As the border spreads inwards, other communities will need to come to an understanding of its mechanisms of control. There are no "one size fits all" tactics or strategies: each affected community must come up with its own response. As we contend with the realities of this growing zone of conflict, we must not forget that we have power to challenge those narratives that are used to control and repress us.

Every time I see a sign proclaiming "We are not criminals" I cannot help but think, *actually we are*. The heavy hand of the state comes down harder on some than others, and those distinctions play out along all kinds of categorical lines, but in a climate of political repression that punishes even the smallest acts of solidarity, all who resist *are* criminals. We are criminals perversely complicit in our own imprisonment. The only silver lining is that we are all complicit in different ways, and so it follows that we are all able to resist in different ways. As I am in the habit of telling my kid, the border is both "for real" and "for pretend." The border is fragile; we draw and redraw it every day. The consequences may be great, but we don't *have* to draw those lines.

NOTES

1   Coalición de Derechos Humanos, "Arizona Recovered Human Remains Project," Coalición de Derechos Humanos web site, http://derechoshumanosaz.net/projects/arizona-recovered-bodies-project/ (2012).

2   "Mixed-status" refers to communities and families composed of documented and undocumented people.

3   George Ann Potter, *Deeper than Debt: Economic Globalisation and the Poor,* (Nottingham: Russell Press, 2000), 8.

4   John E Serieux, and Yiagadeesen Samy, "Introduction: Debt, Debt Relief and the Poorest: Small Steps in a Long Journey," in John E Serieux, and Yiagadeesen Samy, eds., *Debt Relief of the Poorest Countries,* (Piscataway: Transaction, 2002), 37.

5   The terms North and South refer to a divide in socio-economic, political, and discursive power that exists between wealthy "developed" countries (the North) and poor, lesser "developed" countries (the South.) These terms are imperfect but in a post-colonial/neo-colonial era it is useful to have a language, however flawed, to describe in general terms those who are defining the relations of power and those who are being exploited by them.

6   Susan George, *A Fate Worse than Debt,* (Harmondsworth: Penguin Books, 1988), 41–54.

7   Potter, *Deeper than Debt: Economic Globalisation and the Poor,* 12–13.

8   David Ransom, "The Dictatorship of Debt," *New Internationalist,* No. 312 (1999): 7.

9   Potter, *Deeper than Debt,* 72–73.

10   Timothy J. Dunn, *The Militarization of the US-Mexican Border, 1978–1992* (Austin: University of Texas Press, 1996), 21.

11   Dunn, *The Militarization of the US-Mexican Border,* 162.

12   Peter Andreas, *Border Games: Policing the US-Mexican Divide* (Ithaca: Cornell University Press, 2009), xi.

13   Timothy J. Dunn and José Palafox, "Militarization of the Border," in *The Oxford Encyclopedia of Latinos and Latinas in the United States,* Suzanne Oboler, ed., (New York: Oxford University Press, USA, 2006).

14   Senate Committee on the Judiciary, Subcommittee on Immigration, hearing on "Enhancing Border Security," 106th Cong., 2nd Sess., Feb. 10, 2000 (statement of Michael A. Pearson, Executive Associate Commissioner for Field Operations, Immigration and Naturalization Service).

15   Ibid.

16   No More Deaths, No Más Muertes, "A Culture of Cruelty: Abuse and Impunity in Short-term U.S. Border Patrol Custody," No More Deaths website, http://www.nomoredeaths.org/cultureofcruelty.html (September 2011).

17   For an interesting essay detailing Border Patrol tactics see: Anonymous, "Designed to Kill: Border Policy and How to Change It," elenemigocomun website, June 21, 2011, http://elenemigocomun.net/2011/06/designed-kill-border-policy/#more-9174.

18   Other theorists have expressed more eloquently the process of nation-state formation and citizen-identity at length. To list only a few: Franz Fanon, Michel Foucault, Antonio Gramsci, and Antonio Negri.

19   Lauren Gambino, "Program Prosecutes Illegal Immigrants Before Deporting Them," Arizona State University News 21 website, 2010 featured story, http://asu.news21.com/2010/prosecuting-illegal-immigrants/ (2012).

20   "Illegal reentry under Title 8, 1326 of the United States Code was the most commonly recorded lead charge brought by federal prosecutors during the first half of FY 2011. It alone accounted for nearly half (47 percent) of all criminal immigration prosecutions filed. It accounted for just under a quarter (23 percent) of overall criminal prosecutions, surpassing illegal entry (Title 8, 1325) as the most frequently cited federal lead charge. Illegal reentry is a felony offense and results in longer sentences than the second most frequent immigration charge brought this year, illegal entry, which is classed as a petty misdemeanor. During the first six months of 2011, the average prison sentence was 14 months for those

convicted where illegal reentry was recorded as the lead charge." Transactional Records Access Clearinghouse (TRAC), "Illegal Reentry Becomes Top Criminal Charge," TRAC website, June 10, 2011, http://trac.syr.edu/immigration/reports/251/.

21 "Fact Sheet: Delegation of Immigration Authority Section 287(g) Immigration and Nationality Act: The ICE 287(g) Program: A Law Enforcement Partnership," ICE website, http://www.ice.gov/news/library/factsheets/287g.htm.

22 "Secure Communities," ICE website, http://www.ice.gov/secure_communities/.

23 Beau Hodai, "Corporate Con Game: How the private prison industry helped shape Arizona's anti-immigration law," *In These Times*, June 21, 2010, http://www.inthesetimes.com/article/6084/corporate_con_game/.

24 John Biewen, "Corporate-Sponsored Crime Laws," American Radio Works website, April 2002, http://www.americanradioworks.org/features/corrections/index.html.

25 Laura Sullivan, "Prison Economics Help Drive Ariz. Immigration Law," National Public Radio website, October 28, 2010, http://www.npr.org/2010/10/28/130833741/prison-economics-help-drive-ariz-immigration-law.

26 "For communities within 100 miles of the border, police/immigration collaboration is even more widespread and insidious, in large part due to its informal nature. As an example, in the city of Tucson police officers have discretion over whether or not to call the U.S. Border Patrol on anyone with whom they come into contact. Oftentimes this practice takes place prior to arrest or citation, leaving little or no paper trail by which to challenge or document the practice. Every year there are thousands of people deported from Tucson following minor traffic stops or other interactions with police in neighborhoods, shopping centers and public spaces; individuals so detained are immediately taken into Border Patrol custody and frequently pressured into signing a voluntary departure form that expedites their removal from the United States." Geoffrey Boyce and Sarah Launius, "Normalizing Noncompliance: Militarization and Resistance in Southern Arizona," Bad Subject website, http://bad.eserver.org/issues/2011/81/boyce-launius.htm (2011).

27 For more insight on the participatory nature of social control, see the short story by Peter Gelderloos, "The Atrocity," To Get to the Other Side website, October 24, 2005, http://togettotheotherside.org/essays-and-short-stories/the-atrocity/.

28 Valeria Fernández, "New Arizona Law Rattles Immigrant Community," New America Media website, November 30, 2009, http://news.newamericamedia.org/news/view_article.html?article_id=0b54cfcfc7f95adfe97e2e7d2668a037.

29 Social workers have adapted to this situation by creating a strange "don't ask, don't tell" policy in which: "even in circumstances where a legal requirement mandates the disclosure of client information, the client is to be informed, if feasible, before the disclosure is made, of the effects and/or consequences of disclosure. Consistent with acceptable principles of social work practice, it may be appropriate to notify clients in advance of how the new law works so that they will be informed when making a decision whether to remain silent when asked for verification of immigration status or whether to answer 'no' if they have no documentation of their status." National Association of Social Work, "Social Workers, Immigration Policies and State Benefits Introduction," National Association of

Social Workers - Arizona Chapter website, Jan. 2010, http://www.naswaz.com/display-common.cfm?an=1&subarticlenbr=202.

30   Caley Cruz, "Comatose Man Deported to Mexico, Family and Friends Upset," *Phoenix News*, Feb. 24, 2012, http://www.azfamily.com/news/local/Family-and-friend-upset-Phoenix-man-deported-to-Mexico-in-a-coma-140236303.html.

31   Brady McCombs, "68 Arrested in Smuggling Raid: ICE-led Operation Targets Shuttle Firms in Effort to Halt Illegal-Immigrant Traffic," *Arizona Daily Star*, April 16, 2010, http://azstarnet.com/news/local/border/article_3ec9bf86-6f57-5a5b-aa6d-ccebc30e5344.html.

32   Interview with an anonymous community member who was present during the raid, May 2012.

33   Ibid.

34   Brian Scoloff, "Border Patrol Use of Force Policy Scrutinized," *ABC News*, Oct. 19, 2012, http://abcnews.go.com/US/wireStory/border-patrol-lethal-force-scrutinized-17512721#.UI8Ydob4L7w.

35   Rock throwing is frequently cited as justification for lethal force, even in cases where eye witness accounts disprove this claim. Immigrate America, "Cold Blooded Murder by US Border Patrol of US Citizen Carlos La Madrid Confirmed!" Immigration Clearing House website, March 29, 2011, http://immigrationclearinghouse.org/cold-blooded-murder-by-us-border-patrol-of-us-citizen-carlos-la-madrid-confirmed/.

36   Although it was written about a different era and political context, I encourage those interested in examining mass incarceration, the police state, and participatory controls to read the masterpiece by Aleksandr Solzhenitsyn, *The Gulag Archipelago*, (New York: Harper & Row, 1973).

37   Ginger Rough, "Brewer: Most illegal immigrants smuggling drugs," *The Arizona Republic*, June 25, 2010, http://www.azcentral.com/news/articles/2010/06/25/20100625arizona-governor-says-most-illegal-immigrants-smuggle-drugs.html.

38   A moving book on the topic of the drug war is John Gibler, *To Die In Mexico: Dispatches from Inside the Drug War*, (San Francisco: City Lights Books, 2011).

39   Jonathan Clark, "Agent charged with corruption now at center of civil suit over shooting," Nogales International website, March 30, 2012, http://www.nogalesinternational.com/news/agent-charged-with-corruption-now-at-center-of-civil-suit/article_ff762930-7a78-11e1-bf4c-001a4bcf887a.html.

40   Howard Campbell, *Drug War Zone: Frontline Dispatches from the Streets of El Paso and Juarez*, (Austin: University of Texas Press, 2009), 23–24.

41   U.S. Department of State, "Merida," U.S. Department of State website, http://www.state.gov/j/inl/merida/.

42   Ibid.

43   Ibid.

44   Deborah Bonello, "Mexican police in 'torture' class?," *Los Angeles Times*, July 1, 2008, http://latimesblogs.latimes.com/laplaza/2008/07/mexican-police.html.

45 Guy Lawson, "The Making of a Narco State," *Rolling Stone Magazine*, March 4, 2009.

46 According to the School of the Americas Watch website, "The School of the Americas (SOA) is a combat training school for Latin American soldiers, located at Fort Benning, Georgia. In 2001 [it was] renamed the Western Hemisphere Institute for Security Cooperation (WHINSEC)." Many of its graduates have committed atrocities. "Since 1946, the SOA has trained over 64,000 Latin American soldiers in counterinsurgency techniques, sniper training, commando and psychological warfare, military intelligence and interrogation tactics. These graduates have consistently used their skills to wage a war against their own people. Among those targeted by SOA graduates are educators, union organizers, religious workers, student leaders, and others who work for the rights of the poor. Hundreds of thousands of Latin Americans have been tortured, raped, assassinated, 'disappeared,' massacred, and forced into refugee [*sic*] by those trained at the School of Assassins." More information is available on the SOA Watch website http://soaw.org/about-the-soawhinsec/what-is-the-soawhinsec.

47 Chris Arsenault, "US-trained cartel terrorizes Mexico: Founders of the Zetas drug gang learned special forces techniques at Ft. Bragg before waging a campaign of carnage," *Aljazeera*, Nov. 3, 2010, http://www.aljazeera.com/indepth/featur es/2010/10/20101019212440609775.html.

48 Ioan Grilloreuters, "Mexico: Zetas rewrite drug war in blood: Military-style attacks commonplace for 10,000 strong gang army," *The Vancouver Sun*, May 29, 2012, http://www.vancouversun.com/news/Mexico+Zetas+rewrite+drug+blood/6698205/story.html#ixzz1yqaSd6ip.

49 Ibid.

50 Arsenault, "US-trained cartel terrorizes Mexico."

51 Robert J. Bunker and John P. Sullivan, "Societal Warfare South of the Border? Extreme Barbarism, a Death Cult, and Holy Warriors in Mexico," *Small Wars Journal*, May 22, 2011, http://smallwarsjournal.com/jrnl/art/societal-warfare-south-of-the-border.

52 For an interesting expansion of this thesis, see the zine *Desert* by Anonymous. Available from the Zine Library website for free downloading: http://zinelibrary.info/desert.

53 There are too many organizations active on the border to list them all. For information on direct aid, see http://nomoredeaths.org.

DISMANTLING COUNTERINSURGENCY WITH EARTH FIRST!

SASHA ROSS[1]

AN ENVIRONMENTAL INSURGENCY?

At an energy industry conference in Houston, Anadarko Petroleum spokesperson Matt Carmichael gave his audience some important advice: "Download the U.S. Army-slash-Marine Corps Counterinsurgency Manual, because we are dealing with an insurgency."[2]

Carmichael was referring to the opposition against hydraulic fracturing, or "fracking," an extraction process by which chemicals are thrust into the bedrock at high pressure to break the stone between pockets of natural gas. By labeling the public outcry against fracking an insurgency, Carmichael evinces industry's fear of popular ecological movements, as well as the general flexibility of the term itself.

Matt Pitzarella, communications director of the natural gas corporation, Range Resources, attempted to soften the implications of Carmichael's comments: "[The gas industry is] not dealing with insurgents," he insists, "[it's] dealing with regular people who live in towns and want to know what you're doing." However, Pitzarella went on to admit, "We have several former psy-ops folks that work for us at Range, because they're very comfortable in dealing with localized issues and local governments. Really all they do is spend most of their time helping folks develop local ordinances and things like that. But very much having that understanding of psy-ops in the Army and in the

Middle East has applied very helpfully here for us in Pennsylvania."[3] While Pitzarella states that there is no real insurgency, he paradoxically admits that military professionals are pursuing a strategy of preemptive counterinsurgency involving psychological operations on the general public.

According to a recent army counterinsurgency field manual, FM 3-07.22, psy-ops tactics are deployed for three reasons: to "Counter the effects of insurgent propaganda"; "Relate controls to the security and well-being of the population"; and "Portray a favorable governmental image."[4] Psy-ops professionals promote an image of popular satisfaction, compliance, and respect for authorities in order to facilitate the plans of the state or employer.

Another manual, FM 3-24, *Counterinsurgency*, states, "Some elements of culture should be identified and evaluated in a counterinsurgency operation."[5] These elements include history, language, geography, religion, communications, political science, respect for the military, social identities, familial roles, acceptable levels of corruption, education, favorite music and movies, cuisine, and popular folk tales.[6] Psy-ops agents bring an inside perspective into the daily lives of a multitude of social actors, so that industry and law enforcement can learn how to best approach the population.

According to Ben Anderson, professor of geography at Durham University, psy-ops signals the emergence of preemptive counterinsurgency.[7] Its use against the environmental movement indicates the extent to which the U.S. military sees Earth First! and radical ecology as a nascent threat. At a military training exercise for "human terrain teams," students participated in a wargame in which environmentalists—in a secessionist area of Kansas called "Lakeland"—present more of an insurgent threat than secessionists themselves. The scenario was presented this way:

> IATAN, a coal-fired power plant on the Missouri side of the river is one of the main military foci due to 'contention within the community' over the environmental pollution it is causing. Sierra Club and other, more radical groups have been active in this area: ELF [Earth Liberation Front] is one such radical group. Even though there is an elected government and rule of law in Lakeland, there are some 'insurgents' who are 'opportunistic.' That is why the US Army has moved into this area that has broken away from US control.[8]

COIN, THIRD PARTIES, AND THE ENVIRONMENT

COIN LITERATURE ADVOCATES a coordinated media campaign along with direct civic engagement through "counternetworks" that work in opposition to social movements emerging through traditions of popular struggles. Hinging on "third party" groups—astroturfed nonprofits or industry-funded civil society organizations—counternetworks work against social movements in attempts to garner public support for motives of industrial development.[9]

Remember Matt Carmichael, the one who spilled the beans about the gas industry's involvement with counterinsurgency? Carmichael's employer, Range Resources, along with numerous other energy companies, proffers heavy funding and administrative direction to industry front-groups like the Marcellus Shale Coalition (MSC), which provides a perfect example of the "third party counternetwork" functioning to advance the industry agenda.

In 2011, MSC and other networked affiliates of industry interests helped push a bill called "Act 13" through the Pennsylvania state legislature, rewriting zoning laws.[10] They did so with the aid of psy-ops mercenaries and "collaborative efforts undertaken over the past several years." One of those collaborations took place at the highest level of state law enforcement. As leaked correspondence later exposed, the Department of Homeland Security worked with the private intelligence corporation Institute of Terrorism Research and Response (ITRR) to monitor activists who opposed deregulation. The scandal would lead to the removal of Pennsylvania's Homeland Security director, James Powers, but not before Powers' correspondence with ITRR was leaked to the press. "We're not looking for [surveillance professionals] to dump everything on us that occurs in their jurisdiction," Powers explains in one email, "only that which relates to the critical infrastructure. In turn, we'll provide it to you for the analysts to review and make further findings."[11]

In another exchange, ITRR's co-founder, Michael Perelman, warns Powers that the threat of environmental activism casts "shades of Al Qaeda," and that large sectors of the population must be monitored in order to prevent insurgent activities.[12] In 2010, Perelman and Powers distributed Terrorist Bulletins warning against elements within the public debate over zoning, as well as public schooling, recognition of Jewish holidays in high schools, and gay rights.[13]

According to *Alter Press* editor Steven Rosenfeld, "The industry needed the legislature to rewrite [oil and gas] laws because a 2009 decision by the Pennsylvania Supreme Court upheld municipal rights to write zoning laws that excluded oil and gas drilling if it did not fit the community's 'character' and 'special nature.'"[14] Supported by a smear campaign launched by DHS (with the help of ITRR), industry was able to overhaul the zoning laws. According to former Pittsburg City Council President Doug Shields, "Act 13" converted Pennsylvania into "a resource colony for multinational corporations."[15]

The ability of industry to control zoning ordinances marks a paradigm shift towards the *delegation* of planning to business elites acting through local political proxies (third party organizations).[16] This shift relies on commercial and political elites acting in tandem in direct, constructive partnerships that involve local political planning in capitalist growth and industrial development. Urban theory scholar Neil Brenner explains that the modern political economy involves "flexible, site-specific decision-making procedures, funding schemes, zoning specifications, planning guidelines, and regulatory techniques."[17] Using these "site-specific" manipulations, Department of Homeland Security and other state institutions are able to assist industrial operations in building seemingly community-led movements, like MSC, to intervene in political questions, like zoning laws.

In the words of COIN theorist David Kilcullen, "We need to look at our theories of top-down state-building and recognize what empirical evidence from the field is telling us: that bottom-up, community-based, civil-society approaches are having much greater success than top-down, state-based approaches."[18] Kilcullen claims that the decentralization of power necessarily leads to democratic advancement, yet his model functions only on the condition of corporate domination over social mobilizations concerning clean water, land rights, and public space. Rather than grassroots direct democracy, localized political-economic partnerships often lead to more exclusive control over the spatial organization and political life of society, politics, and economy.[19] To conceal the authoritarian and thoroughly militarized structure of development, "astroturfed" nonprofit organizations mediate between the politico-economic partnerships and the population.[20] We already saw how one industry front-group, MSC, actively worked to alter zoning laws in Pennsylvania. Another such group is Anadarko-funded Energy In Depth (EID), which operates as a public relations firm for industry.

EID boasts its grassroots credentials, claiming to be composed of "independent" gas drillers. EID supports the energy industry by publishing convoluted articles smearing concerned citizens for questioning fracking. In one article, "Lenders Bagels," EID attempts to discredit university professors in Utica, an area plagued by the effects of fracking, by insinuating that the academics' status as ivory tower intellectuals separates them from the environment and local communities. "Lenders Bagels," like so many other articles and reports, is a demagogical attempt to distort the public discourse by braiding scientific issues together with religious and ethnic "shifters," moving the discourse from public aims and achievable goals to unrelated issues of prejudice.[21]

Through propaganda, public perception becomes more pliable to industry's alterations of the political and social landscape. Ben Anderson explains:

> "Perception" is normally included in the counterinsurgency literature within a broader category of the "cognitive terrain" or "human terrain" of conflict. In relation to these terrains, population is understood in terms of affectively imbued values, beliefs and attitudes.... Perception is known as a mixture, then, of cognitive and affective. The population is known and engaged as a

collective entity that thinks, feels, and believes, and whose perception mixes with a population's "interests" and "ways of life" in complex ways without being reducible to them.[22]

By monitoring a large number of individuals and strategically altering zoning ordinances and other spatial relationships, COIN identifies and defines an "operational environment," so that operatives can turn that environment into a productive force toward the goals of development—a kind of colonial *umwelt*, or perceptive field, that can be isolated, manipulated, and transformed to shape people's ideas and desires.

GOING BEYOND REPRESSION IN GASLAND

To SAY THAT the same COIN strategy has been deployed in regions around the country would be an understatement. In one telling episode, in March 2012, professor Adam Briggle of the University of North Texas was questioned for teaching a class about the merits of civil disobedience (particularly ecodefense). He was asked by two FBI agents, "Have you heard anything about IEDs [improvised explosive devices]?"[23]

Earth First! in Pennsylvania along with Rising Tide in North Texas and other activist groups have resisted natural gas production and COIN practices by creating resistance nodes, which act as small networks and generate larger networks when functioning together.[24] One example is the Marcellus Shale EF! Network, composed of nodal organizations, such as Finger Lakes EF! and Genesee Valley EF!. These activist groups often have porous borders between them, as individuals work and organize sometimes with several groups at once, using nodes to bring people together for specific actions.

Thus, the groups within the Marcellus Shale EF! Network are autonomous and interlinked, while being semi-distinguished by geographic bioregion. Marcellus EF! comes together at times for intensive operations, such as an important blockade in June 2012 that shut down a fracking drill in the Moshannon State Forest. Involving a tree sitter suspended by anchor ropes blocking the access road, the blockade included dozens of blockaders guarding slash piles of debris while another 50 protestors shut down the entry to the road. Police came armed with assault rifles to disperse the peaceful blockade, but the protest held out for 12 hours of resistance. Although the Marcellus EF! network can mobilize such large-scale events at key times, EF!ers are able to dismantle counterinsurgency most effectively through the extensive day-to-day work of local organizing and land-based activism. As land-use policy and economic structure are reshaping political realities by dispossessing large numbers of people and leaving others without clean water to drink or grow food with, Earth First! is helping communities develop the practical skills to build self-sustaining communities. Instead of focusing on "outsiders," the media must pay attention to individual land owners, councils, and residential districts speaking out against fracking and rezoning.

Earth First! has a long history of forging spaces of escape (or what Andrej Grubacic calls "exilic spaces") within the contemporary political economy of extraction and development.[25] Energized by the Zapatista rebellion in 1994, EF!ers constructed liberated zones to halt destructive logging and realize the art of community in resistance. In 2005, in New Orleans, EF!ers were on hand to use their skills in building Common Ground, liberating territory in the neighborhood of Algiers to help defend and rebuild the Lower Ninth Ward after Hurricane Katrina.

The following year, Earth First!ers from South Florida helped Take Back the Land build the "Umoja Village," creating a place of liberation for the urban homeless. Umoja Village was a shantytown in Miami that addressed the economic causes of homelessness, tying them into the ecological causes of climate change and the many forms of oppression related to both. Showing the way forward for a popular response to the housing market crash, Umoja constructed a small community with group meetings, individual responsibility, and mutual aid. The structure empowered formerly homeless people to live, eat, and work, make community decisions, move toward ecological initiatives such as compost toilets, and have a place to ground their relationships.[26] In opposition to the colonial environment of COIN, Umoja Village presented a visionary place of community and liberation of land.

Also that year, Earth First!ers participated in the No Borders Camp situated at the Calexico/Mexicali border, and more recently have participated in Occupy encampments throughout the U.S. Developing the practice of liberating spaces from the mighty redwoods of Cascadia to urban Miami to the creosote bushes of the Sonoran desert, EF!ers have helped to dismantle the set notions of borders, exploring instead the ideas of biodiversity and bioregionalism as they play out amidst the geographies and networks that exist between and outside of nation states.

NOTES

1   I would like to thank my family for their support, as well as the editors for their diligent work in directing and shaping this article. Thanks also to the *Earth First! Journal* collective, past and present—especially Nettle, Russ McSpadden, Ana Rodriguez, Panagioti Tsolkas, Jacob Richardson, Mike Ludwig, Kenton Cobb, Grizzemily, Jezzabell, and everyone else. Also, thanks to Luke Romano, Niki Berger, Douglas Fur, Rain, Gigi, Karen Pickett, Karen Coulter, Jim, Donny Williams, Darwin, Noel, Brenna, Tucson Food

Not Bombs, the Pigeon Village, Chukshon Earth First!, Everglades Earth First!, Bark, Wetlands Activism Collective, the Brecht Forum, Kazembe Balagun, Vijay Prashad, Luis Figueroa, Maurice Wade, Adam Weissman, and especially Shay Emmons and Francis.

2   Eamon Javers, "Oil Executive: Military-Style 'Psy Ops' Experience Applied," *CNBC*, November 8 (2011), http://www.cnbc.com/id/45208498.

3   Ibid.

4   United States, Department of the Army, *Counterinsurgency Operations (3-07.22)*. (Fort Leavenworth: U.S. Army Combined Arms Center, 2004): 3-3.

5   FM 3-24.2, 1-19-23.

6   Ibid.

7   Ben Anderson, "Facing the Future Enemy: US Counterinsurgency Doctrine and the Pre-Insurgent," *Theory, Culture & Society*, 28 no. 7–8 December (2011).

8   David Price, "Human Terrain Systems Dissenter Resigns, Tells Inside Story of Training's Heart of Darkness," *CounterPunch*, February 15 (2010).

9   Erik Swyngedouw. "Authoritarian governance, power, and the politics of rescaling". *Environment and Planning D: Society and Space* 18 (2000): 63–76.

10 External Affairs Manager, Anadarko Petroleum, speaking to gas industry leaders about community resistance (November 9, 2011). Found in *Marcellus Monthly*, March (2012), www.marcellusprotest.org

11 Will Potter, " Pennsylvania "Eco-Terror" Bulletin is Not an Isolated Case: It's a National Problem," *Green is the New Red*, http://www.greenisthenewred.com/blog/pennsylvania-homeland-security-eco-terror-bulletin/3145/, (accessed September 16, 2010).

12 Sparki, "Shades of Al Qaeda," *Itsgettinghotinhere.org* (November 11, 2010); Comparing environmentalists to Al Qaeda is only a strategic foothold in a war of positions; Powers once declared, "Timothy McVeigh is not a terrorist, just very angry with the US government.... Whether a person is a terrorist or a criminal is irrelevant to me." (See Will Potter, *Green is the New Red: An Insider's Account of a Social Movement Under Siege*. (San Francisco: City Lights, 2012), 47.

13 Marc Levy, "'Appalled' Pa Gov. Shuts Down Reports on Protests," *Palm Beach Post*, http://www.palmbeachpost.com/news/nation/appalled-pa-gov-shuts-down-reports-on-protests-915717.html, (accessed September 15, 2010).

14 Stephen Rosenfeld, "Fracking Democracy: Why Pennsylvania's Act 13 May Be the Nation's Worst Corporate Giveaway," *Alter Net*, http://www.alternet.org/story/154459, March 7 (2012).

15 Ibid.

16 A good, early description of this conversion from the Keynes-Ford monopolist tendencies of political economy toward the current system can be found in Ernst Mandel, *Late Capitalism*, translated by Joris De Bres. (London: NLB, 1976), 243–44.

17 Neil Brenner, *New State Spaces: Urban Governance and the Rescaling of Statehood*, (USA: Oxford University Press, 2004), 247.

18 David J Kilcullen, *Counterinsurgency*, (London: Oxford University Press, 2010): 160.

19 Michael Hardt and Antonio Negri, *Multitude*, (Cambridge: Belknap Press, 2004), 61.

Ben Trott provides a good analysis of COIN in light of Hardt and Negri's ideas, which were formed during the beginning of the Iraqi occupation. See Ben Trott, "Immaterial Labor and World Order," *ephemera* 7, 1 (2007): 219

20 Swyngedouw calls this rescaling of federal standards, multinational corporations, and local political power "glocalization", which is further explained in Bob Jessop, "Liberalism, Neoliberalism, and Urban Governance: A State-Theoretical Perspective," in *Spaces of Neoliberalism,* ed. Neil Brennerand Nik Theodore. (Malden: Blackwell, 2002): 112–116.

21 In his article, "The Prose of Counterinsurgency," Guha describes similar activity occurring in the case of the English army in India. "Organization shifters" in this case, related to the historiographic manipulation of a narrative, "help the author to superimpose a temporality of his own on that of his theme, that is 'to dechronologize' the historical thread and restore, if only by way of reminiscence or nostalgia, a Time at once complex, parametric, and non-linear... braiding the chronology of the subject-matter with that of the language-act which reports it." See Ranajit Guha, "The Prose of Counter-Insurgency," in *Subaltern Studies II: Writings on South Asian History and Society,* ed. Ranajit Guha (Delhi: Oxford Press, 1983).

22 Ben Anderson. "Population and Affective Perception: Biopolitics and Anticipator Action in US Counterinsurgency Doctrine," *Antipode* 42, 13 (2011): 205–236.

23 Justin Bright, "UNT professor, student questioned by FBI," *North Texas Daily*, March 28 (2012).

24 This theory is, to some extent, recognized by Giddens's theory of structuration, presented in his book *The Constitution of Society.* It is also worth noting that Giddens is plagiarized shamelessly within the military's COIN field manual.

25 Andrej Grubacic, "Exilic Spaces and Practices in the Capitalist World Economy," *Review, A Journal of the Fernand Braudel Center* 35, no 2 (Summer 2013), forthcoming.

26 See Max Rameau, *Take Back the Land: Land, Gentrification, and the Umoja Village Shantytown* (Oakland: AK Press, 2013).

COUNTERINSURGENCY AND THE OCCUPY MOVEMENT

GEORGE CICCARIELLO-MAHER

JOURNALIST CHRIS HEDGES RUFFLED THE FEATHERS OF MANY WITHIN AND around the Occupy Movement when he denounced black bloc anarchists as a "cancer" requiring rapid and precise excision.[1] "The corporate state," he argued, "can use the Black Bloc's confrontational tactics and destruction of property to justify draconian forms of control and frighten the wider population away from supporting the Occupy movement," and the movement would be better off without these hypermasculinist, anti-organizational absolutists who "represent no one but themselves." Many, notably anarchist theorist David Graeber, have rightly attacked not only the misrepresentations in Hedges' argument, but crucially its implications: by singling out and denouncing a sector of the movement, by dividing 'good' protesters from 'bad,' this purportedly nonviolent writer was in fact *encouraging* police violence himself (after all, surgical removal of a tumor is nothing if not violent).[2] Less noted, however, is the degree to which Hedges' discourse *literally* does the work of the police by contributing to actual policing strategies as they have developed in recent decades. By grasping the development of these strategies, we will be in a better position to avoid the pitfalls of the hysterical liberalism espoused by Hedges and others, and by understanding our enemies, we will be better prepared to confront them.

FROM FORCE TO INCAPACITATION

COUNTERINSURGENCY (COIN) DOCTRINE has seen parallel developments in the international and domestic sphere, aided in no small part by the mutual imbrication of the two spheres as federal agencies have come to play a larger role in both equipping and assisting the development of local policing strategies.[3] Internationally, this shift in counterinsurgency theory is best expressed in the recent revision, under the oversight of General David Petraeus of the U.S. Army *Counterinsurgency Field Manual* (FM 3-24), which emphasizes the political over the military aspects of counterinsurgency, a focus on the local population rather than the enemy (strictly understood), and the ideological winning of the hearts and minds of the "uncommitted middle" rather than a policy of unrestricted annihilation.[4] However, we must be clear that this new counterinsurgency doctrine is still fundamentally military, and these hearts and minds are not seen as ends-in-themselves, but are rather a means toward ultimately defeating the enemy. For Petraeus and others, good intelligence comes from a friendly native population—the sea within which insurgent fish either flourish or perish—and the goal is therefore to disrupt this insurgent symbiosis.[5]

Just as the U.S. military seeks to win hearts and minds abroad not as a contribution to a more human world but as the best way to win a war against insurgents, so too has domestic policing shifted toward seemingly softer forms in an effort to destroy movements with the velvet glove, albeit not without recourse to the iron fist. Patrick Gillham has recently tracked this shift in protest policing, one driven by a dialectic of policing and resistance that has led to strategic and tactical innovation on both sides. During the 1960s, the policing of protest movements was rooted in a strategy of "escalated force," which was characterized by "mass and unprovoked arrests and the overwhelming and indiscriminate use of force."[6] The public scrutiny generated by this excessive use of force gave rise in the 1980s to a new strategy of "negotiated management," in which police collaborated with the leaders of "professionalized social movement organizations" to regulate highly choreographed demonstrations and the often scripted arrests they involved.[7] Radical organizers soon slipped the yoke of such routinized protest, however, putting forth ambitious demands that exceeded negotiation, pioneering new and more flexible tactics, and refusing to be straitjacketed by either the police or their own 'leaders.' Negotiated management simply could not keep up.[8]

The rigidity of negotiated management was fully laid bare in the 1999 Seattle protests, where police were unable to "prepare for contingencies and allocate resources necessary to control the unpredictable tactics" of demonstrators.[9] Radical organizers thus forced policing agencies to strategically reconfigure once again, the result of which has been what Gillham deems "strategic incapacitation." This approach "emphasizes the application of selectivity whereby police distinguish between two categories of protesters—contained and transgressive—in order to target those most likely to engage in disruptive activities."[10] In other words, contemporary policing strategy has come to rest firmly on a distinction between 'good' and 'bad' protesters, crucially identifying the latter *in potentia*, prior to any disruption. In practice, this often looks like a selective fusion of the two prior policing regimes: negotiation for the good protesters, force for the bad.

However, Gillham insists that this selective use of force—with its preemptive and large-scale arrests and "less lethal" weaponry—has three additional aspects that constitute a qualitatively new regime for the containment and repression of dissent. Firstly, contemporary policies of strategic incapacitation place a much greater emphasis on surveillance prior to, during, and between protests.[11] Secondly, this strategy seeks to consciously manage information, both internally through multi-agency sharing practices, and externally through the media by controlling "the flow of suitable information... using sophisticated public relations tactics."[12] Finally, and crucially, strategic incapacitation seeks to proactively organize space in a way that hinders and hobbles organizers by effectively preventing access to the object of protest (with a greater reliance on the so-called "free-speech zones" of recent years).[13] This is, in short, a potent strategy for the segregation of protesters (the preemptive identification of troublemakers as objects suitable for the use of force), the preemptive justification of their repression (through media smear and fear campaigns), and the preemptive division of space as a marker confirming this division (those who stay where they are told are 'good,' those who do not are 'bad'). Those troublemakers, "whose actions the police cannot predict," represent a non-negotiable excess that must be contained or "neutralized."[14]

The echoes of international counterinsurgency doctrine in this new form of movement policing are direct and unmitigated: where "strategic incapacitation" is premised upon a distinction between good and bad protesters, the revised FM 3-24 similarly seeks "a balance between the discriminate targeting of irreconcilable insurgents and the persuasion of less committed enemies to give up the fight with the political, economic, and informational elements of power."[15] Toward this end, two of the first "contemporary imperatives" for COIN include the management of information and the use of an appropriate (selective) level of force.[16] It is crucial to bear this police-military parallel in mind, lest we forget that this is a war. While FM 3-24 marks the entry of a "kinder and gentler counterinsurgency" into military doctrine if not practice, that does not make it any less violent, but only means that—like strategic incapacitation—the violence is more selective when a "kinder and gentler" façade is politically expedient.[17] Even where the military and police are in fact less violent than in the past, that is not because the police or the army desire a more just and peaceful world: *they want to win*.[18] If we lose sight of this, we get caught up in measuring progress by declining use of force rather than in forms of popular victories, privileging the façade of peace over the need for justice.

In what follows, I discuss the degree to which this shift in policing/COIN strategy has played out in the repression of the Occupy Movement, which began by inverting the terms of counterinsurgency doctrine, beginning with the last element of "strategic incapacitation": the control of space. Not only did the movement set out from a preexisting basis of widespread economic discontent, but it did so in a way that seized territory, threatening to hold it permanently, reversing the equation of who it was who controlled the space, and forcing the state to act: this seizure of space was its strength. Here it was the oppressed doing the occupying, taking space not in the name of imposing a social order on the colonized, but as a fulcrum for attacking privilege. This emphasis on space was not without its problems, but in what follows I want to focus on the *military* importance of this inversion.[19] Here was not simply another march to be choreographed, with a small number of incorrigibles to be preemptively arrested or dispersed by force: the Occupy Movement planted itself territorially and refused to move. Even once camps were cleared, moreover, their specter provided a focal point for demands (especially in Oakland): return to the camp.[20] After all, if FM 3-24 speaks of both "occupations" and "insurgencies," it does so on the assumption that these are opposing terms: that the U.S. will be the occupier and those occupied will resist with insurgent methods.[21] At least in theory, the Occupy Movement sought to be something relatively new: an insurgent occupation.[22]

My analysis draws on two seemingly opposite examples: Occupy Oakland and Occupy Philadelphia. While Oakland and Philadelphia both boast a considerable radical heritage (particularly with the Black Panthers in the former and the Revolutionary Action Movement in the latter), recent years have seen vastly different political conditions in each city. In Oakland, 2009 marked a seismic shift in radical politics with the rebellions that greeted the murder of Oscar Grant at the hands of the police. The self-empowering lessons of mass action in the streets led organizers to break decisively with progressive city leaders and their partners in the nonprofit sector, relying on street mobilizations to force the arrest and trial of Grant's murderer.[23] These rebellions were followed in short order by a wave of university occupations prompted by the further privatization and neoliberalization of the University of California.[24] In other words, Oakland was home to both the "occupations" that preceded Occupy Wall Street as well as the popular, community struggles that had in many ways provided their political lessons and organizational infrastructure.

By contrast, Philadelphia was amid a relative downswing of organizing (an energetic 2009 effort to save public libraries notwithstanding). Many radicals were embedded within either nonprofit reform efforts or the prefigurative communal projects that were in many ways a legacy of the <u>Movement for a New Society</u>, and many black residents were living under the shadow of the Philadelphia Police and the memory of the 1985 MOVE bombing.[25] While both cities were governed by Democrats, Oakland Mayor Jean Quan played the role of the wavering progressive, whereas Philadelphia Mayor Michael Nutter had no such pretenses, and this difference would be crucial. In analyzing these cases, however, we must not let their divergent outcomes and impacts mislead us. While the occupations in both cities began from very different positions of strength and political composition, and confronted a different degree of will on the part of the city and the police, the policing strategies each faced were largely identical.

INCAPACITATING OCCUPY: A DRAMA IN THREE ACTS

The similarity with which Occupy Oakland and Occupy Philly have been repressed testifies to a complete embrace of the "selective" nature of strategic incapacitation. The exceptionally broad nature of the Occupy Movement exacerbated this selectivity in three key ways. Firstly, political leaders from right to left (but especially Democrats) felt obligated to embrace at least some elements of this outpouring of spontaneous, populist dissent. Secondly, the multiplicity of messages and demands emerging from the movement—from liberal tax reform to revolutionary change—allowed elected officials to seemingly embrace the movement (by embracing one part) while simultaneously attempting to destroy it. Finally, the broad nature of the Occupy Movement meant that, in COIN terms, not all occupiers were hard-line insurgents. As a result, the strategy for dividing 'good' from 'bad' protesters would be more ambitious and brazen, attempting to chip away at the unity among the Occupiers while cutting ties to the broader population.[26]

The common script that would play out across the country took the form of a drama in three acts, each intertwined and circulating around a central premise of the new domestic counterinsurgency that is "strategic incapacitation": divide insurgents both internally and from their support base, using media manipulation and managed information, before then subjecting them to the "selective" use of force. I hope that by looking closely at the stages according to which this process played out it might be possible to get beyond some of the limitations of Gillham's arguably more static model of strategic incapacitation. This script is strikingly similar across the map, from Oakland to Portland, Atlanta to Philly: a Democratic mayor plays nice, claiming to represent "the 99%" and to support the Occupation's crusade against big business. But at some point, small hegemonic shifts signal coming offensives.

In a crude and thinly-veiled information war, lies are tossed about like the seeds they are, and the media duly parrots lines put forth by police and city alike. This "chatter" (to turn the language of the counterinsurgents against them) begins to spread surreptitiously: that Occupy is unsanitary, now dangerously so, now downright violent.[27] A murder, a suicide, a rape, or an overdose suddenly brim with political opportunity. With the stage set, all that remains is for the guardians of good order to step in to defend the common good. Something must be done to save Occupy from itself.

ACT ONE: THE FAÇADE OF NEGOTIATION

Under a regime of strategic incapacitation, negotiation does not disappear entirely, but communication becomes both "selective" and "one-way," available only to the 'good' protesters and functioning merely to inform them of decisions made previously by police.[28] In the policing of Occupy, there was more to it than this, as communication strategy was from day one itself a terrain for a struggle to divide and discredit the movement and eliminate the encampments. One cause for the decline of negotiated management in the aftermath of the 1999 Seattle protests was the difficulty of "negotiating" with leaderless movements, and this difficulty was similarly present with Occupy. But rather than making policing more difficult, in the era of strategic incapacitation this difficulty provided fodder for public officials, with permits and the legitimation of certain voices functioning within a media strategy aimed at dividing and discrediting the movement.

When the occupations appeared on the horizon, sparked by the example of Occupy Wall Street, many city officials supported and even encouraged these expressions of discontent while attempting to corral them within the realm of the permitted. Given recent history, Occupy Oakland resolutely refused to even consider applying for a permit: the lesson in popular power offered by the Oscar Grant rebellions was enough to convince a majority that permits were both unnecessary and even dangerous. (On several occasions, OPD used permits to pressure the permit-holders, namely the family of Oscar Grant, to keep protesters in line.) Public officials and political leaders were also banned from speaking at the General Assembly, and perhaps most importantly but controversially, the police were themselves banned from the recently-renamed Oscar Grant Plaza.[29]

In Philadelphia, by contrast, despite an initial outpouring of more than 1,000 people to support the occupation and the direct seizure of City Hall (Dilworth) Plaza, a small number of self-appointed liaisons and ACLU representatives successfully applied for a permit, marking a considerable if rarely mentioned victory for the Nutter administration. Occupy Philadelphia had agreed to play by the rules established by the city, and had crucially handed over its own sovereignty. Ironically, the permit application was only filed *after* the occupiers had forcibly taken the plaza, as though they became frightened of the specter of their own power. According to a former city liaison from Occupy, the mayor's office even offered—in a nod toward negotiated management—to arrange symbolic arrests to stimulate the movement, while also promising that a permit would protect the rightful occupiers from "other groups."[30] The first few nights of Occupy Philly reflected this balance of forces: Mayor Nutter and Police Commissioner Charles Ramsey visited the Occupy camp, with some occupiers even posing for pictures with these ostensibly supportive officials. While some confronted the mayor and distributed pamphlets insisting that "The Mayor and the Police Are Not Our Friends," such warnings went unheeded in the early days of the occupation.[31]

By late October, Oakland city officials were already complaining of a breakdown in communication, but the question of permits and formal communication with the city was in reality but a prelude to the crucial second act.

ACT TWO: DISCREDIT AND DIVIDE

The nexus of city/police officials and the media was central for the destruction of the Occupy Movement. According to Gillham, under strategic incapacitation the media functions not only to discredit movements, but to assist their repression by stoking fear and "rais[ing] expectations that police will need to curtail civil liberties, use force, and make mass arrests in order to minimize violent protests."[32] The function of media messaging and framing strategies toward Occupy was firstly, to document an unwelcome shift from acceptable to unacceptable occupations; secondly, to present the occupiers as unreasonable and unfaithful partners in dialogue; thirdly, to exaggerate the threat posed by the occupations; fourthly, to discredit the movement by dividing it both from the population and within its own ranks; and finally, to prepare the public for the eventuality of a brutal eviction.

It is worth directly comparing the rhetoric delivered by the respective city administrations to their respective media arm. In a public statement on October 20th—five days prior to the first eviction of Occupy Oakland—City Administrator Deanna Santana posted the following:

> We believe that after 10 days, the City can no longer uphold public health and safety. In recent days, camp conditions and occupants' behavior have significantly deteriorated, and it is no longer manageable to maintain a public health and safety plan. These conditions, which have not been sufficiently addressed, include: Fire hazards... Safety hazards: increasing frequency of violence, assaults, threats and intimidation... Denial of access: to emergency personnel to treat injured persons and to police to patrol the Plaza... Sanitation hazards... Health hazards...

Physical damage... As a result of these serious conditions, the Administration has determined that facilitating this expression of speech is no longer viable, nor in the interest of public health and safety.[33]

The media, meanwhile, was contributing in its own significant way to the good vs. bad distinction, decrying aggression toward reporters, lamenting the fact that a national movement had been hijacked by activists and the homeless and "altered to embrace local issues," and openly fostering a division between "legitimate protesters" and "activists."[34] In the run-up to the first eviction of Occupy Oakland, press reports cited anonymous police to document these purportedly dangerous conditions. And prior to the second eviction anonymous leaks warned both of an impending eviction and the "overwhelming force" it would entail, all in an effort to 'soften up' the public to the idea.[35] The fact that these were 'leaked' only serves to obscure the media strategy of making such threats public. This strategy became clear when emails appeared in which OPD Chief Howard Jordan informed the Mayor that crime had actually *declined* around the occupation and discussed how to manipulate this truth, as well as in efforts both prior to and after the effort to reoccupy a space on January 28th.[36] A fatal shooting near the camp on November 10th only provided more fodder for the city in the run-up to the second eviction.[37]

On the opposite coast, the same script played out. After initially expressing support for Occupy Philly, and evidently fooling many Occupiers in the process, Mayor Nutter was re-elected by a wide margin on Tuesday November 8th, freeing his hand for a change in course. The previous week, the Radical Caucus of Occupy Philly had brought forth a proposal to the General Assembly, which simply stated that the Occupy camp would not voluntarily leave in preparation for a scheduled construction project in Dilworth Plaza, and would resist eviction. The proposal seemed to shock many who had been lulled into the false sense of security that liberal tolerance provides, but after extending discussion of a modified proposal for an entire week, a four-hour General Assembly decided almost unanimously to remain in Dilworth Plaza and make preparations for nonviolent civil disobedience in the event of a raid.[38] In a scripted press statement just two days after that vote, Nutter's intentions to divide and conquer were made patently clear, in terms that directly echoed Oakland.

As in Oakland, Nutter spoke of a shift within the Occupy Movement leading to "dramatically deteriorating conditions." As in Oakland, the indicators of this deterioration included "intolerable" health and safety issues, including a recent sexual assault at the camp. And as in Oakland, the embodiment of this deterioration was the takeover of a once-laudable movement (of 'good' protesters) by anarchistic troublemakers ('bad' protesters), and the vast bulk of Nutter's speech was dedicated to emphasizing this division and deepening it with his fear-mongering:

> Occupy Philly has changed…. Occupy Philly is fractured with internal disagreement and disputes. The people of Occupy Philly have also changed and their intentions have changed…. [T]hey told me that they would be peaceful, that they would not be disruptive…. We've seen the rise of new groups as a part of this movement like the Radical Caucus, which is bent on civil disobedience and disrupting city operations. Many of the people that we talked to in the beginning of this event and activity are now gone…. And Occupy Philly has refused to engage in active, regular discussions with us. This change in behavior is no accident. It is a direct result of the fact that this movement has changed and the people have changed…. Occupy Philly has changed, so we must change our relationship with them.[39]

The *coup de grâce* of this entire performance came with regard to the impending renovation of Dilworth Plaza, a project "built by the 99 percent for the 99 percent." While this was clearly an effort to pit Occupy against the community more broadly, it was also a strategy for planting the seeds of political division *within* Occupy and allowing these to play out: debates soon raged within Occupy Philly about the danger of losing labor support (which with a few exceptions had been largely absent from the beginning), neglecting that this rhetoric was simply part of the city's eviction strategy.

Occupy Philly was quick to respond to the mayor's accusations. At a counter-press conference, speaker after speaker dismantled Nutter's claims, piece by piece. The most shocking revelation came from the Women's Caucus, which was quick to highlight the opportunism and hypocrisy of focusing in on the sexual assault as a pretext to attack the Occupation. As a representative of the Women's Caucus told the press, "We asked police for help with the eviction of a sexual predator. The police said, 'It's not our problem. Get your men to handle it.'"[40] This counter-messaging was only a scrambling rearguard effort, however, and despite the fact that Nutter's clear strategy strengthened the resolve of some occupiers and drove out some collaborators, the damage had already been done.[41] According to one self-professed "moderate" who had previously (and naïvely) collaborated with the city: "The Mayor of Philadelphia blatantly lied. All of the people that the city had worked with from day one, myself included, were still there. The only thing that had changed was that we were no longer allowing ourselves to be controlled by a system that served to protect the status quo."[42] The script was written beforehand, and all that remained in question was how divided the movement would be and how much public support it could muster to prevent an eviction.

ACT THREE: EVICT

While we have already seen that the political strategy of elected leaders in Oakland and Philadelphia largely conforms to the strategic incapacitation model in its effort to divide 'good' from 'bad' protesters through the management of media portrayals—reserving the use of force for the latter (at least in theory)—in Oakland this was not, or not primarily, the result of the ineffectiveness of negotiated management.[43] Rather, it was the indiscriminate use of "less lethal" weapons against an April 2003 anti-war demonstration at the Port of Oakland that informed a revision of OPD policy to prohibit some "less lethal" weapons, constrain the use of others, and prescribe negotiation even in cases when laws are being broken.[44] The revised OPD Crowd Control Policy reads in many ways like a guidebook for strategic incapacitation, particularly in its insistence that "all members of a crowd of demonstrators are not the same" (Section VIII, C6).[45] While this revised policy also prescribes mass arrest prior to the use of force and other elements of strategic incapacitation, the evictions of Occupy and the outcry they would spark emerged at the margins of these regulations (neither from following them to the letter nor from blatantly disregarding them).[46] OPD's extensive use of surveillance and infiltration became clear, moreover, with the publicized identification of OPD officer Fred Shavies, who had been operating undercover around the camp, and the later release, under state and municipal law, of OPD's internal documents related to the policing of Occupy.[47] Equally apparent is OPD's selectivity: recently released internal communications reveal an effort to target "anarchists" prior to any illegal activity.[48]

Despite all efforts to strategically incapacitate Occupy Oakland, the first eviction of Occupy Oakland on October 25th became an unmitigated public relations nightmare for Mayor Jean Quan. When occupiers reconvened at the Oakland Public Library and attempted to retake Oscar Grant Plaza, the division between 'good' and 'bad' protesters collapsed: marchers uniformly insisted on retaking the plaza, and police responded with teargas, reducing the downtown area to a hazy warzone. While this already marked a failure of strategic incapacitation, it became a disaster when Iraq War veteran Scott Olson was critically injured and, to make matters worse, a police officer was seen callously tossing a flash-bang grenade into a crowd of demonstrators attempting to rescue him.[49] The idea of a war veteran surviving multiple tours to nearly be killed for protesting was beyond the pale: soon Jon Stewart was lampooning Mayor Quan on *The Daily Show*, Keith Olbermann was demanding her resignation on *Countdown*, and many Occupy supporters had thrown their support behind a previously conservative campaign to recall the Mayor.

It was not the live rounds of Jackson State and Kent State that nearly killed Olson, however, but rather an excess built into strategic incapacitation itself: Olson was struck in the head by a teargas canister fired at close-range.[50] If negotiated management could not contain the will of radical organizers, neither could strategic incapacitation contain the will of individual police officers to do maximum harm with whatever weapons are at their disposal. The first Oakland eviction was therefore *not* a return to the days of escalated (and excessive) force, but rather a situation in which, confronted with intransigent marchers in the streets, OPD officers, commanders, and supporting agencies exceeded the bounds of strategic incapacitation knowing full well that Mayor Quan would bear the brunt of the consequences.[51] When Occupy Oakland retook Oscar Grant Plaza, the fences hastily erected to keep the protesters out were removed and turned into lawn art, symbolically mocking efforts to control space. At a euphoric General Assembly in the reoccupied plaza, more than a thousand demonstrators took full advantage of the momentum provided by police repression—a dynamic Marx reputedly deemed the "whip of the counter-revolution."[52] They declared a General Strike on November 2nd, and an estimated 25,000 people poured out of work and into the streets to shut down the Port of Oakland. Quan had learned a central lesson of the new COIN doctrine the hard way: that "an operation that kills five insurgents is counterproductive if collateral damage leads to the recruitment of fifty more insurgents."[53]

Not only did the perception of excessive force give Occupy Oakland a much-needed shot in the arm, but this dialectic of resistance and repression has also forced innovation in policing techniques akin to the previous curtailment of the escalated force doctrine in the late 1960s. The baton jabs against UC Berkeley students and professors and the infamous pepperspray incident at UC Davis were widely publicized and roundly condemned (here, *Daily Show* coverage again played a key role). After the UC Davis incident, for example, California Governor Jerry Brown ordered a review and revision of Police Officer Standards and Training (POST) guidelines, beginning with an upcoming Crowd Management Summit in San Diego. It was not only excess from above in the form of police violence that pushed this transformation, but also the excess from below of the Occupy Movement's own innovative elements.

According to one headline, Occupy "chang[ed] how police operate," as the large and rapid mobilizations made possible by electronic communication have exacerbated the difficulties that previously surfaced under negotiated management. Moreover, as larger numbers now become potential 'troublemakers,' police agencies are forced to devote heavier resources to mobile policing in their own jurisdictions and "mobile field forces" to respond to increasingly frequent requests for mutual aid police contingents by other municipalities.[54] Even more recent events in Oakland indicate that the selective incapacitation of transgressive elements in Occupy Oakland has increased: the city and OPD undertook a campaign of increased surveillance, targeted arrests, selective intimidation, and more recently, the issuing of "stay-away" orders preventing individuals from returning to Oscar Grant Plaza.[55] More ominously still was the arrest of three Occupy participants who, after an altercation at a march, were charged with a hate-crime to, in the words of one civil rights attorney, "break the movement."[56]

In Philadelphia, given the effectiveness with which Mayor Nutter and the PPD had divided Occupy from the city and even from itself, it would be no surprise when the occupation was removed with a whimper rather than a bang. On November 18th, under threat of eviction from the city and a withdrawal of support from the unions, Occupy Philly voted to do what it thought the city wanted by moving across the street into Thomas Paine Plaza (adorned with a menacing statue of notorious former Police Commissioner, and later mayor, Frank Rizzo). Once again, the occupiers made the fatal mistake of taking the city at its word. Given the tradeoff between a potentially long-term occupation of Paine Plaza and a potentially conflictive eviction of Dilworth, Nutter and PPD opted for the latter and blocked entry to Paine Plaza, forcing occupiers to scurry back across the street in disarray.[57] The permits, the negotiations, and the commitment to protect First Amendment rights were revealed to have been little more than a ruse.

When an eviction order was finally handed down for November 27th, many within Occupy Philly seemed willing to embrace a return to the scripted protests of the past and negotiation with the police: a select few were prepared to passively remain in the Plaza to be arrested, with pathways cleared for a choreographed police action. Nutter's only error in the whole affair was *not* evicting the occupiers that night, but instead waiting until the 30th, by which point anticipation had put nerves on edge and the unpredictability of the action prevented a fully negotiated outcome. The result was instead at least a minor rupture, as somewhat unexpectedly, hundreds engaged in unpermitted marches around Center City, leading to 52 arrests in the early morning hours. But the ease with which the city destroyed Occupy Philly was no accident, and nor was the striking similarity between the scripts played out in Oakland and Philadelphia.

CHARLES RAMSEY AND PERF

IF THE STRATEGY to repress and destroy Occupy Philadelphia played out almost seamlessly, this was not due to the farsightedness of the city's *political* leadership or Nutter's own management skills, but to a different actor entirely: Police Commissioner Charles Ramsey. Not only is Ramsey worthy of discussion in his own right as an emblematic figure in the new policing model of strategic incapacitation, but the shift in policing in Philadelphia also reflects broader nationwide shifts as well as underlying continuities to which we must be attentive.

For years, policing in Philadelphia was epitomized by the combative Commissioner-turned-Mayor Frank Rizzo, whose electoral victories were largely fueled by attacks on the black community.[58] The fact that both a black mayor (Nutter) and black police commissioner (Ramsey) currently preside over the city should not mislead us, however: knowing full well that black police are compatible with white supremacy (and are arguably its best weapon), Rizzo was himself responsible for an influx of black officers into the PPD, and a black mayor (Wilson Goode, who cut his teeth in lawsuits against PPD racism) would preside over the 1985 bombing of the MOVE house. More importantly for my purposes, Ramsey is today the head of the Police Executive Research Forum (PERF), originally an anti-Rizzo organization seeking to reform corrupt and discredited policing practices.[59] But even here I want to insist that, for our purposes, there is more continuity than rupture with the Rizzo legacy.

Charles Ramsey came to the Philadelphia Police Department out of his involuntary retirement amid the fallout surrounding his policing of anti-IMF protests in Washington D.C. in 2002. As Metro Police Chief, Ramsey had shown his dedication to strategic incapacitation when he preemptively arrested hundreds of anti-IMF protesters in Pershing Park.[60] Just two years prior, Ramsey's MPD had used zoning laws to preemptively shut down the convergence center for IMF/World Bank protests, "successfully disrupt[ing] the ability of demonstrators to organize."[61] In other words, Ramsey had proven his ability to destroy movements without resorting to the brute force of the past, and while both he and the D.C. city government were ultimately held responsible for violating the Fourth Amendment, Philadelphia Mayor Michael Nutter was eager to bring this new paragon of policing on board. Prior to the emergence of the Occupy Movement, Ramsey was applying COIN-like measures to policing Philadelphia's black population, largely through an increase of surveillance, foot patrols, and the control of space through stringent and racist curfews. In other words, Frank Rizzo and Charles Ramsey used different means toward the same end: both excelled at destroying movements. So, if our only metric is overt coercion, we run the risk of missing the underlying continuities between escalated force and strategic incapacitation.

It is precisely these crucial underlying continuities that have evaded recent debates about the policing of the Occupy Movement. In a now-controversial piece, Naomi Wolf ties—in a conspiratorial fashion—the blandest anti-corporate demands of Occupy to a purported scheme for top-down corporate/

Congressional/Department of Homeland Security repression of the Occupy Movement. The similarities in messaging and tactics used against the occupations, Wolf insists, would be simply unthinkable without "a full-court press at the top. This was clearly not simply a case of a freaked-out mayors,' [*sic*] city-by-city municipal overreaction against mess in the parks and cranky campers. As the puzzle pieces fit together, they began to show coordination against OWS at the highest national levels."[62] While Joshua Holland has roundly debunked Wolf's factual claims, and Corey Robin has similarly undermined the theoretical foundations of this assumption that repression must begin at the top, something has been missed in this debate over the "facts" and a crucial aspect of this paranoia has gone unnoted, namely, the fact that repression and counterinsurgency need not be brutal at all.[63]

The central object of Wolf's denunciation is none other than PERF, within which Ramsey is a prominent figure, but rather than coordinating a 'brutal' crackdown, PERF was contributing to something arguably more sinister: the expansion of the doctrine of strategic incapacitation and its application to the Occupy Movement.[64] Not only do we need to recognize the shift from escalated force to strategic incapacitation if we are going to be in a position to resist contemporary policing strategies, but focusing on police violence makes it very easy for organizations like PERF to deny the charges. In a press release responding to allegations of coordinating police crackdowns, PERF insisted—quite honestly—that it seeks only to disseminate "best practices" that aim to *reduce*, not *increase*, police use of force in crowd control. Among these "best practices," they refer to precisely the same distinction between 'good' and 'bad' protesters that is so central to contemporary strategic incapacitation: "When dealing with law-breaking protesters, don't forget that thousands of nonviolent protesters are merely exercising their First Amendment rights. So the police must differentiate the lawbreaking protesters from those who are peaceful."[65] All PERF needed to do to assuage liberal hysteria that it was stoking the flames of violent repression was to tell the truth.

After defending PERF's objectives from the critiques of Occupiers, one budding military strategist puts this nicely:

> PERF is in a position much like that of the COIN advocates in the US military. They are saying that the police need to win hearts and minds, they need to have good contacts in the community, they should show restraint even in the face of provocation, they should target the use of their full power as precisely as possible, etc. Ironically, by delegitimizing PERF and perhaps by chilling police chiefs from talking with it, the Occupy folks may well be setting the stage for more police violence and overreactions. Of course, this would serve Occupy well. A good round

of police atrocities could be what really kicks their movement into overdrive.[66]

PERF is perfectly aware that the "whip of the counter-revolution" can be a boon to radicals, and this understanding lies at the heart of both global counterinsurgency doctrine and "strategic incapacitation" on the domestic level. But here liberals fall silent, and the liberalism underlying many of the occupations becomes a serious obstacle. By focusing too directly on brute force, Wolf and others neglect the reality of strategic incapacitation, thereby running the risk of contributing to its effectiveness by lending tacit support to attacks on the so-called violence within the ranks of Occupy and the 'good' vs. 'bad' protester division which underlies police efforts.

WOLF IN THE HEDGES

HERE WE RETURN, of course, to Chris Hedges, despite the ostensible opposition between his rhetoric and that of Naomi Wolf. After all, each seems to direct their paranoia toward different targets: Wolf toward the alleged federal coordination of the crackdown on Occupy, and Hedges toward the anarchist fringe of that movement. However, once we turn from what Wolf and Hedges are *against* to what they are *for*, we find striking similarities. Put simply, Hedges and Wolf both subtly demand a return to negotiated management, or even escalated force: for Wolf, the police should return to their role as protectors of First Amendment rights, and for Hedges the protesters themselves should return to the choreographed routines and even "embrace police brutality."[67] By neglecting the shift in policing strategies and counterinsurgency from outright force and violence, through negotiated management, and on to strategic incapacitation, both ignore the imperative need for a rupture with the existing order if political change is to be possible at all.

Doubly ironic is the fact that Hedges couches his attack on the black bloc in this same language of counterinsurgency: these anarchists are "a gift from heaven to the security and surveillance state," he contends, while naïvely insisting that our relationship toward that state "is not a war." But pressed to provide an alternative, Hedges conveniently retreats to the past, to the strategic opposition between Martin Luther King's nonviolence and Bull Connor's predictably violent response, thereby concealing recent shifts in policing strategy. Contemporary policing is less Bull Connor and more Charles Ramsey, and our strategy must keep pace with that of our enemies. Like Wolf, Hedges conspicuously fails to do so. More troubling than Hedges' neglect of this shift in policing strategy is his contribution—however inadvertent—to its effectiveness. By parroting the fundamental division of strategic incapacitation between 'good' and 'bad' protesters, and by suggesting the surgical removal of the latter, Hedges literally marks the boundary that divides his liberal tolerance from that which is beyond the pale. The implications of this position are not abstract.

I was recently on an Occupy Philadelphia march in solidarity with Occupy Oakland following the encirclement, or "kettling," and mass arrest of protesters during the attempted January 28th building occupation. Several marchers attempted to rile the small crowd up to retake Dilworth Plaza. While Civil Affairs Officers (a notorious unit established in the 1960s to manage protesters) initially attempted to prevent this, they and other officers withdrew, the fence was torn down, and some marchers symbolically reoccupied the plaza for a few moments. Half of the crowd, rather than remaining in the streets, actually *retreated* to the other side, actively denounced the action (mind you, retaking a plaza that had previously occupied), and some even pointed out agitators to the police (others later denounced instigators as possible *agents provocateurs*). These aspiring surgeon's assistants were effectively saying: "There is your cancer! Go and excise it!" The PPD was more than willing to oblige, moving in to surgically arrest two so-called agitators. Hedges himself would have been proud. Even more troubling was the fact that many 'good' protesters seemed not to care that the 'bad' had been removed. When some marchers retreated while singing "This Little Light of Mine," they were mic-checked by a young black woman: "This is no time to celebrate! Your comrades were just arrested! This is disgusting!"

By merely standing in opposition to violence—by the police or protesters—rather than standing *for* the imperative need for social transformation that drives protests to begin with, Wolf and Hedges unwittingly contribute to a double function. Firstly, they obscure the fact that contemporary policing is *not* simply rooted in brute force but instead in the more subtle and selective deployment of force against the 'bad.' Secondly, they themselves contribute to that selectivity by reinforcing the very division that underlies the strategy of strategic incapacitation. Thus they conceal the weapons of our enemies and divide our own forces.

Much has been said about the violence-versus-nonviolence debate within and prior to Occupy, and it is true that we need to defend the violent as well as the nonviolent and accept not only a diversity of tactics but also a diversity of strategies for building the new world. Arguably more important than debating violence within *our* ranks, however, and even more important than denouncing nonviolence as complicit in perpetuating the violence of the existing order, is grasping and opposing the seemingly less-violent policing strategies we might otherwise overlook or, worse still, encourage with our rhetoric. From the perspective of building sustained movements, "strategic incapacitation"—if we fail to recognize how it operates and strategize how to oppose it—could prove even more harmful than the indiscriminate force of the past. In response to such divide-and-conquer tactics, Kristian Williams has argued that, "we need to be prepared to support the guilty along with the innocent."[68] We must also protect the troublemakers, because this is simply not a question of violence or nonviolence, but one of attempts to destroy political movements by violent *or* nonviolent means. We are opposed to both.

Here an important final caveat is in order: counterinsurgency research has been too focused on the rights of the privileged. As Williams puts it, "repression… is not something that happens solely, or even mainly, to activists."[69] There have always been good and bad protesters, and these are distinguished as much by race as by tactical orientation. Surveillance, preemptive arrests, media slander campaigns, and less-lethal—but also more-lethal—weaponry have been nothing new to black movements from the Revolutionary Action Movement and the Black Panthers of the 1960s to the Republic of New Afrika in the 1970s and MOVE in the 1980s, not to mention the more mundane selectivity of stop-and-frisk and racist curfews. Unfortunately, the chasm separating the Occupy Movement from the most oppressed communities has prevented us from taking this lesson to heart. Our enemies who wrote FM 3-24 understand well the need for insurgents to take refuge in the people, in broad movements, to sink our roots deeply into communities and refuse to be moved. Williams continues:

> When facing counterinsurgency, we need to learn to think like insurgents: The antidote to repression is, simply put, more resistance. But this cannot just be a matter of escalating tactics or increasing militancy. Crucially, it has to involve broadening the movement's base of support.[70]

When we have successfully done so, there will be no 'good' protesters, only 'bad.' When the troublemakers outnumber the collaborators, then—and only then—will our own popular insurgency stand a chance.

NOTES

1   Chris Hedges, "The Cancer of Occupy," *Truthdig*, February 6, 2012, http://www.truthdig.com/report/item/the_cancer_of_occupy_20120206/.

2   David Graeber, "Concerning the Violent Peace-Police: An Open Letter to Chris Hedges," *n+1*, February 9, 2012, http://nplusonemag.com/concerning-the-violent-peace-police.

3   Kristian Williams, "The Other Side of the COIN: Counterinsurgency and Community Policing," *Interface: A Journal for and about Social Movements*, May 2011, http://www.interfacejournal.net/wordpress/wp-content/uploads/2011/05/Interface-3-1-Williams.pdf.

4   *The U.S. Army/Marine Corps Counterinsurgency Field Manual* (Chicago: University of Chicago Press, 2007), 35. This development marks the long-overdue entry into counterinsurgency doctrine of what Italian Marxist Antonio Gramsci called "hegemonic struggle," in contrast to a purely coercive or military approach (and here military practitioners are latecomers vis-à-vis the Western Marxists who developed and expanded the concept). The Cold War overshadowed such questions, and while the U.S. defeat in Vietnam certainly raised the right questions, these were set aside and avoided in favor of comforting answers. It was therefore only amidst the Iraqi insurgency that some U.S. commanders sought to revise counterinsurgency doctrine. In this new COIN doctrine, Gramsci's "war of position" assumes a central role in building and occupying the "powerful system of fortresses and earthworks" of hegemonic power that surround and reinforce the besieged state, making a frontal "war of maneuver" less costly and difficult in the end. Antonio Gramsci, *Selections from the Prison Notebooks* (London: Lawrence and Wishart, 1971): 238.

5   Were this not absolutely obvious, it's worth noting that Petraeus has been an outspoken supporter of increased use of military force globally, and as a Colonel in 1997, Petraeus and his co-authors echoed Sam Colt in their insistence, "Never send a man when you can send a bullet." David Petraeus, Damian Carr, and John Abercrombie, "Why We Need FISTs— Never Send a Man When You Can Send a Bullet," *Field Artillery* n. 3 (May-June 1997): 3-5. The revised FM 3-24 was subject to a "vetting session" that included academics, human rights NGOs, and journalists. For an analysis of the Manual's genesis and content, see John Nagl, "Foreword," in *Counterinsurgency Field Manual*, xvi. See also the review symposium dedicated to FM 3-24 in *Perspectives on Politics* 6, no. 2 (2008): 345–60.

6   Patrick Gillham, "Securitizing America: Strategic Incapacitation and the Policing of Protest Since the 11 September 2001 Terrorist Attacks," *Sociology Compass* 5, n. 7 (2011): 637.

7   Gillham, "Securitizing America," 638.

8   Gillham, "Securitizing America," 638–39.

9   Gillham, "Securitizing America," 638.

10 Gillham, "Securitizing America," 640.

11 Gillham, "Securitizing America," 643–44.

12 Gillham, "Securitizing America," 645–46.

13 Gillham, "Securitizing America," 646–47.

14 Gillham, "Securitizing America," 642.

In Gramscian language: war of position for the many, war of maneuver for the few. According to the political theorist Wendy Brown, the roots of this division lie within the predominant discourse of tolerance itself, which serves to mark the powerful as "normal" while discrediting the "unruly" as somehow "deviant," and thereby "legitimates the most illiberal actions of the state." Wendy Brown, *Regulating Aversion: Tolerance in the Age of Identity and Empire* (Princeton: Princeton University Press, 2006), 8.

15 Nagl, "Foreword," xvii. The "paradoxes" of counterinsurgency discussed within the Manual, moreover, reflect the "selectivity" in rejecting a one-size-fits-all approach to insurgents (47-51).

16 *Counterinsurgency Field Manual:* 44-45. We could similarly point to the RAND study which emphasizes the need to "shape human terrain" by influencing popular opinion and thereby "unlock the promise of informational power." David C. Gompert et al., *War By Other Means: Building Complete and Balanced Capabilities for Counterinsurgency* (Santa Monica: RAND, 2008): xxxi, xl.

17 See the critique of the intersection of pacification and security in M. Neocleous and G. Rigakos, eds., *Anti-Security* (Ottawa: Red Quill Books, 2011).

18 Sarah Sewall, "Introduction," *Counterinsurgency Field Manual,* xxxiv.

19 The dangers of uncritically embracing the slogan of the "99%" were skillfully demolished by the late Joel Olson, "Whiteness and the 99%," http://www.bringtheruckus.org/?q=node%2F146.

20 For an analysis of Occupy Portland's spontaneous innovations with regard to space, albeit one which overlooks the realities of contemporary policing, see Lester Macgurdy, "Occupy Portland Outsmarts Police, Creating Blueprint for Other Occupations," *Portland Occupier,* December 15, 2011, http://www.portlandoccupier.org/2011/12/15/occupy-portland-outsmarts-police-creating-blueprint-for-other-occupations/.

21 In line with the *Manual*'s efforts at ideological obfuscation, however, the term "occupier" is explicitly shunned in favor of "liberator." Likewise, the country where operations occur is euphemistically called the "Host Nation." *Counterinsurgency Field Manual,* 162.

22 This was not without precedents, however, and we could apply a similarly paradoxical label to such effective tactics as sit-down strikes, factory occupations, and the community-level occupation in Oaxaca.

23 See Raider Nation Collective, *From the January Rebellions to Lovelle Mixon and Beyond* (Oakland: 2010), which reprints several of my accounts. See also George Ciccariello-Maher, "From Oscar Grant to Occupy: The Long Arc of Rebellion in Oakland," in K. Khatib, M. Killjoy, M. McGuire, eds., *We Are Many: Reflections on Movement Strategy from Occupation to Liberation* (Oakland: AK Press, 2012), 39-45.

24 See *After the Fall: Communiqués from Occupied California* (February 2010), http://afterthefallcommuniques.info/.

25 See Andrew Cornell, "The Movement for a New Society: Consensus, Prefiguration, and Direct Action," in D. Berger, ed., *The Hidden 1970s: Histories of Radicalism* (New Brunswick: Rutgers University Press, 2010): 231–49.

26 In the terms of COIN doctrine, this strategy sought not only to separate the movement from its support networks, but also from its auxiliaries and mass base. *Counterinsurgency Field Manual,* 22, 31.

27 For just one example, see Chip Johnson, "Occupy Oakland demonstration has taken ugly turn," *San Francisco Chronicle,* October 21, 2011), http://www.sfgate.com/cgi-bin/article.cgi?f=/c/a/2011/10/21/BADO1LK9Q2.DTL.

28 Gillham, "Securitizing America," 640, Table 1.

29 "General Assembly Resolutions (Oct 10—Nov 16 Summary)," http://occupyoakland.org/2011/11/general-assembly-resolutions/.

30 Julia Alford-Fowler, "How to Radicalize a Moderate: The story of a former OP City Liaison,"

February 20, 2012), http://davidandgoliathproject.wordpress.com/2012/02/20/how-to-radicalize-a-moderate-the-story-of-a-former-op-city-liaison/.

31 http://multi.lectical.net/content/mayor_and_police_are_not_our_friends_letter_occupy_philly. Two strange elements of an early provocation strategy also deserve mention; firstly, the appearance of a wealthy woman in a fur coat strolling through the camp at night with a butler; secondly, disinformation passed from the police to the early self-appointed liaison group that "Black nationalists" planned to attack Occupy.

32 Gillham, "Securitizing America," 646. See also Luis A. Fernandez, *Policing Dissent: Social Control and the Anti-Globalization Movement* (New Brunswick: Rutgers University Press, 2008).

33 http://www2.oaklandnet.com/OAK031803.

34 Chip Johnson, "Occupy Oakland demonstration has taken ugly turn."

35 Phillip Matier and Andrew Ross, "New police plans to oust Occupy Oakland campers, *San Francisco Chronicle*, November 9, 2011), http://www.sfgate.com/cgi-bin/article.cgi?f=/c/a/2011/11/08/BASA1LS510.DTL#ixzz1ovlPvrxf; Ali Winston, "Notice Warns of Monday AM Raid on Occupy Oakland," *The Informant*, November 13, 2011, http://informant.kalwnews.org/2011/11/notice-warns-of-monday-am-raid-on-occupy-oakland/.

36 "Emails between Oakland officials reveal tensions during Occupy ordeal," *KTVU.com*, January 13, 2012, http://www.ktvu.com/news/news/emails-exchanged-between-oakland-opd-reveal-tensio/nGMkF/.

Prior to Move-In Day, the City released a statement dividing good from bad by encouraging efforts toward "productive" causes rather than resource-draining protests. http://www2.oaklandnet.com/OAK033073. Many noted the irony that one of the causes championed by the City's press release is the nonprofit Just Cause/Causa Justa, which had been one of several groups brutally evicted from an occupied home in West Oakland just weeks earlier. After Move-In Day, which included the temporary takeover of City Hall, police managed the media portrayal of that event by releasing heavily-edited footage that included protesters burning the American flag *outside* City Hall (a *non sequitur* aimed at discrediting the movement).

37 Matthai Kuruvila and Demian Bulwa, "Occupy Oakland: Man Shot to Death Near Camp," *San Francisco Chronicle*, November 11, 2011, http://www.sfgate.com/cgi-bin/article.cgi?f=/c/a/2011/11/10/BAAI1LTA0L.DTL

38 http://occupyphillymedia.org/content/outcome-proposal-vote-november-11-general-assembly.

39 "Text of Mayor Nutter's Statement on Occupy Philly, November 13," *Occupy Philly Media*, November 13, 2011, http://occupyphillymedia.org/content/text-mayor-nutters-statement-occupy-philly-november-13.

40 http://www.citypaper.net/blogs/nakedcity/Occupy-responds-to-Mayor-Nutter.html.

41 The so-called "Reasonable Solutions Committee," which had advocated working closely with the City and police, split openly with Occupy after the proposal to maintain the encampment passed. They went on to negotiate separate permits with the City and in many ways contributed to an atmosphere leading to the violence of the eviction.

42   Alford-Fowler, "How to Radicalize a Moderate."

43   When comparing the evictions of Occupy Oakland and Philadelphia, we need to set aside one important aspect: the dialectic that played out on the national level as eviction of one camp encouraged increased militancy elsewhere. Occupy Oakland was evicted on October 25th and then again on November 14th, and Occupy Philadelphia was evicted on November 30th, and while the Oakland evictions in particular sparked nationwide solidarity actions (as did the excessive force deployed against Oakland's Move-In Day on January 28th 2012), here I will consider these in relative isolation to sketch their local dynamics.

44   ACLU of Northern California, "In Landmark Agreement, Oakland Prohibits Less Lethal Weapons for Crowd Control," November 9, 2004, http://www.aclunc.org/news/press_releases/in_landmark_agreement,_oakland_prohibits_less_lethal_weapons_for_crowd_control.shtml/. This headline is misleading however, as it was only wooden pellets and a variety of less-common weapons and techniques that were fully prohibited.

45   John C. Osborn, "Crowd Control at Oakland Protests: A Visual Explainer," *Oakland Local*, March 1, 2012, http://oaklandnorth.net/2012/03/01/crowd-control-at-oakland-protests-a-visual-explainer/. The policy does, however, limit the targeting of individuals on the basis of prior behavior, but such prohibitions must be taken with a grain of salt.

46   OPD largely followed this policy, with notable exceptions that included the brandishing of weapons prior to issuing dispersal orders, demanding crowds disperse on January 28th while preventing them from doing so, and especially the quick recourse to "less lethal"weapons prior to mass arrests. Of twelve major Occupy operations, only two did not result in the deployment of "less lethal" weapons. Osborn, "Crowd Control at Oakland Protests: A Visual Explainer."

47   For the first, see http://sfist.com/2011/10/31/oakland_pd_officers_spotted_underco.php. When Shavies responded with professions of support for the 99%, many conveniently overlooked the fact that he also defended his work as a police infiltrator (http://vimeo.com/31830746). In other words, some once again fell for the media strategy of those attempting to destroy Occupy. Jennifer Inez Ward, "Police Records Shed Light on Occupy Oakland Action," *Oakland Local*, January 11, 2012, http://oaklandlocal.com/article/police-records-shed-light-occupy-oakland-action. The released documents, videos, and audio footage are available on the City of Oakland's website: http://www2.oakland-net.com/Government/o/OPD/a/PublicReports/OccupyOaklandPublicRecords/index.htm#plan.

48   "Oakland Police Keep Track of 'Anarchists,'" *San Francisco Bay Guardian*, March 14, 2012, http://www.sfbg.com/politics/2012/03/14/oakland-police-keep-track-anarchists.

49   http://www.youtube.com/watch?v=So7Y1FK2BiE.

50   Reports on the "Israelification" of OPD and the fact that OPD trained with Israeli and Bahraini military forces prior to the "violent" raid of Occupy Oakland obscures the fact that such overt coercion simply wasn't the objective of the raid. David Harris-Gershon, "Oakland Police Trained Alongside Bahrain Military and Israeli Forces Prior to Violent Occupy Oakland Raid," *Tikkun Daily*, December 4, 2011, http://www.tikkun.org/tikkundaily/2011/12/04/prior-to-violent-occupy-oakland-raid-oakland-police-trained-

alongside-bahrain-military-and-israeli-border-forces/.

51 OPD had previously declared its intention to investigate Quan when, as a Mayoral candidate, she stood between protesters and police when the verdict was passed down for Johannes Mehserle, Oscar Grant's killer, and she later raised the ire of OPD by insisting that they pay into their own pensions.

52 This phrase is often attributed to Marx, although it never appears in this form in his writings, coming closest in the preface to *The Class Struggles in France*.

53 *Counterinsurgency Field Manual*, 45.

54 Vic Lee, "Occupy movement changing how police operate," *ABC7*, January 9, 2012, http://abclocal.go.com/kgo/story?section=news%2Flocal%2Fsan_francisco&id=8496786. The political fallout from providing mutual aid for unpopular actions has led cities like Berkeley to question the practice entirely.

55 See Decolonize Oakland's "Points of Unity," February 12, 2012, http://decolonizeoakland.org/2012/02/12/point-of-unity/, and "Communiqué," March 18, 2012, http://decolonizeoakland.org/2012/03/18/525/.

56 The defendants were accused of using an anti-gay slur during an argument with a bystander, but claim that she had used racial slurs first. Justin Berton, "Occupy Activists Dispute Hate-Crime Charges," *San Francisco Chronicle*, March 6, 2012, http://www.sfgate.com/cgi-bin/article.cgi?f=%2Fc%2Fa%2F2012%2F03%2F05%2FBAAS1NGGI6.DTL.

57 This was not the victory some suggested, but an abject and depressing defeat, a decision made out of fear that only by coincidence opened more radical possibilities. Efforts to divide the movement with misinformation continued, with Deputy Mayor Rich Negrin even suggesting that the Radical Caucus was negotiating for a permit (http://occupyphillymedia.org/blog/op-ga-notes-saturday-111911).

58 See Omari L. Dyson, Kevin L. Brooks, and Judson L. Jeffries, "'Brotherly Love Can Kill You': The Philadelphia Branch of the Black Panther Party," in J. Judson, ed., *Comrades: A Local History of the Black Panther Party* (Bloomington: Indiana University Press, 2007): 238-247. For a recent account of COINTELPRO activities against Philly SDS in 1969, see Jonathan Valania, "The Phantom Bomb Plot of 1969," *Philadelphia Weekly*, December 22, 2009.

59 Maureen Tkacik, "The Anti-#Occupy/CIA Connection," *Naked Capitalism*, December 12, 2011, http://www.nakedcapitalism.com/2011/12/maureen-tkacik-the-anti-occupy-cia-connection.html.

60 Fernandez, *Policing Dissent*, 3, 134–35. Despite this shift toward strategic incapacitation, however, his overheard comment "we're going to lock them up to teach them a lesson" might belie a certain nostalgia for the spectacular force of the past. http://www.washingtoncitypaper.com/blogs/citydesk/2009/11/18/affidavit-ramsey-ordered-pershing-park-arrests/.

61 Fernandez, *Policing Dissent*, 79–80.

62 Naomi Wolf, "The Shocking Truth About the Crackdown on Occupy," *The Guardian*, November 25, 2011, http://www.guardian.co.uk/commentisfree/cifamerica/2011/nov/25/shocking-truth-about-crackdown-occupy.

63   Joshua Holland, "Naomi Wolf's 'Shocking Truth' About the 'Occupy Crackdowns' Offers Anything but the Truth," *AlterNet*, November 26, 2011, http://www.alternet.org/story/153222/naomi_wolf%E2%80%99s_%E2%80%98shocking_truth%E2%80%99_about_the_%E2%80%98occupy_crackdowns%E2%80%99_offers_anything_but_the_truth/; Corey Robin, "Why Naomi Wolf Got It Wrong," *Al Jazeera*, November 29, 2011, http://www.aljazeera.com/indepth/opinion/2011/11/20111129151234836584.html. Holland comes dangerously close to justifying police coordination as simply another example of "professionals" using national conference calls to go about their business, adding that "such communication is in no way an assault on local communities' autonomy."

64   Shawn Gaynor, "The cop group coordinating the Occupy crackdowns," *San Francisco Bay Guardian*, November 18,2011, http://www.sfbg.com/politics/2011/11/18/cop-group-coordinating-occupy-crackdowns.

65   PERF, "PERF Statement on 'Occupy' Protests," November 20, 2011, http://www.policeforum.org/news/detail.dot?id=2161738.

66   Mark Stout, "The Uproar Over PERF: Occupy Controlling the Information Environment," http://onwarandwords.wordpress.com/2011/11/21/the-uproar-over-perf-occupy-controlling-the-information-environment/.

67   We shouldn't let Wolf's tone divert attention from her fundamentally liberal outlook. Recall, for example, when Occupy Wall Street protesters forcibly shut down a TV set for "Law & Order" that simulated an Occupy encampment, Wolf attacked the action on her Facebook page as "fascism of the left" for censoring "free speech." Post on December 9, 2011, http://www.facebook.com/naomi.wolf.author/posts/303181333048843 .

68   Kristian Williams, personal communication, February 2011.

69   Williams, "The Other Side of the COIN," 108.

70   Williams, "The Other Side of the COIN," 108.

PART FOUR

INFORMATION DOMINANCE

GEOGRAPHY, COUNTERINSURGENCY, AND THE "G-BOMB":
The Case of *México Indígena*

GEOFFREY BOYCE AND CONOR CASH

In 2006 A TEAM OF GEOGRAPHERS FROM THE UNIVERSITY OF KANSAS BEGAN a "participatory" mapping project with Zapotec communities in the Sierra Juarez of Oaxaca, Mexico. The research team, led by Dr. Peter Herlihy, pitched the project to the subject communities as a way to identify and demarcate traditional land use and tenure in order to defend their territories against outside speculation. Yet unbeknownst to these participants, the project, *México Indígena*, was in fact designed to produce digital maps of the "cultural landscape, or human terrain" of Mexico's indigenous peoples.[1] *México Indígena* was the pilot for a research program dubbed the "Bowman Expeditions," sponsored by the U.S. Foreign Military Studies Office (FMSO) at Ft. Leavenworth, Kansas—whose explicit purpose is to gather intelligence on emerging and asymmetric threats to the United States for the purpose of preparing for conflict and maintaining the "peace."

The broader objectives of this research program, overseen by the American Geographical Society (AGS), were to augment U.S. intelligence and counterinsurgency efforts through the generation of diffuse geo-spatial intelligence. As stated in its executive summary, *México Indígena* represented: "the initial step in a much larger concept of reviving a tradition of research by university

scholars providing 'open-source intelligence' on different parts of the world…
[in light of] the unfortunate realization that the United States is now perceived
as a mighty global power crippled by its own ignorance and arrogance about
its dealings with its vast global domain." The document goes on to state:

> Indigenous regions in Mexico, like in so many parts of Latin
> America and around the world, are where rebellions are foment-
> ed, where drugs are produced, where resource pirates operate,
> and where conditions of poverty and despair drive up the high-
> est rates of our migration. Few would disagree that as we move
> into the 21st century, indigenous populations are among the
> most important social actors in struggles of the future of Latin
> American democracies.[2]

In January 2009, a collection of Oaxacan activists, organizers, and residents of the affected community of San Miguel Tiltepec publicly denounced
México Indígena for its military connections and demanded accountability
from those involved and from their colleagues at U.S. universities. This move
has, ever since, generated significant—if muted—controversy within the discipline of geography. The issues involved in this case have, however, often
been treated as exceptional—whether as an issue of individual ethical violations, or as politically dangerous collaboration between scholars and the U.S.
military.[3] In this chapter we will discuss *México Indígena* in greater detail,
and suggest that the actions taken and the statements made by the parties
involved in this scandal help to clarify not only the role of "social science research" in facilitating violence against individuals and communities, but also
the importance of professional identities in shaping the trajectory of research
and its instrumental and political value.

We are living in an era during which the social guarantees of the welfare
state are being openly abandoned and replaced with policies whose logics rest
expressly upon the twin pillars of militarism and "securitization," pillars that
can broadly be understood to operate within a framework of counterinsurgency. Rabid austerity within North American public research institutions, along
with shifts in federal funding priorities toward military and homeland security interests, create significant pressure for academic labor to align with these
agendas. For these reasons, *México Indígena* is alarming and should provoke
reflection within and beyond the discipline of geography. We argue here for
alternative projects of knowledge production whose uses may escape the logics
of neoliberal militarism. We also suggest that *México Indígena* should not be
treated as exceptional, but instead must be understood in terms of institutional
imperatives that align academic labor toward the incorporation of its subjects
into the project of capitalist modernity.

GEO-SPATIAL KNOWLEDGE AND COUNTERINSURGENCY

CARTOGRAPHY IS ONE of the earliest state sciences, enabling and facilitating the administration of territory, centralized planning, and the deployment of military force. As post-colonial theorists like Anne Laura Stoler remind us, advances in cartographic technologies were central to facilitating European navigation and capture of the globe.[4] Geographer John Pickles likewise argues that, as a system for "counting and recording populations" and "defining, delimiting, and mapping space and nature," geo-spatial technologies promote "new practices that are not intrinsic to the new media, but are permitted and facilitated by them: technologies of the body, of the social, of the economy, by which bureaucratic, business, or military functions (and others) can be extended effectively across new territories with effects that previous technologies did not permit."[5]

In the context of the Cold War's "space race" for geovisual supremacy, computerized Geographic Information Sciences and Technologies (GIS&T) fundamentally redefined the nature of cartographic work, enabling the collection of potentially infinite datasets and their near-instantaneous territorial representation. These systems network human operators with electronic processors, advanced software and U.S. government satellites, and have found their way into an endless stream of military, scientific, and industrial applications—from identifying land-change patterns associated with climate variation, to managing resource extraction, to targeting missiles. However, even the most advanced cartographic technologies present an impartial, abstract, and functionally limited dataset. As GIS&T theorist Mike Goodchild points out, despite the panoptic fantasies of military planners— or the dystopian fears of their critics—surveillance technologies like satellites and robotic drones cannot penetrate the spatialities of everyday life, or identify military or security targets, without first having the knowledge that tells them *where* to look, and the analytic capability to intelligently sort the data they collect.[6] The world is not a transparent horizon: visibility is something that must be actively produced. The datasets assembled by a LANSAT 7 satellite, for example, represent informational mountains in which insurgents remain hidden; on its own, this information is useless. It requires interpretation, analysis, and verification, or what GIS scientists call "ground-truthing," to transform global and continuous datasets from "noise" into actionable intelligence.

The labor expended upon these data increasingly assumes colossal proportions. For example, the video produced by a single Predator drone currently requires 19 full-time analysts to process. As sensors become more complicated, the U.S. Marine Corps estimates that they may need as many as 2,000 full-time analysts to regularly process the data generated by a single drone team.[7] The routine use of unmanned aerial drones by the U.S. military in Iraq and Afghanistan; by the Central Intelligence Agency in Afghanistan, Pakistan and Yemen; and by the Department of Homeland Security along the U.S. borders with Mexico and Canada requires a growing cadre of personnel whose task it is to review, process, and share surveillance data—generating additional logistical and bureaucratic hurdles for the useful deployment and management of the technology and the information it produces.

Thus, it is worth noting that by many of the professed rationales of the U.S. government, these surveillance technologies are of modest utility and can do little to halt the actions of a Timothy McVeigh or an Al Qaeda cell. What they *do* facilitate is cooperation between state bureaucracies and military, paramilitary, and extra-military actors by providing information, force, and cover of law to low-intensity campaigns of violence and harassment against targeted communities for the purposes of advancing U.S. corporate and strategic interests.

Writing in 2005, AGS president Jerome Dobson put the issue as follows: "It's one thing to know where each bomb will fall, and GPS can tell you that. It's quite another to know where the people are, and that requires a GIS."[8] As Dobson has argued, the ability to map and understand the human terrain has been one of the most vexing challenges for colonial counterinsurgency and governmentality throughout the era of Anglo-European hegemony, and one that geographers are uniquely positioned to realize.

In its campaigns against the resolute Afghan and Iraqi insurgencies, the U.S. military has sought more and better geo-spatial knowledge through the implementation of Human Terrain Mapping Systems (HTMS). The military's appeals for assistance were met with enthusiastic support from many academic geographers. Dobson specifically has argued that geography could become positioned as a discipline just as integral to the War on Terror as physics was to the Cold War in the aftermath of the atom bomb—a development that he describes as the advent of the era of the "G-bomb."[9]

MÉXICO INDÍGENA AND ITS RECEPTION IN GEOGRAPHY

ALTHOUGH THE ARCHITECTS of *México Indígena* have acknowledged that their program was funded by the Pentagon, both Herlihy and Dobson deny that military planners had any control over the research process, its design, or its outcomes. Yet the location of the program in the Sierra Juarez is suspicious at best.

In 2006 the state of Oaxaca became the home of one of the largest popular insurrections in Mexico since the 1910 revolution. During the uprising, which lasted for more than six months, broad cross-sectors of Oaxacan society joined together to try to force the removal of then-governor Ulises Ruiz Ortiz and popular assemblies assumed control over many of the functions of state and municipal government. In the ensuing repression, 27 participants were assassinated, dozens disappeared, and hundreds imprisoned.[10] It was in the context of this unrest that the architects of *México Indígena* decided to move their operations from the Mexican state of San Luís Potosí to the Sierra Juarez of Oaxaca.

On their website, the architects of *México Indígena* explicitly connect their work to the uprising, stating:

> Since the tumultuous period of political unrest in the summer and fall of 2006, Oaxaca has been in the news as a region where long-standing grievances among many indigenous communities are meshing with other movements in complex ways. Our work will illuminate neglected but important facets of these movements.[11]

Indigenous and rural communities in Oaxaca have been among the most reticent toward the federal government's PROCEDE land reform program, a program that divides communal lands into private allotments that can then be marketized. The *México Indígena* project was designed to study Zapotec communities' resistance to this program, and results were reported directly to the Foreign Military Studies Office on a monthly basis. As they state in their 2006 *Methodological Approaches Report of México Indígena*: "The participatory mapping, or PM, methodology rests on the philosophy that local populations have some of the best and most detailed knowledge of their surrounding lands and resources and that can be collected and interpreted geographically."[12]

In defense of the project, Herlihy has argued that it was intended to benefit subject communities, stating: "Geographical intelligence is needed for peace and prosperity just like it is needed for war and destruction."[13] Yet the kind of peace and prosperity that Herlihy has in mind is revealed through the formative involvement of the U.S. military, Mexican intelligence, and military contractor Radiance Technologies (who served as a fiduciary sponsor), as well as the support of the Smart-port corporation, a Kansas City–based trade company who touted the utility of the project's data for expanding Mexico's transportation infrastructure.

Despite Herlihy's and Dobson's purported transparency about their military connections, the communities in question have denied that these were ever revealed to them, and claim they would not have agreed to participate in the research had they known. In January 2009, local community leaders and NGOs held a press conference following the revelation of the funding sources and institutional connections of the research project. At this news conference, the subject communities issued a list of demands to Herlihy et al. They specifically demanded that all maps produced through the research be returned to the communities, and any unreturned copies be destroyed; and, that the researchers in question apologize for their actions; and that these researchers be held accountable by other geographers and academic colleagues in the United States.[14]

In March 2009 several dozen scholars wrote an open letter to the Association of American Geographers (the discipline's largest professional association) asking for two things: 1) that the organization initiate an investigation into the research project, and 2) that there be a serious, formal, and binding review of a host of issues that the controversy raised.[15] These requests were repeated by the AAG's Indigenous Peoples Specialty Group, who additionally asked the University of Kansas to open an ethics probe.[16]

But the AAG deferred, claiming it lacked the authority to investigate its members' research conduct. Although the AAG convened a committee to revisit the organization's professional ethics statement, adding language on indigenous peoples and geo-spatial technologies, this review avoided altogether the question of military funding and made explicit its status as a nonbinding, advisory document.

The AAG's response has done little to quell the controversy that *México Indígena* stirred. Responding to criticism, AAG president John Agnew wrote in a 2010 editorial:

> Ethics is about people making choices on the basis of weighing the possible consequences for themselves and others of what they do. By definition, ethics cannot be mandated. As a membership organization, the AAG can help make clear what some of the dilemmas will be for those of its members engaged in certain activities. It cannot tell people what they can and cannot do, particularly when the specific projects at issue are organized and funded through a completely different organization. The day the AAG organizes "show trials" will be the day I resign my membership.[17]

This concluding sentence presents explicit red-baiting of *México Indígena* critics, comparing their efforts to pursue intellectual accountability with a Stalinist purge.

The framing of ethics in Agnew's statement is also worth unpacking. Like the concept of ethics embodied in the policies of bureaucratic structures like Institutional Review Boards, ethics here are framed as a safeguard against individual misconduct, without consideration of the larger political context within which research transpires, and without a community or collective understanding of vulnerability, agency, or consent.[18] Within this equation, our conduct and its effects in the world are privatized: only individuals (not institutions) may be held accountable for their choices and their actions, and remedies are likewise individual.[19] Such a conception of ethics views violations as a breach of an implicit contract that would otherwise protect the right of Anglo-American scholars to stalk the world collecting knowledge at will—just as the state, via PROCEDE, would commodify the land to which communities are rooted, confining buyer and seller only through enforcement of the norms of the "free" market.

The above logic detaches ethics from politics, rendering the latter mute. While there is certainly a philosophical distinction to be made between these two domains, as soon as we recognize our responsibility to others—and that this responsibility is also collective—we can no longer defer on the question of politics, or of political action. This is not to suggest that such questions can or should be arbitrated in advance. What is needed is a collective scrutiny of issues, policies, and actions, and for this scrutiny to take place within the context of an open, public debate. But that is precisely what the AAG, and professional geographers more broadly, have resisted doing.

The AAG and its president John Agnew have repeatedly argued that they have neither the power nor the capacity to investigate individual researchers' ethics violations—a claim that may, on its face, be valid. But rather than quelling further controversy, this argument ought to inflame it. After all, Agnew's argument enables a collective withdrawal from accountability or responsibility, an austere sanctioning of the *status quo* and a refusal of reflexivity.

Regardless of individual intention, this evacuation of politics enables the sanctimonious and hypocritical attitude of those within the AAG who would continue to advocate "political neutrality." In practice, such neutrality serves to further align research endeavors with U.S. national security interests, rendering claims about the "protection of human subjects" flaccid. Agnew himself has echoed Dobson in arguing for the utility of geographic research to U.S. strategic and geopolitical interests—despite a career spent denouncing the violence by which such interests are often projected.[20] In an era of university budget cuts, with federal funding priorities increasingly revolving around security and military concerns, such positioning by an AAG president is understandable, although by no means any less alarming. More than anything else, we believe that this conjunction should force those involved in academic work to take stock of our professions and assess our opportunities for collective intervention and for alternative orientations to knowledge production.

DEFUSING THE "G-BOMB" AND CHARTING NEW GROUND: A (PROVISIONAL) CONCLUSION

As MENTIONED ABOVE, *México Indígena* was merely a pilot for a larger, on-going program unabashedly named in honor of Isaiah Bowman, an early -twentieth-century geographer who served as an architect of post-WWII U.S. geopolitical hegemony.[21] In 2005 Dobson solicited $125 million from the FMSO to fund the "Bowman Expeditions," which would resurrect "the early-twentieth-century notion of open-access geographical intelligence, when the U.S. government worked closely with geographers to better understand the world."[22] In response to criticism of the project, Dobson wrote:

> [t]he greatest shortfall in foreign intelligence facing the nation is precisely the kind of understanding that geographers gain through field experience, and there's no reason that it has to be classified information. The best and cheapest way the government could get most of this intelligence would be to fund AGS to run a foreign fieldwork grant program covering every nation on earth.[23]

Elsewhere, Dobson has stated: "My whole rationale for Bowman Expeditions is based on my firm belief that geographic ignorance is the principal cause of the blunders that have characterized American foreign policy since the end of World War II. America abandoned geography after World War II and hasn't won a war since."[24]

The intelligence gathering performed by *México Indígena* researchers is in keeping with the Pentagon's Human Terrain Mapping System, in which the social relationships and human intentions that are seemingly imperceptible to military administrators are assessed by social scientists working alongside soldiers and military advisers. HTMS is seen as especially important for supporting "those operations aimed at stabilizing an area of operations in the aftermath of major combat"[25]—an effort that comprises the largest element of contemporary U.S. military operations. Touted as a bold new initiative by FMSO mouthpieces, in reality HTMS and similar intelligence programs have long existed under various guises; they are essentially a sanitized reboot of the CIA's Vietnam-era Operation Phoenix, under which approximately 87,000 Viet Cong "party cadre" were imprisoned, tortured, or killed.[26]

At the Foreign Military Studies Office, Dobson has been granted a sympathetic audience, briefing General David Petraeus himself on at least one occasion. Since 2006, the FMSO has agreed to fund an expansion of the Bowman Expeditions to at least eight other countries, including: Colombia, Haiti, Honduras, the Dominican Republic, Trinidad and Tobago, Jordan, and Kazakhstan.[27] Despite vocal criticism from a small minority within the

Association of American Geographers, there has been little objection or op-position to this development within the discipline at large. Although a hand-ful of sessions at the 2010 annual meeting of the AAG provided a forum to discuss the *México Indígena* controversy, the only organized group to stake out a strong position on the matter has been the Indigenous Peoples Specialty Group, whose requests for accountability have been largely ignored by the AAG. So much for "collegiality."

The architects of *México Indígena* have publicly argued that "much of the human terrain concept, however controversial, sits at the core of our disci-pline."[28] In this vein, Dobson's argument concerning the contribution geog-raphers might make to the advancement of U.S. geo-strategic interests de-serves to be stressed and expanded beyond a narrow focus on contemporary cases of academic militarism.

As would be obvious to any student of Michel Foucault or of post-colo-nialism, there can be no "innocent" production of knowledge. From their very beginning the disciplines have been oriented toward objectifying the world, policing knowledge, and subjecting people, things, and phenomena to instrumental manipulation. Visibility, intelligibility, and manipulabil-ity are central objectives of the sciences—social as well as physical. That the discipline of geography emerged alongside the entrenchment of capitalism, European hegemony, and the nation-state system is no coincidence[29]; nor should it be seen as such that much university research remains tethered to the interests of the state and private capital. Within the humanities and criti-cal social sciences, it can be attractive to believe that universities represent a bastion of independent thought and inquiry—but often this holds true only in principle.

Because of the structural imperatives associated with our work, we believe that those of us who operate in the academy and maintain emancipatory poli-tics must confront an intractable problem: how are we to approach research and intellectual labor given that the kind of knowledge we produce tends to be more useful to state actors than to the movements we might support po-litically? Recognizing that the relationships between counterinsurgency and academic knowledge, rather than novel or exceptional, cut to the heart of the institutions within which we work, we must find ways to avoid, at once: a cynicism that would normalize collaboration with the military; naïve satis-faction with calls for "professional ethics"; and, hopelessness at the prospect of radical change. This trinity of alienated positions is the *status quo* in the university, and will only produce more of the same.

As Grace Lee Boggs has written: "We need to recognize that the aptitudes and attitudes of people with BAs, BSs, MBAs and PhDs bear a lot of the responsibility for our planetary and social problems."[30] As heirs to a colo-nial tradition, we have much to account for, and confronting even the most obvious academic violence (of the kind that *México Indígena* exemplifies) will remain difficult until we have fully begun to do so. In the meantime, it might be wise to view research as a weapon. Whenever it is being performed or proposed, we should say to ourselves and to our colleagues: "Be careful where you point that thing."

There certainly exist myriad forms of knowledge production that model an emancipatory alternative, and serve to undermine counterinsurgency and the forced imposition of neoliberal policy. A review of such alternatives is beyond the scope of this chapter. But it is worth mentioning, by way of example, that it was activists involved with the English-language Oaxacan news website *El Enemigo Común* who first looked into and uncovered evidence of U.S. military sponsorship for the *México Indígena* project. Their efforts allowed for a direct conduit of communication between the targeted communities in the Sierra Juarez and scholars and activists in the United States. The dissemination of technologies like the internet provide powerful new tools for horizontal information-sharing and collaborative work among geographically disparate groups. We must also recognize, however, that the power of these tools is precisely their popular accessibility, and abandon any claim to unique privilege in our capacity to perform this work.

It is nice to think that we can turn scholarly research, writing, and teaching toward emancipatory ends, but the everyday pressures of the university work-regime run decidedly counter to such efforts. The United States continues investing massive energy and resources in the projection of geopolitical order, and academic scholarship plays a foundational role in this effort. According to anthropologist Catherine Lutz, 25% of all scientists and engineers in the United States work on military projects,[31] and given the secret federal Black Budget, the real figure is almost certainly higher.

We have a responsibility to confront this militarization, even as we recognize that it lies at the origins of our disciplines. Models like the Network of Concerned Anthropologists and the Union of Concerned Scientists provide one set of examples by which collective pressure has been mobilized to challenge professional institutions and articulate alternative political and ethical imperatives. And those of us who happen to work in the academy are uniquely positioned to advance this work. In this period of escalating crisis, austerity, and U.S. military occupation, the most important ethical problem we face is also an expressly political one: that is, to clearly demarcate our commitments, whether to the architects of poverty and mass destruction, or to grassroots peoples around the world struggling for peace, dignity, and justice.[32]

In the Sierra Juarez of Oaxaca the experience of predatory geo-piracy continues to generate organized resistance among the affected communities. In a regional assembly held on July 24, 2011 in San Juan Yagila (one of the principle communities mapped by *México Indígena*), delegates from affected communities issued the "Xidza Declaration Regarding Geo-Piracy," which creates mechanisms for collective decision-making over communal resources and over outside projects proposed for their communities.[33] Through such mechanisms, these communities continue to defend their territory and autonomy. Such organizing should also serve as a reminder that despite technological capability, lack of scruples, and ability to mobilize violence, the architects of U.S. geopolitical hegemony do not always have the last word.

The science, technology, and knowledge in the hands of the powerful continues to develop on its dystopian trajectory. But viewed from another angle, the very scale and magnitude of this effort points to the uncertainty of its success, and suggests just how difficult deciphering the world continues to be for those who would dominate and control it. The fact that alternatives like the 2006 Oaxaca commune, and the sustained struggle for indigenous autonomy throughout the Americas, proliferate in the face of the violence that can be (and often is) mobilized against them, is cause for both hope for the future and skepticism of the hubris that defines intellectual modernity.[34]

NOTES

1   Peter Herlihy, et al. "A Digital Geography of Indigenous Mexico: Prototype for the American Geographical Society's Bowman Expeditions," *Geographical Review* 98, no. 3 (2008): 395–415

2   The *México Indígena* executive summary can be accessed at: http://web.ku.edu/~mexind/ sections%201%20and%202.pdf

3   For further discussion, see: Joe Bryan, "Force multipliers: Geography, militarism, and the Bowman Expeditions," *Political Geography* 29 (2010): 414–16.

4   Anne Laura Stoler, *Along the Archival Grain: Epistemic Anxieties and Colonial Common Sense* (Princeton: Princeton University Press, 2010).

5   John Pickles, "Representations in an Electronic Age: Geography, GIS, and Democracy," in *Ground Truths: The Social Implications of Geographic Information Systems*, ed. John Pickles (New York: The Guilford Press, 1994). See also: Joel Wainwright and Joe Bryan, "Cartography, territory, property: postcolonial reflections on indigenous counter-mapping in Nicaragua and Belize," *Cultural Geographies* 16 (2009):153–78.

6   Nadine Schuurman and Michael Goodchild, "An interview with Michael Goodchild," *Environment and Planning D-Society & Space* 27 (2009): 573–580.

7   Eli Lake, "So much video, so few analysts: Drone footage overwhelming; Pentagon looking for better ways to sift through data," *The Washington Times,* November 10, 2010.

8   Jerome Dobson, "The Dawning of the G-bomb," *Directions Magazine: All Things Location* (2005)   http://www.directionsmag.com/articles/the-dawning-of-the-g-bomb/123453 (accessed April 5, 2011).

9   Ibid.

10   Gustavo Esteva, "The Asamblea Popular de los Pueblos de Oaxaca—A chronicle of radical democracy," *Latin American Perspectives* 34 (2007): 129–44.

11   México Indígena, *Oaxaca Study Area*, México Indígena website, http://web. ku.edu/~mexind/oaxaca_study_area.htm (accessed April 6, 2011).

12   Peter H. Herlihy, Derek A Smith, John H. Kelly, and Jerome E. Dobson, (extract) *México Indígena: Mexican Open-Source Geographic Information Systems (GIS) Project Final Report, Year One*, http://web.ku.edu/~mexind/section%203.pdf (accessed April 6, 2011).

13   Jessica Wicks, "Student activists seek open talks of government funding: Group concerned about intentions of Department of Defense money," *The Daily Kansan* March 25, 2008 http://www.kansan.com/news/2008/mar/25/student_activists_seek_open_discussion_government_/ (accessed April 3, 2011).

14   The full text of the communiqué from the community of San Miguel Tiltepec can be accessed at http://academic.evergreen.edu/g/grossmaz/Position%20of%20San%20 Miguel%20Tiltepec.doc

15   http://academic.evergreen.edu/g/grossmaz/HerlihyLetterSign.pdf

16   http://academic.evergreen.edu/g/grossmaz/IPSGletterAAGboard.pdf

17   John Agnew, "Ethics or militarism? The role of the AAG in what was originally a dispute over informed consent," *Political Geography* 29 (2010): 422–23.

18   See: Melquiades Cruz, "A living space: The relationship between land and property in the community," *Political Geography* 29 (2010): 420–21.

19   There are numerous other problems with Agnew's conception of ethics: 1) It is entirely consequentialist, meaning there are no rules that cannot be over-ridden if the results are good enough; 2) It's entirely voluntarist, e.g. "ethics cannot be mandated"; this perspective makes all scruples super-erogatory (i.e., unnecessary), and amounts to a declaration that accountability is impossible (not for practical reasons, but as a matter of principle); 3) It is also plainly false, since other professions do have enforceable ethical standards.

20   Thomas Gillespie and John Agnew, "Finding Osama bin Laden: an Application of Biogeographic Theories and Satellite Imagery," *MIT International Review*, February 17, 2009.

21   See Neil Smith, *American Empire: Roosevelt's Geographer and the Prelude to Globalization* (Berkeley: University of California Press, 2003).

22   Herlihy et al., (2008) above.

23   Quoted in Cyril Mychalejko and Ramor Ryan, "U.S. Military Funded Mapping Project in Oaxaca: Geographers used to gather intelligence?" *Z Magazine* April 2009.

24   Ibid.

25   Jacob Kipp, et al. "The Human Terrain System: A CORDS for the 21st Century," *Military Review* September–October 2006.

26   Dale Andrade and James Willbanks, "CORDS/Phoenix: Counterinsurgency lessons from Vietnam for the future," *Military Review* March–April 2006.

27   For a list and discussion of contemporary American Geographical Society Bowman Expeditions, see the AGS website: http://www.amergeog.org/bowman-expeditions.htm.

28   Herlihy et al. (2008) above.

29 See Denis Cosgrove, "Prospect, Perspective and the Evolution of the Landscape Idea," *Transactions of the Institute of British Geographers* 10, 1985: 45–62.

30 Grace Lee Boggs, with Scott Kurashige, *The Next American Revolution: Sustainable Activism for the Twenty-First Century* (Berkeley: University of California Press, 2011): 149.

31 Catherine Lutz, "The Military Normal," in *The Counter-Counterinsurgency Manual: or, Notes on Demilitarizing American Society*, ed. Network of Concerned Anthropologists (Chicago: Prickly Paradigm Press, 2009).

32 Lest this comment be taken for vacuous grandstanding, we wish to make clear our belief that this is not a question that can be settled in the abstract, and we would welcome scrutiny of our own work.

33 Oscar Valdivieso, "U.S. army's geo-piracy in Oaxacan communities condemned," *El Enemigo Común* July 27, 2011 http://elenemigocomun.net/2011/07/u-s-army-geo-piracy-condemned/#more-9274 (accessed July 31, 2011).

34 For more information, scholarly debate, and original documents related to the *México Indígena* controversy, visit http://academic.evergreen.edu/g/grossmaz/bowman.html and http://geographyandethics.wordpress.com/.

TARGETING TRANSLATION:
U.S. Counterinsurgency and the Politics of Language

VICENTE L. RAFAEL[1]

WEAPONIZING LANGUAGE

ON JANUARY 2, 2011, *THE WASHINGTON POST* REPORTED THAT THE UNITED States Air Force had unveiled its "new revolutionary surveillance system," calling it, with no hint of irony, the "Gorgon Stare."[2] It consists of a fleet of drone airplanes remotely piloted from the USA, each mounted with nine video cameras at a cost of $17.5 million per drone. Flying continuously over much of the border between Afghanistan and Pakistan, the camera-laden drones are designed to stream high-resolution images of every movement on the ground in real time to soldiers armed with computer tablets the size of an iPad. Video data are stored for future viewing on servers kept in shipping containers somewhere in Iowa. The Air Force has also hired private contractors with backgrounds in televising football games for ESPN and producing reality TV shows to organize the retrieval and replay of images so that "analysts can study them to determine, for instance, who planted the improvised bomb or what the patterns of life in a village are." Touting this immense visual power, an Air Force officer exults, "Gorgon Stare will be looking at a whole city, so that there will be no way for the adversary to know what we're looking at, and we can see everything."[3]

As with the figure of Medusa, Gorgon Stare sees but cannot be looked at. It refuses reciprocity, assuming a position that is as transcendent as it is all-knowing. Thanks to aerial surveillance refined and expanded by digital technologies, the Air Force can claim to monopolize vision itself. It transforms seeing into a weapon targeting anything below. But as the rest of the newspaper article points out, the weaponization of vision is mired in certain complications. The all-seeing Gorgon Stare invariably generates "oceans of information" that cannot be fully processed, overwhelming attempts at mining them for actionable intelligence. Assuming the camera's perspective, soldiers "see everything"—and so see too much. Their vision is checked by the deluge of data. Paralyzed, they suffer the effects of staring out of, only to stare into, the Gorgon's eyes.[4]

As it turns out, the very power of this Air Force Medusa is also its liability. To be effective, high-tech aerial surveillance requires supplemental low-tech means. As another official put it, the video-equipped drones must still rely on "eyewitness reports and boots on the ground." The latter provide views from below by way of face-to-face contacts with the targeted population and a grasp of "local knowledge." "Watching an entire city," another official concedes, "means nothing unless you can put a context to it."[5] To work effectively, the panoptic eye requires the aid of partial vision, fleeting glances and periodic blindness. The latter constitute the crucial materials for the weaponization of seeing. It is precisely the conversion of the local, the particular, and the everyday into weapons of war and pacification that informs the strategic thrust of contemporary U.S. counterinsurgency.

Where conventional warfare has concentrated on the total destruction and unconditional submission of the enemy, counterinsurgency—recognizing the shifting lines between insurgent fighter and civilian population—focuses primarily on "protecting populations."[6] Conventional military doctrine has long regarded combat as the primary role of the soldier who is trained, as one Army officer put it, "to be the wrath of God, able to bring death and destruction anywhere at any time."[7] By contrast, the doctrine of counterinsurgency recasts warfighting in political terms, as a means not only to "clear" the land of insurgents, but to "hold" the population and "build" new institutions to "save" the people from future revolutionary "contaminations." Victory in the context of counterinsurgent warfare is measured not by the number of enemies vanquished but by the increase in trust and sympathy among native peoples that would wean them away from the insurgents' influence.

Counterinsurgency theorists thus argue for a kind of "sociological mission" whereby the invasion and occupation of a country would lead not only to the provision of basic needs such as "food, water, shelter, health care and a means of living," but would also "ensure freedom of worship, access to education, equal rights for women." Indeed, counterinsurgent warfare would bring nothing less than the conversion of the population to such "universal values" as "mercy, restraint, proportional force and just war," providing a "more holistic form of human security" that would include "economic, social, civil and political rights."[8] In countering the "barbarism" of insurgents, American counterinsurgency would "not just dominate land operations but... change entire societies."[9] Such changes would include not only the institutionalization of human rights but also an "environment where business can thrive" and where "providing security" promises to create a "positive business environment... to drive the economy."[10] Thus would counterinsurgency channel popular energies into building a new civil society as the basis of a stable nation-state predisposed to ally itself with the United States.

Just as Hapsburg Spain sought to conquer the Americas and the Pacific through the conversion of native peoples to Catholicism in the wake of the Reformation, so the U.S. empire has sought to dominate the world by seeking to convert its peoples into neoliberal forms of governance in the wake of the attacks of 9/11. Conversion and counterinsurgency go together, both seeking to rid the world of insurgents, religious as well as political, and establishing in their wake a new order of civic life ordered around the broad concerns of the empire. And since both entail the daily "colonization of the life world" of both occupiers and occupied, they have neither temporal limits nor fixed spatial boundaries. Like the project of imperial conversion, counterinsurgency is dedicated to "secur[ing] 'ungoverned spaces' around the globe." Led by the United States, regarded by its military and political leaders as "the indispensable nation," such a mission enjoins American allies with the call for planetary policing and permanent war.[11]

Much has been written about the vicissitudes of counterinsurgency as one of the strategies complementing counter-terrorism in the U.S. occupation of Iraq and Afghanistan. I do not mean to retrace this history nor comment on its historiography as many others already have.[12] Instead, I want to focus on something I alluded to earlier: counterinsurgency as both the process and effect of a certain conversion, which is to say, translation of things into weapons. Given its redemptive ambitions of "saving" native peoples, I'm particularly interested in counterinsurgency's attempts to "weaponize" and "target" one of the most common things in their lives, indeed the very thing that lends to their lives a sense of commonality: their languages.

But we might pause to ask: what exactly does it mean to turn something like language into a weapon? As Deleuze and Guattari have pointed out, there is a close affinity between tools and weapons in that the latter finds its origins in the former.[13] Weapons are tools, but with a difference. Tools once weaponized take on a ballistic quality. They necessarily become projectiles and accumulate speed once they are wielded. That is, they are able to traverse a vector to hit a target, smoothing out spatial distance and overcoming temporal delay. The efficiency and potency of a weapon is thus directly related to its capacity to minimize friction and noise, thereby minimizing the time of its arrival and maximizing the velocity of its trajectory. Weaponization in this sense entails not only the translation, as it were, of one thing into another; it also affects the transformation of the space and time of its deployment, collapsing both to connect with its target.

This brings us to another aspect of weaponization: targeting. Put simply, weapons presuppose targets.[14] Without the latter, there would be no reason for the existence of the former. We could even go so far as to say that targeting, the end of weaponization, is also its condition of possibility. Targets and weapons belong together so that each can become the other: weapons can be targeted and targets refashioned to serve as shields (hence, the root word of "target" in the Greek *targa*, shield) for deflecting the ballistic power of weapons, turning them against themselves as in martial arts. But this also means that weapons can target themselves, backfiring against their users. They can injure and destroy not only others but also those who deploy them. There is thus an element of instability at the basis of weaponization. Reversing their trajectory, they can double back on themselves. Targeting and targeted, weapons are media for expressing in ways both swift and decisive the intentions of their users. However, they can also be an end in themselves, upending in ways both unanticipated and yet inevitable for the end of their user. To weaponize something in view of hitting a target is thus to open oneself up to the risk of being targeted.

In matters of counterinsurgency, talk of weaponization and targeting, with all its attendant seductions and dangers, pops up everywhere. It is particularly striking where the question of the languages and cultures of enemies and occupied populations are concerned. Such talk crystallizes particularly around one of the most important strategic imperatives of counterinsurgency: translation. For example, starting around 2007, the Fort Lewis Foreign Language Training Center near Tacoma, Washington began conducting ten-month courses in Arabic language and culture for members of the Stryker Brigade Combat Team deploying, at least until 2009, to Iraq. The aim of the program was to produce so-called "Language Enabled Soldiers" (or LES) among select members of the brigade.[15] The very term suggests that Arabic is regarded as a kind of special equipment. Knowledge of Arabic, however perfunctory, would set apart some soldiers from their largely monolingual colleagues, endowing them with a capacity to do what others could not. The program itself is consistent with the plans laid out by the Department of Defense's *Defense Language Transformation Roadmap* to develop a "surge capability to rapidly expand language capabilities on short notice." Acknowledging that "language skill and regional expertise" were essential "war fighting skills," the Department of Defense has conceptualized translation as part of what it calls a "critical weapons system."[16]

It is within the context of linguistic militarization that we can understand the training that goes into the making of a Language Enabled Soldier. According to an article written by one of the commanders of the program, the learning of Arabic is set up to be "theater-specific." It involves, for example, practicing Arabic commands in parking lots for regulating traffic through checkpoints, ordering cars to stop and searching their occupants. Soldiers are taught to eavesdrop during routine patrols or while standing guard over prisoners. They also familiarize themselves with "Arabic children's games so they can interact with children… [since] they have often proven to be a sound source of information…. Parents who see soldiers interacting with their children in a benign fashion might be more forthcoming."[17] Armed with rudimentary Arabic, or Pashto, or Dari, as the case might be, the Language Enabled Soldiers are thought capable of establishing rapport with children and their parents, turning them into conduits for intelligence. Speaking the language of the native other, American soldiers can thus target anyone. In this way, they are seen as ideal substitutes for native interpreters. As one of the commanders of the Stryker Brigade pointedly observed,

> We would never contract civilians to man a platoon's machine guns, so why rely on them [native interpreters] for language and culture skills? If we buy into the idea that our nation is at war with Islamic totalitarian terrorists, and culture and language are [a] weapons system important to victory, training soldiers to operate this weapon… is as important to defeating today's enemy as anyone trained to handle critical combat equipment…. [For this reason], the Language Enabled Soldier is as essential as any other part of the intelligence warfighting function.[18]

There are a number of powerful fantasies at work in these remarks. In a profoundly monolingual military, language as such is never thought about except as a marker of foreignness. Seizing hold of the enemy's language is seen as crucial to victory. Translation as the weaponizaton of language, however, is always in danger of falling into the wrong hands, as in the scenario of civilians operating machine guns. If language is to become a weapon, its use must be closely controlled and ideally limited to those with proper training—in this case, the Language Enabled Soldier.

However, as Mary Louise Pratt has shown, fantasies about the military mobilization of translation constantly run aground on the realities of language learning.[19] For one thing, learning a foreign language, especially one as difficult as Arabic, Dari, or Pashto, takes a very long time, far longer than the time of invasions and occupations whose temporal horizons usually contract from one national election to another. Even if the U.S. were to devote considerable resources to producing Arabic-speaking soldiers—whose language skills would at best be elementary—it would find it impossible to transfer these language skills from one theater of conflict to another. It would also be highly impractical for fighters to simultaneously learn the languages of Afghanistan, Pakistan, Yemen, Sudan, Iran, and other areas the U.S. may contemplate invading in search of "Islamic totalitarian terrorists." Designed to be a weapon, the Language Enabled Solider thus becomes obsolete even as he or she is being trained. As one of the readers of a military blog noted, "The Intel community is going to be in so much trouble when they find out that Arabic isn't spoken in Afghanistan."[20] Compounding this strategic dilemma is the fact that the Department of Defense's budget for language training as of 2009 is a relatively meager $181 million, which is less than the price of one F-35 fighter plane.[21]

MECHANIZING TRANSLATION

How THEN DOES the U.S. military respond to the temporal delay and tactical limits of translation? One way has been to turn to computer technologies in order to develop automatic translation systems. Unlike the unavoidably embodied and socially contingent figure of the interpreter, automatic translation devices are thought to be dispassionate and highly manipulable instruments designed to fully comply with the intentions of their users. Imagined by both the military and engineers to have capacities that can outstrip and supersede the cultural difference and divided loyalties of human interpreters, machine translation tends to be idealized as sheer media in the Aristotelian sense of a diaphanous membrane or transparent skin that allows for the frictionless transmission of information vital to victory. They thus come to materialize not so much the perfect weaponization of language as the promise of its future perfectibility.

Compared to the U.S. military's impressive advances in the development of vast surveillance systems and weapons of mass destruction, the deployment of automatic translation systems has been modest in scale though no less ambitious in its goals. Its origins can be traced back to the development of computer systems to gather and translate intelligence after World War II. American and British success in the field of cryptoanalysis—the practice of breaking German and Japanese coded messages during the war—guided the early development of machine translation. Cryptoanalysis regards foreign languages as though they were secret codes whose surfaces can be broken to bring forth hidden messages in the form of statistically arranged patterns. Such mathematical patterns are believed to be evidence of "linguistic universals" supposedly buried in all languages. From the perspective of cryptology, Russian or Mandarin are no more than the instantiation of a universal language or *lingua franca* that could be deciphered and then recoded into English. Computers, along with surveillance systems ranging from satellites to unmanned planes, promised to speed up this process of decipherment by mechanizing translation in ways that would allow for the unlimited accumulation and efficient analysis of information from all corners of the globe. Such promises, however, have never materialized. Mechanical translation projects have developed unevenly from the 1950s, and efforts to arrive at linguistic universals have largely failed along with attempts to capture and crack, as it were, the underlying "code" of natural languages.[22]

Nonetheless, the military's attempts to find technological solutions to the task of translation continues, especially given the counterinsurgent imperative to "protect the population" and work through local cultures. Current research and development efforts around automatic translation devices have been funded and coordinated by the Defense Advanced Research Projects Agency, or DARPA. In 2002, DARPA began a number of projects to deal with the problems of cross-cultural communication in occupied territories. Among these is the Babylon Program. According to the DARPA website,

> The goal of the Babylon Program is to develop rapid, two-way, natural language speech translation interfaces and platforms for the warfighter for use in field environments for force protection, refugee processing and medical triage. Babylon will focus on overcoming the many technical and engineering challenges limiting current multilingual translation technology to enable future full-domain, unconstrained dialog translation in multiple environments.... The Babylon program will [provide] "RMS" or Rapid Multilingual Support [and] focus on low-population, high-terrorist risk languages....[23]

This description has the great virtue of laying out the precise terms for the military mobilization of translation. From Babylon's perspective, the full weaponization of translation entails its technical refashioning into an "interface" and a "platform" from which to launch English and convert it into languages needed to capture targeted audiences. Language here is imagined to be a kind of software, and translation (as an "interface") is understood to work like a computer monitor allowing speakers to see the very structures of intelligibility of other languages reduced to programmable codes. By giving an algorithmic face, as it were, to language, translation as an interface can thus also function as a "platform" from which to manipulate writing and speech. This mechanical model conceptualizes the surge in language capabilities as the complement to the surge of combat forces.

Envisioned to be far more efficient than the Language Enabled Soldier, RMS or Rapid Multilingual Support would, as its name suggests, furnish translations at increased speed with greater accuracy. Not only will translation machines subsume linguistic and cultural differences; they will also close the temporal lag that is seen by the military as impeding the surge of its forces. In so doing, translation machines would come to colonize language itself. Putting an end to the material impediments of difference, delay, and deferral, they would render interpreters obsolete and thereby bring an end to the need for translation as such. One speaks directly and plainly, aiming at his or her listener, and expects to be heard and obeyed, much as one expects attention and compliance when holding a gun in a person's face. In place of the time-consuming, highly contingent, and often volatile practices of negotiation and struggle over meaning and form inherent in acts of translation, this new Babylon sees the triumph of technological systems with which to "enable future full-domain, unconstrained dialog translation in multiple environments."

However, where translation is concerned, the imperial dream of "full spectrum dominance"[24] remains largely a science fiction chimera. The *Star Wars* scenario of intelligent machines having animated conversations with humans and among themselves continues to be perpetually postponed. As of this writing, DARPA has so far only been able to produce a hand-held device called the Phraselator.[25] About the size of a Palm Pilot, the Phraselator provides, as one writer describes it, "a one-way phrase-based voice-to-voice translation" of American English into a target language such as Arabic, Farsi, or Pashto. It is designed in such a way as to accommodate an indefinite number of other languages, which can be programmed into its expandable memory. But like a high-tech tourist phrase book, the Phraselator is unable to translate foreign languages back to English. It is thus severely constrained in its ability to engage enemy combatants or occupied populations. Equipped with noise-canceling microphones, the Phraselator works by means of Automatic Speech Recognition technology, or ASR, which has been widely available for commercial uses over the last two decades.[26] ASR allows the Phraselator to mechanically recognize the English utterances from a wide variety of speakers, breaking these down into their phonetic elements. These are then converted into an interlingua, a kind of third language consisting of a mathematical algorithm that matches the deconstructed bits of English with what it wagers are its corresponding bits in a given target language. Through a voice synthesizer, the machine speaks back the resulting words and phrases of its search in that language.

The range of translatable phrases is largely driven by tactical considerations. The selection tends to be limited to such imperatives as "Show me your identification," "Open your bag," "Stop, or I'll shoot," and the all-purpose declarative "We are the U.S. military. We are here to help you."[27] And since the Phraselator is incapable of translating foreign languages back to English, it can neither interpret responses for their different meanings nor parse descriptions and analysis for their truth content. At best it can issue commands. It can speak, but it cannot listen. For this reason, the Phraselator is less than effective at gathering that most precious commodity of counter-insurgency: information.

Meanwhile, progress in two-way translation systems has been slow and largely limited to medical uses. A device called the Speechalator, for instance, allows doctors to interview non-English speaking patients with simple questions like "Does your x hurt?" The machine then searches its database to posit the entire range of things that "x" might be in the language of the patient and matches it with the most likely English equivalent.[28] But like the Phraselator, the Speechalator is far from achieving "full domain unconstrained translation." It is, for example, susceptible to ambient noise that interferes with its ability to identify and correctly match word fragments and phrases between languages. The Speechalator can thus be deployed only in relatively confined conditions when the din of cross talk and other sounds can be effectively suppressed.

The promise of automatic translation relies on the statistical probability that phonetic sounds in English will match up correctly with corresponding phonemes in the target language. It thus rests on a series of high speed gambles. Underlying the functioning of all automatic speech recognition technologies is probability theory characterized by a high degree of mathematical formalism, which enables machines to make enormous numbers of wagers and compute possible matches of word fragments at great speeds.[29] Nonetheless, such technologies remain incapable of determining the socio-historical contexts that shape and inflect the meaning (or non-meaning) of any given utterance. For this reason, they cannot track the polysemia inherent in speech signaled, for example, by the difference between *what* is said and *how* it is said. Like the Gorgon Stare surveillance system discussed earlier, their great strength lies in the fact that they do not discriminate and can take in any and all data that come their way. Their mode of recognition is quantitative. It could not be any more different from the drama of Hegelian recognition that entails the struggle unto death between two beings, forcing the one who is attached to life to submit to the other who risks everything and becomes the former's master. Rather, recognition here is robustly mechanical, entailing neither political distinctions nor historical memory (and its necessary forgetting). We might think of automatic translation technologies, then, as post-dialectical. They can recognize potentially limitless quantitative relationships but are unable to sort out their qualitative significance. They cannot process irony, for one thing, much less respond to humor. (They therefore know nothing of the wild nature of laughter.) They are unable to understand puns nor sort through the full range of idiomatic and literary expressions fashioned from the ambiguous and unstable use of tropes. That is to say, automatic translation machines cannot account for the poetics, much less the politics, that make up all speech acts. For these reasons, they are perhaps fated to be rudimentary. They remain blunt weapons easily outmaneuvered by their intended targets.

There seems then to be a co-relation between the technological sophistication and practical crudeness of automatic translation systems. This Babylon of counterinsurgency has placed the U.S. military in a position of having to increasingly rely on the very figures it had sought to bypass: native interpreters. Since the invasions of Afghanistan and Iraq, the Americans have looked to private contractors to fill their acute need for native interpreters. Though regarded as essential, the presence of interpreters is also a source of great unease among the troops. They are seen by soldiers as Janus-faced: indispensable aides as much as they are potential spies.[30] They are thus weapons whose effectiveness exists side by side with their dangers. In view of the structurally ambivalent position of the native interpreter—whose relationship to their language is less instrumental than it is existential—the U.S. military has issued a series of protocols governing the proper conduct of translation. Designed to systematically exploit the mediating power of the native translator, these protocols are worth reading closely. They tell us a great deal about American attempts to convert language into a "force multiplier," as well as the ways they multiply the potential failures inherent in such attempts.

THE PROTOCOLS OF INTERPRETING

THE U.S. ARMY/MARINE Corps *Counterinsurgency Field Manual* of 2006 includes an extensive appendix entitled "Linguist Support."[31] It specifically instructs commanders to "protect their interpreters. They should emplace security measures to keep interpreters and their families safe. Insurgents know the value of good interpreters and will often try to intimidate or kill interpreters and their family members."[32] In actual fact, these security measures have been minimal to non-existent. Native interpreters are often compelled to work without protective vests and venture unarmed with soldiers on patrol. They wear sunglasses, caps, and face coverings to hide their identities and assume pseudonyms to protect their anonymity. Many are unable to return safely to their families and often try to escape their homeland by seeking asylum in the U.S. or other countries, receiving little or no help from the U.S. government. As I have written elsewhere, interpreters working for the U.S. military in occupied territories risk permanent exile and estrangement within their own country.[33] The dangers associated with working for the American forces no doubt contribute to the reluctance of native speakers to serve as interpreters.

It is for this reason that they are regarded as "valuable resources" by the U.S. and insurgents alike.

The imperative, both tactical and ethical (where the latter is ultimately at the service of the former), to husband this scarce resource has been the topic of a number of military directives. The *Counterinsurgency Field Manual*, for example, urges commanders to "ensure [that] interpreters understand that they are valuable team members. Recognize them based on the importance of their contributions. Protect interpreters; the insurgents and criminal elements may target them."[34] An army captain who served as Chief of Intelligence Operations in Eastern Afghanistan typifies this regard for what the military refers to as "HNLs" or Host Nation Linguists. "HNLs represent a valuable asset and learning conduit," he writes. As an "asset" in counterinsurgency, they deserve "respect... which will be noticed, passed on and remembered." So it pays to

> take time to share chai with your interpreters and hear their back-stories... rich [with] insights into Afghan history, more valuable than any book in some cases. Listen to their opinion and advice, especially concerning cultural issues. They've experienced a lot and often can be an important guide to the complex relationships between the various tribes and personalities of your province.[35]

Respecting "your interpreter" requires listening to them, not simply giving them orders. It means treating them as "people," not simply as "tools." Yet, the captain also positions the native interpreters as "guides" to local culture and later on as "teachers" of the local language. The task of the translator from this perspective is that of a cultural broker and language instructor. She is thought to mediate the passage of the American soldier through the unknown and uncertain thickets of the occupied territory by giving narrative form to its history and society. The interpreter is thus a kind of native informant whose job is to furnish the military with the medium for gathering intelligence.[36] If the native interpreter has value, it is precisely because she never ceases to be an asset, which is also a kind of spy, a means or an instrument for accumulating what the occupying forces want: information with which to repel insurgents and stabilize U.S. control. Giving translators respect and listening to their views does not therefore alter their fundamental relationship with U.S. soldiers. They continue to work as tools, albeit valuable ones, for the pursuit of strategic ends. Respect merely refines the process of their conversion into weapons of counterinsurgency.

Protecting interpreters, therefore, stems from the same imperative to protect complex weapons systems: they may fall into the wrong hands and be turned against their users. The same paragraph that directs commanders to provide security for their interpreters warns: "Insurgents may also coerce interpreters to gather information on U.S. operations. Soldiers and Marines must actively protect against subversion and espionage...."[37] Put differently, interpreters must be subject to policing as well as protection. They are assets, but also threats to occupying forces. Hence, the manual cautions soldiers when "explain[ing] concepts. They should limit what information interpreters can overhear. Some interpreters for political or personal reasons, may have ulterior motives or hidden agendas. Soldiers and Marines who detect or suspect such motives should tell the commander or security manager."[38] Indeed, there have been reported cases of insurgents posing as interpreters to get into U.S. military bases to gather information and set up ambushes. Private contracting firms such as L-3 and Titan have been known to hire translators, many of them poorly vetted in a rush to fill assigned quotas, linked to the abuses and torture of Iraqi and Afghan detainees. Others, through negligence or sheer incompetence, have failed to properly screen locals hired to work inside the bases.[39] Translators are thus doubly valuable. They are esteemed by the U.S. military because of their scarcity and great utility in the collection of intelligence as much as they are also regarded as valuable targets by those who would seek to challenge and undo U.S. power.

It is not surprising, then, that U.S. forces continue to be ambivalent towards the constitutive ambiguity of the interpreter's position. The latter's social and ontological instability makes them difficult to control in a counterinsurgency context that prioritizes stability. Weaponized, they can target but also be targeted, fire as well as backfire. To guard against such risks, the military has produced a series of protocols to define and direct the proper conduct of translation governing both speakers and interpreters. Such protocols, however, rest on a series of unexamined assumptions about language and translation. They regard language as a mere vehicle for transmitting a speaker's intentions. If handled properly, like a car or a tank, it can be relied upon to transport one's ideas to its intended destination. Similarly, such protocols view translation as a pliant process for transferring meaning and faithfully reproducing the original into its copies. Just as a soldier is trained to be obedient to orders emanating from the chain of command, so the interpreter is expected to be loyal to the speaker whose original words he must convey into their exact copy in another language. As we shall see, these assumptions about the sheer instrumentality of language, coupled with a belief in the mimetic capacity of translation, give rise to unintended effects. Far from securing the relationship between speaker and interpreter, they further expose its unsecurable basis.

We can see such contradictory effects at work, for example, if we turn back to the *Counterinsurgency Field Manual*. Among its basic criteria for selecting native interpreters, it lists the acceptability of the of the translators to the "target audience.... Their gender, age, race and ethnicity must be compatible with the target audience," and so, too, should their "mannerisms." In addition, an interpreter is expected to have a "good reputation in the community," and therefore appear as one "least likely to cause suspicion or miscommunication."[40] At the same time, the translator should act in such a way that does not "distract" his listeners. The latter "should give no attention to the way interpreters talk, only what they say."[41]

An interpreter can connect with his audience only if he first clearly makes visible his social identity. Becoming visible to his listeners is a tactic for disarming them, as it were, of their suspicions and winning their trust. From the American perspective, the effectiveness of a native translator begins with his physical bearing, which can be read by others for signs of his social position. In other words, *how* an interpreter appears matters. It is crucial to establishing the conditions of connectivity with an audience otherwise resistant to being targeted. Seeing the translator, the listener is reassured and thought to become receptive to *what* the speaker has to say.

However, this acknowledgement of the importance of the translator's appearance is negated by another demand: translators must remain discreet. They are expected to act in ways that obscure their way of acting. They must not "distract" their listeners, for distraction is a kind of noise that draws attention away from the *what* to the *how* of a translated utterance. Here, the social identity of the interpreter must be so obvious as to go without saying, unremarkable and therefore unmarked by the audience. Hence, the visibility of the interpreter is meant to produce his invisibility. He is seen by the audience only to be ignored. In this way, soldiers operating through interpreters are able to effectively hit their targets. Indeed, as another set of guidelines from the Center for Army Lessons Learned bluntly puts it: "ideally, the interpreter should be invisible."[42]

This conventional notion of the translator's invisibility takes on an added complexity when fused with the counterinsurgent discourse on linguistic weaponization. What is important to underline here is not only the way invisibility, or what we could think of as stealth, is valued in the conduct of war, but also the way it is produced through the tactical deployment of visibility. So, too, with language: in military terms (which obviously derive from the more common civilian metaphysics of the sign),[43] language works—that is, accomplishes its mission—when its material encumbrances such as grammar, syntax, spelling, sounds, and the like can be controlled to the point that they seem to vanish. They matter so that they can cease to matter. Dematerializing language—rendering it transparent—allows for the unfettered emergence of the meaning and will of the speaker. The interpreter in her visible invisibility is positioned to be an active collaborator in this task. Just as the interpreter is expected to set the way, then get out of the way for the arrival of the speaker's intentions, so language is seen as furnishing the material support for the transfer of ideas and commands, all the while making itself seem immaterial and incidental to such maneuvers. How does this double operation of appearance and disappearance of the translator and the process of translation happen? In a militarized context, how does it succeed and at what point does it fail?

"Interpreters," according the manual on counterinsurgency "should be reliable, loyal and compatible with military personnel.... [They] should be quick and alert, able to respond to changing conditions and situations. They should be able to grasp complex concepts and discuss them clearly and logically." Of course, they must also "speak English fluently."[44] It is easy to imagine that the qualities expected of good native interpreters would not be too different from those associated with U.S. soldiers. Working closely together, soldier and translator share a common fate, exposed to the hazards of war and the exigencies of occupation. But this relationship is clearly hierarchical. As a subordinate alter ego, the interpreter is meant to be the technical extension of the soldier. The former is assigned the role of serving as the latter's faithful representative to the occupied population, one whose fidelity consists of mirroring the tone and gesture of the speaker. "The interpreter," the manual continues, "should watch the speaker carefully. While translating, the interpreter should mimic the speaker's body language as well as interpret verbal meaning."[45] And later on we read that "standards of conduct for interpreters include: being careful not to inject their personality, ideas, or questions; mirroring the speaker's tone and personality; translating the exact meaning without adding or deleting information."[46] Expected to provide the "exact" equivalents for words, the interpreter is also commanded to turn herself into a mirror image of the speaker. She thus becomes who she is not. Like one possessed, the interpreter speaks not as herself but as an other who arrives by way of English *and* who insists on being present in the listener's native language. As the copy of the original, the translator takes on the latter's foreignness, reproducing sounds and movements that emanate from elsewhere. In doing so, the translator becomes like the translation she produces: a putatively faithful rendering of unfamiliar elements into familiar terms. Appropriating its distant origins, the interpreter domesticates a foreign power and brings it forth as something intelligible and accessible to the target audience.

Put differently, translation, as the act of conjuring up equivalents between languages, can easily come across as magical. It evinces a remarkable capacity for linguistic and ontological transformation: becoming someone other than who you are, taking on and taming the language of a foreign presence, reproducing it in one's own native tongue and thereby converting it into something other than what it is. By containing, in all senses of that word, the unfamiliar in the familiar and *vice versa*, the translator thus assumes an uncanny power. It is precisely this power of translation that the soldier must learn to control lest it gets away from him. The interpreter is a "vital communication link between speaker and target audience,"[47] and it is this vitality that must be seized if it is to be successfully deployed. To this end, soldiers are instructed to

> communicate directly to the target audience, using the interpreter only as a mechanism for that communication. One technique is to have the interpreter stand to the side of and just behind the speaker. This position lets the speaker stand face to face with the target audience. The speaker should always look at and talk directly to the target audience, rather than to the interpreter. This method allows the speaker and the target audience to establish a personal relationship.[48]

As the mechanical but no less powerful extension of the American soldier's presence, the interpreter has to be put in his proper place: behind or to the side of the speaker rather than between the speaker and the listener. The interpreter's vital role as a medium of communication—literally as the middle term that brings distances up close, sounding the foreign in the familiar—is acknowledged at the same time that it is suppressed. Again, we see how the interpreter is seen in order to be ignored. Doing so allows the soldier to come forth. Face to face with his target, he appears unarmed, concealing the linguistic power and its embodied agent that makes possible his very ability to speak and be heard. Disarming his target, the soldier can then fire away with confidence. In this idealized scenario, speech gains speed and direction, reaching its audience to the extent that it is propelled by the ever-present but largely unseen machine of translation. Weaponizing speech thus entails harnessing the mediating power of translation as it courses through the interpreter while concealing the process of its exploitation and deployment. The soldier thereby overcomes linguistic difference, converting language itself—English as well as the language of his audience—into a transparent window for the passage of meanings and intentions. Controlling translation, directing and speeding up its trajectory, subordinating the interpreter into a copy, at once visible and invisible, of the speaking self, and subjugating differences between as well as within languages are thus all of a piece in the work of counterinsurgency. In this sense, the manual's protocols for proper translation rehearse the idealized notions of language that we earlier saw at work in the military's attempts to develop automatic translation systems.

THE INSURGENCY OF LANGUAGE

These extravagant fantasies of perfect communication predicated on the mechanization of translation and the subjugation of linguistic difference, however, remain largely unrealized. What is remarkable is how the frustration of this fantasy always already inhabits the very protocols for translation. In the manual on counterinsurgency, one of the most frequently mentioned threats to translation is "distraction." In a section entitled "Good and Bad Practices for Speakers," we read how "speakers should not distract the audience while the interpreter is translating. Avoid pacing, writing on the blackboard, teetering on the lectern, drinking beverages, or doing any other distracting activity while the interpreter is translating."[49] The warning against distraction stems from the fear of disrupting the smooth workings of translation. As it turns out, it is not only the interpreter but the speaker who poses such a threat. Pulled in different directions, the soldier's body is inhabited by other thoughts jockeying for attention. Exposed to a foreign audience, he restlessly anticipates what to say next, besieged by impulses he struggles to control. Recognizing these surging impulses, the soldier might pace, drink, or write. His body, awash in nervous energy, might begin to move in ways at odds with his mind. At that moment, he then appears to be one thing while saying another. Instead of coming across as a unified self in full control of itself and its speech, the soldier appears distracted, which is to say, divided and thus other than himself. The sight of a divided speaker, one who speaks in a language that is not fully his insofar as he is, as it were, not fully himself, brings the soldier in close proximity to the position of the interpreter. Distraction is dangerous precisely because it threatens to blur the distinction between the speaker and the translator and, by extension, between the original and the copy.

To prevent these hierarchical distinctions from being overturned, the manual urges speakers against "Address[ing] the subject or audience in the third person through the interpreter. For example, avoid saying, 'Tell them I'm glad to be their instructor.' Instead, directly address the subject or audience saying, 'I am glad to be your instructor.' Make continual eye contact with the audience. Watch them, not the interpreter."[50] In addressing his audience, the speaker should always do so as an "I" speaking to a "you." The translator, by contrast, is never to be addressed in the second person but must always assume the position of an occluded third term. In this way, the translator is neither a "him" nor a "her" but an "it." It is essential, as we have seen, for the translator to efface him or herself so that the speaker can have a face with which to address his listeners. The danger, however, lies in the constant temptation for the speaker to speak to the interpreter directly. Unsure, perhaps even unnerved by the unfamiliar looks of his audience, the soldier would understandably seek out the familiar face of his interpreter. In doing so, he speaks as an "I" to someone who is supposed to be an "it" but is now addressed as a "you." He inadvertently converts the third term into a second person while placing the listeners in the position of the occluded third. The targeted "you" suddenly becomes the vanishing "it."

Complicating this situation is the fact that the interpreter, as we saw, is expected to echo the speaker and so can only say "I" as a simulacrum of another "I." The interpreter therefore is one who is forbidden to say "I" to refer to himself. He can only do so to refer to an other, the speaker. It is as a not-"I," and therefore as an "it," that the interpreter seems to vanish from view. This invisibility, which is linguistically produced, endows the interpreter with a kind of disembodied presence. Without a body, the interpreter can seem to go through the walls that separate English from other languages. In this sense, the position of the interpreter as an "it" whose invisible and disembodied presence allows it to cross linguistic boundaries seems akin to that of a ghost. But in referring to the interpreter in the second person, the speaker confounds the protocols of address. As a "you," the interpreter's spectral presence is revealed to be a conjuring trick. He now comes across as a specifically embodied person, one who can say "I" and actually refer to him or herself. This confusion of address has important consequences. The interpreter's recovered visibility threatens to uncover the real nature of the relationship between speaker and interpreter as one of dependency; it is in fact the American soldier who is dependent on the native translator, while both are dependent on the workings of language. Meanwhile, the listener, the speaker's target, escapes. He is excluded by having become a third person. By upending the relationship between speaker, interpreter, and listener, the misplaced circulation of pronouns confuses the terms of address and sabotages the proper operation of translation as conceived by the manual.

Perhaps mindful of the uncanny ways by which language, once repressed, returns to haunt the work of counterinsurgency, the manual is replete with advice for speakers—not only on their behavior and mode of address, but also on how to formulate their speech.

> An important first step for Soldiers and Marines communicating in a foreign language is to reinforce and polish their English language skills…. They should use correct words, without idioms or slang. The more clearly Soldiers and Marines speak English, the easier it is for interpreters to translate exactly. For instance, speakers may want to add words usually left out in colloquial English such as 'air' in 'airplane.' This ensures they are not misrepresented as referring to the Great Plains or a carpenter's plane.[51]

Here, the speakers are cautioned less about the ambiguity of another language as the potential treachery of their own. Even before their speech is translated by the interpreter, speakers must first translate it themselves. By "polishing their English language skills," avoiding colloquialisms and slang, soldiers engage in a sort of intra-lingual translation. "Before speaking impulsively," the manual says, "soldiers and Marines should consider what they wish to say." They should not, in other words, blurt out the first things that come to mind but instead convert their thoughts into proper forms of speech. They must follow orders, which is to say, listen to another, higher language issuing from within their own. Doing so entails translating within English, hearing and speaking it as if it were a second language that encapsulates their first. They thus speak as an "I" in possession of its words only to the extent that they speak in another register, in "polished English," and therefore as an other "I" within a language whose sameness is always already fractured into the colloquial and the officially conventional. To speak properly in "correct English" is to split oneself, moving between one's native tongue and its national-official reformulation.[52] In this way, self-division and intra-lingual translation precede any attempt on the soldier's part to engage the native interpreter and his target audience. Such operations are essential, as the manual points out, to guard against the risks of mistranslation. One should add "air" to say "airplane," for example, lest "plane" by itself be confused with a geographical region in North America or a carpenter's tool. In doing so, the soldier avoids mistranslation, which like distraction generates noise that detracts from producing exact translations.

Nonetheless, noise never stops running through languages, making mistranslation not only an inevitable event but a constitutive condition of speech. Colloquialisms and slang are impossible to fully expunge. They invariably seep into every conversation, for they are precisely what give language its social vitality and historical specificity. There is therefore an element of utter wishfulness that infuses the manual's injunction against using,

> terms of surprise or reaction such as 'gee whiz' or 'golly' [since] these are difficult to translate [and] might lose their desired meaning.… Speakers should avoid American 'folk' and culture specific references. Target audiences may have no idea what is being talked about. Even when interpreters understand the reference, they may find it difficult to quickly identify an appropriate equivalent in the target audience's frame of reference. Transitional phrases and qualifiers may confuse non-native speakers and waste valuable time. Examples include 'for example,' 'in most cases,' 'maybe,' and 'perhaps.' Speakers should avoid American humor. Humor is culturally specific and does not translate well.[53]

This catalogue of prohibitions points to the difficulties of controlling language in its totality, whether one's own or the other's. The danger lies not only in being misunderstood in the language of the native other but also in failing to make oneself comprehensible in one's own. Rather than face the risk of losing face, of saying something that deters the interpreter, creating distractions and leaving one's interlocutors mystified, the speaker is commanded to repress those aspects of his language that defy translation. He must therefore keep in mind what remains untranslatable: "terms of surprise," "folk references," "qualifiers," "humor," and so forth. He must labor to keep these out of linguistic exchanges and so accede to the higher language of command that tells him what he "must" do. Doing otherwise would jeopardize the work of translation, understood here as the search for exact equivalents that, by fixing the link between English and native words, would also stabilize the relationship between speaker and audience, occupiers and occupied.

Does the manual locate in the native language of the American soldier a kind of insurgency felt in the very insistence and intractability of what remains untranslatable? As the passage above shows, even the manual's authors fall prey to the insurgency of the untranslatable when they resort to the very features of language that they had targeted for repression. For example, the manual talks of avoiding "qualifiers," such as "for example," but does so by giving examples, such as "for example." Unable to co-opt linguistic difference, it cannot fully recruit English into the task of weaponizing translation. Instead, it calls for the repression of those parts of speech that resist such an operation. That such calls are repeatedly issued along with warnings about distractions and mistranslations suggests the extent to which they fail to be heard and heeded. It is this recurring failure and continued resistance of language to the commands of counterinsurgency that guarantees that translation will misfire and miss its targets, whatever and wherever they may be.

TRANSLATING OTHERWISE

THE CHRONIC FAILURE of counterinsurgency to weaponize language, whether its own, English, or the other's, tends to generate catastrophic effects. Targets are missed or misconstrued, accidents abound, deaths proliferate while no one is held accountable. As I have been suggesting, the resistance of language to weaponization is not incidental but structurally built into the very discourse and practices of counterinsurgency. That counterinsurgency harbors the very elements of its own undoing can be understood in at least two ways. On the one hand, as military leaders and engineers tend to think of it, the intractability of language could be regarded as a kind of noise that adds to the friction of war: merely a technical problem that can be fixed with greater application of resources, financial and technological, and a strengthening of political will. On the other hand, we could think of the insurgency of language as evidence of the possibility of another kind of translation practice at work. Operating *in between* the lines of imperial commands, it would be a kind of translation that evades targeting, spurring instead the emergence of forms of life at variance with the biopolitical prescriptions of counterinsurgency. Where might we see this occurring? In what follows, I conclude with one such instance.

On March 1, 2011, American-led NATO helicopter gunners killed nine Afghan boys between the ages of nine and fifteen as they collected firewood in the remote mountains of Kumar province in eastern Afghanistan, mistaking them for Taliban insurgents who had earlier fired at American troops.[54] The killings followed in the wake of an increase in the number of civilian deaths caused by American-led forces throughout Afghanistan since the troop surge in 2009. "Regrettably there appears to have been an error in the handoff between identifying the location of the insurgents and the attack helicopters that carried out subsequent operations," an official NATO statement explained. General David Petraeus, commander of NATO forces, issued an apology to the families of the boys and to the people of Afghanistan for this "mistake," saying that "These deaths should have never happened." Mistaking children for insurgents, the helicopter gunships addressed them accordingly, sending a message whose force could not be denied. The targeted audience of this fully weaponized speech act were not expected to respond. But something else happened: they spoke back, or at least some of them did.

One of them was Hemad, an eleven year old who survived the attack. He spoke to the reporters of the *New York Times* through an interpreter who remains invisible and unnamed:

> We were almost done collecting wood when suddenly we saw the helicopters come. There were two of them. The helicopters hovered over us, scanned us and we saw a green flash from the helicopters. Then they flew back high up, and in a second round they hovered over us and started shooting. They fired a rocket which landed on a tree. The tree branches fell over me and shrapnel hit my right hand and my side.

Hemad goes on to say that the tree branches hid him and probably saved his life. It also gave him a vantage point from which to witness the helicopters "shoot the boys one after another."

Thanks to the work of translation, the boy's words reach beyond the village and across the globe for others to hear. What comes to us is a story as spare and unadorned as it is vivid and unnerving in its effects. It is a minimalist retelling of counterinsurgency from the point of view of a member of the population it is supposed to protect. Rendered by the translator and the newspaper editor in grammatically correct English, it nonetheless conveys a semantic excess. The English makes legible the boy's Pashto, yet the meaning of its content remains elusive. We recognize the words and can make sense of the form, but we can barely comprehend the implications of what has been said. We get instead a number of incommensurable possibilities: we sense, for example, an enormous senselessness, or an unforgivable act, or the monstrous effects of the most precise and controlled use of advanced weaponry. All of these imply that translation does not necessarily bring meaning to the surface for us to see. Rather, as Walter Benjamin once put it in a different context, "meaning plunges from abyss to abyss until it threatens to become lost in the bottomless depths of language."[55] Unable to ground meaning, translation leads to its falling away. Hemad's story is translated not to establish exact equivalents between his Pashto and our English and thereby allow his intentions to come forth. Rather, like an interlinear translation, what comes through is the inexactness and ambiguity of a message contained in a grammatically correct form. Hidden from view, Hemad witnesses the helicopter gunship do its work, addressing the boys by turning them into targets. He hears the pilots speak, as it were, delivering their message swiftly and directly. Shooting the boys "one after another," the pilots recognized the boys as in some sense mirror reflections of themselves: uniform, undifferentiated, and replaceable parts of an enemy army accessible through the insistently mechanical speech of a war machine. Overcoming their fear of death, the pilots could now incorporate it as the substance of their message, transmitting death itself to those who earlier they thought had threatened them with it. In return, they expected nothing back, no response, just the silence and stillness of those they targeted.

The technical precision and unerring accuracy of the computerized gunships were meant to deliver an unequivocal message. As weaponized media of communication, the guns translated and transmitted the pilots' intention, bypassing the need for human interpreters. On-board guidance systems automatically located the targets without the mediation of local guides, and so could deliver the pilots' message without delay. However, the message was delivered to the wrong address, to a "you" that was meant to be someone else. The pilots did not mean to kill these children. The children just got in the way of the pilots' desire to impose what they deemed to be their sovereign will. This getting in the way is retrospectively reckoned as an accident that absolves the pilots of criminal intent. They made mistakes and merely misspoke. The pilots meant to kill those they were sure deserved to die. Their intentions, borne of rational calculation and moral certainty, were legitimate—so it might be argued—even if their realization proved to be horribly otherwise. The pilots meant what they said, they just did not mean it to be directed to those who ended up receiving the full force of their speech. This disjunction between a message and its address, between the pilots' decision and their larger design, could not but stimulate other kinds of responses beyond the calculations of counterinsurgency.

Embedded in the newspaper story is one such response from an Afghan shopkeeper, Ashabuddin:

> As soon as we heard about the attack on the village's children, all the village men rushed to the mountains to find out what really happened. Finally, we found the dead bodies. Some of the dead bodies were really badly chopped up by the rockets. The head of a child was missing. Others were missing their limbs. We tried to find the body pieces and put them together. As it was getting late, we brought down the bodies in a rope bed. We buried them in the village's cemetery. The children were all from poor families; otherwise no one would send their sons up to the mountains despite the known threats from both insurgents and Americans.

As with Hemad's story, Ashabuddin's narrative in its English translation comes across as dry and bereft of affect. He hears about the attack and connects it with the missing children. Along with other village men, he searches for them and eventually finds them, or rather, what remains of their bodies. They see the signature, as it were, of the pilots' language in the boys' "chopped up" limbs. One can only assume that the sight of dismembered bodies would cause anyone to recoil in horror. But Ashabuddin's story continues in the same flat tone as he talks of the men collecting body parts, bringing them down and burying them. The men in effect reverse the work of targeting. Where the helicopter gunships scattered the bodies of those they addressed, the villagers seek literally to recollect them, binding them together so that they could be buried and thus rejoined to the living. Mourning their loss, the villagers rearticulate the identity of the pilots' targets: "The children were all from poor families."

In hearing this story translated into English, we are once again faced with the workings of a kind of interlinear translation. Just as an interlinear translation seeks to preserve the ambiguity of the original text, safeguarding its mystery and intimating its inexhaustible possibilities for meaning,[56] so Ashabuddin's account comes across as intelligible while simultaneously suggesting something that lies behind or beneath it that can neither be seen nor grasped. It imparts, which is to say, divides and shares, a story about the impossibility of restoration and recuperation. Attempting to "find body pieces and put them together," the villagers in Ashabuddin's narrative are left with a sense of something, indeed of many things, missing. He says of Khalid, his fourteen-year-old nephew who was among those killed, "He was studying in the sixth grade of the orphanage school and working because his father had died four years ago due to a long-term illness. His father was a day laborer. He has thirteen sisters and two mothers. He was the sole breadwinner of the family. I don't know what would happen to his family and his sisters and mothers."

Gathering the boys and burying them brings no closure but instead intensifies uncertainty about the future, and thus about uncertainty itself. The story and its translation allow us to see that we do not see, conveying a semantic excess that remains impervious to narrative domestication. This imperviousness is perhaps what is indicated by the affect-less tone of Ashabuddin's voice rendered in English. Translation in this case is faithful to the original, bringing the story up close, so close as to make it profoundly foreign to us, just as it remains irreducibly strange to the Afghan man who tells it. Moving between the lines of Pashto, the English translation conveys a story that remains inassimilable to larger narratives of war just as it proves inhospitable to our attempts to render war familiar and banal. "I don't know what would happen…," Ashabuddin says, and neither do we. We apprehend war's violence and its remorseless violation of life even as we are unable to comprehend, much less adequately respond to, its effects.

There is, then, in Ashabuddin's story something else that reveals itself, the nature of which we can never be certain, but which nonetheless reaches us. It might be that in the living's attempts to recover the dead and rejoin their missing parts we glimpse at the persistence, even emergence of another kind of life, one that is not reducible to the language of targeting and weaponization. Much less is it likely, therefore, for this other life to submit to the "saving power" of American counterinsurgency that demands the rational re-ordering and deployment of all life in the war against terror. Or perhaps, it is the voice of those who, speaking in the midst of occupation, find themselves living so intimately with death that they can hardly draw the line that separates them from those they've lost. Barely able to mourn, it comes across as flat and empty of affect. Yet, this voice is just as likely to call for the other's death. As the newspaper article points out, a few days after the killing of the boys, small crowds of people both in the village and in the capital of Kabul gathered to protest, chanting "Death to America! Death to Obama and his colleagues and his associates! Death to the American government!"[57] Uttered from below, whether in Pashto or its English translation, "death" is less a kind of weapon as a token return, a way of giving back to America what America has left behind in Afghanistan. Rhetorically sounding out a death sentence, such chants understandably call for revenge. As such, they redefine Afghan relations to the U.S.

We can imagine the chants overturning the discursive hierarchy of counterinsurgency, placing the population in a position of judging their putative protectors. We might even speculate that such calls for revenge bring forth the possibilities of a life that speaks of an afterlife beyond imperial occupation. Or, restraining our wishfulness, we might pause to consider that they could be merely the traumatized, automatic responses to the inexplicable and unjustifiable loss of life, and perhaps even of an afterlife. We who are dependent on translation's fidelity to the vagaries of the original can never be sure. Translation *detains* us, in all senses of that word, and we can only continue to attend to that which reaches us but which nonetheless remains resistant to the weaponizing impulses of counterinsurgency.

NOTES

1   A different version of this essay appeared in the journal *Social Text* (Winter 2012/2013).

2   Ellen Nakashima and Craig Whitlock, "With Air Force's New Drone, 'We Can See Everything'," *Washington Post*, January 2, 2011, http://www.washingtonpost.com/wp-dyn/content/article/2011/01/01/AR2011010102690.html.

3   Ibid. As of this writing, the development of drone-mounted surveillance systems has continued unabated, fueled by the anticipation of future permanent wars and by the sublime sums of money gushing forth from the U.S. Department of Defense. A recent example is the "Global Observer," which can fly for days up to an altitude of 65,000 miles, well beyond the reach of anti-aircraft missiles, and is capable of surveying as much as 280,000 square miles, "an area larger than Afghanistan, at a single glance. That would give the Pentagon an 'unblinking eye'." It would surpass the visual capacity of satellites, but would cost about $30 million each. See W.J. Hennigan, "Drones Becoming Speedier, Deadlier," *Seattle Times,* January 12, 2011, A3.

4   One result of the blindness caused by data overload is the use of weapons of mass destruction against unintended targets such as women and children. Such tragic and criminal miscalculations are all too common in the use of unmanned airplanes. See for example, Thom Shankel and Matt Richtel, "In New Military, Data Overload Can be Deadly," *New York Times,* Jan. 16, 2011, http://www.nytimes.com/2011/01/17/technology/17brain.html?src=me&ref=homepage.

5   Nakashima and Whitlock, "With Air Force's New Drone, 'We Can See Everything'."

6   As Michael Hardt and Antonio Negri point out, in this new era of permanent and postmodern war, the unmatched capacity of the U.S. military to visit cataclysmic destruction on its enemies must be accompanied by a flexible capacity for constructing new social orders and subjectivities with which to replace what had been decimated. So-called "stability operations" are thus meant to "protect" populations from insurgents and rebuild the country by providing it with the infrastructures—ranging from schoolhouses to a parliament, from a police force to regular trash collection, from functioning banks to

anti-corruption laws—with which to ward off insurgency and integrate the nation-state into the global order sanctioned by the U.S. and the U.N. Borrowing from Foucault, Hardt and Negri refer to the negative, destructive sovereignty of the U.S. military as "bio-power"—i.e., the power over life and death—and its productive, counterinsurgent efforts as attempts at co-opting the biopolitical—i.e., the totality of social relations that are produced, reproduced, and shared in common on a daily basis. See: Michael Hardt and Antonio Negri, *Multitude: War and Democracy in the Age of Empire*, New York: Penguin Books, 2004, 36–62.

Though I concur with Hardt and Negri, I do not follow their terminology. But as will become obvious in the rest of this essay, my treatment of translation and language is not so foreign from what they consider to be the realm of the biopolitical.

For an extended illustration of how the work of counterinsurgency seeks to appropriate and exploit the power of the biopolitical to the extent of claiming (and failing in many instances) to cast itself as its source, see United States, Department of the Army, *The U.S. Army/Marine Corps Counterinsurgency Field Manual (FM 3-24)*, Chicago: The University of Chicago Press, 2007. We will take a closer look at this text below.

7   See George E. Anderson III, "Winning the Nationbuilding War," *Military Review*, September-October, 2004, 47–50, 50.

8   The quotations come from Kalev Sepp and Robert Tomes, cited in Jonathan Gumz, "Reframing the Historical Problematic of Insurgency: How the Professional Military Literature Created a New History and Missed the Past," *The Journal of Strategic Studies* Vol. 32, No. 4, 553–88, August 2009, 561–62; and Sarah Sewell, "Introduction to the University of Chicago Press Edition: A Radical Manual," United States, *The U.S. Army/Marine Corps Counterinsurgency Field Manual*, Chicago: University of Chicago Press, 2007, xxx.

9   John A. Nagl, cited in Gumz, "Reframing the Historical Problematic of Insurgency," 562.

10   United States, *Counterinsurgency Manual*, Table 5–6, 173.

11   Sarah Sewell, "Introduction," xliii; and see especially Chapter 5, "Executing Counterinsurgency Operations," 151–197. The notion of the U.S. as "the indispensable nation"—a reiteration of one of the sacred tenets of U.S. nationalism, American exceptionalism—is from former Secretary of State Madeleine Albright and has been echoed by counterinsurgent theorists such as John Nagl. See Tara McKelvey, "The Cult of Counterinsurgency," *The American Prospect;* Nov 2008; 19–22. Or, as Hardt and Negri put it, "War must become both procedural activity and an ordering, regulative activity that creates and maintains social hierarchies, a form of bio-power aimed at the promotion and regulation of social life." *Multitude*, 21.

12   The literature on counterinsurgency is massive and varied. Here, I can only cite a small handful of what I've found to be useful accounts that deal both sympathetically and critically with the history of contemporary U.S. Counterinsurgency. See for example David H. Ucko, *The New Counterinsurgency Era*, (Washington DC: Georgetown University Press, 2008); Andrew J. Bacevich, *Washington Rules: America's Path to Permanent War*, (New York: Metropolitan Books, 2010); David Kilcullen, *The Accidental Guerilla:*

Fighting Small Wars in the Midst of a Big One, (Oxford & New York: Oxford University Press, 2009); John A. Nagl, *Counterinsurgency Lessons from Malaysia and Vietnam: Learning to Eat Soup with a Knife*, (Westport, CT: Praeger, 2009); Robert M. Cassidy, *Counterinsurgency and the Global War on Terror: Military Culture and Irregular War*, (Westport, CT: Praeger, 2006); Jonathan Gumz, "Reframing the Historical Problematic of Insurgency: How the Professional Military Literature Created a New History and Missed the Past," *The Journal of Strategic Studies* 32, no. 4 (2009): 553–88; John Kelley, Beatrice Jauregui, Sean Mitchell and Jeremy Walton (eds.) *Anthropology and Global Counterinsurgency*, (Chicago: University of Chicago Press, 2010); David Price, *Anthropological Intelligence: The Deployment and Neglect of American Anthropology in the Second World War*, (Durham: Duke University Press, 2008); Nicholas Mirzoeff, "War Is Culture: Global Counterinsurgency, Visuality and the Petraeus Doctrine," *PMLA* 124 no. 5 (2009): 1737–46; Derek Gregory, "The Rush to the Intimate: Counterinsurgency and the Cultural Turn," *Radical Philosophy* 150 (July/August 2008): 8–23.

13 Giles Deleuze and Felix Guattari, *A Thousand Plateaus: Capitalism and Schizophrenia*, translated by Brian Massumi, (Minnesota: University of Minnesota Press, 1987), 395–400. For a more detailed historical development of the process of weaponization, see Manuel de Landa's *War in the Age of Intelligent Machines*, (New York: Zone Books, 1991), especially 11–126.

14 For this discussion of targeting, I'm indebted to the work of Samuel Weber, *Targets of Opportunity: On the Militarization of Thinking*, (New York: Fordham University Press, 2005).

15 Harry D. Tunnell IV, "Developing a Unit Language Capability for War," *JFQ: Joint Forces Quarterly* issue 51, 4th quarter, (2008), 114–16. All further references to this essay will appear in the main body of the text.

16 United States, Department of Defense, "Defense Language Transformation Roadmap," United States Department of Defense website, http://www.defense.gov/news/Mar2005/d20050330roadmap.pdf (accessed January 3, 2005).

17 Tunell, "Developing a Unit Language Capability for War," 115.

18 Ibid, 116.

19 Mary Louise Pratt, "Harm's Way: Language and the Contemporary Arts of War," *PMLA*, v.124, no.5, (2009), 1515–31.

20 See "3AJK" 7/23/09 comment on Joshua Foust, "Unfit Interpreters," *Registan.net*, http://www.registan.net/index.php/2009/07/23/unfit-interpreters/ (accessed July 23, 2009).

21 This information comes from Max Boot, as cited in David H. Ucko, *The New Counterinsurgency Era*, 87. In 2007, the first generation of F-35 planes cost $220 million each. As of 2010, the manufacturer, Lockheed Martin, Corp., dropped the price to $111.6 million each. See "Pentagon Details Cost of F-35 Fighter," *Reuters*, http://www.reuters.com/article/idUKN1627640520101217 (accessed Dec. 17, 2010).

22 For a penetrating history of cryptology and cryptomachines, see Manuel de Landa, *War in the Age of Intelligent Machines*, 206–15. See also Jonathan Slocum, "A Survey of Machine Translation: Its History, Current Status, and Future Prospects," in Jonathan Slocum, ed., *Machine Translation Systems*, (Cambridge: Cambridge University Press, 1988), 1–48.

23 DARPA, "Babylon Program," http://www.infowar.net/tia/www.darpa.mil/iao/Babylon.htm.

24 United States, Department of Defense, "Joint Vision 2020 Emphasizes Full Spectrum Dominance," http://www.defense.gov/news/newsarticle.aspx?id=45289, (accessed June 2, 2000).

25 The company is called Voxtec. See their website for the company's history and for technical details regarding the development and use of the Phraselator, http://www.voxtec.com/phraselator/.

See also Ann Harrison, "Machines Not Lost in Translation," *Wired*, http://www.wired.com/science/discoveries/news/2005/03/66816 (accessed March 9, 2005).

For brief but incisive cultural critiques of the Phraselator, see Rosalind Morris, "Images of Untranslatability in the U.S. War on Terror," *Interventions*, v.6, no.3 (2004), 401–23, especially 420; and Mary Louise Pratt, "Harm's Way," 1519. Pratt makes the astute suggestion that the Phraselator is descended from the analog technology of sixteenth century Spanish conquistadors called the *requerimiento*, a pronouncement read to native peoples demanding their submission and conversion to Catholicism, refusal of which would incur a military response. Separated by five centuries, both technologies are nonetheless "instrument[s] of pure interpellation."

26 For a short history of Automatic Speech Recognition technology, see B.H. Juang and Lawrence R. Rabiner, "Automatic Speech Recognition—A Brief History of the Technology Development," (no date), http://www.ece.ucsb.edu/Faculty/Rabiner/ece259/Reprints/354_LALI-ASRHistory-final-10-8.pdf.

27 See Mike Hanlon, "Mobile Technology: PDA Based Translator for Field Use," in *Gizmag.com*, http://www.gizmag.com/go/1833 (2003); and Katherine Mieszkowski, "How Do You Say 'Regime Change' in Arabic?" *Salon.com*, http://www.salon.com/technology/feature/2003/04/07/phraselator (accessed April 7, 2003).

28 For technical descriptions of the DARPA-funded development of the Speechalator, see Alex Waibel, Ahmed Badran, Alan W. Black, *et. al.*, "Speechalator: Two-Way Speech-to-Speech Translation on a Consumer PDA," *EUROSPEECH 2003*, Geneva, http://www.cs.cmu.edu/~awb/papers/eurospeech2003/speechalator.pdf.

Also, Yuging Gao, "Speech-to-Speech Translation," (2003), on the *IBM Research* website, http://domino.research.ibm.com/comm/research.nsf/pages/r.uit.innovation.html

29 See Juang and Rabiner, "Automatic Speech Recognition," 12–21.

30 See for example, Vicente Rafael, "Translation, American English and the National Insecurities of Empire," *Social Text* 101, v.27, no.4 (Winter 2009), 1–23.

31 *Counterinsurgency Field Manual*, Appendix C, 335–346.

32 FM 3-24, C-19, 340.

33 See Rafael, "Translation, American English and the National Insecurities of Empire."

34 FM 3-24, Table C-2, 346.

35 Captain Don Moss, "The Hidden Engagement: Interpreters," *Small Wars Journal* (2010): 2. http://smallwarsjournal.com/blog/2010/05/the-hidden-engagement-interpre/

36 For a series of sustained critiques on the militarization of anthropology and ethnography, see the essays in Kelley, *Anthropology and Global Counterinsurgency*.

37   FM 3-24, C-19, 340.

38   FM 3-24, C-15, 338-339; C-20, 340.

39   See Moss, "The Hidden Engagement," 4; Pratap Chatterjee, "Outsourcing Intelligence in Iraq: A CorpWatch Report on L-3/Titan, http://www.corpwatch.org/article. php?id=15253, (accessed April 29, 2008).

40   FM 3-24, C-7-8, 337.

41   Fm 3-24, C-8, 337.

42   United States, The Center for Army Lessons Learned, "How to Communicate Effectively Through Interpreters: A Guide for Leaders," *News from the Front*, Nov.–Dec. (2003), http://www.au.af.mil/au/awc/awcgate/army/using_interpreters.htm.

43   Here I am thinking especially of what Jacques Derrida has referred to as *logocentrism* and his compelling critique of the metaphysics of the sign as it informs the history of Western thought. See especially Jacques Derrida, *Of Grammatology*, translated by Gayatri Chakravorty Spivak, (Baltimore: Johns Hopkins University Press, 1976); *Limited, Inc.*, (Evanston, IL: Northwestern University Press, 1988); *Writing and Difference*, translated by Alan Bass, (Chicago: University of Chicago Press, 1978).

44   FM 3-24, C-12, 338.

45   FM 3-24, C-33, 343.

46   FM 3-24, Table C-1, 342.

47   FM 3-24, C-32, 343.

48   FM 3-24, C-37, 344.

49   FM 3-24, Table C-2, 346.

50   FM 3-24, Table C-2, 346.

51   FM 3-24, C-38, 344.

52   See Rafael, "Translation, American English, and the National Insecurities of Empire," for a discussion of the historical roots and political ramifications of this split.

53   FM 3-24, C-39-44, 344-345.

54   Alissa J. Rubin and Sangar Rahimi, with an Afghan Employee in Jalalbad, Afghanistan, "Nine Afghan Boys Collecting Firewood Killed by NATO Helicopters," *New York Times*, March 2 (2011), http://www.nytimes.com/2011/03/03/world/asia/03afghan.html?_r=1&scp=1&sq=afghanistan%20killings&st=cse.
      The rest of what follows comes from this article.
      It is worth noting that the killing of civilians by manned and unmanned aircraft has been all too frequent in the U.S. war in Afghanistan and Pakistan. For a brief summary of the more recent events, see Kathy Kelley, "Incalculable," *Huffington Post*, March 4 (2011), http://www.huffingtonpost.com/kathy-kelly/afghanistan-war-casualties_b_831190.html

55   Walter Benjamin speaking of Holderlin's translation of Sophocles in "The Task of the Translator," in *Illumination,* translated by Harry Zohn, (New York: Schocken Books, 1969), 69–82. The quote appears on p.82.

56   Ibid., 81–82. Benjamin here is also thinking of one of the exemplars of interlinear translation, the Septuagint scriptures, where the books of the Old Testament appear with a Greek translation situated in between the lines of the original Hebrew.

57 Rubin and Rahimi, "Nine Afghan Boys"; Patrick Quinn, "Karzai Rejects US Apology for Killing of Nine Afghan Boys," Associated Press, in *Huffington Post*, March 6 (2011), http://www.huffingtonpost.com/2011/03/06/karzai-rejects-us-apology-afghanistan-boys-killed_n_831972.html.

WHO NEEDS THE NSA WHEN WE HAVE FACEBOOK?

EVAN TUCKER

ANONYMOUS VS. ANONYMOUS

IN THE SUMMER OF 2011 THE DECENTRALIZED HACKER GROUP ANONYMOUS announced that they wanted to kill Facebook. The YouTube video announcing the attack proclaimed:

> Your medium of communication you all so dearly adore will be destroyed. If you are a willing hacktivist or a guy who just wants to protect the freedom of information then join the cause and kill facebook [*sic*] for the sake of your own privacy. Facebook has been selling information to government agencies and giving clandestine access to information security firms so that they can spy on people from all around the world. Some of these so-called whitehat infosec firms are working for authoritarian governments, such as those of Egypt and Syria. Everything you do on Facebook stays on Facebook regardless of your "privacy" settings, and deleting your account is impossible, even if you "delete" your account, all your personal info stays on Facebook and can be recovered at any time.... Facebook knows more about you than your family.[1]

Complicating matters, other individuals claiming affiliation with Anonymous denounced the video and said that it was a hoax. Things got ugly when this rival faction published information about a person who had allegedly called for the Facebook attack. Of course, the date for the attack came and went and Facebook was not destroyed. But the threat resurfaced again in January of 2012 and the recriminations resumed.

It appears that the most vocal portion, if not the actual majority, of those in Anonymous champion the importance of social media. Yet the call for the destruction of Facebook seems to suggest a crumbling consensus on the value of the medium. Some of the concerns expressed in the Anonymous communiqué have been raised in the wider society, but they seem to be drowning under a flood of fawning press coverage, awestruck over Facebook's latest innovation. But the radical call to action brings to light a dark side of social media that neither innovation nor regulation can erase.

WHAT'S WRONG WITH FACEBOOK?

SOCIAL MEDIA IS unlike any other surveillance technology that has ever existed.[2] Through its innovative organization and display of information, it offers users an unparalleled sense of self-expression and social connection. Its seductively simple platform enables people to share information about themselves and the people they know without a second thought.

Since the collection and organization of large volumes of data is typically the most challenging aspect of a surveillance operation, the advent of social media has been a boon for law enforcement and others with an interest in managing the people they intend to control and/or profit from. Social media has also been a gold mine for advertisers, who pay top dollar for the information that users voluntarily provide. For these reasons, user privacy is not part of the business model. The service is free only because the user is the product.

Since the website Friendster was launched in 2002[3] the use of social media websites has expanded tremendously, with Facebook alone claiming over 800 million users.[4] The influence of social media has been frequently discussed, but rarely critically. So far as I have seen, there has been no comprehensive, public examination of the negative impacts that social media has on our lives, communities, and political movements.[5]

There are four serious problems with social media. These are:

1. Information is not secure. All user-submitted content is controlled by corporations, which freely share it with the government and sell user information to other businesses.

2. The amount of information generated is enormous. Social media's popularity and ease of use have created an ever-expanding data-base—larger than any in history—allowing the government to pros-ecute more people and businesses to extract more profit.

3. User profiles are nothing more than dossiers voluntarily created and published by the subject. A self-created dossier can be more revealing than one created by an intelligence agency.

4. Social media automates and simplifies the mapping of interpersonal associations and social networks.

Social media normalizes relentless record-keeping of our lives and tracks us like never before. These sites give governments and businesses access to information that they would never have the time or resources to acquire on their own. It also avoids the scandal associated with the exposure of mas-sive surveillance programs, because the subjects of these dossiers are the same people who produce and disseminate them.

While some users may take self-censoring steps to mitigate the problems, these four aspects are interconnected and inherent to the technology. If you use social media and don't provide much information about yourself, your profile may not be much use to the government, but it probably isn't much use to you, either.

Let's consider the problems in more detail:

1) INFORMATION IS NOT SECURE. ALL USER-SUBMITTED CONTENT IS CONTROLLED BY CORPORATIONS, WHICH FREELY SHARE IT WITH THE GOVERNMENT AND SELL USER INFORMATION TO OTHER BUSINESSES.

In a 2006 article about Myspace, *Newsweek* aptly described it as "a searchable, public scrapbook of images, affiliations and written exchanges" that hands law enforcement data on millions of "potential suspects, witnesses or vic-tims."[6] The privacy implications are astounding, though many people feel that their information is secure because they have chosen a privacy setting that limits access to their profile.

Myspace and all similar websites have so-called "privacy policies." These policies are little more than memos to users hinting at the privacy violations that await them. (And, of course, the terms and conditions are subject to change at any time). In its privacy policy, Myspace indicates that it records user IP addresses for "security purposes." Their privacy policy acknowledg-es that the company will provide a user's personal information to "comply with the law or legal process" and that they will "access or disclose" it if they think it necessary to "protect the safety and security of Users of the Myspace

Services or members of the public" or for "risk management purposes." The meaning of "risk management" is left unexplained.[7]

Facebook's privacy policy states: "We receive data about you whenever you interact with Facebook.... When you post things like photos or videos on Facebook, we may receive additional related data (or metadata), such as the time, date, and place you took the photo or video." Their policy later states, "We receive data from the computer, mobile phone or other device you use to access Facebook. This may include your IP address, location, the type of browser you use, or the pages you visit.... When we get your GPS location, we put it together with other location information we have about you (like your current city). But we only keep it until it is no longer useful to provide you services."[8] Keep in mind, however, that Facebook is not just providing *you* a service; many other people would like that information and Facebook's privacy policy makes it clear they will share the data they collect on you if they believe it is necessary:

> We may share your information in response to a legal request (like a search warrant, court order or subpoena) if we have a good faith belief that the law requires us to do so. This may include responding to legal requests from jurisdictions outside of the United States where we have a good faith belief that the response is required by law in that jurisdiction, affects users in that jurisdiction, and is consistent with internationally recognized standards. We may also share information when we have a good faith belief it is necessary to: detect, prevent and address fraud and other illegal activity; to protect ourselves and you from violations of our Statements of Rights and Responsibilities; and to prevent death or imminent bodily harm.[9]

So the company's "good faith" is all that stands between the wealth of data they collect about you, and anyone who asks for it.

Since business and law enforcement prefer accurate information, Facebook does its best to verify what you submit. This issue of identity verification hit the headlines in the fall of 2011 when author Salman Rushdie had his Facebook account deactivated after the company demanded proof of identity. Facebook demanded that Rushdie change the name on his account to his birth name, Ahmed Rushdie, despite his being a world-famous author who has published under the name Salman Rushdie for decades.[10]

Pressure from law enforcement has influenced this effort to force people to use their birth names. But it is not the only reason. Linking a person's "authentic identity" to their Facebook page has become an important part of Facebook's business model. According to Somini Sengupta of the *New York*

Times, "Forrester Research recently estimated that companies spent $2 billion a year for personal data." Companies like Facebook hope to peddle users' real names as a virtual passport to be used to sign in to over 7 million websites and applications. As Sengupta points out, "it gives Facebook a trail of valuable information about the reading, listening, viewing and buying habits of its users."[11] This information is the product in a multi-billion dollar industry that creates financial incentives for minimizing user privacy and anonymity.

A Federal Trade Commission (FTC) complaint alleges that Facebook has violated users' privacy in a variety of ways including: continuing to display photos that users have deleted, changing privacy settings without permission, and selling users' information to third parties despite claims to the contrary. According to Michael Liedtke of the Associated Press, Facebook is "trying to make money by mining the personal information that it collects to help customize ads and aim messages at people…." Liedtke also points out, "That strategy has been working well as Facebook prepares to sell its stock in an initial public offering that's expected next year." During the period of the privacy violations, Facebook's revenue increased from $777 million to $4.3 billion.[12]

Facebook is not alone. Both Google and Twitter have likewise been the subject of FTC complaints for how they have handled users' information.[13]

2] THE AMOUNT OF INFORMATION GENERATED IS ENORMOUS. SOCIAL MEDIA'S POPULARITY AND EASE OF USE HAVE CREATED AN EVER-EXPANDING DATABASE—LARGER THAN ANY IN HISTORY—ALLOWING THE GOVERNMENT TO PROSECUTE MORE PEOPLE AND BUSINESSES TO EXTRACT MORE PROFIT.

Despite the FTC's action against social media companies, government agencies often rely on these sites to get private information about users. Companies like Myspace are quite comfortable assisting these agencies. In 2006, *Newsweek* reported that "a 20 member, 24/7 law enforcement team fields 350 calls a week from its rolodex of nearly 800 agencies, helping them surf the site." The article goes on to say, "Communication between cops and the two-year-old company has surged this year, with Myspace now contributing to about 150 investigations a month, according to Jason Feffer, its vice president for operations." The same article states that "under Justice Department guidelines, anything posted online is fair game." Myspace ought to be familiar with Justice Department guidelines since they hired former federal prosecutor Hemanshu Nigan to monitor the site.[14]

Social networking sites have become such a rich source of information that law enforcement agencies now prepare trainings on how to use them for investigations. In March 2010, the Electronic Frontier Foundation received documents through the Freedom of Information Act regarding a Justice

Department presentation entitled "Obtaining and Using Evidence from Social Networking Sites." The documents indicate some of the ways the U.S. Department of Justice uses social media: "Reveal personal communications; Establish motives and personal relationships; Provide location information; Prove and disprove alibis; Establish crime or criminal enterprise."

One section title asks, "Why go undercover on Facebook, Myspace, etc"? The text provides the following answers: "Communicate with suspects/targets; Gain access to non-public info; Map social relationships/networks." In a section on witnesses, where the authors ominously proclaim "Knowledge is power," they urge attorneys to "Research all witnesses on social-networking sites" and "Advise your witnesses: Not to discuss cases on social-networking sites; To think carefully about what they post."[15] Ironically, if everyone took their advice, the Justice Department would probably find these sites much less useful.

Also among the documents the Electronic Frontier Foundation received was a 2010 Department of Homeland Security memo entitled "Social networking sites and their importance to FDNS." (FDNS stands for Fraud Detection and National Security.) It states:

> Narcissistic tendencies in many people fuels [*sic*] a need to have a large group of "friends" link to their pages and many of these people accept cyber-friends that they don't even know. This provides an excellent vantage point for FDNS to observe the daily life of beneficiaries and petitioners [*sic*] who are suspected of fraudulent activities…. This social networking gives FDNS an opportunity to reveal fraud by browsing these sites to see if petitioners and beneficiaries are in a valid relationship or are attempting to deceive CIS [Citizenship and Immigration Services] about their relationship. Once a user posts online, they [*sic*] create a public record and timeline of their activities. In essence, using Myspace and other like sites is akin to doing an unannounced cyber "site-visit" on a petitioners and beneficiaries [*sic*].[16]

It's not just the Feds who are catching on to the social media craze, either. All types of law enforcement agencies can register for the Social Media Internet Law Enforcement (SMILE) conference—an annual gathering for investigators looking to "add another weapon to… [their] arsenal." The conference website claims that agencies are using social media in areas such as "community policing, recruitment and retention, investigations, crime prevention, reputation enhancement / management as well as others." In addition to these areas of emphasis the 2012 SMILE conference offers to educate cops on how to use social media for explicitly political purposes. Their website reads, "This (the fourth) SMILE Conference will also emphasize *the changing role between law enforcement, social activists and traditional media*. Tuesday will offer an entire day of topics covering social activists' interference with investigations, maintaining public order, and mass surveillance in an open source world."[17]

The case of *U.S. v. Eric McDavid* et al. offers us an early example of this "changing relationship between law enforcement, social activists and traditional media." In 2006 McDavid and his codefendants, Zachary Jenson and Lauren Weiner, were arrested and branded as eco-terrorists due to the efforts of an FBI informant called "Anna." The informant traveled to activist gatherings and protests from 2003–2005 trying to gather information and encouraging attendees to break the law. According to FBI agent Nasson Walker, "the information she has provided has been utilized in at least twelve separate anarchist cases."[18]

The FBI's motivation for pursuing McDavid can be summed up by the first line about him in the criminal complaint: "Eric McDavid, age 28, is an anarchist…." The word "anarchist" appears in the fifteen-page complaint no less than twenty-six times.[19]

After the three were arrested, it came out that the government was monitoring the Myspace accounts of Jenson and Weiner. (McDavid did not have one).[20] In the discovery process, the government turned over printed copies of Jenson and Weiner's Myspace pages, including all of their blog posts, comments, and friend listings. The criminal complaint that charged the three with "conspiring to damage or destroy certain property by explosive or fire" referred to Zachary Jenson's Myspace page and quoted from it extensively. The complaint states:

> Jenson, like McDavid, is security conscious and is careful not to disclose information on his website regarding his politically-motivated illegal activity. In one journal entry, Jenson recounts illegal activity he conducted somewhere in the San Francisco Bay Area. A verbatim text of the entry, dated May 21, 2005, reads as follows:
>
> "what happened friday night can't be told here online. it can only be told in person, so everyone back home will have to wait because of security. imagine: music blaring, kids running in the streets, dancing and shouting, adrenaline surging, cops right behind us. we ran fast. and you know what kind of tags were left upon the concrete. yeah, you know."
>
> The FBI JTTF [Joint Terrorism Task Force] has researched the above-described incident and concluded that it took place

at a protest in downtown Palo Alto, CA. During this incident, dumpsters were moved and overturned in the streets, store windows were broken, and graffiti was sprayed on walls and sidewalks. Photos of the protest obtained through a public source depicts an individual spray-painting the phrase, "pandas are sexy" onto a sidewalk. Jenson's web page contain(s) numerous references to pandas and the "panda house," Jenson's name for his former residence....[21]

Clearly Jenson's concerns about security were warranted, even if his response to them was idiotic.

At Zachary Jenson's bail hearing, his Myspace and LiveJournal accounts were referenced frequently. A straight-faced prosecutor announced that on Jenson's Myspace page he admitted to being a "ninja" and an "assassin," thus proving that he was too dangerous to be released on bail. The prosecutors also used information from Jenson's Myspace account to argue he had no residence and no ties to a particular geographic community and was therefore a "flight risk." No independent corroboration was required for these claims because they were Jenson's own words. Jenson was denied bail.

Weiner was released because she quickly agreed to cooperate with the government and testify against her codefendants. Her family posted the $1.2 million bail.

McDavid, like Jenson—and partially *because of Jenson*—was also denied bail. Though McDavid did not have a Myspace account, Jenson's Myspace page was offered as representative of McDavid's behavior and as a source of insight into his activities. The criminal complaint states: "Jenson's site also contains several journal entries in which he documents his interactions with McDavid. Information from Jenson's journal entries corroborates reporting from the CS [confidential source] regarding McDavid and Jenson's travels."[22] Documents obtained through a FOIA request make it clear that the government was using Jenson's Myspace to track McDavid's whereabouts and obtain information about who his friends might be.[23] Even though McDavid had no Myspace page of his own, Jenson did the damage by putting information about McDavid on his page. McDavid was ultimately sentenced to nearly 20 years in prison.[24]

McGregor Scott, the U.S. Attorney who aggressively pushed for the prosecution of McDavid, went into private practice in 2009 and was retained in 2011 to represent Facebook from his Sacramento office. Ironically, Scott represents Facebook in one of the few reported cases where they are *refusing* to turn over user information. This time it is being requested by defense attorneys to prove juror misconduct.[25]

3] USER PROFILES ARE NOTHING MORE THAN DOSSIERS VOLUNTARILY CREATED AND PUBLISHED BY THE SUBJECT. A SELF-CREATED DOSSIER IS MORE REVEALING THAN ONE CREATED BY AN INTELLIGENCE AGENCY.

When testifying in McDavid's trial, "Anna" stated that her first attempt at infiltrating an activist meeting failed because her appearance did not adequately resemble the people she was trying to deceive. Though she never explained how she finally got it right, it's clear that social media was an important tool for validating her false identity and keeping tabs on the people she met. But the abundant and well-packaged information people have on their profiles has an even more important use for informants.

In their 2005 ethnography of anarchists in *Studies in Conflict and Terrorism*, Eugene police officer Chuck Tilby and University of South Florida psychology professor Randy Borum state that "infiltration is made more difficult by the communal nature of the lifestyle (under constant observation and scrutiny) and the extensive knowledge held by many anarchists, which require [sic] a considerable amount of study and time to acquire."[26]

The success of law enforcement infiltration tactics hinges on believability. If police or informants cannot convincingly impersonate anarchists (or environmentalists, animal rights activists, etc.), then they cannot gain the trust of those people. Without the opportunity to build trust quickly, the ability to manipulate people is severely diminished. Social networking websites could be the ideal text for the necessary study. By offering complete profiles of individuals in social and political groups it gives informants all the information they would need to pose as a member of that group.

Police and prosecutors are unabashed about their regular and widespread reliance on social networking sites. Police can create false profiles for surveillance purposes, but ordinary social media users who do so can be severely punished. (In 2006, a thirteen-year-old girl from Farmington, Connecticut was charged with criminal impersonation because she created a Myspace profile of her principal.[27]) While the sheer number of Myspace profiles may give the impression that there are too many people to effectively monitor, some police agencies are becoming increasingly proficient at dealing with enormous amounts of data. The technology news website *DailyTech* reports that the NYPD plans "to mine social media sites like Facebook, Twitter and Myspace in order to find criminals bragging about a crime they've committed or planning to commit a crime." This is part of a growing trend of tech-savvy law enforcement agencies that have realized they can do more than manually look through these public dossiers. According to *DailyTech*, "New York isn't the only city with positive results from data mining social networks. London's rioters and looters have used Twitter and BlackBerry messages this week to choose targets to burn or loot. Police have been able to use the social networks to find pictures of these criminals."[28]

This data mining is not just used for police work, but for intelligence purposes as well. In a 2012 article about the U.S. government monitoring social media all over the world, Kimberly Dozier of the Associated Press discovered the massive amount of information the CIA is able to collect and process. She reported that, "the CIA is following tweets—up to 5 million a day." Analysts then cross-reference the data with both publicly available information and surreptitiously acquired intelligence to create reports for the White House.[29]

Students from junior high to college are among the millions monitored on social networking. As the *New York Daily News* reports, "A New Hampshire teen discovered that free speech actually comes with a price." In May of 2011, thirteen-year-old Shayne Dell'isola was suspended from Rundlett Middle School in Concord, New Hampshire after posting on her Facebook that she wished Osama Bin Laden had killed her math teacher.[30]

Connecticut Attorney General Richard Blumenthal put it simply: "the illusion of privacy is simply self-delusion on the part of young people." Blumenthal argues that "there is absolutely no reasonable expectation of privacy, which is the test under the law for the requirement of a warrant before the police should use it as evidence."[31]

The more people offer up their personal lives to the internet, the deeper the intrusions become. In January 2008, Myspace made an agreement with fifty Attorneys General, promising to "enhance the ability of law enforcement officials to investigate and prosecute Internet crimes," and to develop "identity verification technology" for the site. A press release from the National Association of Attorneys General also stated there will be scrutiny of "every image and video uploaded to the site."[32]

One of Facebook's methods for scrutinizing every image on their site is using facial recognition software that can automatically identify people in photos. According to Sarah Jacobsson Purewal of *PC World*, "Sure, you can 'opt-out' of the service, but it's a pretty weak consolation. After all, opting out won't keep Facebook from gathering data and recognizing your face—it'll just keep people from tagging you automatically." This technology could potentially make a person identifiable in any picture of them posted to Facebook, including pictures posted without their knowledge or permission. A person does not even need a profile to be identified. Purewal goes on to describe this as "Facebook's way of creating a huge, photo-searchable database of its users. And yes, it's terrifying." Every time a photo is tagged on Facebook, info is added to their massive database of information about the 90 billion photos that they host. And remember: once they have this information, they can give it to anyone they want to.[33]

But it is not only the companies and law enforcement examining young people's profiles. According to the *Boston Globe*, eleven high school athletes were suspended from participating in school sports after a parent found pictures on Facebook of them using alcohol and tobacco. The parent down-loaded the pictures and turned them over to the school administration. According to Superintendent Joseph F. Casey, "We are not trying to interfere with what happens outside of schools…. [But] if you're going to represent the school we expect you to uphold that image 24/7." In addition to the athletic suspensions, the school is trying to determine the location of the photos, so that the owners of the house can be prosecuted for allowing underage drinking. If convicted, they could face up to a year in jail and a $2,000 fine.[34]

Universities across the country have indicated that they regularly look at Facebook and will expel students if they see evidence of violations. One student, Cameron Walker, was expelled from Fisher College in Boston for a Facebook post that criticized a campus police officer. Walker later admitted he "was naive about Facebook, because it wasn't affiliated with a university."[35]

Like other government agencies, schools not only monitor social media to control people's behavior, but also to manage dissent. In response to protests against fee hikes, the University of California-Davis created the "Student Activism Team" to spy on students and campus organizations they believed to be involved in the protests. This became public knowledge after a former student received 280 pages of documents through the California Public Records Act detailing some of the University's surveillance activities.[36]

Given the budget crisis that precipitated the protests, it is unlikely that the University has unlimited funds for spying on students. The abundance of up-to-date protest information on Facebook allowed the University to maximize the efficiency and effectiveness of its response. In one email, Associate Director of the Center for Student Involvement Ann Reynolds Myler states, "As we monitor facebook and website announcements to get a better idea of activities for the day, we will finalize the shift schedule for our 16 member resource team."[37] Though schools have rushed to capitalize on the wellspring of intelligence that social media provides, they are just one of many institutions concerned with amassing knowledge to control subject populations.

4) SOCIAL MEDIA AUTOMATES AND SIMPLIFIES THE MAPPING OF INTERPERSONAL ASSOCIATIONS AND SOCIAL NETWORKS.

According to the U.S. Army, one of the key tasks of counterinsurgency is to understand how members of a targeted population interact with each other. The U.S. Military uses a technique called Social Network Analysis to map people's relationships and their connection to any insurgency or political movement. According to Army Field Manual 3-24, "For an insurgency, a social network is not just a description of who is in the insurgent organization; it is a picture of the population, how it is put together and how members interact with one another." The manual goes on to explain the importance of this process by pointing out that Social Network Analysis:

helps units formalize the informality of insurgent networks by portraying the structure of something not readily observed. Network concepts let commanders highlight the structure of a previously unobserved association by focusing on the preexisting relationships and ties that bind together such groups. By focusing on roles, organizational positions, and prominent or influential actors, commanders may get a sense of how the organization is structured and thus how the group functions, how members are influenced and power exerted, and how resources are exchanged.[38]

In the documents obtained by the Electronic Frontier Foundation, the Justice Department indicates that the ability to "[m]ap social relationships/networks" is one of their primary purposes for using social media. Nowhere is this practice more damaging than in the communities branded with the "gang" or "terrorist" labels.

These labels are defined in part by the beliefs and associations of those being targeted for surveillance, harassment, and prosecution. A crime becomes gang or terrorist activity based on the alleged intentions or loyalties of those accused. When people have this "gang member" or "terrorist" label thrust upon them, activities that would ordinarily be considered legal become illegal, and illegal activities are dealt with much more severely. Relationships, behaviors, and aspects of appearance that are not themselves criminal are used to criminalize communities and support legal interventions.

The California Penal Code defines gangs in the following way:

> any ongoing organization, association, or group of three or more persons, whether formal or informal, having as one of its primary activities the commission of one or more of the criminal acts … having a common name or common identifying sign or symbol, and whose members individually or collectively engage in or have engaged in a pattern of criminal gang activity.[39]

Unfortunately the "common identifying sign" is often race, as the individual accused of membership need not himself have participated in a crime and the "informal" nature of the "gang" leaves little opportunity to disprove membership. Communities targeted for anti-gang efforts often face police occupation and shootings, more frequent arrests, enhanced charges, longer sentences, and further isolation in prison.[40]

According to the *Victorville Daily Press*, officials from the San Bernardino Sheriff's department regularly use Myspace to "track and identify gang members." The Gang Unit of the Sheriff's department began using Myspace after hearing about the success other law enforcement agencies had with the website. The gang unit uses the profiles of individual Myspace users to get the District Attorney to seek gang enhancements (which increase the length of prison sentences) for people being prosecuted for other crimes. It is unclear if these people would even be considered gang members were it not for their Myspace accounts.[41]

Besides the public goal of prosecuting Internet crimes, law enforcement also uses data from social networking sites to map and analyze political movements and subcultures. Social media makes association more transparent and therefore easier to criminalize. It offers the raw materials for these state-constructed identities.

In 2006, Southern California animal rights activists found out how seemingly innocuous postings on their Myspace pages can have severe consequences. In November of that year, Santa Monica Police, in cooperation with the FBI, raided the homes of eight animal rights activists, trashed their residences, took thousands of dollars worth of property, and ultimately filed no charges. The activists' problems with law enforcement began when they were served with restraining orders to force them to stay away from the property and employees of the beverage company POM Wonderful. POM Wonderful was, at the time, engaged in animal testing and was the subject of regular protests. The restraining order was roughly eighty pages long and included photographs, text, and links from the Myspace accounts of the eight people whose homes were later raided. The information from the Myspace pages was collected by a law firm working for POM Wonderful and included pictures of people passing out information about veganism, attending unrelated protests, and drinking beer. These pictures—along with links to websites such as veganoutreach.org and ecoprisoners.org—were meant to prove that these people were dangerous and supported direct action. While none of the information was linked to any actual crime, all the activists were served with restraining orders, and just over a month later, their houses were raided.[42]

Though much of this chapter focuses on the government's nefarious use of social media, private industry is another culprit. Some businesses engage in surveillance for their own purposes, while others capitalize on the government's outsourcing of intelligence activity. Private security firms are hired to engage in surveillance on behalf of government, so that the dirty work of spying can be done off the books. Little is known about the surveillance practices of businesses in general, and how they use social media in particular. Most of what we know about the government's uses of social media comes from the glimpses gained through the Freedom of Information Act and the cops' propensity to brag about it to the press. The activities of businesses are not covered by the Freedom of Information Act and they are rarely willing to give their secrets up in public. But sometimes those secrets are leaked or stolen, as in the case of private security firm HBGary Federal.

Aaron Barr, the CEO of HBGary Federal had a plan to identify members of the hacker group Anonymous and sell the information to the FBI. Anonymous describes itself as a "decentralized network of individuals focused on promoting access to information, free speech, and transparency."[43] They caught the attention of the FBI in 2010 when they shut down the websites of Visa, Paypal and Mastercard in retaliation for cutting off services to the independent news organization Wikileaks.

Barr felt that social media sites were invaluable tools for mapping networks of hackers and uncovering their identities. He even presented a talk at a Justice Department conference about using social media and "specific techniques that can be used to target, collect, and exploit targets with laser focus and with 100 percent success."[44] Despite this brazen boasting he was not successful—in fact, quite the opposite.

Barr created fake Twitter accounts and Facebook profiles to befriend people he believed were "leaders" in Anonymous. He had planned to expose Anonymous members at a February 2011 security conference in San Francisco where he was scheduled to give a talk entitled "Who Needs NSA when we have Social Media?" But he was never able to give that talk. By the time the conference rolled around Aaron Barr and HBGary were in ruins. Anonymous had hacked into HBGary's computer system and made the information they found publicly available online.

Bragging about his efforts in the press unleashed a backlash from Anonymous that cost Barr his job and crushed the company he worked for. Anonymous taunted him with the fact that the information he planned to sell to the FBI was all bogus: "please note that the names in the file belong to innocent random people on facebook, none of which are related to us at all...."[45] Barr was close to erroneously implicating people in hacking activities that they had nothing to do with.

When Anonymous made all Barr's emails public, it became clear that HBGary Federal had been contracted by the U.S. government to create software that would generate fake social media profiles to manipulate public opinion. According to Darlene Storm in *Computerworld*, "It could also be used as surveillance to find public opinion with points of view the powers-that-be didn't like. It could then potentially have their 'fake' people run smear campaigns against those 'real' people." [46]

The leaked emails also indicate that HBGary Federal was hired by the Chamber of Commerce to engage in campaign of sabotage and disruption against their enemies. HBGary's plan included using social media to cause infighting, sway public opinion, and gather information on union activists, their friends, and their families, including their children.

Those activities are summed up well in a letter written by about a dozen members of Congress calling for investigation in the matter. The letter states:

> The emails indicate that these defense contractors planned to mine social network sites for information on Chamber critics; planned to plant "false documents" and "fake insider personas" that would be used to discredit the groups; and discussed the use of malicious and intrusive software ("malware") to steal private information from the groups and disrupt their internal electronic communications.[47]

One of HBGary's partners in corporate-espionage-for-hire is a Silicon Valley based software company called Palantir. After HBGary's emails were leaked by Anonymous it became clear that Palantir worked with them to prepare a proposal on ways to attack, embarrass, or discredit opponents of the U.S. Chamber of Commerce and Bank of America.[48] Palantir products and services have wide use beyond corporate smear jobs. Palantir's clients in government include agencies such as the NYPD, LAPD, CIA, FBI, and the U.S. Army. The secret of Palantir's success is its ability to take enormous disparate data sets and organize them to create extremely comprehensive pictures of individuals and communities. For example in Afghanistan the U.S. Military uses Palantir to plan counterinsurgency operations. According to a report in *Bloomberg Business Week* the Army can

> type a village's name into the system and a map of the village appears, detailing the locations of all reported shooting skirmishes and IED, or improvised explosive device, incidents. Using the timeline function, the soldiers can see where the most recent attacks originated and plot their takeover of the village accordingly.

Their data aggregation software has domestic applications as well. According to the same report, "the FBI can now instantly compile thorough dossiers on U.S. citizens, tying together surveillance video outside a drugstore with credit-card transactions, cell-phone call records, emails, airplane travel records, and Web search information."[49]

Social media clearly offers a mother lode of information for this handmaiden of repression.

THE REVOLUTION WILL NOT BE FRIENDED

FACEBOOK'S DEFENDERS MAKE the argument that the technology plays a crucial role in the struggle for freedom worldwide. Since the uprising in Tunisia,

NYU professor Clay Shirky has emerged as one of social media's major public proponents. In Shirky's view, "the political effect [of social media] is principally in allowing people, who are discontent[ed] with their government, to find each other, to coordinate their feelings and to decide to take action."[50] In the introduction to an interview with Shirky the blog *OnlineJournalism* proclaimed, "social media can do everything from cause revolutions to create whole new political parties when done right."[51]

While it is true that people can connect and organize through social media, its use can come with costs such as constant surveillance, arrest, expulsion, deportation, and incarceration. These costs are often downplayed or ignored while the benefits are overstated.

In this vein, much has been made of the role of social media in the uprisings in the Middle East. Visiting Stanford Scholar Evgeny Morovoz suggests that "Perhaps the outsized revolutionary claims for social media now circulating throughout the west are only a manifestation of western guilt for wasting so much time on social media: after all, if it helps to spread democracy in the Middle East, it can't be all that bad." Morovoz has argued that the successful use of social media in countries like Egypt has been largely because the disintegrating regimes have not been very tech savvy. In his article "Smart Dictators Don't Quash the Internet,"[52] Morovoz notes that countries like Russia and China have used social media as a way to manage dissent, identify opponents, and to cripple the communication system of the opposition. Russia, China, and Vietnam have all set up their own social media systems that are controlled by the government and compete, often quite successfully, with Facebook and Myspace. And countries that have experienced recent uprisings with dissidents using social media have learned their lesson: Syria and Iran do not shut down social media websites, they recognize their value as sources for information about the opposition.[53] Likewise, after riots took place throughout England in August of 2011, British Home Secretary Theresa May began to meet with Facebook, Twitter, and Research In Motion to discuss how they can help the British government in times of unrest.[54]

Social media surveillance is not just for riots and revolutions. The government also uses it for managing its citizens and maintaining stability. The purpose of counterinsurgency is not just to put down revolt, but to make sure it never happens.

Malcolm Gladwell argues that "high-risk activism" is an important element of political movements (ranging from the American Civil Rights Movement to the Italian Red Brigades), and that it is necessary for people to have strong ties to engage in this kind of activism together. Social media, in contrast, promotes *weak* ties. In his *New Yorker* article on the subject, Gladwell states, "It makes it easier for activists to express themselves, and harder for that expression to have any impact. The instruments of social media are well suited to making the existing social order more efficient. They are not a natural enemy of the status quo."[55]

In response to Gladwell, Steve Sherman argues that media has always been important for social movements and that these movements must adjust to technological change to be successful.[56] But let me be clear: my argument is not against social movements using media or technology. I am arguing that social media, specifically, is unlike any technology that has existed before, and that the collection of corporations that has come to be called "social media" is dangerous and destructive.[57]

As activists, we may want to reach as many people as possible and gain approval for our marginalized causes, but too often we have lost sight of the effects of the tools we use. The fact that people see social media as a tool for social change is more a triumph of marketing than the result of some digital revolution. Social media is a powerful tool for the very institutions that we are at war with, the people that seek to exploit and oppress us. Embracing it has resulted in our willing participation in a process of surveillance that we should be actively resisting.

FROM COUNTERINSURGENCY TO COUNTERINTELLIGENCE

OF COURSE SURVEILLANCE can be a two-way street. In an article about social media and law enforcement, the website *Government Technology* observed, "Although social media can help enlist public support it can also turn on a dime and do the opposite." Their prime example is from Albuquerque, New Mexico where a "police officer involved in an on-duty shooting brought discredit to himself and his department when reporters discovered that he listed his occupation as 'human waste disposal' on a Facebook profile."[58]

Similarly, in October of 2011, the Twin Rivers Police Department in Sacramento, California came under scrutiny when reporters found pictures on Facebook of t-shirts produced and sold by the police union. Those shirts showed a picture of a small child inside a cage with the caption "U raise 'em, We cage 'em."[59] When the photos went public, it exposed the cops' sadistic attitude toward children and their contempt for people in the community, adding to the tension between the police and the population. Within two weeks Police Chief Christopher Breck was put on paid administrative leave without explanation.[60]

According to the *San Francisco Chronicle*, at a recent conference San Francisco Police Commander Richard Corriea told, "the 100 or so police bosses that it was crucial they adopt strong social media policies to avoid security gaffes. A quick survey showed that almost none of the chiefs had implemented such policies."⁶¹ The SFPD learned their lesson the hard way: In December 2011, participants in Occupy San Francisco learned of an imminent raid on their camp by reading a police officer's Facebook and Twitter posts.

These blunders point to one of the only legitimate uses of social media—intelligence. That is its true function and that is why we must remove ourselves from it. Yet law enforcement and government officials are no less foolish than the rest of us. It appears that they expose, embarrass, and incriminate themselves on social media as much as anyone else does. Since social media is a corporate project with a track record of government cooperation, we are at a distinct disadvantage. Yet as long as they continue to present us with information that can help us fight repression and injustice, we must seize it. The task is to find a way to do this without exposing ourselves in the process.⁶²

KNOWLEDGE IS POWER

THE USE OF social media increases the risk of surveillance, repression and incarceration. It is a gold mine for anyone—from cops to school officials to private businesses—looking to collect information. It makes students easier to manage, movements easier to dismantle, and all kinds of people more likely to be harassed or arrested by law enforcement. As Christian Parenti said in his book *The Soft Cage,* "With a little imagination one can see that no matter how mundane, surveillance is also always tied up with questions of power and political struggle."⁶³

Yet, the dangers of surveillance are often waved away by people who think that they have nothing to hide. This carefree, and sometimes self-righteous, attitude relies on the assumption that the collection of information is an essentially neutral process, and only has negative consequences for those committing crimes. But it is through the very act of surveillance that crime is produced.

Philosopher Jeffrey Reiman argues that the idea of "crime" is created through agents of the law defining certain acts as crimes and certain people as criminals. Reiman asserts that the concept of crime is an important tool to allow the wealthy and powerful to maintain control over everyone else without really keeping us safe. In his book *The Rich Get Richer and the Poor Get Prison,* Reiman argues that "on the whole, most of the system's practices make more sense if we look at them as ingredients in an attempt to maintain rather than reduce crime."⁶⁴

Surveillance is one of these practices. By dramatically enhancing the government's ability to surveil people, social media users enhance the government's ability to produce crime. While clearly there are acts labeled criminal that are both real and harmful, the designation of "crime" is not always linked to demonstrable harm: the notion of "crime" requires no such objective criteria. As Reiman points out there are numerous factors in people's lives—such as unsafe working conditions, denial of healthcare, pollution, and high-level fraud—that are rarely considered crimes but cause enormous amounts of harm. "Crime" exists because the state has the power to stand in judgment over people's lives. As the government gains increasing access to those lives through surveillance, their arena of power expands.

Social media creates a relationship of confession and observation between a government and its subjects that facilitates the production of crime. It allows the government and their corporate masters (or minions) unprecedented access to our lives, to our communities, and to our movements. The damage this does outweighs any perceived benefits from increased "communication" or "free" publicity. Joining the site is free, but that is because your relationships, your activities, and your life have become the product. The inclusion of the "knowledge is power" formulation in the Justice Department's training notes should serve as a reminder that the government is empowered, in part, through the collection of information on its subjects. As we accumulate as much knowledge about ourselves as possible, and serve it up to businesses and the state, we give them more power over our lives, voluntarily and necessarily.

We must withdraw our consent from this repressive practice and not accept surveillance as a norm. The Department of Homeland Security mocks users for their narcissism. The Department of Justice says that everything posted online is fair game. The Connecticut Attorney General says that any idea of privacy on social media sites is just an illusion. These are the people who benefit from our use of social media and their proclamations about its dangers offer us compelling reasons to stay away.

While I agree that social movements need media, it is not uncommon for some movements to abstain from activities that have been considered normal social practices (as the use of social media has become). Movements have boycotted elections,[65] or run people for political office who then refuse to serve;[66] many individuals abstain from voting completely.[67] Some activists refuse to talk to corporate media.[68] And of course many activists refuse to talk to law enforcement under any circumstances.[69] These are but a few examples of instances when political groups or social movements refuse to participate in normal social practices that harm their interests. In many of these cases, the social movements argue that everyone should participate in their chosen tactic to deny the state legitimacy and power. That is precisely what I am advocating: that regardless of political or social affiliation, we reject the minor conveniences that participating in this insidious system of surveillance affords us, in order to deprive businesses and the government of some of the power they have over our lives. Remember: they need us more than we need them.

When the renegades of Anonymous called for the death of Facebook they were not the first to recognize the damage that is caused by participating in social media. But they may have been the first to challenge us to engage in collective struggle to resist it. Now we must step us to this challenge, and determine what form that struggle will take.

NOTES

1 Rosie Gray, "Anonymous Wants To Destroy Facebook," *The Village Voice*, Aug. 9, 2011, http://blogs.villagevoice.com/runninscared/2011/08/anonymous_wants.php, (accessed June 25, 2012).

2 For the purposes of this article, I define social media as a system of internet-based, user-generated profiles that emphasize the mapping of connections between people and amassing large amounts of personal information. According to this definition websites such as Facebook, Myspace, Twitter, LiveJournal, and Google+ are social media and websites such as Youtube or Indymedia are not.

3 Christopher Nickson, "The History of Social Networking," *Digital Trends*, Jan. 21, 2009.

4 Lori Andrews, "Facebook Is Using You," *The New York Times*. Feb. 4, 2012.

5 In this article I have chosen to focus primarily on the problems encountered by people using social media in the United States. For this reason my criticisms of social media use and admonitions to avoid it are directed at Americans. I will leave it to people outside of the United States to determine if these criticisms are applicable to their movements and their lives.

6 Andrew Romano, "Walking a New Beat," *Newsweek*. Apr. 23, 2006.

7 Myspace Privacy Policy, http://m.myspace.com/settings/privacy.wap?bfd=offdeck&p=11, (accessed Jan. 15, 2012).

8 Facebook Privacy Policy, http://www.facebook.com/about/privacy/your-info#inforeceived, (accessed Jan. 15, 2012).

9 Facebook Privacy Policy Block Quote, http://www.facebook.com/about/privacy/other, (accessed Jan. 15, 2012).

10 Somini Sengupta, "Rushdie Runs Afoul of Web's Real-Name Police," *The New York Times*. Nov. 14, 2011.

11 Ibid.

12 Michael Liedtke, "FTC: Facebook Misled Users on Privacy," *Telegram.com*, Nov. 30, 2011.

13 Ibid.

14 Romano, "Walking a New Beat."

15 John Lynch and Jenny Ellickson, "Obtaining and Using Evidence From Social Networking Sites," United States Department of Justice, Computer Crime and Intellectual Property Section, Mar. 16, 2010, https://www.eff.org/files/filenode/social_network/20100303_crim_socialnetworking.pdf, (accessed Jan. 16, 2012).

16 United States Department of Homeland Security, Citizen and Immigration Services, "Social Networking Sites and Their Importance to FDNS," July 20, 2010, https://www.eff.org/files/filenode/social_network/DHS_CustomsImmigration_SocialNetworking.pdf, (accessed Jan. 16, 2012).

17 SMILE Conference, Advertisement, *SMILE-A LAwS Communications Event.* LAwS Communications. http://lawscommunications.com/smile, (accessed Jan. 16, 2012).

18 *U.S. v. Eric McDavid* et al. criminal complaint. Case # 2:06-MJ-0021, Jan. 17, 2006, http://supporteric.org/sacramento_affidavit___crim_complaint.pdf, (accessed Jan. 20, 2012).

19 Ibid.

20 The informant had a Myspace account that she continued to log on to after their arrest, and FBI case agent Nasson Walker had a Myspace account that he used regularly.

21 *U.S. v. Eric McDavid* et al. Idiosyncratic capitalization in the original.

22 Ibid.

23 Documents from the FBI on Eric McDavid obtained by the author through the Freedom of Information Act.

24 Social networking can continue to haunt people even after they leave prison. On September 16, 2010, a year and a half after his release from prison, environmental and animal rights activist Rodney Coronado was sent back on a probation violation. His offense? Accepting a "friend request" from another activist on Facebook. According to the government, by accepting this request Coronado had violated a provision of his probation that prohibited "associating" with any activists, as well as using an "unauthorized" computer. Adam Federman, "The Persecution of Rod Coronado," *Counterpunch,* Sept. 1, 2010.

25 Andy Furillo, "Sacramento Judge Delays Contempt Decision against Facebook," *Sacto 9-1-1, The Sacramento Bee,* Oct. 11, 2011.

26 Randy Borum and Chuck Tilby, "Anarchist Direct Actions: A Challenge for Law Enforcement," *Studies in Conflict & Terrorism* 28.3 (May–June, 2005): 201–23.

27 In Our Towns, "Impersonation Charged," *Courant.com.* Oct. 25, 2006.

28 Tiffany Kaiser, "NYPD Looks to Mine Social Networks for Info on Criminal Activity," *DailyTech,* Aug. 11, 2011.

29 Kimberly Dozier, "AP Exclusive: CIA following Twitter, Facebook," *Yahoo! News.* Associated Press, Nov. 4, 2011.

30 Larry McShane, "Facebook Post Wishing Osama Bin Laden Killed Math Teacher Gets New Hampshire Teen Suspended," *New York Daily News,* May 19, 2011. The school refused to comment on the issue, citing student privacy restrictions. It is ironic that the school would invoke privacy as a way to avoid defending their actions rather than as something that would prevent intrusions into a student's personal life.

31 Tracy Gordon Fox, "Extra Eyes Watch Online," *Hartford Courant,* Oct. 29, 2006.

32 "Nation's Attorneys General Announce Nationwide Agreement With Myspace Regarding Social Networking Safety," *NAAG News.* National Association of Attorneys General, Jan. 14, 2008.

33 Sarah Jacobsson Purewal, "Why Facebook's Facial Recognition Is Creepy," *PC World*. June 8, 2011.

34 Sean Teehan, "Facebook Photos Bring Suspensions," *Boston.com*. May 8, 2011.

35 Harvey Jones and Jose Hiram Soltren. "Facebook: Threats to Privacy," Massachusetts Institute of Technology, Dec. 14, 2005, http://groups.csail.mit.edu/mac/classes/6.805/student-papers/fall05-papers/facebook.pdf, (accessed Jan. 16, 2012).

36 Cory Golden, "Students Accuse UCD of Trying to 'infiltrate' Protest Groups," *The Davis Enterprise*, Apr. 13, 2011.

37 Anne Reynolds Myler, "RE: URGENT: October 7th Day of Protest," Message to Griselda Castro and Brett Burns, Apr. 21, 2011. Email. http://www.scribd.com/doc/53581856/part-2-of-3-UC-Davis-Docs-Reveal-Officials-Surveillance-and-Infiltration-Tactics-During-Campus-Fee-Increase-Protests.

38 Army Field Manual 3-24 Appendix B: B15, B17.

39 California Penal Code Section 186.22 (f) "criminal street gang" http://law.onecle.com/california/penal/186.22.html, (accessed Jan. 22, 2012).

40 Kim Strosnider, "Anti-Gang Ordinances After City of Chicago v. Morales: The Intersection of Race, Vagueness Doctrine, and Equal Protection in the Criminal Law," *American Criminal Law Review* 39.1 (2002): 101–46. *Race and Anti-Gang Ordinances*. The University of Dayton School of Law, Winter 2002.

41 Katherine Rosenberg, "Myspace: A Place for Gangs," *Victorville Daily Press*, June 6, 2009. Gang unit head Detective Jeremy Martinez says, "They have since taken down that page. I don't know if they got smart or what, but the individual pages are still active. That's how I'm identifying, or trying to identify the gang members. It's a great tool.... Sometimes you get lucky and it has a good photo of them, or it lists where they live or what school they go to.... A few of them actually put their real names." Nowhere does the detective say that these "37 suspected gang members" are wanted criminals or that their Myspace profiles offer evidence of crimes.

42 Author's interview with one of the targets of the raid, Justin Hand. August, 2008

43 Anonymous Analytics, "Who We Are," *Anonymous Analytics*. July 20, 2012. http://anon-analytics.com/.

44 Nate Anderson, "How One Man Tracked Down Anonymous—And Paid a Heavy Price," *Wired.com*. Feb. 10, 2011.

45 Ibid.

46 Darlene Storm, "Army of Fake Social Media Friends to Promote Propaganda," *Computerworld*, Feb. 22, 2011.

47 Brad Friedman, "Democrats Call for Probe Into Chamber's Shady Plot to Sabotage Progressive Organizations." *AlterNet*, Mar. 1, 2011.

48 Eric Lipton and Charlie Savage, "Hackers Reveal Offers to Spy on Corporate Rivals," *The New York Times*, Feb. 11, 2011.

49 Ashlee Vance and Brad Stone, "Palantir, the War on Terror's Secret Weapon," *Bloomberg Business Week*, Nov. 22, 2011.

50 Marco Werman, "Clay Shirky and the Political Power of Social Media," *The World*, Public

Radio International, Jan. 21, 2011.

51   Anonymous, "Clay Shirky on Twitter and the Social Media Revolution," *The Online Journalism Blog*. Paul Bradshaw, Nov. 7, 2009.

52   Evgeny Morozov, "Smart Dictators Don't Quash the Internet," *The Wall Street Journal*. Feb. 19, 2011.

53   Ibid. On the other hand, prior to an August 2011 protest, Bay Area Rapid Transit (BART) Police shut down cell phone service in its downtown stations to prevent the protesters from coordinating their actions through social media. Michael Cabanatuan, "BART Admits Halting Cell Service to Stop Protests," *SFGate*, Aug. 13, 2011.

54   David Meyerm "Twitter, Facebook and RIM 'look Forward' to Riots Talks," *ZDNet UK*, Aug. 12, 2011.

55   Malcolm Gladwell, "Twitter, Facebook, and Social Activism," *The New Yorker*, Oct. 4, 2010. Evgeny Morovoz points out that those strong ties existed between activists in the Middle East before the recent uprisings: "The collaborations between Tunisian and Egyptian cyber-activists—so widely celebrated in the press—were not virtual, either. In the space of a week in May 2009, I crashed two (independently organised) workshops in Cairo, where bloggers, techies, and activists from both countries were present in person, sharing tips on how to engage in advocacy and circumvent censorship…." He further elaborates: "There were many more events like this—not just in Cairo, but also in Beirut and Dubai. Most of them were never publicised, since the security of many participants was at risk, but they effectively belie the idea that the recent protests were organised by random people doing random things online. Those who believe that these networks were purely virtual and spontaneous are ignorant of the recent history of cyber-activism in the Middle East…". Evgeny Morozov. "Facebook and Twitter Are Just Places Revolutionaries Go," *The Guardian*, Mar. 7, 2011.

56   Steve Sherman, "Why Social Media—Even Twitter and Facebook—Matters," *Left Eye On Books*, Feb. 17, 2011.

57   Morozov, "Smart Dictators Don't Quash the Internet."

58   Wayne Hansen, "How Social Media Is Changing Law Enforcement," *Government Technology*, Dec. 2, 2011.

59   Melody Gutierrez, "Controversial T-shirts Puts Twin Rivers Police Department in the Spotlight Again," *The Sacramento Bee*, Oct. 31, 2011.

60   Bill Lindelof, "Twin Rivers School Police Chief Placed on Administrative Leave," *Sacto 9-1-1*, *The Sacramento Bee*, Nov. 10, 2011.

61   Vivian Ho, "S.F. Cops Accidentally Leaked Occupy Raid Plans," *San Francisco Chronicle*, Jan. 10, 2011.

62   For more information about computer security visit https://help.riseup.net/en/security and http://www.earthfirstjournal.org/section.php?id=4.

63   Christian Parenti, *The Soft Cage: Surveillance in America : From Slavery to the War on Terror*, (New York: Basic, 2003).

64   Jeffrey H. Reiman, *The Rich Get Richer and the Poor Get Prison*, (Needham Heights: Allyn & Bacon, 2001).

65 Thomas Fuller, "Main Opposition to Boycott Myanmar Election," *The New York Times*, Mar. 29, 2010.

66 Republican Sinn Fein, "Elections and Abstentionism." *Republican Sinn Fein*. Jan. 22, 2012, http://www.rsf.ie/election.htm.

67 Vagabond Theorist, "Why I Don't Vote," *Infoshop News*, Nov. 2, 2010.

68 Dahlia Lithwick, "How OWS Confuses and Ignores Fox News and the Pundit Class," *Slate Magazine*, Oct. 26, 2011.

69 Katya Komisurak, "Legal Briefing for Activists at the Republican National Convention," *Just Cause Law Collective*, Center for Constitutional Rights, 2007.

PART FIVE

CONSPIRACY CHARGES
AND TERRORISM TRIALS

BUILDING CONSPIRACY:
Informants in the Case of Eric McDavid

JENNY ESQUIVEL

> *"The power to offer a temptation to crime is the power to decide who shall be tempted. It can be and often has been used as a way for the Government to eliminate its enemies...."*
> —*Professor Paul Chevigny, "A Rejoinder,"* The Nation[1]

INFORMANTS ARE AT THE HEART OF THE U.S. JUDICIAL SYSTEM. AS ALEXANDRA Natapoff points out in her book *Snitching: Criminal Informants and the Erosion of American Justice*, "Snitching is paradigmatic of the American criminal process because it embodies three of its distinctive characteristics: secrecy, discretion, and the dominance of plea bargaining."[2] Informants have long been integral to the functioning of the police in the U.S.—most notably in the "war" on drugs. Since 9/11 there have been a series of high-profile cases related to a different kind of war. As the "war on terror" has ensnared countless individuals, Muslims in particular have borne the brunt of this war on ideas. But perhaps seeing an opportunity to expand long-standing investigations, to respond to increasing pressure from industry groups whose pockets were being affected, or to give the impression of "success" in their new war the state also intensified its gaze on the animal rights, environmental, and anarchist movements. From December 2005 and into 2006, nine people were arrested by the FBI and charged with a series of arsons, most of which had occurred in the Pacific Northwest. Four others were indicted, two of whom have since been captured and two whom have not. "Operation Backfire" was the culmination of years of (mostly fruitless) investigation. A break in the case came in 2004 when Jacob Ferguson, threatened with being charged with an arson at a car dealership (known as the "Romania II" fire[3]), decided to fully cooperate with the Feds. Ironically, Ferguson had no involvement in that fire. But he had been on the Feds' radar since 2001 when a roommate of his, Heather Coburn, reported him to the police as a suspect when her truck went missing. (The truck was later found a block away from the house.) When another activist went to the police requesting reports on both the "stolen" truck and Romania II, the cops began drawing links between the two. Ferguson later submitted to an interview with the Feds after being subpoenaed to a Grand jury in October 2001. He was subpoenaed again in 2002, but they still were not getting the information they needed to build a case. That wouldn't happen until Ferguson decided to cooperate in 2004.

At the behest of the FBI, Ferguson traveled the country to visit his old friends and comrades and reminisce about actions they had participated in together. All the while, he was wearing a wire. These conversations fed the government a wealth of information it wouldn't otherwise have had access to. After Ferguson's sentencing in 2008, the prosecuting attorney told the media that Ferguson's assistance broke what had been, up until that time, a "wall of silence" about the case. "Only through the assistance of Mr. Ferguson, did the pieces of this mosaic come together," Kirk Engdall said.[4] Without Ferguson's cooperation, the government might never have succeeded in cracking the case.

Operation Backfire has been identified by many within environmental and animal rights circles as the beginning of the "Green Scare"—a term that refers to the targeting of these movements by local and federal law enforcement for harassment, arrest and prosecution. The "Green Scare"—whether or not one chooses to use that particular moniker—is certainly alive and kicking. And in fact, it could easily be argued that it began long before the arrests in 2005.

Since 9/11, the government has shifted vast amounts of money and resources to the task of "fighting terrorism." In 2011, the *Los Angeles Times* reported that federal and state governments were spending as much as $75 billion a year on "domestic security."[5] In a paper detailing these expenses, Professors John Mueller and Mark Stewart write, "federal expenditures on domestic homeland security have increased by some $360 billion over those in place in 2001."[6] Much of this has been used to "expose, disrupt, misdirect, discredit, or otherwise neutralize" environmental, animal rights, and anarchist "organizations and groupings, their leadership, spokesmen, membership, and supporters." This language is actually from a 1967 internal FBI memo concerning "black nationalist, hate-type organizations." The memo was unearthed—along with several thousands of other pages of FBI documents—when COINTELPRO was exposed in 1971. Today, the language the FBI uses in reference to its new enemy #1 is chillingly similar. In a statement issued to Congress in 2005, FBI Deputy Assistant Director John Lewis stated, "Together with our partners, we are working to detect, disrupt, and dismantle the animal rights and environmental extremist [*sic*] movements that are involved in criminal activity."[7]

True to their word—at least in this instance—the Feds have waged all-out war against anyone and everyone who poses a threat to industries engaging in the destruction of the environment or the torture and abuse of animals (or the bureaucracies and state structures that support them). And this has certainly not been limited to folks engaged in illegal activity. In 2006, six people known as the SHAC 6 were convicted of conspiracy to violate the federal Animal Enterprise Protection Act. (SHAC stands for Stop Huntingdon Animal Cruelty, a campaign against Huntingdon Life Sciences.) The six were not accused of actually engaging in any "terrorist" acts themselves. Rather, they were alleged to have operated a website that reported on and expressed ideological support for protest activity against Huntingdon Life Sciences and its business affiliates. The government's case against them centered on the idea that above-ground organizers of a campaign are responsible for any and all acts that anyone engages in while furthering their goals.

In February 2006, Rod Coronado was charged with distribution of information relating to explosives, destructive devices, and weapons of mass destruction. This charge stemmed from a lecture he gave in 2003, in which he answered a question about how he made an incendiary device used in an action for which he had already spent four years in federal prison. After a jury deadlocked on the charges, the government threatened to charge Rod with the same thing—for a different speech. Understandably exhausted by fighting legal battles for so many years, and ready to move on to life with his family, in December 2006, he accepted a plea bargain (one that did not require him to cooperate with the government); he was sentenced to 12 months in prison (a "bargain" compared to the five-to-ten years he could have received at trial).

These examples are two among many. The Green Scare is far-reaching and constantly changing. In January 2006, it took yet another menacing turn.

On Friday, January 13, 2006, Eric McDavid, Zachary Jenson, and Lauren Weiner were arrested in Auburn, California, and charged with conspiracy to destroy public and private property by means of fire or explosives. The three were labeled "eco-terrorists" and accused of being members of an Earth Liberation Front (ELF) cell. Their arrest was the direct result of an FBI informant, a young woman by the name of "Anna," who was paid over $65,000 by the FBI to befriend activists, fabricate a crime, and implicate them in it. Zachary Jenson and Lauren Weiner caved under the threat of twenty years in prison and agreed to cooperate with the prosecution in exchange for a plea deal that would drastically reduce their sentences. This cooperation included testifying against Eric at his trial and providing the government with information on people unrelated to the case, as well as an agreement to testify at secret grand jury proceedings, should the government request it.[8] On September 27, 2007, after receiving faulty instructions from the court, a jury found Eric guilty. On May 8, 2008, he was sentenced to nineteen years and seven months in prison. Eric's is one of the two longest sentences of any environmental prisoner we know of in the United States, including people who pled guilty to multiple arsons spanning several years.[9] Eric, in contrast, was accused of nothing more than thinking or talking about the "wrong" things. For more information on Eric and his case, please visit www.supporteric.org.

Unfortunately, since Eric's arrest there seems to have been an increase in the number of cases involving the use of informants and entrapment. In order to better protect ourselves and our comrades from future government abuses and imprisonment, we need to arm ourselves with the knowledge and information necessary to guard against infiltration. There are a number of lessons from Eric's case that could be useful to this end.

Before we begin, however, a quick note about fear: It's easy to feel "paranoid" in today's political environment. While it is critical that we maintain a high level of security consciousness, we must also be aware of how fear can infect and destroy our movements. The Feds have a long history of using this fear as a tool of repression—effectively manipulating and coercing us into internalizing their mechanisms of policing. Not only is this damaging to each of us on a very personal level, it also carries with it the very real possibility of alienating us from each other, pulling apart tightly knit communities, and causing our movements to unravel from the inside. This process can destroy a movement faster than any outside, physical force ever could. In light of this, all of the information below is offered with a very important caveat: there is almost no such thing as a fool-proof snitch test, and none of the observations below should be considered as such.

It is not my intention to instill fear and provoke immobility. That would be counterproductive. Instead, I wish to offer some insight, based on my own experiences with this particular case, about possible warning signs. In the pages that follow, you will find explanations and descriptions of cop behavior, as well as some background details. I urge you to draw your own conclusions. Keep in mind that this is not a checklist. None of these behaviors, taken on its own, could be considered "proof" of someone's identity as an undercover/snitch/informant. Misidentifying someone as an informant is an incredibly serious error.

Finally, by way of explanation and in the interest of transparency, a few details about the author: I am Eric McDavid's partner. He and I met in August of 2004, which, coincidentally, is the exact same time that he met "Anna." I also met Anna—and Zachary Jenson—at this time. Much of what follows is informed by my personal experiences with the three of them. Jenson and I were once close friends. We traveled together, he stayed in my home on more than one occasion, and I did support work for him after his arrest (until he started cooperating). Anna and I had very limited contact for a very short period of time. We met in August of 2004 at a CrimethInc gathering in Des Moines, Iowa, and spent a small amount of time together there. From there, friends and I traveled to the Republican National Convention (RNC) in New York. Anna, Jenson, and Eric all met us in NYC and we spent much of the week together. After the RNC, I lost all contact with Anna and only knew of her through my friendships with Jenson and Eric. Jenson, Eric, and I remained in contact and grew rather close. Eric and I became partnered (officially) right before Eric's arrest.

After Eric was arrested, I became deeply involved in his support—which also meant doing a fair amount of work for his lawyer. Some of that work included transcribing the dozens of hours of surveillance footage turned over by the prosecution in discovery. Those transcriptions, along with testimony given at trial, provide a wealth of information about Anna and how she operated. Much of what follows is gleaned from these sources.

ANNA: A CASE STUDY

WHEN ANNA INTRODUCED herself to Jenson and Eric in August, 2004, she was fairly new on the scene. She had no real previous contacts or connections, but claimed to possess specific skills and to have experience with "direct action." During the time she worked for the FBI, Anna played the role of a medic at various protests and gatherings. She wore the garb and carried basic first aid supplies—despite having no medical training and having done no independent study of herbs, tinctures, or other natural medicinals. During Eric's trial, Anna stated, "I wore the attire of a street medic. However, if someone came to me for aid, I always passed them off to someone else."[10/11] Clearly, this ruse had the potential to put people in real need of medical care in danger. Anna claimed to have a specific skill, but was unable to demonstrate any real knowledge about it or practical application of it.

Anna also spoke in veiled terms about her participation in previous actions. In fact, she implied to Eric, Jenson, and Weiner that she had been involved in fairly serious direct actions in the past, and passed herself off as someone with "experience"—with skills and knowledge that could be useful to people planning actions. If someone boasts and brags about illegal things they have done in the past, they are, at the very least, a danger to themselves and those around them. This kind of behavior would almost certainly draw the attention of any informant who might be within earshot—whether or not the person doing the bragging is actually an informant herself. If the person's bragging is based in fact, they could be getting themselves (and those around them) in serious trouble. Even if what they are saying is untrue they are drawing unwanted attention to themselves and their friends. And this kind of behavior could point to more deep-seated character flaws that are less than desirable when choosing people to work with.

While Anna was usually reticent to divulge the details of her own life to comrades, she had no problem probing others for information about theirs. She asked many questions—about people's political history, how they became involved, who they knew, what actions they had participated in. Anna asked about all of these things with alarming persistence. She sometimes said that she was conducting an informal study, or that she was just curious about how different people became involved in the anarchist movement. She asked Eric on numerous occasions whether he knew whether Ryan Lewis had "help" with the ELF actions for which he was accused, in an apparent attempt to solicit an admission from Eric. Eric's response was the correct and solid, "I don't know, and I wouldn't tell you if I did."

DISPOSABLE INCOME

ANNA HAD SEEMINGLY endless supplies of cash. She paid for the group's food when they were together. She paid for Weiner's plane tickets to California in November 2005, so she could meet with the others—a meeting that only happened because of Anna's urging, done at the behest of the FBI. She drove Weiner and Jenson from D.C. to California in January 2006. The computers the group was using were supplied by Anna (and the FBI, which later confiscated them). She paid for the cabin they were living in. When the group went shopping for groceries and supplies, Anna pulled out $100 bills and gave them to the others to make the actual purchases. (This allowed her to claim during trial that the money for shopping came from Eric and Weiner's pockets.)

In an interview with Madelynn Amalfitano in 2010, Weiner explained,

> I saw it like a very personal, like she wanted me to be there through this moment. She was paying for me to be there, so it's like, you know, someone pays for you to go on vacation with them, they want you to enjoy it with them… So it's almost like you're indebted to them… and this is why I was uncomfortable with her paying for so many things. You become indebted. And not just indebted, but dependent as well. I had no money outside, of you know, what she was giving me.[12]

Anna's explanation for her startling wealth was that she had worked as a stripper. She also claimed to have worked in a chemistry lab at her school (although no one looked into her story to see if it checked out). Even if both of these lies had been true, it is highly doubtful that Anna would have been able to afford all these large expenses, as well as completely support four people indefinitely, without the seemingly bottomless pockets of the FBI.

ERRATIC BEHAVIOR

ANNA HAD A tendency to disappear and reappear sporadically. Often people wouldn't hear from her for months at a time, then she would come back on the scene, asking for help finding specific people or advocating confrontational, risky behavior. Anna first appeared at the protests against the Free Trade Area of the Americas in 2003. From there her handlers sent her to the G8 in Georgia, the 2004 Democratic National Convention, the 2004 CrimethInc convergence in Des Moines, and the 2004 RNC in New York. But after this flurry of activity, Anna disappeared for months. According to her testimony at trial, the Feds did not call her again until January 2005 to see if she could attend the inaugural protests, and then again in June 2005 to see if she could attend the Philadelphia BioTech protests. During much of this time, Anna was not in contact with her "friends." She claimed that she did not stay in contact with Eric and Jenson after August 2004 until Eric started emailing her in 2005. She initiated contact with them at BioTech in Philly in 2005, where they were all physically reunited. Before that, in May 2005, Anna began emailing her contacts in an effort to track Eric down. The transcripts from her trial testimony read:

> **Q.** [Mark Reichel, Eric's lawyer] Okay. Now, why would you have written, if you did, an e-mail to someone in May saying, you know, where is McDavid and Ollie, I'm trying to get a hold of them?
>
> **A.** [Anna] I was attempting to gain further access into the protest groups and the groups that I had previous contacts with. I had not been undercover within those groups for a lengthy period of time. And I was attempting to use the contacts that I had once known to gain further access to the groups.[13]

In the same email exchange referenced here, Anna offered up the following to one of her contacts:

What's up in your corner of the world? I've been trying ot [*sic*] track you down for a while—the Halliburton Shareholders Mtg is comign [*sic*] up soon in Houston. Anythign [*sic*] "fun" planned?? :) I'd love to have a party, if you know what I mean....[14]

And in a later email:

Brutal—It'll be a reunion! :) DO you guys need anything? Supplies, paint, chains, nials [*sic*], pipe, anything? Tar and Feathers? Like I said, disposable income, so ask around all your contacts. It'd be safer to bring from outside as well. So what are we gonna' do? :)[15]

Here Anna is emailing someone she barely knows and whom she hasn't spoken with in months, asking about other activists, advocating illegal activity, and offering to provide the funds to make it happen. That all of this happened at all is a bit alarming. The fact that she was presumably trying to "plan" illegal activity over email should have been even more disturbing.

SURVEILLANCE

ACCORDING TO HER testimony at trial, at the beginning of her work with the FBI Anna's main method of communication with them was her cell phone. At this point in time, she was not (as far as we know) wearing a wire, and relied on text messaging to update them about her whereabouts, the plans the group was making, where they were headed next, etc. Because of this, she was overly reliant on her cell phone—she frequently disappeared to make phone calls and was loath to be anywhere without it. When the group was living at the cabin in Dutch Flat, they asked her repeatedly to turn off her phone, but she never complied.

Based on transcripts handed over in discovery, we also believe that Anna had a wire in her bag, making her reluctant to go anywhere without it.

The car that Anna was driving, which was the group's sole source of transportation during their stay in Dutch Flat (and was also the car in which she ferried Jenson and Weiner across the country), was wired with audio and video surveillance. Because the device was housed in the radio console, she claimed that the stereo was broken. This claim probably should have provoked skepticism as they were still able to hook up their iPods to listen to music in the car. At one point, during a conversation between Anna and Weiner, Weiner voiced concern that Anna's car might be wired. Anna reassured her that it was not, and feigned offense that Lauren could think she wouldn't know whether or not her own car was secure.

The bottom line here is this: There is no way for someone to be certain that their car is or is not bugged (unless the someone in question is the person who did it). If someone insists their car is not bugged, they are either foolish or lying. Weiner was talking to a person she considered to be a trusted friend and her response to Anna's reply (acceptance) was understandable. Unfortunately, her decision to act on the belief that the car was *not* wired was very detrimental. Even if a person has every reason to believe that a particular space is not wired (a car, a house, an office…), they should never under any circumstances talk about illegal activity or say otherwise incriminating things about themselves or others in such places.

Because the laws about surveillance (not that these laws are always followed) require that the "source" be present in the room while recording, and because the government is not supposed to record in private areas of the house (bedrooms and bathrooms), Anna insisted on sleeping in the living room during her stay at the cabin in Dutch Flat. This allowed the Feds to monitor and record her at all times—even while she was sleeping. It also, presumably, gave them more "air time" because she was almost always in the community space. The night before their arrest, the group insisted that Anna claim a more private space for herself in the cabin; they thought it would help her relax and be happier. Knowing that the group would be arrested the next morning, she told them that she would sleep on the couch for one more night, then move elsewhere the following night.

Anna was constantly asking her companions to repeat themselves—so much so that Eric jokingly commented at one point about her need for hearing aids. During one conversation, Anna became quite confrontational about the group's communication style, going so far as to tell them that they needed to look directly at her when talking to her (more than likely in an effort to get a better recording). Sometimes the ears you are speaking up for might not be the ones you can see in front of you.

WORD GAMES

WHEN A PERSON lies for a living, they become pretty adept at it, but when they're lying 24/7, they're bound to slip up once in a while. Anna told a lot of stories—and they didn't always add up in a logical way. Anna was "arrested" at the RNC in 2004. Interestingly, the other people she was with at the time who, like her, had their bags searched, were *not* arrested at that time. She then told a number of people that she had been separated from other arrestees and "interrogated" by the police. Later, when Weiner was asking her about it in Dutch Flat, Anna responded that she had been quickly released and had dinner with a friend that night. That was not the story that Weiner had originally heard from other people, and it certainly did not match the stories told by other people after an RNC arrest; many of them were in custody for two days or more.

Anna was incredibly skilled at manipulation. One way she manipulated people was to put words into their mouths in an attempt to get them on tape saying damaging things. For example, Anna would have a conversation with Jenson, say something encouraging violence or "revolution," then in a later conversation with Weiner, Anna would tell her that it was Jenson who had made statements about violence or revolution. The following conversation between Anna and Jenson, recorded in the car, is a good example of this. In the following transcripts, "S" is the "source" (Anna) and "Z" is Zachary Jenson. Lauren Weiner is presumably asleep in the back seat. [IA] indicates that the dialogue was inaudible.

> **S:** Like I pretty much think that all of us are revolutionaries. I think that, even though we haven't really said it, we all are hoping for one thing, this country and [IA] the world [IA]

> **Z:** Yeah.

> **S:** Yeah. I think, even though we haven't really said it, I think all of us are hoping that these actions join the bigger picture and help that. Are a part of that revolutionary action. Like Ren [Weiner] was saying, start this, and then someone will pick up what we're doing and then another person will pick up and keep going. And maybe we'll have started a revolution.[16]

Later, during the same car ride, after Jenson moves to the backseat and Weiner joins Anna up front, we hear a strikingly similar conversation.

> **S:** Brings me to two separate but equal points that Ollie [Jenson] and I talked about earlier. He and I, rather he, talked about how even though none of us have said it [IA] even though none of us have really said it, that doing this—and I think you went into it a little bit—um, was kind of a first step on hoping to draw out that long and windy road toward revolution.[17]

This conversational ju-jitsu served a couple of different purposes. First of all, it was a tool she used to try and convince the others in the group that they were all "on board" and committed, when in fact she was the one pushing the group and keeping them together. It was also an attempt to confuse the others about conversations they had engaged in, making them think they had said things that *she* had actually said. She would then later try to get them to agree that they had said something or suggested a particular course of action, so that it would be caught on tape as "their" idea.

Occasionally, this would backfire on her. Here is an excerpt from a conversation recorded at the cabin in Dutch Flat:

> **A** [Anna]: Here's a question for you. Do you remember at CrimethInc in Des Moines, at the skillshare on guerrilla warfare, they talked about attacking federal institutions?
>
> **E** [Eric]: Oh, in Indiana.
>
> **A:** And state government. Yeah.
>
> **E:** I wasn't there, at that one.
>
> **A:** I remember you guys all talked about… I totally remember this conversation.
>
> **E:** Really? Cause I …
>
> **A:** Cause we worked at the skill share, where I think [redacted] was, and he talked to us about it
>
> **E:** Yeah…
>
> **A:** And…
>
> **E:** What do you remember?[18]

Anna was later questioned on the stand about this exchange:

> **Q.** [W]hen you asked him that, that's kind of a reaffirmation, you wanted to get something on tape from him about that, right?
>
> **A.** Correct.
>
> **Q.** And it just didn't get on there, right?
>
> **A.** Correct.

Q. In fact, the opposite got on there, correct?

A. Correct.[19]

In some instances, Anna took this tactic a step further and tried to get them on tape participating in specific actions. On January 12th, the day before their arrest, the group was boiling bleach in an attempt to follow one of Anna's bomb "recipes." (The effort ended in failure when the bowl they were using broke). Anna became clearly agitated when Weiner and Jenson refused to participate:

S [Anna]: Why don't you guys come out here and be a part of this?

L [Weiner]: Ollie is looking up what the other shit is in that salt.

S: Whatever.

L: Like, we are. Don't worry. I just don't want to, you know, inhale bleach fumes. I feel safe in the house...

S: That's not the point. You're supposed to be deconditioning yourself as you said. You're supposed to be out here. Being part of this.

L: I told you I'm going to be standing pretty far back.

S: You need to be strong. You need to surprise yourself...

L: I'm not going to get bleach poisoning by standing over it, alright.

S: There's no bleach poisoning.

L: If I don't have to do anything right now, I could see it from here.

S: What do you want to do to be part of this?

L: Uh, I'll measure out the...

S: How about, how about, she, you can measure out the salt, what about, um, helping filter.

L: Alright…

S: Well, that's a good idea. A real good idea. Everyone wants to be a equal part of this, right? They need to help. They need to help. You know it.

E [Eric McDavid]: You don't. Nobody needs to do anything, Anna. People are going to do what they feel like they need to do.

S: They've said they wanted to.

E: You don't have any control over it.

S: They've said they wanted to. So—

E: Yeah, but, how, it's not your place to make them hold onto their word; that's their place.

S: No, but you can help them. Everyone needs a little help.

E: Sometimes, it's true. But not all the time.[20]

Anna testified at trial that while this was happening she was actually moving furniture around the house in an attempt to give the surveillance cameras a clearer view.

PUSHING, CAJOLING, ENTRAPPING

PERHAPS THE MOST alarming of Anna's traits was her constant pushing to plan more, say more, and do more. If ever there was a lull in the conversation, Anna would be the one to push it back into focus. She berated the group on multiple occasions for not sticking to a plan, and was constantly suggesting what the group should do next. Whenever anyone showed signs of unease or hesitation, Anna was there to harass them into participation. At one point she asked the group if they were "copping out" and was insistent that they "stick to a damned plan." The following conversation occurred the night before Eric, Jenson, and Weiner were arrested. It is very typical of the conversations the group was having throughout the entire week they were at the cabin together. The group was talking about "targets" and their desire to take things down a notch.

S [Anna]: So where do dams, power stations, gas stations and banks, where do they fit into it?

E [Eric]: That could even fit like, within the next year....

S: What!

E: What are you thinking?

S: Ah, nothing.

E: Big shuffle a little too big for you?

S: I'm just upset that we lost the Forest Service one.

E: Eh.

L [Weiner]: We haven't lost it.

E: It's still there, it's not going anywhere.

S: I guess I'm just different than you guys. I like to do this, this and this [makes vertical steps with hands]. I don't like this amorphous crap. I don't like it. I don't like it at all.

E: Ok.

S: And I don't like how I always have to change to your guys' stuff.

E: Yeah.

S: I don't like that. I wish one day we could keep the damned plan. I wish one day you guys could stick to a list. I don't like having to bend to fit your schedules.

L: We're all bending.

S: Why can't one day you guys say, hey, this is what we want [movement of hands]. That's me.

L: The thing is, we're all bending.

S: Yeah? I don't see it…

E: Sorry you don't see that, but, I mean, we just totally, I mean, Ollie had an issue, and I had to change my perception of it, because he's part, he's part of this.

S: Yeah.

E: And so it's kinda' like, ok, we're moving too fast for him, we got too much stuff going on for him. We got to slow down, back it down.

S: I understand slowing down, but I still don't like how we're not saying, hey, you know, sure let's slow it down, we have years, two years, three years to do this. Fine. Why can't we say hey, in these two years, three years we're going to try to do this. And then we'll move up to this, and then we'll move up to this. Ok.

L: I thought that was what we were doing.

S: No you're not. Cause you said "Oh I don't want to put a hierarchy on it, I don't want to put a level." So—

L: Because we don't want to say one thing is more important than the other.

S: You are saying that one is more important than the other.

E: From my perception, that's what we said.

S: Ya, you're saying we're going to try out all this, and then we're going to move to this. And then once we feel we're bad-ass enough, then we are going to move to this. That's what I'm looking for. That's what I'm hoping to hear.

L: Well that's pretty much what we're doing!

E: That's kinda' like, what I was trying to get my point around. I'm sorry if I miscommunicated that.

S: Yeah.

E: That was like, what I was trying to say.…

L: What you just said is what I understand is now, we're all together.

S: Ok, good. Well I—don't understand. What're we gonna do, and then what, and what's up here [indicating levels with hands]?

E: All right!

S: What are we working towards?

L: You want a goal.

S: Yeah, I would like a damn goal.[21]

The conversation continued to degenerate. And, of course, the tone of a conversation is difficult to convey through a transcription. Suffice it to say that Anna was very combative and emotional.

Later in the evening:

S [Anna]: Tomorrow, what were we planning on doing tomorrow? Are we still planning on doing anything tomorrow? Or should I just stop thinking about plans?

E [Eric]: Hmm.

L [Weiner]: I would love it if you stopped talking.

S: I would love it if you guys followed a plan! How about that?

E: All right, how about we talk about tomorrow after dinner. Would that be ok?

S: Whatever, yeah.

E: No? You want something right now?[22]

Anna was incredibly pushy and displayed an alarming unwillingness to listen to others' concerns. These are destructive, unhealthy patterns in any relationship and should never be tolerated—regardless of whether or not you are planning actions together.

Anna also constantly suggested new targets or attempted to get the others to clarify what their targets and priorities were (a difficult task, since they apparently didn't have any). In doing this, she was likely attempting to get Jenson, Weiner, and Eric on tape advocating specific actions against specific targets, which the government could later use against them at trial. It is clear when listening to the tapes that these conversations would never have happened without Anna's insistence. She was, in effect, creating the government's case for them and manufacturing the very crime for which she would never be arrested or charged.

JENSON AND WEINER

ONE OF THE most difficult aspects of Eric's arrest, trial, and conviction is figuring out what role his former codefendants played throughout the ordeal. Their role during trial was clear and obvious: they became the tools of the state, testifying against Eric in a desperate attempt to save their own skins. But Weiner and Jenson's testimonies were drastically different—in both style and content. While Weiner seemed less willing to perform for the government and almost relieved to tell a version of the story that more closely resembled the truth, Jenson's testimony was a shockingly obvious, well-rehearsed act. At times he seemed desperate to give the prosecutors what they wanted and needed to hear, even if it meant spewing lies about his former friends. What led them to this? Were there warning signs, or things that could have offered clues along the way that, if the unthinkable happened, betrayal might be the outcome?

Throughout the time the group spent together, Weiner talked just as much, if not more, than Anna. Her zealousness, in retrospect, was just a show of bravado—she was trying to prove herself to others. At one point, she lied to the group about putting graffiti up in the bathroom of a Glaxo Smith Kline building, and about throwing a brick through a window during the World Bank protests in Washington, D.C. In her proffer and on the stand, Weiner said she was "pretending" to impress Anna and the others. Weiner seemed particularly inclined to this kind of behavior because of (what she perceived as) her close relationship with Anna. At one point during trial, Eric's lawyer questioned Weiner about that relationship:

> **Q** [Mark Reichel] What I'm getting at is you liked Anna a lot, right?
>
> **A** [Weiner]. Yeah, she was a big sister to me.

Q. Right. And there was a period in January in Dutch Flats where you were acting to make her happy, right?... You would—when I say acting, I mean doing something different than what you really felt or meant?

A. Yes... I was always trying to impress her.[23]

Jenson testified that he, too, was "acting" during his time with Anna and the others.

Q [Mark Reichel]. Well, let me ask you about the issue of anybody in the group lying to each other, okay?

A [Jenson]. Okay.

Q. Okay. In late January just before the arrest, okay?... At that time frame. You testified here today that you felt reluctant or hesitant at some point, right?

A. That's true.

Q. Okay. And is it fair to say that you certainly didn't want the group to know that, right?

A. Yes, that's true... I was still saying things to make them think that I was 100 percent good to go for it.

Q. So you were saying things to make them think that you were 100 percent good to go for this whole thing, right?

A. Yeah.

Q. Were you hesitant about it a little, deep down inside, basically?

A. Yes.

Q. Okay. Reluctant?

A. Yes.[24]

All of this points to an all-too-common group dynamic whereby people feel pressured to "prove" their dedication and commitment to "the cause."

Talking shit and being "hard core" is not proof of one's deeply-held beliefs, but rather it is indicative of insecurity and possible weaknesses to be exploited by the state. People need to understand the seriousness of some forms of direct action and the consequences they face if caught; they need to realize that action is not a game. If someone is feeling hesitant or reluctant about a given course of action, those concerns should be voiced immediately. And they need to have the courage to make decisions for themselves—without acting because of others' perceived wishes or desires. If we can't stand up for ourselves amongst friends, how can we be expected to do it when we're up against the state? If people aren't able to get past the bravado and fully internalize (as much as one can without actually being there) what it means to be in prison, there is a much greater likelihood of them snitching and destroying the lives of others. It's easy for folks to talk about how prison is "no big deal"—but going up against the state *is* a big deal.

BACK TO BACKFIRE

IN EXAMINING WHAT makes codefendants turn on each other, it is useful to look at the statements made by activists-turned-informants about what they did and why they did it. While many of these statements are nothing more than excuses for people turning on their friends, there are also some valuable lessons.

In a statement released in December 2007, Darren Thurston (convicted for an attempted liberation of wild horses at a Bureau of Land Management facility) wrote about his experiences after being arrested and what he perceived to be the main causes of the avalanche of cooperation that ensued. He points to six distinct causes: 1) the FBI/government planting rumors and spreading misinformation about the defendants, 2) indictees being alienated from the activist community, 3) a lack of support for grand jury resistors, 4) a crossover between "cells," 5) attorneys pushing defendants to cooperate, and 6) the isolation of prisoners from their support and community (lack of clear communication). Some of these are more relevant than others for the purposes of this article.

Thurston claims that "the government purposely dropped names, details, and misinformation in affidavits and at bail hearings in a very successful campaign to cause confusion, sow infighting, and cut off support for those in prison... With the availability of open publishing and the proclivity of activists to pass along gossip, these FBI-started rumours became 'facts' in no time—even among long-time credible activists."[25] This is classic, textbook COINTELPRO behavior and should not come as a surprise to experienced activists. But, obviously, not everyone was prepared for this sort of sideways assault.

Meanwhile, folks on the outside engaged in damaging banter and chatter in public forums, which no doubt aided the Feds in their mission to recruit new snitches in the Backfire cases.[26] Planting rumors is certainly not limited to the post-arrest stage of repression. In December 2010, the blog "Green is the New Red" cited a document uncovered through a FOIA request in which an agent is interviewing an undercover source working within the animal rights movement. The agent's report about the interview reads: "The Animal Rights Movement does little research on newcomers into the movement and basically goes with its gut instinct as to whether a person is an informant or not. Organizers of the Animal Rights Movement *can be discredited and removed from the scene by planting rumors that they are plants and/or informants.*"[27]

Thurston points out that the first people to flip in the Operation Backfire cases were those who were already alienated from the activist community. They were more likely to talk to Ferguson when he was traveling the country, trying to get his old comrades to reminisce about their past (while he was wired). They were also willing to cooperate with the government much more quickly than the others.

For example, Stan Meyerhoff and Jenn Kolar—both long alienated from the communities they used to work in—were the first to flip (after Ferguson, of course). Meyerhoff was allegedly promising cooperation within an hour of his arrest on December 7th, 2005. Kolar apparently walked into an FBI office in Colorado two days later to turn herself in and offer assistance. The first issue—the reminiscence with former comrades—is easy enough to address by the adherence to the most basic of Security Culture principles: never talk about past actions. That is obviously more complicated than it sounds. But weighed with the possible ramifications of such seemingly friendly conversation, it is the only secure option. The second issue, however, is much more complex. It raises myriad issues around class, privilege, and the ability of an entire movement to engage the passions of those involved for a lifetime commitment. That does not mean that people have to be committed to engaging in direct action for a lifetime—or that they have to be in engaged in any action at all for a lifetime. What it does mean, however, is that if people feel connected enough to the issues and the people involved, they will not be willing to trade their freedom for someone else's when the shit hits the fan.

Often, the first sign that the Feds are involved in an investigation is when activists, their friends, families, or loved ones begin receiving subpoenas to a grand jury. While there is much in Thurston's account that feels nauseatingly akin to finger-pointing, he was correct in identifying support for grand jury resistors as an integral component to any strategy against informing, snitching, and repression in general. If people are solidly supported during this stage, it could, in a best case scenario, block the Feds in their efforts at gathering information that could result in indictments. And even if indictments do come down, the support that was built and nurtured during this early phase can be a powerful starting point for a larger campaign. When people know they will be supported—because they have already experienced it—they are much more likely to stand firm.

The issue of crossover between cells is reflective of the larger problem. Obviously, if none of the Backfire defendants had cooperated in the first place, the crossover wouldn't have mattered. Unfortunately, the very first people to flip in these cases—Jake Ferguson and Stan Meyerhoff—were involved in more than one cell, and so were able to provide information about multiple people. The lesson here is obvious. Small is beautiful. The fewer people involved, the less potential there is for a security breach.

Attorneys are notorious for pushing people to take cooperating plea deals. In fact, they are schooled in it. Without plea deals, the criminal "justice" system would come to a screeching halt. Trials are expensive, time consuming, and just plain cumbersome for everyone involved—including the government. And lawyers. We must also keep in mind that most lawyers do not have a real understanding of what motivates activists and the principles that drive their decision-making. Most attorneys would probably claim that they are looking out for the best interests of their client (which certainly do not include those of "the movement" or their client's codefendants). And in the mind of an attorney, that usually means the shortest possible sentence, regardless of what kind of soul-crushing compromise one has to make in the process. Political prisoners should be clear with their attorneys from the beginning about what is and is not acceptable to them in this realm. And if an attorney is resistant to that at any point, we need to remember that attorneys can—and sometimes should—be fired. It is hard enough to fight the state—we shouldn't have to fight our lawyers, too.[28]

In his statement, Darren Thurston also points out that the isolation prisoners endure makes it incredibly difficult to have open, honest lines of communication between prisoners and their supporters. That is undoubtedly true. It is also not a coincidence. The state knows very well that people who are isolated are much more likely to make decisions they might not otherwise make. That is why it is essential that nothing be reported on as "fact" until there is undeniable documentation about a person's status as a cooperator (a plea agreement, for instance). We should never make assumptions about what a person in prison is doing based on their desire to not speak publicly about their case—and we should most definitely *never* take the government's word about what a person in prison is doing or the decisions they are making. As frustrating and confusing as it is, dealing with arrest and imprisonment often means long periods of waiting and uncertainty. When we jump to conclusions, we run the risk of damaging our communities, the work we do and the people with whom we have relationships.

Meanwhile, it is essential that we do everything within our power to reduce the prisoner's sense of isolation. That is, in part, why prisoner support is such an incredibly important component of any real struggle or resistance movement.

Thurston goes on to say, "I chose this path because I thought I was strong and smart enough to do battle in the interview room with the Feds. I admit I made mistakes—I got tricked and cornered on a couple issues."[29] The implicit sentiment here is that he was *not* strong enough and smart enough to take on the Feds in the interview room. I would posit that no one is. It's not that the Feds are inherently stronger or smarter—it's that they are trained in the art of manipulation and coercion.

He is not the first to take on this challenge and fail miserably. In an interview with documentary filmmaker Madelynn Amalfitano, Lauren Weiner stated, "at that point, I had listened to every tape and read every transcript. And I knew that they were—that there were things not in there that I could testify to… So I saw it as an opportunity for me to tell the truth. All of it. Unfortunately I didn't realize the system didn't quite work like that. And I wouldn't be given the opportunity to do that."[30]

Thurston closes his statement by saying, "I deeply wish all of my co-defendants had refused to co-operate at the onset of this case so others wouldn't have had their hands tied."[31] Placing the blame for his cooperation on others is a transparent attempt at exoneration. The fact that four other defendants in these cases were able to obtain noncooperation plea agreements makes that clear.

LESSONS LEARNED

THERE ARE A number of lessons to be learned here, and a number of things that may seem obvious but could bear repeating.

In regards to communication, it is critical to remember that there is virtually no such thing as 100% secure email. Eric, Jenson, and Weiner were convinced that by using offshore email accounts, they could circumvent government spying. Clearly, that is pointless when one of the people you are communicating with is a government agent. They also continued to use traditional providers, such as Hotmail (as well as their supposedly "offshore" accounts), for a large proportion of their communications. Their emails were quickly handed over by those corporations—as well as their complete contact lists stored in those accounts. (The warrants specifically requested the contact lists.) Many of the emails seized were completely irrelevant, but were handed over to the Feds anyway.

Phones can be (and are) easily tapped and used as listening devices. In late 2006, a U.S. District Judge ruled that the FBI can use people's cell phones as a "roving bug." That means that they can remotely switch the cell phone microphone on and use it to eavesdrop on nearby conversations—without the person who owns the phone having any way of knowing. The phone doesn't even have to be powered on for this to work. Some people believe the only way to ensure a phone is not being used as a monitoring device is to remove the battery completely.[32]

It is imperative that one knows one's friends—especially if one chooses to work with them in actions that might land them in jail. Eric and Jenson met Anna in August of 2004 and were not arrested until January 2006. They knew Anna for a year and a half before they were arrested; they emailed her, talked to her on the phone, traveled with her, stayed with her at community spaces during gatherings, stayed with her in Weiner's apartment during the protests of the BioTech conference in 2005 and at Eric's parents' house later that year, and, finally, lived with her in a cabin for a week before their arrest. Clearly, they thought they knew her. But through all of this, they never met her family or her friends. They never had dinner at her house or met her dog. They never met her at her job, to make sure it existed. They never visited her at school, either. And they paid dearly for it. Any of these things, taken on its own, wouldn't seem all that alarming. I certainly have friends whom I have never visited at work. I don't mean to say that we need to undergo serious investigation of everyone we befriend. But people who are engaging in illegal action should be certain that the folks they are working with have stories that check out.

In many ways, it seems as if the devastation wrought by informants could be greatly mitigated by practicing and fostering healthier communication and group dynamics. We need to remember that confidence and self-esteem are distinctly different from bravado. The former are desirable traits in any companion. The latter can be not only an annoyance but also incredibly destructive—for both the person displaying it and the people around them. Both Jenson and Weiner were lacking in confidence and self-esteem, as is evidenced by the statements they made in their proffers and on the stand. They almost always caved to Anna, even when she was telling them about their own previous experiences. Their inability to stand up for themselves, or make decisions for themselves, left Anna's manipulative behavior unchecked; she ended up controlling the show. The first time the group tried to talk to Anna about their reluctance was the night before they were arrested. It is quite possible that the FBI finally knew, without a doubt, that the conspiracy they had spent so long trying to construct did not really exist. And so they made their move. If the group had found their courage in dealing with Anna before that time, it is possible they never would have been arrested.

We need to treat each other with basic respect. It is always a terrible idea to push people to action if they are reluctant. Quite simply, this is not something a good friend would do. Yet it is something Anna did relentlessly. By the time of their arrests on January 13th, it was clearly making the rest of the group incredibly uncomfortable, but they continued in their attempts to placate her. If someone is repeatedly pushing others to illegal action—action with which they are clearly uncomfortable—their motives and intent should be questioned. Challenging each other and ourselves to do the right thing are integral components to social struggles. But bullying other people to participate in illegal action (which could result in significant jail time) is unacceptable.

Besides being an unhealthy relationship pattern, it is possible that pushing people to do things they don't want to do could make it more likely that someone will flip after arrest. People must feel committed and dedicated to the work that they do—without bullying or guilt-tripping. Otherwise they most certainly will not have the inner courage and strength to withstand the stress of imprisonment.

Abusive bullies have no place in our movements or our communities. Whether or not they are working as informants, these people are disruptive and destructive to the work we do. We need to be clear that they are not welcome. That would not only make us safer from government spying, it would also make us healthier within our own communities. And the healthier we are, the more able we are to do the work that matters to us.

Eric was the one most willing to contradict Anna—but he was ultimately unwilling to cut ties with her despite her almost abusive behavior. That was in part, perhaps, because of his romantic interest in her. We must remember that romance is not indicative of "safety." Eric was involved with Anna, on some level, during the time they knew each other. He wrote her love letters, they had conversations about their relationship, and they shared some level of physical intimacy. During her testimony at Eric's trial, Anna stated that the FBI's Behavioral Analysis Unit gave her a six-page questionnaire to fill out about Eric's "personality, his behavior, personal habits, actions he has done, things he has said."[33] Presumably the information from this questionnaire was then used by the Feds to help her respond to his advances in a way that would keep him interested. In short, she led him on. It's possible that Eric's interest in Anna led him to trust someone (and say things) he otherwise wouldn't have—something the government is more than happy to use as a tool.

Eric's lawyer filed a motion accusing the government of misconduct related to Anna's manipulation of her relationship with Eric and his desire for romance. The government's response cited various cases in which informants had been used in the most devious ways—including providing people with drugs, threatening to kill a defendant's friends if they did not follow through on a drug deal, and paying for bomb-making materials. As for intimate relationships, the government's response stated, "The Ninth Circuit has held that the government is permitted to exploit intimate relationships in the context of an undercover investigation. In *United States v. Simpson*, the informant pretended to be a close personal friend of the defendant for over five months during which time she had sex with him on a regular basis."[34]

Informants are paid to lie. The insane myth about cops having to tell you if you ask them "are you a cop?" has infected our movements with a complacency and self-assuredness that is completely unwarranted. Whether or not you have ever actually believed that particular lie, its essence has permeated our discourse and practice for far too long. There is no "test" for informants—the government can and will do anything in their pursuit of a conviction. They don't have to try to cover their tracks or downplay their outrageous behavior. Instead, they simply cite all of their previous fucked-up behavior, which the courts have upheld.

In a similar vein, you don't feel good about someone you are potentially going to work with, you should not work with them. We need to remember to trust our intuition. One of the eeriest moments recorded in the dozens of hours of surveillance in Eric's case is an exchange between Jenson and Anna in the car ride out west. Jenson is talking to her about whether or not her experience in the National Guard (apparently another fabrication) made her more enthusiastic about direct action:

S [Anna]: So, um, I feel immensely for the individuals that I interacted with, like the poor suckers like me, that are over in Iraq right now, that freakin' they had no control and nothing to do and they got fucked... But um, for the institutions and the really, the overarching reasons and the bigger picture behind all that, yes, it does make me seethe with anger. Really want to fix it, do something, change something, you know... That make sense? I mean, if you're asking if it made me angry and wanna, you know, destroy it, then the answer would be yes.

Z [Jenson]: Alright.

S: What got you thinking on that?

Z: I don't know I was having a, I had a really silly paranoid thought last night while I was really stoned.

S: Oh. What?

Z: That um, that you were still like mentally fucked up from being in the National Guard... And you were like, going crazy and like leading us all into this.

S: Oh, no. Are you kidding? I'm fucking not your leader.

Z: I know, I know. But like, coaxing us into [IA] persuading us… But then I realized like, hey, that is a really silly paranoid thought.

S: Yeah, it is. I haven't done any coaxing.[35]

Zach's "paranoid" thought was actually incredibly close to the mark. Anna was, indeed, coaxing them into something. Unfortunately, his drug use allowed him an excuse to dismiss a rather astute observation.

We must ensure that we do not overcompensate for our paranoia. Luce Guillén-Givins gives an insightful account of organizing protests against the 2008 RNC in St. Paul in *Conspiracy to Riot in Furtherance of Terrorism*. She writes about several experiences with undercover informants throughout the organizing process and notes that she was not alone in her suspicions of them. "Nonetheless, we didn't have any 'smoking gun' with which to keep him ['Panda'] out and, while I wanted to exclude him anyway based on a gut feeling, the group had been clear that we weren't empowered to go on instinct alone."[36] Later, she writes about a discussion within the "Welcoming Committee" about another informant: "I felt crushed in this moment, almost wholly defeated by the groupthink that was so clearly creating an environment where people were pressured into feigning trust and affinity with people they had good reason to suspect and fear."[37]

Luce's account points to two very real obstacles for the organizing and work that we do. The first is the power issues so often prevalent in group dynamics—patriarchy, racism, classism, ageism, heteronormativity, etc. These can make it incredibly hard for people to speak openly and honestly about their concerns. If they do speak, they are often ignored or belittled. (And privileged people are often hesitant to raise concerns for fear of looking racist, sexist, or whatnot.) For a movement that often prides itself on autonomy and the power of individual action, we still have a long way to go in overcoming the groupthink that Luce so poignantly details.

The other obstacle to be overcome is the conflict between our desire to keep our work open to newcomers and our very real concerns about security. There needs to be an open, honest dialogue about how to accomplish that. Obviously, different groups have different structures, goals, lifespans, strategies, and tactics. All of that should inform any decisions made about how to balance openness with security. And, of course, there are times when it is wholly inappropriate for a group to be open to anyone other than its creators.

Security culture needs to be revived, respected, and deeply embedded. Jenson, Weiner, and Eric talked about security culture a lot—but Jenson and

Weiner both failed pretty miserably in actually carrying it out. In 2010, Will Potter posted on his blog, "'Security culture' has been cited in court cases and Congressional hearings as a source of frustration for FBI agents."[38] However, he notes the discovery of FBI documents indicating that formerly security-conscious activists are failing to follow their own protocol. The FBI documents he cites reads: "the day of those strict rules may be passing. Source believes that many of the younger activists do not subscribe to these strict requirements as they are extremely inconvenient."[39] Trading security for convenience can have devastating results.

That was clearly illustrated in the Operation Backfire cases. In the course of his travels about the country in 2005, Ferguson was able to get a number of those involved to reminisce about their previous actions—talking not just about themselves, but about others who were involved. Because these folks trusted someone working for the Feds, most of them are now in prison.

The recent explosion of social media sites is another example of the destructive power of our conveniences. Myspace pages and, more recently, Facebook pages have repeatedly shown up in court documents. Both Jenson and Weiner had Myspace accounts, and these were monitored by the FBI and used against them. Pages and pages of the discovery consisted of print-outs from these easily accessible logs of Jenson and Weiner's whereabouts, their thoughts, and their plans. This "evidence" most certainly played a part in the judge's decision to deny Jenson bail. And if he had been released, it is quite possible that, free from the confines of a cell and minus the added stress and pressure of incarceration, he might not have decided to cooperate with the government.[40]

In defiance of the most basic of Security Culture tenets, Lauren Weiner had a terrible habit of talking about her other friends who were (she claimed) involved in illegal activity. This practice was made evident through both the discovery in Eric's case and a subsequent FOIA request we filed after his arrest. Obviously, everything she said to Anna was eventually sent to—if not immediately heard by—the FBI. While curbing this terrible habit certainly wouldn't have done much to protect Weiner herself from this particular informant, it would have most definitely saved her friends from whatever kinds of repression ensued.

The bottom line is this: Never talk to others about illegal activity unless you yourself are currently engaging with them in it. In the classic zine, *Security Culture: What it Is, Why We Need It and How We Implement It*, the authors list four common examples of security-violating behaviors: lying (telling someone you did an illegal action that you didn't do), gossiping (telling people details of actions you were not personally involved in), bragging (about actions you have participated in), and indirect bragging (telling people you want to remain anonymous or stay underground—indicating that you are involved in direct action without actually talking about it). The edition referenced here was revised in 1999, so none of this is new. Yet probably everyone reading this essay has known people who have displayed some or all of those behaviors. I knew two: one was a government informant and the other was Eric's former codefendant, Lauren Weiner—who started cooperating with the government less than two weeks after her arrest.

The zine also has a list of topics which are inappropriate for conversation:

- your involvement or someone else's involvement with an underground group

- someone else's desire to get involved with such a group

- asking others if they are a member of an underground group

- your participation or someone else's participation in any action that was illegal

- someone else's advocacy for such actions

- your plans or someone else's plans for a future action

As previously noted, Anna loved talking about these things.

We could write volumes about informants, how they work and how better to protect ourselves. There is, unfortunately, a wealth of experience to draw from. But ultimately our best protection is a real, solid commitment and dedication to each other and the work that we do. Perhaps that sounds oversimplified and idealistic. Certainly it won't keep informants from attending our events or even infiltrating our groups. But it would go a long way toward minimizing the havoc they wreak while simultaneously strengthening our movements and our work.

Building and nurturing this kind of commitment and dedication is no small task. It means we have to work tirelessly at improving our communication skills and group dynamics. It means we have to address issues like racism and patriarchy, which still manage to infect our communities. It means we need to learn how to overcome our lack of self-esteem and to make decisions for ourselves. It means we need to become stronger people, with a more solid sense of integrity. Then we need to ensure that the people we work with are held to the same standards.

And we need to remember why we do the work we do. If we lose that connection, we lose everything. When people who are in jail lose that connection—or if they lost it before they were arrested—they have no incentive to stand strong against the state. In his sentencing statement to the court,

Zachary Jenson wrote, "I believe that, while I was in jail, I was presented with the opportunity to explore spirituality, to better myself, and to move past the dead rut of the anarchist movement... I had time to myself to reflect on my life and where it was taking me. It helped influence my decision to cooperate and plead guilty." He goes on to say,

> I have learned that the love of the spirit is far more potent and valuable than the despair and selfishness of the anarchist movement. I have learned that every human being, no matter any distinction, deserves the utmost respect and compassion. During the time I was a part of the movement, I was among peers who accepted and loved me. I found validation and security among these people. However, I would later learn after pleading guilty, after getting away from them to have my own thoughts, that these people accept you for your ideology rather than your essential self. To turn against the ideology of the movement means ostracism and exile... I can't consider them my friends anymore after rejecting me for wanting to live my life for myself and not for them.[41]

Jenson's statement is interesting for a couple of different reasons. It is clear that Jenson had no idea before going to jail who he was as a person or what mattered to him. To be fair, many people don't at the age of 20. It seems that he identifies his participation in "the movement" as more a matter of happenstance, void of any political or philosophical underpinnings. He was there because he felt "accepted" and "validated." While it is certainly reassuring that our communities feel open to people who might have felt alone and isolated before, we need to be realistic about the implications when thinking about who we will and will not work with when the repercussions have the potential to be so severe. Jenson was a pleasant fellow. I was actually rather fond of him before he flipped on Eric. But he never struck me as anyone you could depend on in a pinch. To be frank—he smoked a lot of pot, was often lost in daydream, and lived life rather whimsically. He had a very flimsy sense of self—which is why Anna was so successful at manipulating him and keeping him involved in the alleged "conspiracy," even though (by his own admission) it was not anything he really wanted. In short—he was never truly passionate about the issues that he was purportedly working so hard to solve. And that is a huge reason why, in the end, he chose to cooperate with the prosecution.

Jenson also claims that people in "the movement" accept you for your ideology, and not for your essential self. Again—that seems like a hollow proclamation coming from someone who so clearly didn't know his own "essential self." Instead, he spent time trying to talk bigger and more militantly than he was actually feeling. How could he expect others to know his "essential self" through all of this acting and bravado? I'm not trying to trash talk someone who could be (and has been) very easily demonized. What I'm getting at here is the importance of having the strength to base our words and our actions on our own internal realities, recognizing when other people do and don't do that, and then choosing to work only with the former group. What Jenson doesn't seem to realize is that for people with a strong sense of self, what he is referring to as "ideology" is (for many) a natural extension of one's "essential self."

Without a deep connection to the things we fight for and the people we fight with, we will never be able to withstand the pressure the state puts on us. We need to recognize, think about, and talk about, the role that privilege has played in many of these "Green Scare" cases—specifically, how easy it is for folks to reintegrate after they "mess up." When people still feel like they have something to lose—a good job, a wealthy family, etc.—and they can get it all back by simply betraying their friends, their principles, and their integrity, it becomes much easier for them to dissociate. This movement is largely young, white, and middle- (to upper-) class. When the going gets tough… many get going, because they can, because they have something else to go back to.[42]

In November 2008, Eric wrote a piece addressing some of these issues:

> No matter what choices we make, we're always allowed back into the fold [of privileged society]. The deeper the deviation, the trespass: the higher the toll for return. Actually at that point, the cost is irrelevant (made stark by some of the [Green Scare] cases) because all that matters is the return to comfort: that familiar (given level of) freedom. And who couldn't relate to the choices made? We've been shown repeatedly the outcome: "it's only natural."
>
> From my perspective the type of Death we're Dancing with here is the fear of letting go—letting go of what we've been taught (programmed) defines us—that which we are to hold most sacred.
>
> What are the definitions which define your reality?
> What choices do they open before you?
> And which are closed?
> What unfolds because of those choices?
> Basically: How do you wish to Live your Life?
> Under whose discretion?
> What is it you hold Sacred?[43]

Unless we are making choices based on who we really are and what we really hold sacred, we will never be able to withstand the repression that comes about from some of those choices. If we aren't personally prepared to deal with the consequences of illegal action, we have no business making those kinds of choices. It only endangers us and our comrades.[44]

In 2011, Eric wrote about his experiences in jail and prison. He said,

> i was persynally prepared 4 what came w/isolation, having done the necessary wk on myself = the internal exploring, healing & nourishing needed 2 survive & dance w/the trauma of B'n raised N this culture; w/the effects from the shock & continuous trauma of B'n caged all i would've had 2 fall bk on would B those culturally programmed traits we're all raised with, such as identification w/the oppressor, mob mentality, & submission 2 authority... my receiving those weekly stacks of mail did wonders which i'm perpetually grateful 4, but w/out the anchor of knowing, loving, & B'n aware of who i am—how could i've stayed true 2 the intentions of my Heart?...[45]

Eric knew who he was and what he held sacred before he went to prison. Jenson and Weiner, clearly, did not. Because of this, Eric was able to maintain his integrity and stand strong against the state. He continues to do so, seven years into his sentence.

Informants are an integral part of the state's strategy in its war against activists. Infiltration not only aids the authorities in their gathering of "intelligence," it also helps them undermine our movements by inserting destructive individuals into our communities. Unfortunately, it often has the desired effect of instilling fear and mistrust. But what we must remember is that our greatest strength lies in our real connections with each other and the world we live in. To move forward effectively we must ensure that we are nurturing those connections and building stronger communities. After all, without them, what are we fighting for?

NOTES

1   Paul Chevigny, "A Rejoinder," *The Nation*, Feb. 23, 1980, at 205, quoted in Alexandra Natapoff, *Snitching: Criminal Informants and the Erosion of American Justice* (New York: New York University Press, 2009), 151.

2   Natapoff, *Snitching*, 6.

3   "Romania II" was the second arson at the Romania Chevrolet dealership in Eugene, Oregon. The arson was meant to be an act of solidarity with Jeff "Free" Luers, who spent over 9 years in prison for the first arson at the dealership.

4   William McCall, "Radical 'Snitch' in Western Arsons Gets Probation." Associated Press, June 3, 2008, http://www.katu.com/news/local/19507819.html, (accessed July 26, 2012).

5   Kim Murphy, "Is Homeland Security Spending Paying Off?," *Los Angeles Times*, August 28, 2011, http://articles.latimes.com/2011/aug/28/nation/la-na-911-homeland-money-20110828 , (accessed July 26, 2012).

6   John Mueller and Mark G. Stewart, "Terror, Security, and Money: Balancing the Risks, Benefits, and Costs of Homeland Security" (paper presented at the Annual Convention of the Midwest Political Science Association, Chicago, IL, April 1, 2011).

7   U.S. Senate Committee on Environment & Public Works, 109th Congress, *Oversight on Eco-terrorism specifically examining the Earth Liberation Front ("ELF") and the Animal Liberation Front ("ALF")*, (2005) (statement of John Lewis, Deputy Assistant Director, Federal Bureau of Investigation. http://epw.senate.gov/hearing_statements.cfm?id=237817.

8   Their plea agreements can be found online at: http://supporteric.org/documents.htm.

9   Marie Mason was sentenced in 2009 to almost 22 years in prison for two acts of arson related to GMOs and logging.

10   Complete transcripts of Eric's trial can be found on his website at: http://supporteric.org/documents.htm.

11   United States v. McDavid (No.2:06-cr-00035). Trial Proceedings: Reporter's Transcript, 401.

12   Lauren Weiner, unpublished interview with Madelynn Amalfitano, January 5, 2010.

13   United States v. McDavid (No.2:06-cr-00035). Trial Proceedings: Reporter's Transcript, 413–14.

14   United States v. McDavid (No.2:06-cr-00035). Trial Proceedings: Defense Exhibit A-2.

15   Ibid.

16   United States v. McDavid (No.2:06-cr-00035). Government Discovery: CD H (audio recording), January 5, 2006.

17   Ibid.

18   United States v. McDavid (No.2:06-cr-00035). Government Discovery: CD A (audio recording), January 9, 2006.

19   United States v. McDavid (No.2:06-cr-00035). Trial Proceedings: Reporter's Transcript, 444.

20   United States v. McDavid (No.2:06-cr-00035). Government Discovery: Transcripts from D14, Session 8, 3–4. January 12, 2006.

21   United States v. McDavid (No.2:06-cr-00035). Government Discovery: D17 (video recording), January 12, 2006.

22   United States v. McDavid (No.2:06-cr-00035). Government Discovery: D18 (video recording), January 12, 2006.

23   United States v. McDavid (No.2:06-cr-00035). Trial Proceedings: Reporter's Transcript, 874–76.

24   United States v. McDavid (No.2:06-cr-00035). Trial Proceedings: Reporter's Transcript, 1022–25.

25 Darren Thurston, "Fired Back", December 21, 2007, http://resist.ca/sites/resist.ca/files/firedback.pdf, accessed December 11, 2012):13.

26 The point here is not to place blame on any particular individual or group; the decision whether or not to cooperate with the prosecution ultimately lies only with the person being charged with a crime. But it is useful to identify the conditions under which a particularly situated defendant found noncooperation to be untenable.

27 Will Potter, "FBI File Reveals Discussion of Discrediting Animal Rights Activists by Planting Rumors," *Green is the New Red*, December 6, 2010, http://www.greenisthenewred.com/blog/fbi-file-reveals-discussion-of-discrediting-animal-rights-activists-by-planting-rumors/3282/, emphasis added by Potter.

28 This point has led many to the conclusion that we need more "activist" lawyers. That is obviously beyond the scope of this chapter, but it is a point worth exploring.

29 Thurston, "Fired Back," 19.

30 Lauren Weiner, interview with Madelynn Amalfitano, January 5, 2010.

31 Thurston, "Fired Back," 19.

32 Declan McCullagh and Anne Broache, "FBI Taps Cell Phone Mic as Eavesdropping Tool," *CNET News*, December 1, 2006, http://news.cnet.com/2100-1029-6140191.html.

33 United States v. McDavid (No.2:06-cr-00035). Trial Proceedings: Reporter's Transcript, 578.

34 United States v. McDavid (No.2:06-cr-00035). Government's Consolidated Opposition to McDavid's Motions to Dismiss the Indictment, Document 169, March 13, 2007, 30.

35 United States v. McDavid (No.2:06-cr-00035). Government Discovery: CD H (audio recording), January 7, 2006.

36 Luce Guillén-Givins, "The RNC Welcoming Committee," in *Conspiracy to Riot in Furtherance of Terrorism: The Collective Autobiography of the RNC 8*, ed, Leslie James Pickering (Arissa Media Group, 2011), 224.

37 Guillén-Givins, "The RNC Welcoming Committee," 233–234.

38 Potter, "FBI File Reveals Discussion of Discrediting Animal Rights Activists by Planting Rumors."

39 Ibid.

40 For more on the dangers of social media, see Evan Tucker's essay, "Who Needs the NSA When We Have Facebook?" in this volume.

41 United States v. McDavid (No.2:06-cr-00035). Zachary Jenson, Sentencing Declaration to the Court, Document 379, December 2, 2008. This is an interesting statement coming from someone who had just complained about his former comrades' selfishness. I would argue, instead, that people were not angry at him for wanting to live his life for himself, or because he renounced his politics but rather, people were angry because he chose to save his own skin by throwing his best friend to the wolves. Maybe that was just part of his studies in spirituality....

42 Of course, these aren't the only reasons that people snitch on one another. The state will always find pressure points and apply force accordingly. For some, that may involve the

risk of losing their children or their home. For others it may involve the risk of deportation. The list is endless. Part of our responsibility as people involved in struggles for social change is to figure out how to prepare ourselves and each other for these attacks and to take care of each other when they occur. Without the support of our communities, resisting the state can be an almost insurmountable task.

43 Eric McDavid, November 2008, http://supporteric.org/writings.htm, (accessed December 8, 2012).

44 I am not saying that we should not support people facing repression for actions we may disagree with strategically, or people who have merely gotten in over their heads. But we should pause before taking action and think critically about our responsibilities—to ourselves and our communities—in the event of arrest.

45 Eric McDavid, "Toward a Re-Cognition of Choice," Zine, 2011.

A CURIOUS CASE:
Long Island Radicals Confront the Green Scare

KEVIN VAN METER WITH TEAM COLORS COLLECTIVE
AND FRIENDS[1]

THE FOLLOWING REPRESENTS A SAMPLING OF INDIVIDUALS WHO HAVE BEEN arrested in the United States during the roundup of radical earth and animal liberationists commonly referred to as the "Green Scare":[2] Jeffery "Free" Luers, Craig "Critter" Marshall, Jacob Conroy, Darius Fullmer, Lauren Gazzola, Josh Harper, Kevin Kjonaas, Andy Stepanian, Daniel McGowan, Jonathan Paul, Joyanna Zacher, Nathan Block, Eric McDavid, Marie Mason; and then, there is Conor Cash.[3]

The first fourteen are currently, or have been until recently, serving lengthy prison terms. This list would be considerably longer if it included more recent arrests, or those who have cooperated with the prosecution. What is curious about the fifteenth name, and the case of Conor Cash, is that he is the only one who has not been incarcerated: the only one not to become a political prisoner.

On February 15, 2001 the Federal Bureau of Investigation (FBI) arrested Conor Cash and charged him as the ringleader of the Long Island cell of the Earth Liberation Front (ELF). Four years of legal proceedings were followed by a two-week trial. Cash faced 40 years in prison. Instead, he won a swift jury acquittal. Cash is one of the only Green Scare defendants who is not in jail and there are a number of important reasons for this, beyond his innocence.

Primarily his success flowed from previously existing conditions like a well-organized movement constructed by dense relationships and connections with progressives on Long Island. The success of the support campaign is attributable to the particular form of community organizing the members utilized, coupled with an intelligent and well-conceived defense strategy. Rather than serving as a counter to other support campaigns, this essay seeks to complement and augment work done elsewhere with the purpose of providing lessons for current political organizing in general and political prisoner support work in particular. Through an analysis of the case and the political struggles surrounding it, we hope to pull out relevant lessons for activists and others seeking to understand strategies of state repression and insurgent organizing.

OVERVIEW OF THE PERIOD IN QUESTION

IN ORDER TO present the case and draw out relevant lessons, I have created three chronologies: Local Activism and the Counter-Globalization Movement, the Earth Liberation Front on Long Island, and the Case of Conor Cash. The chronologies cover the period from late 1997 through the end of 2004, and naturally overlap a great deal.

The organization Cash was a part of on Long Island, the Modern Times Collective, functioned as a node of the counter-globalization movement and addressed particular, local issues. This local activism can be periodized into two phases: the first, "activist" phase begins in April 1998 and ends in late August of 2000; the second, "community organizing" phase continued from late August 2000 until early 2005. Additionally, the counter-globalization movement has its precursors in the 1990s and first appeared as a small-scale insurgency in the streets of Seattle on November 30, 1999. This cycle of protest would largely dissipate by the summer of 2001—prior to September 11, 2001—and figures into the period of repression beginning in 2000, as well as the case against Cash.

Our second chronology looks at the ELF on Long Island. The ELF carried out most of its actions during a relatively short period from July of 2000 until January of 2001. The third and final chronology will explore the case against Cash. He was arrested on February 15, 2001, with additional charges being added shortly after September 11. His trial began May 10, 2004, and he was acquitted ten days later.

The particulars of these chronologies, especially the diary of ELF actions, might initially seem to be tedious, but they will be used to indict the FBI and U.S. Attorney's office in a clear framing of Cash for his participation in both local struggles and an international cycle of protest.

LOCAL ACTIVISM AND COUNTER-GLOBALIZATION

IN ORDER TO understand the charges against Cash and the subsequent solidarity campaign that led to his acquittal, it is important to describe the context these arose in, as Long Island has a peculiar political environment. During the late 1990s and early 2000s, the region had some of the most "significant inequalities of opportunity across racial and economic lines" in the United States.[4] Being in one of the most expensive places in the country to live, with little rental stock, housing costs are extreme in relation to wages, which have stagnated for the past 40 years. The public transit system moves commuters east and west from one end of the island to New York City, but there are few ways for anyone else to travel north and south without a car, creating a transit nightmare for working-class and poor people, as well as middle-class youth. With little public space and no geographic or political "center," struggling to create a life outside of suburban culs-de-sac and shopping malls is quite difficult. Fighting for social change in a decentralized space, with such an atomized and segregated population, is incredibly difficult.

Long Island was home to America's first major experiment in suburbia. Suburban Long Island was specifically designed to prevent upheaval and urban problems. Historically, Long Island is segregated by race and class; people of color were denied home ownership through both legal prohibitions and a deeply embedded arsenal of more subtle forms of discrimination.[5] These practices have a continuing and decisive presence in its life and politics.

While the region was affected by the civil rights and women's liberation movements, and student demonstrations against the Vietnam war, by the mid-1990s there were only a few areas of left and radical struggle. These included immigrant day labor organizing in the El Salvadorian community; anti–police brutality, prisoners' rights, and hip hop among the African American population; and a small group of radicals that developed out of do-it-yourself (DIY) punk scene and the confutation of elements that became the counter-globalization movement. The latter, made up predominately of middle-class and working-class white youth, is the community that Cash and his support group arose from and worked within. There was, and continues to be, a progressive and liberal element but their scope of action is extremely limited.

MODERN TIMES AND THE COUNTER-GLOBALIZATION MOVEMENT

THE MODERN TIMES Collective (MTC) came together on April 11, 1998, and sought to bring various existing radical efforts and ideas into one organized body.[6] As the only organization of extra-parliamentary left and the only radical project among white, middle- and working-class youth (excepting only the local chapter of the Animal Defense League, or ADL), MTC drew a large number of participants from the DIY punk and hardcore counter-cultures and other neighboring sectors of the community. Maintaining a relationship with the ADL, Modern Times periodically cosponsored events for the League and worked in solidarity with its members who were accused of Animal Liberation Front (ALF) and other actions, including Andrew Stepanian. Stepanian would later become a political prisoner himself as part of the Stop Huntingdon Animal Cruelty 7 (SHAC 7)—six activists and an incorporated organization targeted for their animal rights organizing. From late 1997, with activity predating the collective, until 1999 approached, most of the MTC activities included Food Not Bombs meals, work with different international solidarity and Anti-Racist Action networks, solidarity with the local day labor community through the Workplace Project, attending Reclaim the Streets, Critical Mass, and anti-war protests in New York City and beyond, periodic potlucks and political educational events, and regular outreach at concerts and other cultural events.

By the fall of 1999, with major global and national winds shifting, the MTC began participating in what would later be called the anti-, or as I prefer, counter-globalization movement, following the involvement of some collective members in the Reclaim the Streets street occupation on June 18, 1999—referred to as J18, a formula that would be repeated throughout this cycle of protest. In the lead-up to the N30 (November 30, 1999) Seattle World Trade Organization protests, the collective participated in planning meetings and educational forums in New York City and elsewhere in the Atlantic region.

The oft-touted slogan spray painted on buildings around Seattle, "We are Winning," found its way eastward, and many of the collective's members were caught up in the excitement surrounding the possibility of "winning." At the same time, and for the same reasons, the government grew fearful about the counter-globalization movement. The Seattle WTO Summit had been anticipated as a triumph for left-of-center Democratic President Bill Clinton. Instead, in the midst of police riots and teargas, the government had to declare a civil emergency before the President could give a speech ceding political space to the protesters.[7]

Following the WTO protests, the work of the Modern Times Collective was concretized when the A16 (April 16, 2000) World Bank / International Monetary Fund protest was announced, and the collective brought returning veterans from Seattle to Long Island for training purposes. Upon returning from A19 in Washington, D.C., Modern Times immediately began planning their own local Reclaim the Streets (RTS) action for May Day, 2000, with help from members of the Direct Action Network, who coordinated the N30, A19, and other counter-globalization protests. It was collectively decided that holding the street during the May Day RTS action would require a 23-foot tripod—a civil disobedience tool with an activist perched on the top of it.

"If I can't dance its [*sic*] not my revolution!" declared the broadsheet distributed by the MTC leading up to the May Day street party (held May 6, 2000). The broadsheet concluded, "This is a non-permit[ted] demonstration of our power!" Beyond the "if I can't dance" slogan the paper included quotes from German anarchist Gustav Landauer, the Situationist International, Pyotr Kropotkin, Friedrich Nietzsche, Abbie Hoffman, and a number of chants common to the counter-globalization movement. The broadsheet didn't only describe "what and why"; it also provided a history of the International Monetary Fund, World Bank, neoliberalism, a history of May Day, and situated the concepts and politics within an understanding of the local environment. The RTS-style action that followed included a short march where Conor Cash took the role as the tripod sitter. He, as well as a dozen others, were arrested for disorderly conduct.

In mid-July 2000, MTC traveled *en masse* to Philadelphia to prepare for the protests against the Republican National Convention. Spending considerable hours on reconnaissance missions to sites of planned civil disobedience, attending trainings, coordinating with other activists, and building civil disobedience devices known as lock boxes, the collective was setting up a base of operations for the near 60 people the MTC would have on the ground during the protests. A highway on-ramp was chosen as the site of an occupation with a "lock down" and support blockade. Cash was arrested along with over two-dozen others. It was one of the only successful blockades during the RNC.

Shortly thereafter, over Labor Day weekend of 2000, the MTC held its customary three-day conference, as it had two years prior. A number of other participants noted surveillance of the event. The MTC dissolved itself at this gathering—though it would put out a newspaper called *Modern Times* a few months later—and sought a shift in the nebulous group's organizing strategy from a protest mobilization orientation to a community organizing approach. Herein the MTC dropped the self-identified anarchist label, created networks through various sub- and counter-cultures, and began to strengthen bonds with both neighboring communities and others in struggle. It is these relationships that would play out in the support campaign for Cash.

When the ELF and ALF began a concerted wave of actions in the fall of 2000 this newly reconstituted group of activists responded. At this time, in a piece entitled "Special Report: Long Island activists under attack," the former-MTC, through its periodical, summarized the repression they faced: "From surveillance and visits to activists' homes, to the illegitimate incarceration of a vocal animal rights activist, those young people who have tried to make the world a more just place for all have had the attempted disruption of their lives and activities."[8]

The article continued to summarize the history of the FBI's Counter Intelligence Program (COINTELPRO) of the 1950s–1970s, expressed solidarity with Andrew Stepanian, and summarized the harassment of MTC members. The authors naïvely believed it would deflect attention away from the MTC. The paper also included an open letter from the MTC titled "Real Radicals Don't Destroy: They Create," which argued:

> The recent tactics employed by the [ELF], while they focus on an issue we are concerned about, are ineffective as far as creating a democratic environment where community members have power over, and direct participation in, the affairs that impact them.
>
> Creating an environment of fear and intimidation by means of arson is not conducive to the development of an empowered community. Instead, it leaves the mission of building a sustainable future to a few anonymous crusaders, who may or may not take into account the issues their communities would like to voice. Furthermore, arson puts at risk the lives of volunteer firefighters and innocent community members who are not profiting from suburban sprawl.[9]

While the statement was consensed upon by the collective's membership, the organization received harsh criticisms from other radicals in the counter-globalization movement, who believed that the MTC was going against the agreed upon acceptance of "diversity of tactics"—the approach of accepting a wide range of tactics, including property destruction, which became increasingly popular as the counter-globalization protest cycle peaked. The MTC believed at the time that the Long Island political environment required base-building approaches before any sort of clandestine direct action could have any effect, and correctly assumed that the repercussions would be placed at the doorsteps of MTC and ADL members.[10] Less than three weeks later, the FBI would arrest one of the core organizers of the Modern Times Collective.[11]

EARTH LIBERATION FRONT ON LONG ISLAND

THE ELF ANNOUNCED itself on Long Island on July 7, 2000, when two acres of genetically engineered corn at Cold Spring National Laboratories were destroyed; an additional eleven actions continued until construction equipment was set ablaze on January 14, 2001. In addition, there were far more ALF actions during this time.[12]

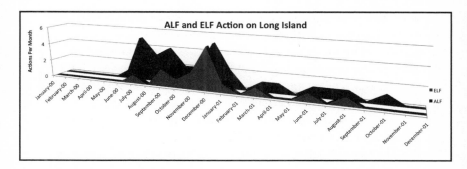

On January 17, 2001 three teenagers were arrested as the Long Island cell of the ELF. All three would cooperate with the prosecution, and two would testify against Cash. Moreover, as there were other actions that the ALF and ELF claimed, but that are not connected to that cell, it seems likely that there was a second cell, or perhaps "lone wolf" members acting autonomously.[13]

For our purposes here, we begin this chronology with the cell made up of those witnesses who cooperated against Cash. In late November and early December 2000, the ELF committed a series of arsons in eastern Long Island under the spray painted slogan "if you build it, we will burn it." Beginning on September 26, 2000, the Long Island cell of the ELF committed twelve acts in total in a campaign against suburban sprawl. The group began with lock gluing and window breaking before escalating to arsons.[14] Additionally, an action claimed jointly by the ALF and ELF on December 7, 2000 resulted in smashed windows and anti-meat slogans being spray-painted at the McDonald's headquarters in Eastern Long Island. A remaining "diary of actions" can be determined from available statements and press reports:[15]

1. September 2000, Eastern Long Island: A reported act of vandalism at a construction site. (It is possible this action was fabricated, as neither a record in the local press nor any communiqué can be located.)[16]
2. September 26, Coram: Signing themselves "the elves," the ELF claimed to have damaged homes under construction and a bulldozer at the site.[17]
3. October 21, Moriches: Nineteen ducks were liberated from Titmus Duck Farm.[18]
4. November 11, Coram: Construction sites were vandalized using techniques that "involved monkeywrenching vehicles, pulling up survey stakes, smashing windows and leaving spray painted messages."[19]

5. November 24, Coram and Miller Place: Windows were smashed at construction sites, and a bulldozer vandalized.[20]

6. December 1, Middle Island: Windows were smashed, survey stakes were pulled, and "anti-sprawl" graffiti was spray-painted. The communiqué is the first to call attention to the Long Island Pine Barrens, an ecosystem under threat from development and whose preservation as been a contentious issue in the region for decades.[21]

7. December 9, Middle Island: The Long Island cell of the ELF escalates tactics to include arson as condos were burned. A communiqué stated that "all of the incendiaries ignited successfully and the resulting fires gutted almost 16 nearly completed luxury homes, which were to be sold at several hundred thousand dollars each."[22]

8. December 19, Miller Place: "[A]nti-urban sprawl messages were spray painted on the walls, then accelerants were poured over the house and lighted. Let there be no mistake that this was a nonviolent action and the house was searched for any living thing before being set alight. This is the latest in a string of actions in the war against urban sprawl."[23]

9. December 29, Mount Sinai: "If you built it, we will burn it" is spray-painted in a new suburban development and three additional homes are set on fire. The communiqué stated, "This action was done in solidarity with Josh Harper, Craig Rosebraugh, Jeffrey "Free" Luers and Craig "Critter" Marshall, Andrew Stepanian, Jeremy Parkin, and the countless other known and unknown activists who suffer persecution, interrogation, police brutality, crappy jail conditions, yet stand strong."[24]

10. January 14, 2001, Middle Island: In a final action, the Long Island Cell of the ELF burned a pickup truck and construction equipment.[25]

In addition to these ten actions, the cooperating witnesses admitted to "put[ting] glue in the locks of a furrier's store in Miller Place" though it is likely that they were referring to the ALF-claimed action in nearby Mount Sinai on September 15, 2000.[26]

Looking at a map of Long Island, one can see that all of these actions occurred within five miles of each other. Therefore, the police investigation focused on a relatively small area. While Cash lived in Brooklyn at the time of his arrest, he had lived with his parents in the hamlet of Sound Beach periodically during the preceding months, which is just a few miles north and eastward from where these actions took place.

To briefly mention the national context: two days following the December 29 arson, and on the other side of country, the ELF burned the offices of Superior Lumber outside Eugene, Oregon. This was to be one of the most spectacular attacks by the ELF cell that would eventually be rounded up during Operation Backfire, and both the press and the FBI increased their rhetoric as a result of what they presumed to be a clandestine organization operating nation-wide.

Until the December 9 arson, there had not been a news report of the ELF activity on Long Island. On December 13, *New York Newsday* began coverage with a less-than-dramatic headline—"Group Claims Role in Fire"—which appeared in the back of the paper and referenced the jointly claimed ALF / ELF action of December 7.[27] *Newsday* would respond, a bit late, on December 18 with an editorial titled "Long Island Is No Place for Environmental Terrorism":

> No amount of sloganeering or self-righteous posturing can justify such forms of protest. Suffolk police are actively investigating all of the incidents. This is one investigation worth a significant investment of resources in order to carry it to the arrest stage. Then it is worth carrying to trial, conviction and sentencing severe enough to curb this lawless trend now before anyone, anywhere gets the idea that such behavior is tolerated on Long Island.[28]

Additional arsons would follow the next day, on December 19, and again on December 29, spurring another, more conciliatory editorial, "Ecoterrorism / Setting fire to new Suffolk homes is hardly the right way to protest the environment." Running on January 2, 2001, as a direct response to the previous actions, it referred to the "If you build it, we will burn it" slogan:

> There is nothing charming about this message, nothing tender, nothing ghostly and most of all nothing sporting about this admonitory scrawl. It is part boast and part threat, and it was left behind by arsonists who set fire to four empty new homes in that Mount Sinai development.

The piece then concluded by chastising Long Island's political leadership for their failure to adequately address the issue of sprawl:

> As to the underlying land-use questions on which even reasonable people can disagree, it is clear that the Town of Brookhaven, site of these incidents, has consistently failed to administer its land-use planning with care or discretion.[29]

The tone of the two editorials is remarkably different, with the second being more of an appeal to address the issues underlying the ELF actions. The following day, the Long Island Builders Institute, a trade association and lobbying group, offered a $10,000 reward for the arrest and conviction of the culprits.[30] The press coverage of the issue even moved into the realm of the "human interest story" when on January 4, 2001, *New York Newsday* ran "Terrorism Off the Beaten Path," a rambling article on the "story around the story."[31] Then on the night of the final arson, *60 Minutes* ran a piece on the ELF with the tagline "The elusive eco-terrorists have destroyed $37 million worth of property and now have begun targeting the American suburbs." By the final fire, the Long Island cell of the ELF had caused $358,000 in damages, and in a January 14 communiqué, the group proclaimed its support for Andrew Stepanian, who was then currently serving time the county jail.[32]

Between the regional paper *New York Newsday*, the Builders Institute, and national media attention, the local police and FBI were certainly feeling pressure to catch the ELF.

"IF THEY TAKE YOU IN THE MORNING": THE CASE OF CONOR CASH

ON FEBRUARY 15, 2001, the FBI and Suffolk County Police entered a residence in Brooklyn, New York and arrested Conor Cash. They had gone to his parents' home in Sound Beach that morning as well. Without a warrant, and brandishing automatic weapons, they tossed the place. With the continuous harassment of the collective and raids in the prior week, additional arrests were expected. Noted civil rights attorney Fredrick Brewington had by then been put on retainer by a number of the MTC core members. Brewington represented Cash at his hearing and negotiated the defendant's release on $250,000 bail. Cash didn't spend more then a few hours in custody and was never questioned.

Immediately following the tragedy on September 11, 2001, the FBI utilized the prevailing fear to bring additional charges of "providing material support" to "terrorists." Anonymous sources told *New York Newsday* that "it was coincidental that an anti-terrorism statute was used against Cash so soon after the attacks on the World Trade Center and Pentagon. The government had planned for several weeks to bring the additional indictment...."[33] Cash was the first person in the United States to be charged as a "domestic terrorist" after September 11. In a press statement rare to this case, Brewington said the government was trying "to force the young man to plead guilty."[34]

The following section is broken up into two parts. First, Cooperating Witnesses and Pre-Trial Developments will look at the cooperating witnesses—beginning with their initial detection, briefly exploring their similarities with other government informants, and detailing their cooperation with the government. It then continues into related pre-trial developments locally and nationally. The second part, *U.S. v. Conor Cash*, will specifically deal with the trial, starting with an early support-group win, then moving to the government's case, and attempt to turn a MTC member into an informant. It continues with the testimony of cooperating witnesses and the FBI agent in charge of the case, and concludes with the testimony of the Deputy Assistant Director of the FBI to a Senate Committee during the latter part of the trial. While the chronology is looser than in the previous two sections, it is intended to explore particular themes and issues in their own context.

COOPERATING WITNESSES AND PRE-TRIAL DEVELOPMENTS

"WE ARE WINNING" was spray painted at the site of one of the December arsons, which happened to be across the street from the high school two of the ELF cell members attended;[35] the third participant connected with the cell at an environmental rally, though the record doesn't state which one. Although some details remain shaky to this day, it is certain that all three cooperated with the prosecution: two specifically against Cash. All three were under eighteen years of age and white middle-class males; two had parents who were police officers. One would plead and disappear, while the remaining two testified against Cash at trial. A mysterious fourth, a female named "Courtney,"[36] whose father was a New York City Detective and part of the JTTF, was referenced as part of the cell, but according to government testimony she was never charged, or even questioned.[37]

Unlike the Operation Backfire defendants, the Long Island cell of the ELF did not research its targets or choose targets as part of a larger campaign. Rather, theirs was an amateurish and unrefined targeting of any housing development under construction. However, as would prove to be unfortunately common with Operation Backfire, George Mashkow III, Jared McIntyre, and Matthew Rammelkamp took a plea and cooperated with the government.[38] As of this writing, of the thirteen activists indicted in the original Operation Backfire roundup, four had taken non-cooperating pleas, three have not been apprehended, one has plead guilty but appears not to be cooperating with the government, one would commit suicide while in jail, and the remaining four have cooperated with the government against the other defendants. This is where the similarities between the cases end, however, as Cash has always maintained his innocence and would be found not guilty at trial.

It is clear from press reports that Jared McIntyre was boasting to classmates about the activities of the ELF. This led the Suffolk County Police and FBI to search his home, which led them in turn to George Mashkow, who was the first of the group to agree to cooperate with the prosecution.[39] It was clear from January 9, 2001 forward that the ELF cell members were working with the government, and after nearly a month of silence, on February 2, 2001, *New York Newsday* announced "Teen Guilty of Arson / LI eco-terrorism suspect negotiates plea agreement." The article stated:

> In a breakthrough in the wave of arson and vandalism in Suffolk County claimed by the [ELF], a Coram teenager [Mashkow] who is believed to have played a key role in the incidents pleaded guilty to arson late Friday in a secret court hearing, according to several sources familiar with the case.
>
> Jared McIntyre, a senior at Longwood High School in Middle Island and the son of a New York police sergeant assigned to that department's School Safety Division, also agreed to cooperate with investigators probing the ELF incidents, the sources said.

The article continued,

> The other three suspects—described as another teenager at Longwood [Mashkow], a 16-year old at Middle Island High School who lives in Miller Place [Rammelkamp], and a young adult acquaintance [possibly "Courtney"]—are all in various stages of negotiations for plea bargains with federal prosecutors, the sources said.[40]

Additional news reports confirmed that all three were cooperating with the FBI.[41] This would be the first conviction of an ELF member in the United States, and these arrests were only the second such occurrence.

Embarrassingly, the vast underground network of ALF and ELF cells, this terrorist conspiracy that the FBI would eventually call the nation's "number one domestic terrorist threat," turned out to be teenagers. Cash himself was only nineteen, and the *Boston Globe* article that appeared the day after his arrest called attention to the fact that he was "the only legal adult of the group" and "was charged with aiding and abetting the actual arson."[42] Radical press such as the *Earth First! Journal* would pick up the story too, albeit with numerous discrepancies and distortions.

A few months following Cash's arrest, on May 21, 2001, two fires raged simultaneously in the Pacific Northwest. It was a $3 million night for the ELF. An office and a number of trucks at Jefferson Poplar Farms in Oregon, and the office of Professor Toby Bradshaw at the University of Washington burned. Both actions, according to the communiqué, were against the genetic engineering of trees.

Back on Long Island, the ELF struck at an Old Navy store on March 5, 2001; then again at Bank of New York on June 13, 2001. They then returned to Cold Spring Harbor National Laboratory on August 21, 2001 to smash windows, causing $15,000 in damages.[43] ADL activist Andrew Stepanian was being followed this entire time, which was publicly acknowledged on February 1, 2002.[44] McIntyre would be jailed for violating his bail agreement with the FBI and U.S. Attorney's office after he admitted that Cash was innocent in an online exchange with another activist.[45] Imprisoned on July 29, 2003, McIntyre was still sitting in jail when Cash's trial started—at the request of Assistant U.S. Attorney Timothy Driscoll, who was prosecuting Cash. Driscoll was not the first prosecutor to pick up this case; he was the seventh U.S. Attorney to lead the charge against Cash, and it was he who subpoenaed a half dozen MTC activists in early May of 2001.[46]

The case of the "United States of America—against—Connor Cash, Defendant" began and resolved itself before either the SHAC 7 arrests in May 2004, or the initial Operation Backfire round-up in December 2005.

U.S. V. CONOR CASH

ON MAY 10, 2004, the *U.S. v. Conor Cash* began. The former MTC members launched a court support campaign, bringing young activists from across Long Island to attend the two-week proceedings. But most important was the group's ability to garner support from professors, professionals, white-haired senior citizens from the local peace movement, the immigrant rights community, and the clergy. With every pew seat taken, the massive presence became a fact that the jury, judge, and prosecutor could not ignore—in fact, the judge commented on the size of the crowd.

This presence would benefit Cash's case in another significant way. While leaving the court building, Cash's mother overheard one juror state to another that "we should send these kids to Iraq"—"these kids" meaning those in the galley. Brewington was able to use this utterance to exclude a clearly prejudicial juror from the trial at the start of the third day of hearing evidence. *New York Newsday* reported: "The juror, who was not identified, told U.S. District Jude Thomas Platte that she had said of backers of Connor Cash, 22, of Sound Beach, that 'they should send these kinds who are anti-American across to Iraq to see what's going on over there. Then they would not be against our government'."[47]

The government investigation, as revealed at trial, focused on a simplistic equation, summarized like this: "Cash as tripod sitter of the MTC May Day protest equals Cash as leader." Several people helped build the tripod for May Day, but since Cash was the only one able to climb to the top of the civil disobedience device and hold his location upon it for an extended period of time, he was given the task on the day of the action. The theme of Cash as leader was transposed from the May Day action to the ELF, as the government applied their understanding of hierarchical organizational forms in trying to explain how three teenagers, the cooperating witnesses, kept them on the run for four months. During FBI Counter-Terrorism Division/JTTF Special Agent Joseph Metzinger's testimony (explored at length later), he was asked by Brewington, "And sir, would it be accurate to say that Mr. Cash became a target of the Suffolk County Police Department based on him being on top of that teepee?" Metzinger responded, "I believe the Suffolk County Police Department decided to target Mr. Cash, probably for that reason, yes."[48]

Following the arrest of a dozen MTC members at the May Day action, the local county police separated MTC member Jon Berg from the rest and held him in a single cell rather then the general holding cell where the rest were questioned. This suggested prior surveillance, which was confirmed when one of the arresting officers admitted that they had been following the MTC. Four months later, the FBI visited Berg at home. His girlfriend was pregnant at the time, a fact of which the Feds were aware. They asked him to become a paid informant. Berg declined. He later testified: "Well, once the questioning was done, they asked me in so many words if I would become involved in the ELF. I believe the words they used was I would be heavily compensated, and that I made a joke and asked them how much, and they said it depends on what you find out."[49] Berg was first contacted in late summer by the FBI— "Around that time, September, August," he testified—which is important to note as this was weeks prior to the string of ELF actions they would later prosecute Cash for.

Jared McIntyre had been imprisoned for lying about an instant messenger exchange he had with another activist, screen name "X Tyler Durden," where he stated quite clearly that Cash was innocent.[50] This was a violation of his cooperation agreement, and challenged the U.S. Attorney's bases for prosecution. He was sentenced to a year in jail and was called to the witness stand in an orange jumpsuit. McIntyre was badly beaten while incarcerated and began his scripted testimony by stating that Cash had provided the gasoline for the December 29 arson. But upon on cross examination, McIntyre flip-flopped, stating:

> **D:** [Defense attorney]: and at bottom of page 4 [reading the instant messenger exchange], you wrote these words, didn't you, "I told them he didn't know." You're referring to Mr. Cash, right?
>
> **M:** [McIntyre]: Yes, I was.

D: [Defense]: "And that he was about as guilty as my mom when she drove me to the thrift store and I bought the shoes that I used." You wrote that, right?

M: [McIntyre]: Yes, I wrote that.[51]

Further along in the questioning it continued,

D: [Defense]: And then you wrote, "they're tired of dragging in minors and want some more adults, so that's why they brought in Connor, so the ADL is under intense scrutiny." You wrote that, right?

M: [McIntyre]: Yes, I did.[52]

McIntyre would bumble the rest of the testimony, not able to answer a simple question of when he was lying—on the stand during direct questioning or in the multi-page instant message he sent to an ADL activist. He was required to provide the government with "substantial assistance" in testifying against Cash, but was unable to remember exact dates unless they related to the case against Cash.[53] The strength of the defense attorney's approach to questioning and analysis, the vigilance of Cash's mother in recalling the juror's utterance, and the fellow activists' reporting of McIntyre's statement had a major impact on the case; the force of the community was also felt through their direct presence in the courtroom.

The testimony of Matthew Rammelkamp preceded McIntyre's testimony, but unlike McIntyre, Rammelkamp recanted with ease. On direct questioning, Rammelkamp would answer "yes" when asked about Cash's involvement, but upon cross examination by Brewington he stated that he was "coerced" by the FBI into implicating Cash. With both of the prosecution star witnesses providing, at best, questionably reliable testimony, Driscoll would have to rely on the lengthy testimony of Metzinger, who admitted that Cash had been followed for his activism months prior to any ELF action. Additionally, the testimony of Detective John Vohs would try and establish the credibility of video evidence from a Hess gas station, where Driscoll claimed Cash purchased gasoline on behalf of Rammelkamp and McIntyre for the December 29 arson.[54] Vohs was over 100 yards away from the Hess station, and stated that Cash filled a gas can. Though the prosecution presented only stills of this video evidence, the reliability of this evidence would play out shortly in a major turning point for the trial.

During his testimony at Cash's trial Special Agent Metzinger, beyond confusing the ELF and Earth First!, offers an interesting utterance that is well outside the line of questioning. Herein he ties the series of counter-globalization actions into the developments on Long Island and the government's concern about the trajectory of struggle. He testified,

> In April of 2000, I was sent with another investigator to Seattle, pursuant to the riots that occurred out there at the World Trade Organization. There's still a lot of damage to the downtown area, so the anarchists' statement was all over downtown. The FBI in Seattle, the state police in Seattle, the police showed us photographs and explained to us what happened. I met with the Los Angles FBI and the Philadelphia FBI [sites of the forthcoming protests against the DNC and RNC] and police pursuant to the criminal conventions occurred in that city, with the anarchists' statement were painted on the street and the buildings. [*sic*] In May 1st...
>
> [Defense attorney, Question: Which year, please?] May 1, 1999, they had the May day to occur in Manhattan, a bunch of different groups came together in Manhattan to protest and the anarchists' statements were spray painted in several places around the city.
>
> [Defense attorney, Question: I appreciate that. My question to your, sir, is how many tattoos like that have you seen?].[55]

Brewington was questioning Metzinger in regards to the Circle A tattoo that adorns Cash's shoulder.

A key witness for the defense, Dr. Stephen Duncombe, professor of the politics of media and culture at New York University, would testify about the symbolism of the "Circle A" and its importance in the punk culture that Cash was part of. On the night before he was to testify, Metzinger and another FBI agent visited Duncombe at his office in a clear attempt at intimidation. While the court refused to charge Duncombe as an expert witness, his testimony provided clarification on the "Circle A" showing that it was a widely used symbol.

In the midst of the trial, on May 18, 2004, John E. Lewis, deputy assistant director of the FBI's Counter-Terrorism Division, testified before the Senate Judiciary Committee about the "domestic terrorist threat," mentioning Cash by name. Lewis stated:

> In February 2001, teenagers Jared McIntyre, Matthew Rammelkamp, and George Mashkow all pleaded guilty, as adults, to Title 18 U.S.C. 844(i), arson, and 844(n), arson conspiracy. These charges pertained to a series of arsons and

attempted arsons of new home construction sites in Long Island, NY, which according to McIntyre were committed in sympathy of the ELF movement. An adult, Connor Cash, was also arrested on February 15, 2001, and charged under federal statutes for his role in these crimes. Cash is currently on trial in federal court for charges of providing material support to terrorism. The New York [JTTF] played a significant role in the arrest and prosecution of these individuals. Despite these recent successes, however, FBI investigative efforts to target these movements for identification, prevention and disruption have been hampered by a lack of applicable federal criminal statutes, particularly when attempting to address an organized, multi-state campaign of intimidation, property damage, threats and coercion designed to interfere with legitimate interstate commerce, as exhibited by the SHAC organization.[56]

While Lewis would present the case as a success, less than two days later, Cash would be acquitted. After the jury entered their deliberations, they requested the full copy of the videotape from the Hess station, rather than the stills provided by the prosecution. As the video was being set up, Brewington and his assistant council noticed major discrepancies between the video about to be shown to the jury, the stills entered as evidence, and the video provided in the discovery phase. The tape had clearly been doctored. Brewington threatened to pursue a declaration of mistrial if the evidence was admitted. The following day, in an unprecedented move, the judge threw the tape out. Within a few hours, Cash would be free from all charges and Brewington announced, "This is what democracy looks like."[57]

SOLIDARITY CAMPAIGN & POST-TRIAL POLITICAL DEVELOPMENTS IN LONG ISLAND

THROUGHOUT THE TRIAL, Brewington was able to construct a counter-narrative to the prosecution's version of MTC, Cash, and his supporters. Herein he was able to describe projects to feed the homeless, educate the community, provide space for young people to congregate, and protest in ways that did not include property destruction. Rather than simply challenging the inaccuracies and distortions in the prosecution's case, the defense told its own story. This was particularly clear with the screening a twelve-minute documentary called *Modern Times: Building Community in America's First Suburb*.[58] This documentary film included footage nearly identical to that the police took of the MTC May Day protest, as well as commentary on the group's purposes, clearly defining it as a public organization; it allowed Brewington to argue that the MTC, and hence Cash, had nothing to hide.

A substantive support campaign developed as an extension of the former-MTC's organizing strategy. In one of its first acts, the group held a discussion session with a set of older activists, which had initially been planned to inform Long Island's peace and justice community about the repression Cash was facing. But it shortly became an outpouring of stories told by older activists about the times they had been visited and threatened by the FBI in the 1960s and after. Numerous intra-community meetings were held, with and without Cash, to plan tasks leading up to and during the trial. An important component of these meetings was the expression of fear and upset that this was happening to the community in general, and Cash in particular.

In order to build court support, the group held one-on-one sessions with members of the peace and justice community, the immigrant rights movement, local academics, clergy, and other progressives; this effort resulted in a diverse crowd attending each day of trial. Members and staff from the Long Island Alliance for Peaceful Alternatives and other peace groups, as well as the Workplace Project, attended many of the trial's eight days. Herein the group expanded and leaned on existing relationships that had been developed over years of relationship building and community organizing. Indeed, these preexisting and meaningful relationships had developed *prior* to the period of repression, and it is doubtful that the MTC and its successor organization would have been able to build such bonds *during* the wave of repression.

In the three years between Cash's arrest and trial, the MTC had morphed into the Long Island Freespace, a nonprofit organization that held educational, political, and cultural events. This community organizing, rather than activist protest, approach allowed the group to expand its base in a period of repression, when, elsewise, many organizations often contract. During the trial itself, the support group cooked meals for the Cash family, and coordinated supporters to be with Cash during trial breaks and in evenings to provide anything he might need as well as a compassionate ear to listen. The vigilance of the group was also important, as the FBI/Suffolk County Police Department videotaped the comings-and-goings of support group members at the courthouse and followed many of them home and elsewhere. Additionally, two obvious plants attended the early trial dates and asked to join the long-dissolved MTC; they were collectively ignored.

In regards to the defense, having Brewington represent Cash was decisive. Brewington was a veteran of local civil rights struggles, had worked alongside William Kunstler reviewing the COINTELPRO papers, and was greatly respected on Long Island. It was the relationships the organizers of the MTC and Long Island Free Space had, as well as Brewington's prior relationship with Cash, which secured his position as defense attorney. Brewington advised the support group on all matters and many of the group's strategies were run through him first. For instance, it was Brewington who argued that the support group should not speak to the mainstream press about the case or related developments. He argued that the case would be tried in court, not in the press, and that any press statement could in fact harm them at trial or with any attempt to get the prosecution to drop the charges. The support group complied with his request. Additionally, the support group sought to tightly control the discussion and the image of the case in the radical press. Only four articles appeared with the group's participation, one at Cash's arrest, one on the onset of trail, and two following; the first was written by an anonymous activist, one of the articles was written by a support group member following Cash's acquittal, and the other two were penned by New York City–based journalist and supporter Eric Laursen.[59]

While the success of the defense counsel, support group, Cash family, and community surrounding them certainly contributed to the acquittal, these are not the only factors to consider. First, the core support group members, and many in the community, were able to take the entire two weeks off of work or adjust their work schedules, for the entirety of the trial. That, along with the fact that the Long Island Freespace was able to pay Cash and a co-organizer [the author, Kevin Van Meter] for the duration, is a situation not necessarily available to others facing repression. Additionally, being a white male charged in a case around development and environmental issues provided Cash certain privileges when facing an all-white jury, and these cannot be discounted. In a segregated place such as Long Island, with a long history of intense racial prejudice, one can assume that (for instance) a black or brown defendant, charged in a case focusing on the prison industrial complex, police violence, or issues of poverty, would have been treated substantially differently.

COUNTERING COUNTERINSURGENCY

IT IS USEFUL to consider this particular case in the larger context of repression and the strategies of counterinsurgency (COIN) utilized by the state apparatus. Since we have entered a period of "permanent repression," begun by at least the late 1970s, it is important to consider the social movement developments and waves of repression over the past three decades. Describing the shift between previous periods of repression and the current period, Ken Lawrence states,

> The difference today is [the state's] belief that insurgency is not an occasional, erratic idiosyncrasy of people who are exploited or oppressed, but a constant occurrence—*permanent insurgency*,

which calls for a strategy that doesn't simply reply on a police force and national guard and an army that can be called out in an emergency, but rather a strategy of *permanent repression* as the full-time task of the security forces. This difference has been elaborated theoretically largely as a consequence of the Indochina war, which gave this strategy its name: *counter-insurgency*.[60]

A state of permanent repression does not simply relate to political insurgencies or peasant movements of the Global South, but rather a society of control and a generalized state of siege upon the domestic, civilian population as part of a larger reorganization of power relations and the development of neoliberalism.[61] Herein we draw upon a small but growing literature on counter-counterinsurgency.[62] While this literature specifically addresses the foreign intervention apparatus of the United States, it has clear domestic ramifications.

It is important to note that *permanent* does not necessarily mean *consistent* or *continuous*. While the state itself is on permanent deployment, the apparatus of the state (local police agencies, FBI / JTTF, and private security) shifts to address particular threats as well as to respond to the environment in which it finds itself. A political environment can swing support against particular forms of repression, or against repression itself—which is where political organizing comes in.

When the state attempts to repress a radical movement, that does not necessarily mean that the movement has launched an insurgency, despite the oft-repeated activist myth that repression is always a direct reaction to our success. There are three stages of insurgency: proto-insurgency, small-scale insurgency [when insurgency grows beyond the initial insurgents] and major insurgency [when struggle is generalized across the population].[63] Both the ELF and the counter-globalization movement reached the level of small-scale insurgencies in their own way, within their own logic. But in neither case was repression *necessary* to decompose the movements, though it was the path chosen by the state; the latter movement was decomposing itself due to internal contradictions and dispersion of energy in significant ways. Rather, the wave of repression apparent in the Green Scare and related prosecutions is intended to prevent *new forms* of proto- and small-scale insurgency from emerging during a period when movements are at a low level of composition (density of relationships, organizational forms, strength *vis-à-vis* capital and the state).[64] It is clear that the state apparatus was surprised by the emergence of the ELF and the counter-globalization movement domestically. After all, by the late 1980s and early 1990s the forces of neoliberalism were triumphantly announcing the "end of history," meaning that the era of revolution and unrest had come to an end.

On May 10, 2001, in light of the increasing power of radical protests and organizing with the counter-globalization movement, the federal government declared Reclaim the Streets, of which Modern Times was an active part, a terrorist organization. An FBI report explained,

> Anarchists and extremist socialist groups—many of which, such as the Workers' World Party, Reclaim the Streets, and Carnival Against Capitalism—have an international presence and, at times, also represent a potential threat in the United States. For example, anarchists, operating individually and in groups, caused much of the damage during the 1999 World Trade Organization ministerial meeting in Seattle.[65]

In addition to the FBI report, the RAND Corporation produced a book in 2001 titled *Networks and Netwars: The Future of Terror, Crime and Militancy* which had three chapters dedicated to radical movements of the time.[66] RAND was advising law enforcement and government agencies in regards to the threat posed by the Seattle cycle of protest, black bloc anarchists (who were featured in two of the chapters), and the ELF. Specifically on the question of the state being caught off guard, one of the chapters locates the success of Seattle in the "utter surprise and confusion during the initial confrontation."[67] The collection does not specifically address the peak of this cycle of protest and, unfortunately, the literature on the subject from the perspective of its participants does not chart this decline either.

The counter-globalization movement peaked and then dissipated before September 11, 2001. The international Carnival Against Capital held on June 18, 1999; Earth First! ecological defense in the Pacific Northwest; and a related developments in the U.S. all fed into the N30 Seattle demonstrations. This rupture continued with April 16, 2000, against the International Monetary Fund and World Bank (IMF/WB) in Washington, DC; May Day the next month; and the Republican (Philadelphia) and Democratic (Los Angles) conventions in August. By August 2000, the MTC consciously removed itself from the protest-centric arm of the counter-globalization movement to focus on grounded, local issues. The Direct Action Network, which played a major role in Seattle and the events listed above, collapsed within the following year. While in the immediate aftermath of September 11, the IMF/WB protests planned were "canceled" by left organizations planning it—though a small group of anarchists continued with the action—it is questionable what good another summit protest would have done. The next major action, the World Economic Forum Protests in New York City in early February 2002 were so well managed by the state that they had little effect. When the same forces assembled for the Free Trade Area of the America protests in 2003, and the conventions a year later, it was clear that the state had gained the upper hand and that the cycle of protests had become a poor reflection of its previous anti-summit theatre. Between 2001 and 2003 U.S. radicals were engulfed in mass-based anti-war movement with few structural similarities to the counter-globalization movement.[68]

However, despite all the evidence, activists continue to believe that September 11 ended the period of struggle. This story is problematic for two reasons: first, it concedes too much power to the state to shift the terrain; and second, it provides an inaccurate account of the ability of the counter-globalization movement to ground itself and develop outside of the summit cycle of protest. The second point runs against the myths activists often tell about themselves; they would rather put the blame for movement disintegration on the state than on their own inability to build wider circles of struggle.

While the environment for organizing had certainly changed following September 11, the communities facing direct repression were overwhelmingly Muslim and members of immigrant groups. Movements in Europe and the Global South, when it was clear that attacks on capital and the state at the site of large conventions weren't working, shifted focus to issues of precarity and issues grounded in various communities; but that did not happen in the United States.

The way activists have framed of this period of repression ignores both historical and current examples of how repression has been directed against communities of color. Commenting on the "Green is the New Red" line, Claude Marks states "as an explicit part of that, there is an omission of anything that would care to look at the racial politics of the United States."[69] He follows this comment with the missing history of COINTELPRO, predominately used against communities of color and indigenous movements, and he goes on to critique the "Green Scare" conceptualization for not including the current wave of repression against Muslim and immigrant communities. There is also a larger apparatus of repression that has resulted in the dramatic increase in the prison population: and the wave of deportations directed at immigrant communities as a response to the strength of the migrant and immigrant rights struggles, perhaps best illustrated by the 2006 May Day protests. Including these realities would provide a clearer picture of the state's strategy.[70]

Taking the larger context into account, it seems that during a period of movement decline the state did two things. First, it utilized counterinsurgency strategies to prevent the development from a proto- to a small insurgency; and second, it applied lessons learned from countering the autonomous struggles of the insurgents during the previous peaks of activity. As it entered its decline, the counter-globalization movement simply stopped innovating tactically and was unable to generalize its struggles to larger sectors of the population.

LESSONS FOR POLITICAL ORGANIZING

IN DRAWING OUT the lessons for political organizing, political prisoner support, and surviving repression, there are few points as important as the development of relationships outside of our own immediate, radical circles. It was because of the concentric circles of both political and personal relationships that the MTC sought out and furthered prior to a period of repression that it was able to utilize after Cash's arrest and through his trial. Since the collective and its successor organization, the Long Island Freespace, held numerous community-based dialogs and cultural events that drew a substantial crowd from beyond Long Island's white, middle-class and working-class subculturally defined youth, it had regular contact with much larger communities than its own. Additionally, the MTC actively engaged in solidarity and participated in coalitions with peace groups, unions, immigrant rights organizations, and other community initiatives over a period of five years before Cash's arrest. Engaging in community organizing beyond the borders of subcultural radicals, and doing so prior to a period of repression, was decisive—since it is from the wider circle of personal relationships that active solidarity could be drawn. Furthermore, this approach directly counters key strategies of counter-insurgency—the questions of legitimacy and center of gravity.[71] Herein the insurgents incorporate the struggle over legitimacy into their pre-repression organizing and attempt to seize the center of gravity as an "operation against the state."

The support campaign around Cash, with direction provided in part by Brewington, decided internally to take a different approach than other such campaigns at the time. Many of those convicted during the Green Scare utilized the attention of their cases to talk about environmental destruction or animal rights. The priority of our campaign was Cash's freedom and, as trial approached, acquittal. Too often radicals utilize periods of repression to further a particular cause or issue. The argument we used was this: the cause will still be there following the case. Clearly this needs to be decided autonomously by each defendant and their support group. Those facing political repression should have control over the approaches they take to defend themselves—excluding, of course, snitching and cooperating with the prosecution—and their autonomy in these decisions should take priority over the ideological positions of the movement.[72]

By extension, it is important to emphasize the responsibility that the radical press and fellow radicals have to the individuals facing repression and the support group that speaks for the defendant or prisoner. While the Cash support group would not engage or speak to the mainstream press, it did seek out relationships with the radical press, and as previously mentioned, four articles appeared with the group's consent. However, the coverage in two additional articles that appeared in the *Earth First! Journal* were poorly researched and filled with misinformation, which could have been damaging at trial.[73]

Of course, it is not as though Cash's support committee did everything right either. We needed to do more specifically and consistently address the trauma and Post Traumatic Stress Disorder associated with repression and incarceration, as well as secondary trauma of support group members. As stated above, the development of technical assistance, knowledge, and financial resources needed to be implemented *prior* to confrontations with the state and a period of repression. Often radicals suggest that resistance should be "expected"; so should repression. Next time, let's be prepared for it.

In the end, McIntyre would be sentenced to three and a half years, in addition to a year already served. Mashkow would be imprisoned for a year and a day. And Rammelkamp would spend six months in jail. That's practically nothing compared to the 40 years faced by Cash. But, following his acquittal on May 20, 2004, Cash was free. And soon thereafter, the Long Island Freespace would open a new social center, with Cash as a staff member.

Of course we would rather that this case was not so curious, that there would be further acquittals and new victories. At the ten-year anniversary of Cash's arrest, this is the first time this story has been told, and it is our hope that it helps others survive the repression they face.

NOTES

1   While Conor Cash was consulted during various stages of this chapters construction, the views expressed herein are the author and author alone. *The Curious Case of Conor Cash* was the title given by conference organizer Will Munger to a presentation by Conor Cash and Kevin Van Meter at the "Counter-Counterinsurgency Convergence" held at Reed College from April 8–10, 2011. That event marked the first time either would speak publicly about the case and the talk served as the impetus for writing this chapter. *A Curious Case* is the result of years of collective organizing and collaborative thinking; and as a member of the support group around Cash, I participated in countless discussions, strategy sessions, meetings with legal counsel, documentary endeavors, and group therapy sessions. While the brunt of the trauma was experienced by Conor and the Cash family, we all carry the wounds of secondary trauma with us. Team Colors Collective and Friends—Conor Cash, Stevie Peace, Benjamin Holtzman, Craig Hughes (whose editing and support assisted greatly with this chapter)— arose from this trauma and *A Curious Case* is the result of its collaborative work. I would like to acknowledge the editors of this volume for their patience and support; and I want to express my respect and appreciation to the Cash family for allowing me to tell this story now at the ten-year anniversary of Conor's arrest. Furthermore, the manuscript was greatly improved by suggestions from Daniel McGowan, Robert Lepley, Tom Buechele, and scott crow.

2   The author believes that labeling this wave of repression the "Green Scare," in allusion to the Red Scare, is historically inaccurate and that the comparison does more to dilute our understanding than to clarify. However, the term is used throughout *A Curious Case*

because it has gained wide usage to describe this wave of repression. See Craig Hughes & Kevin Van Meter, "Is Green the New Red?: Thinking about political repression today" in *Left Eye on Books* (September 22, 2011); available online at: http://www.lefteyeonbooks. com/2011/09/is-green-the-new-red-thinking-about-political-repression-today/ (accessed January 22, 2012); Will Potter, *Green is the New Red: An Insider's Account of a Social Movement Under Siege* (San Francisco: City Lights, 2011).

3   Note throughout *A Curious Case*, Conor's first name is spelled with one 'n' as this is his correct, legal spelling. In the press, both mainstream and radical, as well as the indictment and court documents Conor is spelled with a double 'n', as "Connor." I have not corrected this error when it appears in the quoted original.

4   Institute on Race and Poverty, "Racism and the Opportunity Divide on Long Island," (July 2002); available online at: http://www.eraseracismny.org/downloads/reports/ER_ IRPFullReporttextonly.pdf (accessed July 13, 2011).

5   Conor Cash. "Decomposition and Suburban Space," *Affinities: A Journal of Radical Theory, Culture, and Action* (Winter 2010); available http://journals.sfu.ca/affinities/index.php/affinities/article/view/26 (accessed August 20, 2011).

6   The author initiated this first meeting along with Craig Hughes. Conor Cash joined the collective just prior to J18. In its earliest pamphlet, the collective stated its mission as such: "Modern Times: Long Island activist collective; is an umbrella organization of many diverse groups that are joining in a union of mutual aid, solidarity, and decentralization. The united purpose of this organization is to revolutionize society toward a just and free existence. A society with out hierarchal power, oppression, marginalization, wage-slavery, cruelty, discrimination, and environmental destruction. Our separate movements, especially in the historically inactive regions of the hyper-capitalist nations, at present are dissociated and financially strapped. By working together locally we can create a great resistance to the powers at bay" [errors appear in the original].

7   Robert Collier, "Clinton Urges Fairer Trade / He says WTO should hear out demonstrators"; San Francisco Chronicle (Dec. 2, 1999); available at http://articles.sfgate. com/1999-12-02/news/17708441_1_wto-world-trade-organization-result-in-trade-sanctions (Accessed July 30, 2011).

8   Credited to the Mustache, Cheap Sunglass and Comb-Over Conspiracy (in actuality, Kevin Van Meter). "Youth Activists under Attack," *Modern Times*, Volume 1, Number 2 (Winter 2000; published January 25, 2001).

9   Ibid.

10   Hindsight, a decade later, provides a different understanding: if multiple MTC members had been involved in the ELF and ALF, the statement would seem like a dismissal of our support for imprisoned activists. Additionally, the statement didn't properly reflect the opinions of the MTC and its members as to the use of clandestine actions generally; the concern was simply how such acts would function in the specific political context on Long Island. It can be taken now, as it was then, as a defensive move on behalf of the MTC.

11   As the SHAC 7 arrests occurred in early May 2004 and "Operation Backfire" followed in December, the case of Cash fits into dynamics of a wave of underground direct action and

subsequent repression that took place on Long Island during this same period. Operation Backfire was the name given to an FBI investigation targeting the ELF and ALF, resulting in the arrest of thirteen individuals between December 2005 and January 2006, and additional arrests following. It would be the largest case to date of activists targeted as part of the Green Scare. Likewise, the aforementioned Stepanian was arrested on February 3, 2000 and sentenced to six months in the county jail on November 17, 2000, on the dubiously credible charges of smashing fur store windows. His sentence came following a long campaign of harassment.

12 Between 1997 and 2008, the ELF claimed responsibility for eleven or twelve Long Island actions, depending on sources. The vast majority took place in the latter part of 2000. During this time period the ALF claimed 72 actions, with fifteen between September 2000 and January 2001 alone—the height of ELF activity. On December 7, 2000, the ELF and ALF jointly claimed an action at the McDonald's corporate headquarters in Haupauge, NY; this is included in both totals. See: Peter Young, *Animal Liberation Front Complete U.S. Diary of Actions: The First 30 Years* (Voice of the Voiceless, 2010); Craig Rosebraugh. "ELF in Long Island: Suburbia Burns!" *Earth First! Journal* (Brigid, 2001); "Diary of Actions—2000" Earth Liberation Front Press Office, http://www.earthliberationfront.org/doa2000.html (accessed August 18, 2011).

13 Cash was only charged with providing gasoline for the December 29, 2000 action, and planning an arson to complete the duck liberation at the Titmus Duck Farm that took place on 21 October, 2000. These charges initially amounted to arson conspiracy and aiding and abetting arson. The three cooperating witnesses were charged with an additional three arsons and claimed responsibility for a seventh. However, the cooperating witnesses stated that they didn't participate in the July 7, 2000, action against genetic engineering or the additional twenty-one ALF actions in Long Island during this time period. Following the arrest of Cash and the three cooperating witnesses, the ELF claimed responsibility for March 5 and June 13, 2001, actions. Both included smashing windows and spray painting slogans. The ELF returned to Cold Spring Harbor National Laboratories on August 21, 2001, smashing windows. See: Robert E. Kessler, "Sources: ELF Acts Grew More Violent / Bid for publicity drove an escalation" *New York Newsday*, February 14, 2000 (A04); Douglas Long, *Ecoterrorism* (New York: Facts On File, Inc., 2001). A note on Douglas Long's *Ecoterrorism* is certainly in order, as the author has no accreditation or training in the field, misconstrues numerous facts, and repeatedly refers to Cash as "activist and arsonist" regardless of his acquittal. Long's book is one of the only ones in print that discusses the case.

14 This account excludes an earlier action on July 7, 2000, against what was suspected to be genetically engineered corn at Cold Spring Harbor National Laboratory, which the cooperating witnesses stated they did not commit and local activists believe was the work of others, from outside of Long Island.

15 Note that errors in the communiqués appear in the original.

16 This action is mentioned in Craig Rosebraugh's "ELF in Long Island: Suburbia Burns!" piece in the *Earth First! Journal*—but with the numerous other distortions and inaccuracies in the article, to be addressed later, the claim is dubious.

17 Earth Liberation Front Communiqué dated Sept. 26, 2000; http://www.earthliberation-front.org/comm092600.html (accessed August 18, 2011).

18 Young, *Animal Liberation Front Complete U.S. Diary of Actions: The First 30 Years.*

19 Rosebraugh, "ELF in Long Island: Suburbia Burns!"; Earth Liberation Front Communiqué dated Nov. 11, 2000; http://www.earthliberationfront.org/comm111100.html (accessed August 18, 2011).

20 Earth Liberation Front Communiqué dated Nov. 24, 2000; http://www.earthliberation-front.org/comm112400.html (accessed August 18, 2011).

21 Earth Liberation Front Communiqué dated Dec. 1, 2000; http://www.earthliberation-front.org/comm120100.html (accessed August 18, 2011).

22 Earth Liberation Front Communiqué dated Dec. 9, 2000; http://www.earthliberation-front.org/comm120900.html (accessed August 18, 2011).

23 Earth Liberation Front Communiqué dated Dec. 19, 2000; http://www.earthliberation-front.org/comm121900.html (accessed August 18, 2011).

24 Earth Liberation Front Communiqué dated Dec. 21, 2000; http://www.earthliberation-front.org/comm123100.html (accessed August 18, 2011).

25 Michael Luo & Robert E. Kessler, "Teen Suspected in Eco-Attacks / Sources: FBI raids family's home" *New York Newsday*, January 17, 2001 (A03).

26 Kessler, "Sources: ELF Acts Grew More Violent / Bid for publicity drove an escalation"; Young, *Animal Liberation Front Complete U.S. Diary of Actions: The First 30 Years.*

27 Michael Luo and J. Jioni Palmer, "Group Claims Role in Fire," *New York Newsday*, December 13, 2000 (A51).

28 Editorial. "Long Island Is No Place for Environmental Terrorism," *New York Newsday*, December 18, 2000 (A36).

29 Editorial. "Ecoterrorism / Setting fire to new Suffolk homes is hardly the right way to protect the environment," *New York Newsday*, January 2, 2001 (A30).

30 Kara Blond, "Builders Hit Back Over Attacks / $10,000 offered or info on environmental arsonists," *New York Newsday*, January 3, 2001 (A04).

31 Paul Vitello, "Terrorism Off the Beaten Path," *New York Newsday*, January 4, 2001 (A08).

32 Robert E. Kessler, "Teens Admit Arson Link / 2 agree to cooperate in investigation of ELF," *New York Newsday*, February 2, 2001 (A31); Rosebraugh, "ELF in Long Island: Suburbia Burns!"

33 Kessler, "Terrorism Charge In Teen Arson Case," *New York Newsday*, September 27, 2001 (A24).

34 Ibid.

35 Stephanie McCrummen, Robert E. Kessler. "FBI Collects Evidence Near Teen's School / Also probing other suspects in eco-terrorism attacks," *New York Newsday*, January 18, 2001 (A04).

36 The author could not find a last name for this individual; "Courtney" is all that is listed in the materials I have access to. Additionally, it is not clear if this first name is correct or if it is a pseudonym.

37 *U.S. v. Conor Cash*, testimony, p. 459–63, 476, and 523.

38   Robert E. Kessler, "Sources: Teen Linked To ELF May Bargain," *New York Newsday*, January 19, 2001 (A38); Robert E. Kessler, "Teen Guilty of Arson / LI eco-terrorism suspect negotiated plea agreement," *New York Newsday*, February 10, 2001 (A05); Kessler, "Teens Admit Arson Link / 2 agree to cooperate in investigating the ELF."

39   Ibid; Michael Lou & Robert E. Kessler, "Teens Suspected in Eco-Attacks / Sources: FBI raids family's home," *New York Newsday*, January 17, 2001 (A03); McCrummen & Kessler. "FBI Collects Evidence Near Teen's School / Also probing other suspects in eco-terrorism attacks"; Kessler, "Sources: Teen Linked To ELF May Bargain"; Robert E. Kessler, "Source: 2nd Teen's Home Raided," *New York Newsday*, January 21, 2001 (A05).

40   Robert E. Kessler, "Teen Guilty of Arson / LI eco-terrorism suspect negotiates plea agreement," *New York Newsday*, February 10, 2001 (A05).

41   Kessler, "Sources: ELF Acts Grew More Violent / Bid for publicity drove an escalation," *New York Newsday*, February 14, 2001 (A04); Kessler, "Teens Admit Arson Link / 2 agree to cooperate in investigation of ELF."

42   Fred Kaplan, "Four Charged in Radical Group Arson," *Boston Globe*, February 16, 2001 (A21); Robert E. Kessler, "Suspect Pleads Not Guilty," *New York Newsday*, February 16, 2001 (A04); Anthony Ramirez, "Metro Briefing," *The New York Times*, February 16, 2001 (Section B; Column 1; Metropolitan Desk: 4); Associated Press, "4th Teen arrested in environmental attacks," *Times Union (Albany)*, February 16, 2001 (B2); Al Baker, "A Federal Case in Suffolk: Eco-Terrorism of Adolescence in Bloom?" *The New York Times*, February 18, 2001 (Section 1, Column 2; Metropolitan Desk: 33).

43   Editorial. "Use Activism, Not Vandalism, to Aid the Environment," *New York Newsday*, September 6, 2001 (A42).

44   Sean Gardiner, "This 'Bunny Hugger' Has a Tail, Too / Animal-rights activist: Cops are following me," *New York Newsday*, February 1, 2002 (A25).

45   Robert E. Kessler, "Witness Jailed For Lying About E-mail," *New York Newsday*, July 30, 2002 (A22).

46   FBI agents delivered a half-dozen subpoenas to MTC activists arrested at the May Day 2000 demonstration, and clearly hadn't penetrated the group any deeper since no other MTC associated people were subpoenaed. Unlike the grand jury resistance strategies chosen by other radicals at the time and currently, on the advice of Brewington, the MTC members showed up at what turned out to be a questioning room with Driscoll, Metzinger, and another FBI agent. It is unclear if a grand jury was even empaneled, but Driscoll was stonewalled, with each MTC member requesting a lawyer from the public defender's office, and then providing nothing but static to their questions. It should be noted that the strategy of resisting grand juries and refusing to speak is now common among radicals, but it was not at the time. The MTC saw the history of resisting grand juries as taking place 30 years prior and amongst a nationalist current it did not identify with.

47   Robert E. Kessler, "CENTRAL ISLIP Juror dismissed for remarks in activist case," *New York Newsday*, May 13, 2004 (A38); *U.S. v. Conor Cash*, testimony: 308–327.

48   *U.S. v. Conor Cash*, testimony: 514–515.

49   *U.S. v. Conor Cash*, Berg testimony: 598.

50   Kessler, "Witness Jailed For Lying About E-mail."

51   *U.S. v. Conor Cash*, testimony: 235–236.

52   *U.S. v. Conor Cash*, testimony: 240.

53   *U.S. v. Conor Cash*, testimony: 280–281.

54   *U.S. v. Conor Cash*, testimony: 370–374.

55   *U.S. v. Conor Cash*, F.169 Court Transcript: 531.

56   Congressional Testimony, *Animal Rights: John E. Lewis*, Federal Document Clearing House, May 18, 2004.

57   Robert E. Kessler, "CENTRAL ISLIP in environmental terrorism case," *New York Newsday*, May 21, 2004 (A38).

58   *Modern Times: Building Community in America's First Suburb*. VHS. Directed by Suzanne Shultz (New York, NY: 2000).

59   Anonymous [Andrew Stepanian], "Long Island Activist Targeted By The FBI," *Earth First! Journal* (May 1, 2001); Eric Laursen, "Hard Times for Modern Times," *In These Times*, May 14, 2004; available at http://www.inthesetimes.com/article/1518/ (accessed August 27, 2011); Kevin Van Meter, "Reclaimed Freedom: Activist Community Beats FBI Repression," *Earth First! Journal* (Lughnasadh, 2004); Eric Laursen, "Strong Island Rising," *Indypendent*, June 19, 2004; available at: http://nyc.indymedia.org/en/2004/06/39169.html (accessed August 27, 2011).

60   Ken Lawrence, *The New State Repression,* (Portland: Tarantula, 2006), emphasis in the original.

61   This period coincides with fundamental shifts in other institutions, as a full expression of neoliberalism, in what Gilles Deleuze called "societies of control." See Gilles Deleuze, "Postscript on the Societies of Control," *October*, No. 52 (Winter 1992): 3–7.

62   Network of Concerned Anthropologists, *The Counter-Counterinsurgency Manual: Or, Notes on Demilitarizing American Society* (Chicago: Prickly Paradigm Press, 2009); see also David H. Price, *Weaponizing Anthropology,* (Oakland & Petrolia: *Counterpunch* & AK Press, 2011).

63   Frank Kitson quoted in Kristian Williams, "The other side of the COIN: counterinsurgency and community policing," *Interface*, Vol. 3(1): 81–117 (May, 2011).

64   Specifically on "class composition" see: Harry Cleaver, *Reading Capital Politically,* (Oakland: AK Press, 2000).

65   Congressional Testimony, Louis J. Freeh, "Threat of Terrorism to the United States," May 10, 2001; available at: http://www.apfn.org/apfn/fbi_terrorism.htm (accessed January 22, 2012).

66   John Arquilla and David Ronfeldt, *Networks and Netwars: The Future of Terror, Crime and Militancy* (RAND Corporation, 2001); available at: http://www.rand.org/pubs/monograph_reports/MR1382.html (accessed January 26, 2012).

67   Paul de Armond, "Netwar in the Emerald City: WTO Protest Strategy and Tactics", Ibid., 202.

68   Preemptive raids, arrests, and a media blitz, as well as the "Miami Model" of a militarized police force managing public space with a huge presence, was tested in the immediate

aftermath of the 1999 Seattle protests. The state learned to address the counter-globalization movement's "decentralized, nonhierarchical, network-based movement" strategies. These lessons were implemented with increasing accuracy as the state *learned* and the movement implemented the same strategies, with less and less grounding. The movements simply stopped innovating. See Luis Fernandez, *Policing Dissent: Social Control and the Anti-Globalization Movement* (New Brunswick: Rutgers University Press, 2008), 137; Jarret Lovell, *Crimes of Dissent: Civil Disobedience, Criminal Justice, and the Politics of Conscience* (New York: New York University Press, 2009).

69   Walidah Imarisha and Kristian Williams. "COINTELPRO to COIN: Claude Marks Interview," in this volume.

70   As I have previously argued in Craig Hughes & Kevin Van Meter, "Is Green the New Red?: Thinking about political repression today," *Left Eye on Books* (September 22, 2011); available online at: http://www.lefteyeonbooks.com/2011/09/is-green-the-new-red-thinking-about-political-repression-today/ (accessed January 22, 2012).

71   Michael Freeman and Hy Rothstein (eds.) *Gangs and Guerillas: Ideas from Counterinsurgency and Counterterrorism* (Naval Postgraduate Technical Report); available at: http://www.nps.edu/Academics/Schools/GSOIS/Departments/DA/GGBook.html.

72   This point was discussed at length with Green Scare political prisoner Daniel McGowan in a letter to the author (dated September 9, 2011).

73   The first appeared in the Brigid 2001 (Winter) issue, written by Craig Rosebraugh of the North American Earth Liberation Front Press Office, and was entitled "ELF in Long Island: Suburbia Burns"; it incorrectly counts the number of ELF actions, and (worse) lists one that was only claimed *after* the cooperating witnesses began working with the government. In the following issue, "Elfers Arrested In New York" mistakenly claims that "Rammelkamp and McIntyre did not implicate anyone or answer questions." Neither article mentioned that Rammelkamp and McIntyre were cooperating with the government, a simple fact documented in the mainstream press for months. Anonymous, "Elfers Arrested in New York," *Earth First! Journal* (May 1, 2001); Anonymous, "4 Arrested in Long Island, NY for ELF Activity," *Resistance*, Volume Two, Number 1 (Spring 2001).

FROM REPRESSION TO RESISTANCE:
Notes on Combating Counterinsurgency

LUCE GUILLÉN-GIVINS, LAYNE MULLETT, AND SARAH SMALL

ON AUGUST 30, 2008 WE WERE AWAKENED EARLY IN THE MORNING BY THE SHRILL *ring of the telephone. The news on the other end of the line wasn't good: police were currently raiding three houses occupied by radical activists preparing to protest the Republican National Convention (RNC). Thinking our house would be next, we quickly packed up our belongings and headed out. We had been up late thanks to a raid on our convergence center the night before and were not eager to spend any more time with the police, the sheriff's department, or the Secret Service.*

Unfortunately, our success in avoiding the police was short-lived. Within 72 hours, eight local organizers were rounded up and eventually charged with "conspiracy to riot in furtherance of terrorism." The next few days saw over 800 arrests as thousands of people protested in the streets of St. Paul.

What followed was a two-year political and legal battle. We learned that the raids and arrests marked the culmination of almost two years of police activity and involved multiple informants, surveillance teams, and undercover officers. In discovery we obtained thousands of pages of meeting notes, emails, debriefings and reports, hundreds of photos, and hours and hours of audio recording that the police had collected on our activities. Clearly the state had been intensively monitoring local activists since the convention was announced, and likely continues to do so to this day.

Our experiences dealing with the aftermath of the RNC protests and related legal charges led us to think more deeply about the nature of policing and state repression, and what radical movements can do to counteract these attacks. In particular we were concerned with the more insidious elements of state intervention that work to undermine and co-opt movements along (and in conjunction) with the spectacle of police violence and mass arrests. We began to understand these tactics as a form of domestic counterinsurgency.

WHAT DOES COUNTERINSURGENCY LOOK LIKE?

Though counterinsurgency has been something of a watchword in the global "war on terror," its domestic applications are more obscured. Unlike in places where insurgency is already occurring, counterinsurgency strategy in the United States is primarily focused on preventing insurgent movements from taking root. This means that the state must work to create social conditions that make radical organizing difficult, and engage in constant (though sometimes low-intensity) disruptions of any activity that has the potential to threaten the existing power structure. These disruptions can range from COINTELPRO-style[1] assassinations like the murder of Fred Hampton[2] and lengthy prison terms for political dissidents, to surveillance and data collection on a wide range of public activities. Counterinsurgency can be the cops kicking down your door, but it can also be the co-optation of community organizing, the increasing capacity for sophisticated data-collection, the mapping of social networks, and the paid informant sitting quietly through meetings.

Activists generally remember to take basic security precautions, such as not sending sensitive information over email or discussing specific illegal actions at open meetings. What we often fail to do is address the group dynamics that make us vulnerable to disruption and infiltration, or make plans for how we can support each other when we are facing repression down the road. We tend to ignore the inevitable low-level intervention of the state in our movements, as well as the heightened repression meted out against other communities, until the moment we are confronted with "hard" tactics, such as brutality, prosecution, and imprisonment. Thus, our movements are only putting energy into combating repression when the battle is more than half over, past the point at which we would stand the best chance of winning.

This tendency may, in part, be due to the fact that activists often think there is a choice between the tactics and strategies that bring about repression, and those that avoid it. We believe that this distinction is a false one. While it's true, for example, that breaking a bank window is more likely to generate a rapid police response than circulating a petition, *any* campaign that mounts a potentially successful challenge to existing power structures, regardless of its tactics, will face some form of repression. Our reality is this: we can fight to win, and in so doing encounter state repression, or we can limit ourselves to ineffective modes of activism and agitation in the false hope that this will keep us safe. Counterinsurgency can be brutally effective, and coming to terms with this reality can easily lead to fatalism. But while we can't avoid being subjected to counterinsurgent methods, we can take a comprehensive approach (as the state does) and work to affect the terrain of attack.

If we're serious about growing revolutionary movements with the capacity to effect long-term, radical change, then we have to move beyond a purely defensive posture, wherein our efforts are primarily reactive, into an era of proactive movement building. One way to think about this challenge is to conceive of the conditions that would need to exist in order for insurgent movements to thrive, and to create those conditions within the arenas of radical struggle in which we are already engaged. By steadily laying this groundwork, we can better position ourselves to seize the moments when the state tries to pin us down as opportunities not just to resist, but to actively fight back.

We have by no means developed an exhaustive list of what those necessary conditions might be, but we have sketched out some of the lessons that we've learned. First, we believe that it is not possible to avoid counterinsurgency while working to create radical social change. Police harassment, arrests, and imprisonment are elements of virtually every successful social struggle and we must prepare for and confront this reality. Second, we believe that our approach to resisting counterinsurgency must be holistic; that is, we can't just focus on outsmarting the state. Instead, we must also transform the way we work and take care of each other, and learn to work together across our many differences. And finally, we believe that we can turn moments of state repression into opportunities to build and strengthen our movements.

We rely heavily on examples from the RNC 8 case, but also bring in other, much more severe, instances of state repression faced by the Puerto Rican independence movement and other national liberation struggles, as well as more recent cases falling under the umbrella of the "Green Scare." In so doing, we don't mean to suggest any direct parallel between the various examples. Rather, we've chosen this range of examples both because they draw on our personal experiences and because we feel that they help to provide a more comprehensive view of the sorts of state repression to which radicals today are vulnerable. We have included our more personal experiences and reflections individually in italics, and our broader analysis in the regular text.

WHERE WE'RE COMING FROM

Luce Guillén-Givins: *In 2006, I started organizing with a group called the RNC Welcoming Committee. We were Twin Cities anarchists and anti-authoritarians who came together to develop protest infrastructure against the 2008 Republican National Convention in St. Paul, Minnesota. From August 30 through September 1, 2008, seven other people and I (the "RNC 8") were arrested and charged with multiple counts of conspiracy and terrorism for our roles in organizing for the protests. Most of us were arrested before the protests even began and were held in jail until they were over. None of us were charged with actually* doing *anything; conspiracy charges are based on what the state believes we said, thought, and intended to do. At the peak of the prosecution, we were charged with four separate felonies: "conspiracy to riot," "conspiracy to commit criminal damage to property," "conspiracy to riot in furtherance of terrorism," and "conspiracy to commit criminal damage to property in furtherance of terrorism." We faced up to 12 years in prison if convicted.*

Along with many dedicated supporters, we spent two years waging a massive legal and political campaign to get the charges dropped. In what I think was our biggest unqualified victory, the County Attorney buckled to public pressure and dropped the terrorism charges against us less than six months after filing them. In August of 2010, one of our codefendants decided to cut his losses and plead guilty to a single gross misdemeanor. He chose to serve a short term in jail, rather than a longer period on probation. Despite our disappointment in his decision to take a plea, the fact that he had so much room to negotiate—without testifying against the rest of us—was a sign of the power our support campaign wielded. A month later, and with only a month left before trial, the State dropped all of the charges against me and two of my codefendants. A few weeks after that, the four remaining codefendants each pled guilty to a single gross misdemeanor. They were sentenced only to probation and community service, a massive reduction from the charges the State had pursued at a cost of over $250,000 and more than three years of police and legal work.[3]

We also had other successes over the course of those two years. We contributed to the demise of the County Attorney's gubernatorial campaign, and built some unlikely alliances with people and organizations in Minneapolis and across the country. The successes of our support campaign were only possible because we used our fight as a vehicle for capacity-building. As the case and support campaign progressed, opening new doors in terms of radical networking and solidarity, our experiences pushed us to start fleshing out this idea of capacity-building as a starting point for thinking about resistance to counterinsurgency. The ideas sketched out in this article are predicated on the belief that this can be a winning strategy for revolutionary movements.

Layne Mullett: *Sarah and I live in Philadelphia, but temporarily relocated to Minneapolis before the RNC to help prepare for the protests. Upon returning to Philly, we knew that we wanted to continue fighting for our friends who were facing terrorism charges in Minnesota. However, the context for resisting state repression in Philadelphia during this time was somewhat different than in Minneapolis. Philadelphia has a long history of racist police violence and has also been the site of some of the most dramatic repression in recent U.S. history (most notably the MOVE bombing in 1985[4]). Philadelphians had even had their own experience hosting the RNC, where scores of protesters were beaten and jailed by police. But in 2008, many leftist organizations were focused on other issues, and state repression was low on the list of priorities.[5]*

Sarah and I knew that we wanted to publicize the case and generate political and financial support for the RNC 8, in part because Luce is a close friend, but also because we believed that the use of terrorism charges against people organizing public protests set a dangerous precedent that could extend well beyond Minnesota. However, we knew that getting people on the East Coast to support eight anarchists from the Midwest was going to be a hard sell. For the RNC 8 case to feel relevant in Philadelphia, our work would have to be done in a way that went beyond advocating for those eight defendants and moved towards strengthening our ability to fight state repression in general.

Traditional forms of support for people facing political charges include fundraising for bail and legal expenses, showing support in the courtroom, holding events to raise awareness, and engaging in public advocacy to try to affect the outcome of the case. We wanted to do all these things, but do them in a way that shed light on a wide range of resistance to repression. Using this approach would, we hoped, allow us to incorporate RNC 8 support into our already existing political work rather than diminishing our capacity to carry that work forward.

While in some historical moments fighting specific instances of state repression has helped build movements,[6] it can often make people feel worn down and isolated. We wanted to counter this tendency, and instead attempt to:

1. *connect this case to a legacy of repression against political movements across generational, racial, and ideological lines, and use the RNC 8 support work as a platform to raise awareness and funds for others facing state repression and imprisonment,*

2. *help create the conditions for a movement in Philadelphia that was more prepared to combat repression, and*

3. *make connections between political prisoners/state repression and broader anti-prison and social justice movements.*

As we moved forward we carried each of these goals with us, and tried to develop our activities to meet them. What took shape, in its best moments, mirrored some of the ideas outlined in this essay.

KNOWING OUR HISTORY

THE FIRST NECESSARY condition of fighting counterinsurgency is an awareness and critical analysis of state repression. We cannot defend against an enemy we haven't anticipated, nor can we effectively strategize if we don't have an understanding of what we're up against. Those of us who are likely to be targets of counterinsurgency operations—and it is important to stress how broadly that likelihood applies—are better positioned to deal with attacks against us if we start out with a strong analysis of what we might face.

The history of repression in the United States is older than the state itself, and this repression mirrors an equally long legacy of resistance. Yet one of the striking aspects of activist responses to counterinsurgency tactics is an expression of total shock. How many times have we seen the same thing play out?— the look of confusion and disbelief clouding someone's face as they talk about a recent political arrest or prosecution, stating that they "never thought this could happen here," or wondering what happened to "democracy."

The truth is that many activists in the U.S. are startlingly unaware of the country's brutal legacy of repression.[7] There are several major factors at play here, but among the most significant are high turnover rates and generational divisions. Cycles of entry into and burn-out from radical movements are often as short as a few years, and the sharing of lessons across these micro-generational divides is shoddy, at best. In a society where radical histories are buried and distorted, the lack of intergenerational engagement undermines our best chance at knowing our own histories. For example, there are currently over 70 leftist political prisoners in the U.S.,[8] mostly people who have been struggling behind bars for decades; yet many of us can only name one or two of them. It's sobering to think that people who struggle for revolutionary liberation in this country today wouldn't know about people who've spent years in prison for doing the same. Not only does this rob our comrades of the support they need and deserve, it also prevents us from gaining the wisdom and insight that comes from learning about and talking with previous generations of dissidents and freedom fighters.

Luce: *In Minneapolis, prior to the RNC, work had already been done within the anarchist community that put the issue of state repression on the table in a historically grounded way. Twin Cities activists (viewed collectively) were experienced with state repression: A decade before the RNC, Minneapolis was witness* *to one of the largest police actions in the state's history—a raid on the Minnehaha Free State.*[9] *In 2000, some of the same people who had been integral to the Free State were targets of another massive police operation, in response to protests at a conference of the International Society for Animal Genetics.*[10] *In each of these incidents, radical activists were severely brutalized by police in violently theatrical raids, and the ISAG raid was followed by serious criminal charges against one of the organizers. (As it happens, he would later be one of the RNC 8.) Yet frequent burnout meant that few who were actively involved in organizing against the RNC were fully cognizant of this recent history, and even fewer had been around to experience it first-hand.*

Those of us in the RNC Welcoming Committee were acutely aware of this problem, and felt that our capacity was limited by the disproportionately small presence of older activists with more experience. We were also critical of mass mobilization organizing that lacked roots in local communities, feeling that too often large mobilizations brought with them a traveling show of radicals who skillfully implemented infrastructure for the protest but ignored local campaigns, communities, and histories of struggle. When they left, the skills went with them, the local community was left to deal with the fallout of the protests, and no meaningful exchange between "locals" and "out-of-towners" occurred. We wanted the RNC to be different, both by strengthening our local work and by contributing to the political development of the thousands of people we hoped would come through. So as one of our first group projects, we gathered submissions and published "The Struggle Is Our Inheritance," a zine chronicling some major events in Minnesota's radical history.

The zine begins, "Substantive, radical change is only accomplished with a firm understanding of the past."[11] *It covers a range of topics, such as the 1934 Teamsters' Strike, the emergence of the American Indian Movement in the '70s, and rural Western Minnesota's anti-power line movement.*[12] *The production of the zine was educational for those of us involved, and its publication helped to foreground the idea of a radical heritage in the organizing against the RNC.*

I also worked with a group called EWOK! (Earth Warriors are OK!) that was active in supporting Green Scare prisoners.[13] *We put on many well-attended fundraisers and educational events to that end, bringing speakers from across the country to talk about their experience dealing with state repression. The speakers we brought over the course of the group's life, including Ramona Africa,*[14] *Sara Jane Olson,*[15] *and Leslie James Pickering,*[16] *amongst others, represented a range of movements and eras of state repression. We also created and distributed a zine documenting past instances of FBI harassment of earth and animal liberation activists in the Twin Cities, basic "know your rights" information, and more in-depth analysis of how to deal with government disruption and interference.*

Sarah Small: *After the RNC, one of the first things we started to plan in Philadelphia was a large event that would raise awareness and money for the*

RNC 8, but we didn't want it to focus only on their case. At that time there were eight former Black Panthers, dubbed the "San Francisco 8," who were facing charges stemming from the killing of a San Francisco police officer in 1971. The original charges against them had been dismissed in 1975 after it was revealed that the case was based on statements that one of the defendants made after he and two of his codefendants were tortured for several days while in the custody of the New Orleans Police Department. The USA PATRIOT Act[17] made it possible for these bogus charges to be brought against the same men decades later, in 2007.[18] The Patriot Act also played a role in the RNC 8 case: additional felony charges were added through the use of "terrorism enhancements" under Minnesota's version of the law. In fact, the charges brought against the RNC 8 were the first time the Minnesota Patriot Act was ever used.

We wanted to bring the two cases together to highlight the fact that repression against anarchists is not exceptional; it mirrors strategies the state has used to attack other movements (and is often less severe than the repression visited on struggles led predominately by people of color). It was important to engage in a campaign that saw different cases of repression as interlinked, and we wanted to make sure that our work on behalf of the RNC 8 helped generate support for others facing state repression as well. We decided to make the event a joint fundraiser, with the proceeds split between the RNC 8 and the SF8 defense funds. Layne and I knew it would be challenging to pull off such a large event on our own, so we teamed up with a couple of local activists with similar goals and politics.

We convened a panel of speakers who were part of different radical movements, including representatives from the RNC 8, the SF8, the Puerto Rican Independence movement,[19] and the sole adult survivor of the MOVE bombing. The panel was called "Conspiring for Change," in reference to the fact that most of the panelists had either faced conspiracy charges or were involved in fighting for others facing them. This event was successful, both as a fundraiser and as a way to situate today's anarchist and radical movements within the context of a long legacy of struggle against the state. It also sowed the seeds of some new political relationships that would deepen and grow over the next few years. This effort led to the formation of a new group, which we named the Wild Poppies Collective after a poem by former political prisoner Marilyn Buck.[20] The collective has worked together since 2009, organizing educational events and actions about prisons, state repression and political prisoners.

UNDERSTANDING THE SCOPE OF DOMESTIC COUNTERINSURGENCY

JUST AS IT is important for us to make connections across generations of activists that have experienced repression, it is equally important for us to understand that counterinsurgency tactics do not only target existing political movements. Perhaps the most devastating counterinsurgency efforts are those designed to prevent movements from emerging in oppressed communities. The state does this in part by enacting social, legal, and policing strategies that criminalize and incarcerate poor people and people of color. Any analysis of repression that does not include the 2.3 million people in prison in the United States, or the fact that black people are incarcerated at a rate more than five times that of whites,[21] will lead us to false conclusions about how to resist repression. We can and must make our fight against overt repression of political movements tie back to the realities of mass incarceration and the legacy of white supremacy.

Incarceration rates began their dramatic increase in the late 1970s in the wake of massive radical social struggles, especially in black, Latino and Native communities. White supremacy plays a major role in upholding existing power structures, and efforts to fight white supremacy are met with particularly harsh repercussions from the state. Some of this repression is immediate and obvious—from 1968 to 1971, the FBI was either directly or indirectly involved in as many as 40 murders of Black Panthers.[22] And the American Indian Movement and its supporters were targeted even more intensely, with the state playing a role in 69 murders on the Pine Ridge reservation alone between 1973 and 1976.[23] But backlash against these movements is also mobilized through racially coded policies like "the War on Drugs," which was officially launched by Ronald Reagan in 1982 at a time when drug use was actually *decreasing*, and which led to massive imprisonment of people of color and, to a lesser extent, poor whites.[24] The War on Drugs itself increased the state's capacity for counterinsurgency, particularly in poor urban communities, as millions of dollars in federal funding was directed towards militarizing local police departments.[25] And the drug war was just one component of the conservative "law and order" policies that were specifically designed to create a conservative backlash against the civil rights and liberation movements of the preceding decades, and to prevent such movements from emerging in the future.

The expansion of the prison industrial complex shapes the context in which we operate and affects our ability to imagine what kind of resistance is possible. We believe that genuine efforts at fighting counterinsurgency must acknowledge the profound effect that mass incarceration has had on crushing resistance movements. And we also believe that the fight against mass incarceration is critical, both inside and outside the prison walls. We take inspiration from the many political prisoners who have been part of anti-prison movements and who continue to remind us that the entire prison system must be a central target of our struggles. As the recent prison strikes at Pelican Bay and across the nation prove, not even the most repressive conditions can stop the development of organized resistance. It is our job as radicals on the outside to amplify this resistance and help it grow.[26]

Layne: *The Wild Poppies Collective saw the struggle to free political prisoners as intimately connected to fighting the prison industrial complex. We felt that freeing political prisoners was one aspect of a larger struggle against state repression and mass incarceration, but initially found it hard to make these connections manifest themselves in practice. In 2010 we became aware of Pennsylvania's plans to build three new prisons and expand several others across the state. That seemed like an opportunity to broaden our work, and in 2011, the WPC helped launch a campaign against the prison expansion projects. The campaign, called Decarcerate PA, is demanding a moratorium on prison construction, a reduction in the prison population, and the reinvestment of money in our communities. Our hope is that this campaign can help build a united front against mass incarceration in Pennsylvania, and that successful decarceration efforts could lead not just to the release of political prisoners but to many others targeted by the racist police state.*[27]

Of course, global and domestic counterinsurgencies have taken on new dimensions since September 11, 2001. Globally, the U.S. has waged two long-term and official wars of occupation, in Iraq and Afghanistan, while escalating the practice of unofficial, imperialist warfare throughout much of the world, including increased drone strikes and other military operations in Pakistan and Yemen.[28]

Though we do not believe that the post-9/11 era represents a *fundamental* change in the character of repression employed by the American state, neither do we want to downplay the sweeping and insidious nature of the domestic mechanisms of repression enacted under the banner of a global "War on Terror." The past ten years have seen a massive wave of legislation on both the federal and state levels aimed at criminalizing entire communities (namely, Muslims, Arabs, and immigrants as a whole), as well as a shift towards codifying tactics that police agencies previously employed illegally.[29] Thousands of people, mostly Muslim men, have been imprisoned indefinitely in military prisons abroad and in civilian prisons within the U.S., many without even a nominal guarantee of due process.

The post-9/11 era has also shaped the prison system—for example, with the creation of "Communications Management Units" designed to severely restrict communication with the outside world. People held in the CMUs are permitted only one 15-minute phone call a week, and are barred from any physical contact during the few visits they are allowed. Muslims (primarily of Middle Eastern descent) make up the vast majority of the CMU population, though the units also house other inmates, including a few earth and animal liberation prisoners. People are held in the facilities for a number of reasons, such as involvement in prison organizing, drug convictions, various supposed communication infractions, and alleged or actual affiliations with foreign and domestic groups—on both the right and left—classified as "terrorist organizations."[30]

CMUs are one of the clearest examples of how various and often separate targets of counterinsurgency—Arab Muslims, Black people, and radical activists, for instance—are being subjected to similar counterinsurgency tactics. Through building an understanding of the connections between different targets of counterinsurgency we can decrease exceptionalism in our movement and illuminate potential coalitional organizing strategies. Recognizing these intersections and the common enemy that has created them is critical for building mass support for incarcerated people whether they are considered political prisoners or not. In building revolutionary movements in the United States, we must address the systemic nature of white supremacy, xeno- and Islamophobia, and state repression, and use these intersections as a place to create unconventional alliances and new fronts of struggle.

HONESTY ACROSS IDEOLOGIES

OFTEN, CONVERSATIONS ABOUT creating broad-based support for leftist causes are infused with the belief that we have to compromise or hide the most radical elements of our political analysis and activities to avoid alienating "the masses." We reject this idea for two reasons: First, there is no homogenous "mass" of people. We live in a diverse society, and no single message or framing will or should appeal to everyone. And second, we believe that we can develop broad-based support through being as open and up-front about our politics as possible. This support is necessary as counterinsurgency attempts to isolate and marginalize radical voices and actions. Speaking as anarchists, we know that many people disagree with us, our arguments, and our visions for the future. However, disagreement need not be avoided and, when handled thoughtfully, is a critical component of political engagement and development—on both sides. The harder gap to bridge is the one created by false pretense: no one likes being lied to, especially not based on the condescending assumption that they couldn't "handle" the truth. And in addition to the risk of alienating potential supporters and comrades through dishonesty, we lose unexpected opportunities for affinity and solidarity when we fail to present ourselves and our politics in a transparent manner.

Luce: *There are lots of examples of the benefits of political honesty, but a few from RNC organizing stick out in my mind. Our first endeavor in preparing for the RNC was to construct an explicitly anarchist force that other groups had to grapple* *with, in one way or another. We weren't always well received. But more often than not we were able to gain recognition and respect amongst other anti-RNC organizing groups, in part, because we were the first group to emerge publicly in opposition to the convention, and in part because of our sheer determination. By the time the large, leftist anti-RNC coalition held a conference to gather endorsements for the opening day march, we had already been active for over a year. We took our place at the table as anarchists and, because we had made genuine and serious contributions to the body of anti-RNC efforts, even groups whose tendency would have been to write us off had little option other than to recognize us.*

The Welcoming Committee's commitment to holding space for anarchists at the RNC meant that far more anarchists came to the protests than would have otherwise, and they came having already put time into preparing for the block-ading strategy[31] that had been collectively agreed upon at the national meetings leading up to the RNC. The respect that we earned from other local organizations, however uneasily it was given, helped pave the way for real support after some of us were arrested and as the RNC 8 case (and, to a lesser extent, other felony cases) proceeded through the court system.

The eight of us were falsely accused of conspiring to do some extreme and ridiculous things, including saving buckets of urine for months prior to the convention to throw at cops, planning to kidnap delegates, and running a "terrorist training camp." Alongside these accusations, our anti-authoritarian politics were put in the spotlight. Ramsey County prosecutors thought that other anti-RNC protesters and the public at large would be shocked and horrified, both by the beliefs we actually held and by the absurd things we were accused of doing. They banked on the assumption that our allies would turn against us and, frankly, this would have been a reasonably likely outcome. But the fact that we made ourselves visible—anarchist politics and all—for almost two years before had given fellow activists time to get used to us and even develop an affinity with us. We weren't the scary anarchists of legend, descending on a good city from elsewhere, hell-bent on wreaking havoc, and our work over those two years had at the very least earned us the chance to tell our side of the story.

I also benefited personally from this approach at my job. At the time, I had been working in a college cafeteria on and off for six years. While I didn't walk around my workplace trying to convert people, I was open about my political beliefs and activities. When my mug shot flashed across the local news and I was publicly branded a terrorist, my coworkers and managers—who might otherwise have bought the state's narrative—had an honest relationship with me to counterbalance the hype. I didn't lose my job or suffer any repercussions, suspicion, or harassment at work (as happened to at least one co-defendant), and my manager even held my position during the time I was unavailable as a result of my arrest.

REJECTING FALSE DIVISIONS, CREATING GENUINE SOLIDARITY

ONE OF THE ways that the state suppresses movements is through exploiting existing divisions, and creating false ones, within potentially insurgent communities. Counterinsurgency employs the "good protester/bad protester" dichotomy as a way of manipulating people—both those who are politically engaged, and those who aren't. In this model, the state pits activists against each other, granting some of them (the "good ones") a measure of legitimacy but pinning it to their willingness to help undermine the work of the "bad ones." The idea is that maintaining a cozy relationship with the state will be an incentive for certain activists to delegitimize others, diverting attention from the oppressive nature of the system while accomplishing the goal of isolating and destabilizing radical movements. The dichotomy is often tied to tactical differences, exemplified in media coverage of mass mobilizations where cops, city officials and reporters talk about how the "good protesters" who will be marching peacefully are in danger of being overshadowed by the "bad protesters" who will vandalize things.

Whereas in previous decades protests were often either repressed or simply ignored, the post-911 era has seen the emergence of a more sophisticated model of protest policing. This model, sometimes called "strategic incapacitation," is designed to neutralize specific protesters while maintaining an appearance of the freedom of speech and assembly. According to sociologist Patrick Gillham, strategic incapacitation

> is characterized by the goals of "securitizing society" and isolating or neutralizing the sources of potentially disruptive protest actions or events. These goals are primarily accomplished through (1) the use of surveillance and information sharing as a way to assess and monitor risks, (2) the use of pre-emptive arrests and less lethal weapons to selectively disrupt or incapacitate protesters that engage in disruptive protest tactics or *might* do so, and (3) the extensive control of space in order to isolate and contain disruptive protesters whether actual or potential.[32]

From a policing perspective, this model is most successful if the people who have been identified as the "good protesters" will voluntarily vilify the other protesters in the media and provide the police intelligence on more radical protest activity. The strategic incapacitation model can also create rifts in coalitions of protesters who otherwise might work together effectively despite different tactical or ideological approaches.

To avoid playing into the state's hands, we have to inoculate our movements with the belief that what we have to gain through solidarity is more valuable than what we might gain through divisiveness. This doesn't mean that we can, or should, avoid meaningful conflict, but that we have to think more deeply about the *causes* of that conflict and the most constructive methods of dealing with it.

Luce: *One of the most enduring legacies of anti-RNC organizing is what we call the "St. Paul Principles." In our conversations with anarchists who had been a part of organizing for past mass mobilizations, we heard one issue come up over and over again: the nonviolence pledge. That is, it was not uncommon for major players in a given mobilization to require a pledge of nonviolence as a precondition to formal involvement in the protest organizing. This pledge easily (and to some extent, by design) becomes a wedge driven between groups that might otherwise have worked well together.*[33]

Many of us in the Welcoming Committee felt that it was important to avoid any sort of nonviolence pledge for two reasons. One was a matter of principle: though we saw no strategic value in violent protest at the RNC, there was an overwhelming rejection of pacifist ideology within the group and a belief that nonviolence pledges do more harm than good for radical organizing. The other reason was merely practical: we wanted to avoid being backed into a corner where a refusal to sign any sort of pledge cut us out of general anti-RNC organizing, or where the adoption of such an agreement turned off some of the anarchists we intended to make space for at the protests. So we decided to preempt the whole situation by approaching the other major organizers and proposing a different set of protest agreements—one that foregrounded solidarity and noncooperation with the state.

The St. Paul Principles went as follows:

1. *Our solidarity will be based on respect for a diversity of tactics and the plans of other groups.*

2. *The actions and tactics used will be organized to maintain a separation of time or space.*

3. *Any debates or criticisms will stay internal to the movement, avoiding any public or media denunciations of fellow activists and events.*

4. *We oppose any state repression of dissent, including surveillance, infiltration, disruption and violence. We agree not to assist law enforcement actions against activists and others.*

When we conceived of the St. Paul Principles, we expected an uphill battle, in particular because our blockading plans roughly coincided with the big anti-war march on the first day of the convention. To our surprise, several of the major groups organizing the march were enthusiastic about the idea. The St. Paul Principles were integrated into the endorsement of the big march, which had the effect of bringing on board some of the groups who would otherwise have been most inclined to impose and enforce a nonviolence pledge.

Beyond being divided over tactics, radical movements are often deeply divided by ideological differences. Without minimizing these differences, it is important to struggle to find common ground. When we become too dogmatic or only seek out alliances within our own political milieu, we fail to learn from the experiences of other movements. We also deny ourselves the chance to create a broad and diverse base of support for our own struggles.

Luce: *Prior to the RNC, I identified a strategic value for the anarchist movement here in fostering better relationships with non-anarchist groups. But it wasn't until I had the privilege of watching the fruits of that labor, both at the protests during the RNC and in the community response to legal fallout afterwards, that I truly felt the necessity of such cross-movement solidarity. There is a huge difference between having an intellectual commitment to bridging ideological and social gaps in our movements, and holding a genuine sense of solidarity. Most organizing groups had agreed to the St. Paul Principles before the RNC, but the agreement was often rife with mutual wariness. After the convention, this uneasiness dissipated, and in its place, a sense of collective struggle started to emerge. Signing on to the principles had seeded the idea of this collective struggle, and as the eight of us and the Welcoming Committee as a whole were attacked by the state, other "signatories" felt that they were under attack by extension. Support for our defense was far more diverse than support for our previous organizing had been. And though the St. Paul Principles were specific to the RNC protests in letter, even today people invoke them explicitly in discussions of ongoing community work in the Twin Cities, and model new protest agreements after them across the country.*

Genuine cross-movement solidarity is especially powerful insofar as its growth nurtures and sustains new work in unpredictable ways. While maintaining a critical approach to political and tactical differences, we should also make intentional strides towards opening ourselves up to these new—and sometimes unconventional—alliances. This work has to take place both on the level of personal transformation, and as a matter of organizational culture.

Luce: *While developing the RNC8 support campaign we decided to frame our defense within a broader analysis of state repression, and to intentionally tie it to ongoing political work outside of the defensive realm. For example, we planned most of our events as joint fundraisers, whether with other legal defense funds or* groups engaging in proactive political work. Our insistence on using this model was occasionally a point of frustration for some within the defense committee, who felt like they had signed up to support the RNC 8 and, instead, got stuck with the responsibility of supporting a whole movement. But in the end, members of the defense committee voiced an appreciation of the collective efforts at pushing the boundaries of our support; it made the often mundane work of fundraising and courtwatching more meaningful, and provided ways for people to bring their own political priorities to the table. The practice of continually pushing a narrative that anchored our case to a bigger analysis of repression lent our support work more of a feeling of the mutual aid that is sometimes lacking in legal defense campaigns.

A striking example of this, in my mind, came about in the fall of 2009. Carrie Feldman and Scott DeMuth, two people many of us were friends with, and who had been involved in anti-RNC work among other things, were subpoenaed to a grand jury in southern Iowa relating to an ongoing investigation of an Animal Liberation Front action that had occurred several years prior. Scott and Carrie were initially positioned to receive relatively little support, since the case came seemingly out of nowhere, and animal rights activity receives a chilly reception in many parts of the left. But despite their case having only a circumstantial connection to the RNC, we piggybacked support for the two of them onto RNC 8 infrastructure, hoping that the goodwill afforded us would be extended to them. Our supporters as a whole were remarkably open to this, and it greatly expanded the scope of solidarity for Scott and Carrie as their case progressed.[34]

In September of 2010, as Scott's case was nearing resolution and our own trial date approached, I had a moment of thinking that this local spell of overt repression was finally drawing to a close. Then, on September 24th, I woke up to the news that the FBI was raiding several houses around the metro area. The situation that has unfolded in the time since is this: Two dozen activists, most of them in Minneapolis and Chicago, were subpoenaed to a federal grand jury investigating alleged "material support for terrorism."[35] Based on search warrant affidavits, it appears that the targets of the investigation have been chosen because of their international solidarity work, especially in support of Palestinian liberation. For some of them, an additional and overlapping component of the investigation seems to be their membership in the Freedom Road Socialist Organization.[36] All have refused to cooperate with the grand jury.

Many of these new targets had been active supporters of the RNC 8 as our case progressed. Over the course of our own support campaign, we had started cooking a free meal for supporters once a month as a gesture of appreciation for their work. The meals provided a monthly space for those dealing with the RNC aftermath to gather unencumbered by the obligations of fundraisers, speaking events, and meetings, and the sense of community fostered at these dinners was hugely beneficial to all of us, emotionally and psychologically. As our friends dealt with their own unfolding political case, some of the RNC 8 and the folks who were involved in *our defense committee were looking for meaningful ways to provide support and decided to start organizing a similar monthly meal for them. I think this sort of activity would have been unlikely prior to the RNC, but the work we've all engaged in together has built a feeling of solidarity strong enough to nurture new, cross-movement bonds.*

One of the subpoenaed activists once said to me, "We're standing on your shoulders." While we can't reasonably take any credit for their noncooperating stance, this statement illustrates the extent to which RNC 8 support work injected new attention to state repression in the Twin Cities and established a set of expectations about how to deal with it. The work that went into both our case and Scott and Carrie's cases had become a local reference point for principled resistance to state repression by the time these subpoenas were issued, providing both inspiration and concrete models for possible radical responses.

Layne: *Another positive outcome from doing RNC 8 support in Philadelphia was the development of a lasting relationship between the Wild Poppies Collective (WPC) and local Puerto Rican Independence activists. One of the WPC members had a previous relationship with the National Boricua Human Rights Network and invited a long-time independence activist to speak on the Conspiring for Change panel. Following the panel, we became involved in the campaign to free Carlos Alberto Torres and Oscar López Rivera, the two longest held Puerto Rican political prisoners in the U.S.*

As we learned more about this history, it quickly became clear that there was a lot to learn from the independence movement, both because of their unwavering militant non-collaboration with the state and because they are one of the few movements that has successfully freed the majority of their political prisoners.[37] In order to support these ongoing struggles, the WPC held events featuring former political prisoners from the Puerto Rican movement and hosted discussions about colonialism in Puerto Rico.[38] These generated support, at least in our immediate political circles, among people who were not previously thinking about U.S. colonialism as a present-day reality. Had we been thinking about the RNC 8 support campaign in a more narrow way, or if we had only sought relationships with other anarchists, we would have missed this opportunity to deepen our understanding of anti-colonial struggles and learn from others who had been fighting state repression for decades.

Sarah: *In 2010, Layne, Luce, and I, along with another member of the WPC, traveled to Puerto Rico with a delegation from Philadelphia to celebrate the release of Carlos Alberto Torres. Before his release, Torres was one of two remaining political prisoners out of a group of Puerto Rican* independentistas *who were arrested during the early 1980s and accused of being members of the Fuerzas Armadas de Liberación Nacional (FALN). While a highly successful campaign resulted in Bill Clinton commuting the sentences of eleven FALN prisoners in 1999, Torres and* *his co-defendant Oscar López Rivera remained in prison. Torres' release after 30 years was an occasion of enormous celebration. His freedom, as well as the release of the 11 political prisoners in 1999, was the culmination of decades of work by the Puerto Rican independence movement and their allies. Part of their success lay in building a campaign that worked on multiple fronts, from gaining the support of Nobel Laureates and religious and political leaders,[39] to staging protests and acts of civil disobedience, to building alternative institutions like clinics and schools where the history of anti-colonial resistance could be taught.[40]*

We felt incredibly lucky to be invited to participate in Torres' homecoming. At the time, Luce was still facing two felony charges, and we thought it would be fitting for us to celebrate the release of a political prisoner before she might herself become one. It was an amazing opportunity to learn from a successful 30-year campaign as well as to talk about the upcoming RNC 8 trial. But what we got from our time in Puerto Rico, more than any specific strategy lessons, was the inspiration that came from being with so many people who have fought for their independence with ferocity and love and who were willing to extend their love and support to others in the struggle. And while Oscar López Rivera remains in prison, we continue to fight for his release.[41]

On our last night in Puerto Rico we were eating dinner with two independentistas who had worked for decades for the freedom of the political prisoners. As we were celebrating Carlos' release, and talking about the upcoming RNC 8 trial, one of them said to Luce, "If you go to prison, we'll be there in Minnesota to celebrate when you get out." This was the kind of cross-movement, inter-generational solidarity we had set out to build when we started working on the RNC 8 case, and it came about because we sought out the chance to work in solidarity with people across ideological and cultural divides.

CREATING THE CONTEXT FOR NONCOOPERATION

To SUCCESSFULLY RESIST counterinsurgency we need to develop a context that both demands and supports noncooperation with the state. At its most basic, noncooperation means refusing to give any information on movement activities to law enforcement, or to aid in their investigation and targeting of political movements. There are a few components that are necessary to actively support and build a culture of noncooperation. The first is education. We need to teach each other why noncooperation is so important, and what it looks like in practice. The second is figuring out how to support each other as we experience fear. And the third is developing relationships and movements that can be sustained over the long haul.

There are numerous ways that people choose to engage in noncooperation, ranging from declining to answer questions in police interviews to becoming fugitives to avoid criminal prosecution. The principle of noncooperation with law enforcement is crucial to maintaining political integrity. It has proven to be an extremely effective method of limiting the damage done by, and even incapacitating, investigations aimed at weakening radical movements. In particular, the principle of noncooperation and its effectiveness has shone in the history of resistance to grand juries. Examples of grand jury resistance abound, including in the Black liberation movement, earth and animal liberation movements, and anti-war and international solidarity movements, just to name a few.[42]

The Puerto Rican Independence Movement has an especially strong tradition of grand jury resistance. Puerto Rican activists and their supporters have faced numerous rounds of grand jury subpoenas, beginning in the 1930s, and reoccurring during high moments of struggle in the 1950s, 1970s, and 1980s, and most recently in 2007.[43] Generations of independence activists and their supporters have refused to cooperate with grand juries, even when they are jailed for contempt of court. This has limited the amount of information that the state has been able to gather about movement activities. And when faced with the realization that the threat of imprisonment was not enough to gain compliance, the government at times has even been forced to withdraw grand jury subpoenas.[44]

However, developing this kind of consistent noncooperation takes some serious work on our part. We can't just assume that people in our movements already know that they shouldn't talk to the FBI or testify before a grand jury, even if they recognize the state as an enemy. Sometimes people cooperate with law enforcement or talk to the cops because they believe they have "nothing to hide" or because they think they can "outsmart" them by only giving information that is assumed to be widely known or publicly available. But while we can't always know exactly what information the state has or how it will be used, we do know that data collection is a first and vital step in counterinsurgency efforts. Providing information to activists about the principles behind non-collaboration and how to respond when the state shows up at your door can help foster a movement that is able to withstand this kind of intervention.

Luce: *For a lot of younger people who became involved in anti-RNC organizing, EWOK! materials and events were what introduced them to this idea, and it played a big role in the fact that no one from Minneapolis turned informant during the RNC or its aftermath. In our work, we highlighted the destructive nature of cooperation with the state. We emphasized that our movements do not have the capacity to deal with the devastating effects of snitching and collaborating—the seeds of deep distrust, the grand jury subpoenas, the criminal indictments and prison sentences—and promoted the idea that we cannot afford to support people who collaborate.*

EWOK! did such a thorough job of saturating the south Minneapolis punk and anarchist scene with this information that it became somewhat routine for us to get calls when folks in town (or sometimes, in other states) were harassed by the FBI or subpoenaed to grand juries and wanted help finding legal support and getting the word out. In 2007, the FBI approached a kid who had been arrested for graffiti and asked him to infiltrate vegan potlucks looking for information on anti-RNC organizing because he "looked the part." Though he wasn't involved in political work, he knew he had the right to refuse. He had seen the EWOK! zine and, rather than help the feds, he contacted us with his story, even passing on the business cards and phone numbers of the FBI agents who had propositioned him. EWOK! was able to spin this into a number of local mainstream media stories, further expanding awareness of the state's use of informants and of the specific repressive efforts already underway.

Sarah: *Because many younger activists and organizers in Philadelphia were not experiencing direct state repression, there was a lack of consciousness about the possibility of state action against us. Wanting to use this moment of relative calm to help people prepare for the possibility of future repression, the Wild Poppies Collective put together a workshop designed to both teach about the legal aspects of grand jury resistance and also talk about the psychological aspects of dealing with counterinsurgency.*

For the grand jury portion of the workshop we brought in a radical lawyer, Soffiyah Elijah, who has represented political prisoners since the early 1980s and who was able to speak to participants about the specific ways that grand juries are used to gather information about movements.[45] She outlined some of the most effective strategies for resisting grand juries and dealing with the judicial system. Two former political prisoners, Laura Whitehorn[46] and Ricardo Jiménez,[47] helped facilitate the workshop and also led us in a discussion about the emotional aspects of dealing with imprisonment. We wanted to open up space for people to talk openly about fear, instead of just falling back on bravado or ego to get through scary situations. Bravado may look good in the streets, but can quickly fall apart once activists are facing interrogations or long prison sentences. However, building structures of support where we can sustain each other emotionally through difficult situations creates a much stronger foundation for noncooperation over the long term.

Whitehorn and Jiménez spoke not only about the details of their cases, but also of how they were able to cope emotionally with the intense situations they found themselves in after being arrested. By openly talking about the fears and challenges they faced during their arrests and their time in prison, these older activists opened up space for workshop participants to ask questions about how to face these fears head on. During the question and answer session, one younger activist asked Whitehorn how she had kept herself together emotionally in the days after her arrest in 1985, when she was being kept in isolation, unsure of what would happen to her or her comrades. Whitehorn responded that she had sung songs from her childhood to pass the time and help calm her nerves. This story left a lasting impression on me because it served as a reminder that we all have internal resources that we can use to make it through extremely stressful situations, but we need to be open to the fact that these resources may not come in the forms that we expect.

Fostering fear is a key part of the psychological dimension of counterinsurgency strategy. When people cooperate with police investigations, it is often because they are afraid of the consequences and don't truly believe that the movement will give them the support they need. Of course, people are responsible for their own actions, and the movement cannot afford to support those who decide to collaborate. But when so many people in the last decade have felt compelled to snitch, it must be because we as a movement are doing something wrong. We need to create more opportunities to talk about the psychological effects of state repression, and how we can successfully counteract them. Finding ways to support people who are in scary situations and also teach ourselves how to handle our fear is absolutely essential in building movements that can effectively and strategically respond to our current conditions. Learning to cope with fear does not mean simply showing bravado in the face of repression. Instead we must learn to create spaces that allow us to be vulnerable with each other and be honest about our weaknesses and apprehensions. Building this kind of support helps keep us true to our beliefs and vision even in the face of extreme consequences. It is not enough to believe in our cause; we must also learn to believe in each other.

The development of trust and support should be strong enough to stand the test of time. The Green Scare cases make the necessity of building long-lasting relationships within our movements very clear. In Operation Backfire, the authorities were able to flip a single person and send him around the country wearing a wire, to find his former comrades and get them to talk about the actions they had done together. Eventually, more than two-thirds of the Backfire defendants turned informant, which has created a snowball effect: the informants offered the state new leads in investigations that had gone cold years ago, meaning more and more people have been prosecuted and, in turn, many of them have snitched, producing even newer leads and cases.

One of the factors in the state's success was the passage of several years between the ELF actions and the arrests. There are two implications: First, it meant that people had grown complacent, believing that they were in the clear; having dropped their guard, they were vulnerable. The state's successful strategy in this instance speaks to the ever-present possibility of repression, and reminds us of the dangers of waning vigilance. The state is both patient and proactive, and repression doesn't stop just because a group is no longer active.

Second, the time lapse between the actions and the indictments in the Operation Backfire cases meant that many of the defendants were no longer active in radical environmental struggles and had stepped back from the movement as a whole. The minority of defendants who steadfastly refused to cooperate were people who had remained deeply involved in social justice movements, or who had retained strong personal relationships to people and communities that are committed to noncooperation. Most of the snitches in Green Scare cases have been people who no longer had a deep connection to any radical movement that would hold them accountable. Many defendants were facing multiple life sentences for actions they took as a part of a struggle that was no longer present in their daily lives. In this context, it's easy to see how an internal moral code alone wasn't enough to keep all of them from informing on each other.[48]

Ultimately, the responsibility for their actions rests on the shoulders of the snitches themselves, but the cooperating Green Scare defendants highlight weaknesses in our movements. We have to ask ourselves hard questions about whether or not we foster an environment that is both supportive and challenging, especially as people's politics, tactics, and the nature of the movement itself develop and change over time. We must build accountability with each other, because making choices to protect our movements in the face of serious consequences runs counter to the ways that we have been socialized to conceive of our self-interest. When the movement is weak, it can be difficult for people to realize that the decisions we make *do* have an impact on our collective future. Therefore, it is essential that we create relationships that are both supportive of personal and political growth *and* are able to deepen, grow, and maintain accountability over the long-term. There is no foolproof way to insulate ourselves from future risk, but we can give ourselves an advantage through thoughtful, constant nurturing of strong relationships and healthy communities.

REAL SECURITY CULTURE

WE NOW KNOW there were two paid informants and two undercover cops who had infiltrated the Welcoming Committee, as well as an activist from Texas who had already been flipped by the FBI but was only outed through his role in an RNC-related case.[49] There were also numerous informants used in the Green Scare cases. Some of them had been operating in radical communities for years and were flipped by the Feds,[50] but at least one was a paid infiltrator from the beginning.[51] Adhering to traditional security culture guidelines, such as never indulging in discussions about past illegal activity for nostalgia's sake or never engaging in clandestine activity with people who you couldn't vouch for, would have mitigated the damage done by some of these informants. But we believe that our movements need to be operating with a much broader conception of what keeps us safe and secure. Healthier group dynamics not only allow us to function better collectively, but also make it easier to spot those who are being intentionally disruptive.

While going through the recordings made by the informants in the RNC 8 case, it became clear that the comments that would be most damaging when played in court were not ones having to do with the actual protest planning. Instead, what seemed most useful for the prosecution were the multiple examples of macho posturing in which organizers were discussing actions that they clearly had no intention of, or capacity for, carrying out. Had the group actively discouraged this kind of talk, rather than tolerating or encouraging it, the state would have been stripped of the empty, inflammatory sound bites that constituted the backbone of their case.

Luce: *The Welcoming Committee's internal operation was highly dysfunctional, characterized by things like monopolies on information, grossly uneven workloads, and fraught interpersonal power dynamics. This situation made us especially vulnerable to infiltration and ill-equipped to deal with it. Most of the informants didn't fit in to the group socially or culturally, but rather than being domineering and provocative, they tended to sit on the sidelines, listening and asking questions and hiding behind the explanation that they were "inexperienced." In this way, they played on people's sympathies, and thus weren't held accountable for behaviors that really weren't okay, such as making incredibly sexist comments or refusing to contribute to the group's work.*

The FBI informant preyed on younger and less experienced people who felt that their work and opinions were not valued within the larger group. In big meetings, he was quiet and unassuming, while also at times being quite inquisitive. This made some people feel like he genuinely cared about what they thought and did. FBI recordings showed that as he gained those people's trust, he started to push conversations in dangerous directions, subtly needling and prodding people into posturing about criminal activity well beyond the scope of the organizing they were actually engaged in.

As the RNC unfolded and we realized who the informants were, it became clear that they were all people who had raised alarms for many of us over the course of their involvement and who, with a better internal process, we would have been able to kick out early on. Those of us who were particularly suspicious had taken steps to limit our contact with some of these individuals, protecting ourselves individually but failing to protect the group. And as the eight defendants pored over audio and video surveillance obtained through legal discovery, these suspicions were validated as it was apparent that the FBI informant in particular had behaved in ways that were unacceptable. Those who were closer to the informants had the chance to learn vital information about their lives and behaviors that they withheld from the larger group. Much of this information—what they were doing with their free time, how they appeared to make money, who they were getting close to—didn't necessarily appear suspicious on its face. But when pieced together with the intuitive reactions some of us had, it created an overall picture that clearly suggested these people were informants.

After the RNC was over and the informants had been discovered, I became aware of one particularly glaring example of the dangerous gap in our group communication. It came out that the FBI informant had failed to go through the vouching process that the rest of us completed in order to attend an important strategy meeting a few months prior to the convention.[52] Two different groups of people—a subcommittee he worked with, and the individuals handling registration for the conference—had attempted to get references and background information on him, and he evaded all of their inquiries. The subcommittee dropped the issue, figuring that the folks handling vouches would resolve it; and, in turn, the registrars let his failure to complete the process on their end slide because they figured his subcommittee wouldn't have let him in if he weren't vouched for. The two groups never talked to each other about this, though, and unbeknownst to everyone else, he was admitted to the session in violation of the security protocol we had agreed on. He was the only local informant present, as the protocol had successfully weeded out the others, and he secretly recorded the entire meeting, adding fodder to the prosecution's case against us down the line.

It's doubtful that we would ever have found definitive evidence against most of the infiltrators in the Welcoming Committee, but there was enough out there to justify a decision not to work with any of them. I believe we would have gotten to the point where we felt comfortable making a group decision to kick them out well before the RNC, and before much of the damage was done, if we had prioritized the work of building internal trust and respect and, essentially, of caring for each other.

It is significant that many informants who have been "outed" in the last several years have had reputations for highly problematic and even abusive behaviors. The most notorious of these cases is Brandon Darby, the Texas-based FBI informant mentioned above, who had a reputation for being violent, patriarchal, egotistical, dishonest, and aggressively disruptive. His position and abuse of power in post-Katrina New Orleans' Common Ground collective drove a lot of people, particularly women, out of the organization.[53] While Darby is perhaps an archetypal informant in exhibiting these traits, other recent informants have displayed a different—but still problematic—array of behaviors. Andrew Darst, the FBI informant in the Welcoming Committee, was extremely unreliable, emotionally manipulative, and dishonest. Chris Dugger and Marilyn Hedstrom, both also Welcoming Committee infiltrators, sat through months and months of meetings but refused to share in the collective workload in any measurable way; Dugger was also confronted for having made numerous explicitly sexist remarks but then not held to account for his failure to change.[54] And "CS Anna," the FBI informant used to entrap and convict Eric McDavid, was emotionally abusive, and constantly crossed boundaries and violated consent by pushing Eric and his codefendants to engage in highly risky, illegal activity.[55]

None of these are behaviors we should tolerate, whether someone is working with law enforcement or not. And perhaps if we took these issues more seriously, some of these informants wouldn't have been able to establish a foothold in radical organizing circles in the first place, while others might have been forced out later on.

Additionally, we need to examine the challenges that substance abuse and addiction pose to community safety. A striking example of this is the story of Jacob Ferguson, a former member of the ELF whose transformation into a paid government informant was the turning point in Operation Backfire. His long-standing heroin addiction was no secret amongst folks in Eugene, Oregon, where he lived. But he kept the depth of his substance abuse problems from some of the people he was working with on ELF actions, and those who *were* aware apparently declined to intervene. Hence, he was able to participate in highly risky, clandestine activity, and the people he worked with placed their freedom in his hands. Several years later, when an unlucky chain of events brought him into contact with law enforcement, his drug activities gave them a point of leverage and his intimate knowledge of ELF activity became his ticket out.[56] At numerous points along the way, the people around Ferguson made poor decisions by failing to treat his addiction seriously enough, and the result has been a devastating process of prosecution, snitching, and imprisonment. How best to deal with these issues is an open and complicated question, but the pattern of ignoring or minimizing the seriousness of addiction, or isolating it as a personal problem instead of a community concern, produces dangerous consequences.

REAL COMMUNITY SAFETY

As a movement, we need to build upon the idea that we don't just need to keep the cops out. We need to create models of genuine community safety and accountability that don't replicate either the macho posturing or the punitive discipline of the system we are trying to overturn. We must address conflict and trauma, combat systemic oppression and inequality, and establish systems to care for each other in times of hardship. Negative interpersonal dynamics and oppressive behaviors are serious problems that need to be dealt with in their own right, and also insofar as they leave us vulnerable to disruption by government forces.

While we believe that radical movements should be able to protect themselves and function outside of criminal legal apparatuses, we often lack the skills and the will to address conflict and abuse head-on. At the same time, many radicals, recognizing that cops are dangerous to the communities they police, are working to build alternative forms of justice and methods of harm reduction. There are organizations imagining and developing ways to create genuine community safety by building upon methods of handling conflict that have long existed in communities that haven't been able to rely on the police, as well as finding new ways of addressing various forms of violence.[57] Those of us struggling against overt forms of political repression would do well to learn from these movements. Our communities are often torn apart by abusive behaviors, sexual assault, and other forms of interpersonal violence, and these divisions are easily exploited by infiltrators. We become less vulnerable when we have methods in place to honestly address the conflict and violence that emerge as we are working, struggling, and living together.

Layne: *One of the things I got out of reflecting on my experiences organizing against state repression is the need to develop proactive, visionary movements that can not only withstand state intervention, but are also creating new ways of building organizations and communities. We started out trying to build support for the RNC 8 while they were facing protest-related legal charges, which was in many ways a pretty narrow and specific goal. But through doing that work we made connections with a lot of people who were approaching issues of state repression from a multitude of perspectives, from fighting for national liberation to developing models of transformative justice and envisioning a world without prisons or police. Each of these components has something extremely valuable to offer for fighting counterinsurgency. The trick is to figure out how to combine these elements into a comprehensive strategy that can not only withstand counterinsurgency tactics, but can also move us forward towards creating genuinely insurgent, revolutionary movements here in the United States.*

I think that ideas of transformative justice, of finding ways to actually deal with harm outside of the criminal "justice" system, are crucial to this project. Envisioning and enacting real alternatives to the dysfunctional, soul-destroying systems that people are subjected to under capitalism can give us some of the tools we need—in particular the ability to communicate about difficult issues and create systems of accountability to each other—that make our movements strong enough to withstand state repression and much more likely to resist infiltration.

Fighting oppression should be primary in our work, and not just a means to avoiding repression. Racism, sexism, homophobia, transphobia, classism, and ableism are not "side issues"; they exist both within and outside of our movements, and we cannot successfully fight the state while ignoring these realities. Indeed, what point would there be to toppling the state while leaving its mechanisms of oppression in place?

The more time that women, people of color, and queer and trans people must spend fighting for the space to be heard, respected and valued within the movement, the less time and energy we have available for fighting the state. Conversely, the more we find ways to struggle against systemic oppression, the more space is opened up for people to feel safe participating in the struggle. A vision of safety for everyone is inextricably tied up with our vision of liberation. In this context, safety does not mean that we will never experience trauma, but real "security culture" involves creating spaces where people feel comfortable participating and bringing their full selves to the work. It is essential that we work to build communities capable of supporting people as they take calculated political risks. The more we support each other and hold each other accountable, the better positioned we will be to channel our creativity and energy into taking risks that, while they may lead to repression, can move us towards the goal of revolutionary change. Creating supportive communities and safer spaces is not just an end in itself; it creates a context where we are able to fight for a world without oppression, even in the face of heightened attacks from the state.

CONCLUSION

WE DON'T MEAN to suggest that honesty, cooperation, and a good history lesson are all that's required to wage a successful revolution in the United States. However, we do believe that without a commitment to these things, victory will be impossible. And while we would have preferred not to spend two years engaged in a time-consuming and costly legal battle fighting trumped-up charges against the RNC 8, the lessons we learned were invaluable. Our connections to other struggles are deeper, our analysis is stronger, and we believe that the movements that we are a part of have grown as a result of these experiences.

In this chapter, we have proposed a proactive strategy for protecting our movements from counterinsurgency methods. We see the following as key components of that strategy: understanding both our history and our current context, valuing honesty across ideologies and rejecting false divisions, and committing to noncooperation and to fostering real security culture and community safety. This list is neither foolproof nor exhaustive, but we believe that it can take us at least part of the way towards turning moments of repression into opportunities for movement building.

While the devastating effect that repression can have should not be underestimated, we also believe that repression has the potential to act as a force-multiplier, expanding instead of curtailing the possibility for resistance. Of course, this is only true to the extent that we refuse to be daunted by increasingly high stakes. We might be afraid, but we should accept that fear will be a part of the process of building a world based on justice and love.

The function of counterinsurgency is to make us believe that the cost of resistance is always greater than the potential gains of fighting for liberation. But we can change the calculus. We can turn moments that are supposed to destabilize and drain our movements into moments that allow us to grow, become more expansive, learn our history and create new alliances. We can use these moments to educate our communities about how to fight repression, build strength in moments of fear, and tap into an amazingly rich and inspiring history of resistance. And these actions can move us from resisting repression to sowing the seeds of tomorrow's insurgencies.

NOTES

1   In 1956, FBI Director J. Edgar Hoover launched a domestic counterintelligence program known as COINTELPRO. COINTELPRO had a wide range of targets on the left, from the Communist Party-USA, Martin Luther King, and the Southern Christian Leadership Conference, to the Black Panther Party and the American Indian Movement. The expressed goal of COINTELPRO was to destroy targeted organizations by increasing divisiveness and causing intense interpersonal and political disagreements. The FBI did this in subtle ways by provoking feuds between activists and organizations, and when those tactics failed they resorted to force and coercion. The program targeted right-wing organizations like the Ku Klux Klan, too, but the nature of the FBI's approach to these groups was qualitatively different. See Ward Churchill and Jim Vander Wall, *Agents of Repression: The FBI's Secret Wars Against the Black Panther Party and the American Indian Movement* (Cambridge: South End Press, 2001) and Ward Churchill and Jim Vander Wall, *The COINTELPRO Papers: Documents from the FBI's Secret Wars Against Dissent in the United States* (Cambridge: South End Press, 2001).

2   Fred Hampton was a leader of the Chicago Black Panthers. On December 4th, 1969, he was murdered in his sleep by the Chicago Police Department. See Jeffrey Haas, *The Assassination of Fred Hampton: How the FBI and the Chicago Police Murdered a Black Panther* (Toronto: Lawrence Hill Books, 2009).

3   For more information on the RNC 8 case, see *Conspiracy to Riot in Furtherance of Terrorism: The Collective Autobiography of the RNC 8,* Leslie James Pickering, ed., (Arissa Media Group, 2011).

4   In 1985, the Philadelphia Police Department dropped a C-4 bomb on a house owned by the MOVE family, a Black liberation organization that advocated a "back-to-nature"

lifestyle. The bombing killed 11 of the inhabitants, including five children, and destroyed 60 nearby homes. Margot Harry, *Attention, MOVE! This is America* (Chicago: Banner Press, 1987).

5   A notable exception is the International Concerned Family and Friends of Mumia Abu-Jamal, a Philadelphia-based organization that is led by Pam Africa and advocates for the release of Mumia Abu-Jamal. For more information see: www.freemumia.com.

6   For example, the Black Panther Party was popularized on a national level through their campaign to free party founder Huey Newton. Also, in the 1970s the Puerto Rican independence movement in the U.S. was built at least in part through a successful campaign to free five Puerto Rican Nationalists, one of whom was imprisoned for attempting to assassinate President Truman in 1950, and four of whom had fired guns on the floor of Congress in 1954. See: David Hilliard and Lewis Cole, *This Side of Glory: The Autobiography of David Hilliard and the Story of the Black Panther Party* (Boston: Little, Brown and Company, 1993) and Dan Berger, "The Real Dragons: A Brief History of Political Militancy and Incarceration, 1960s to 2000s," *Let Freedom Ring: A Collection of Documents from the Movements to Free U.S. Political Prisoners*, ed. Matt Meyer. (Oakland: PM Press and Kersplebedeb, 2008), 15–19.

7   For those looking to learn more about this history, a great place to start is the documentary film *COINTELPRO 101*, directed by former political prisoner Claude Marks. It provides a broad outline of the effects of government repression against U.S.-based movements in the '60s and '70s. *COINTELPRO 101*. DVD. Directed by Claude Marks. (San Francisco, CA: The Freedom Archives, 2011).

8   Jericho Movement, "Prisoners," Jericho website, http://www.thejerichomovement.com, (accessed February 28, 2012).

9   The Minnehaha Free State was the work of a loose coalition of radical environmentalists, neighborhood organizers, and Native American activists who joined together in the summer of 1998 to stop the reroute of Highway 55 through park land, Native sites of spiritual and historic importance, and neighborhoods in South Minneapolis. To this end, for almost 16 months, they illegally occupied empty houses and park land in the middle of the planned reroute. On December 20, 1998, over 800 police officers raided the Free State, violently arresting over two dozen people. Another encampment was set up two days later and lasted through the following December. Ultimately, the reroute went through. See RNC Welcoming Committee, *The Struggle Is Our Inheritance: A History of Radical Minnesota* (2007), 71–75. Available for download at: http://zinelibrary.info.

10   The annual ISAG conference, a meeting of academics and corporate representatives, was met with two days of rowdy, unpermitted protests leading to over 100 arrests, a violent house raid, felony charges, and individual exclusion orders on released demonstrators. Individual exclusion orders bar specific named individuals from attending certain events or being in certain locations, where their presence would normally be a legal right protected by the U.S. Constitution. See RNC Welcoming Committee, *The Struggle Is Our Inheritance*, 82–83.

11   RNC Welcoming Committee, *The Struggle Is Our Inheritance*, 2.

12   In 1974, small farmers in Western Minnesota began working through civil channels to stop construction of a 453-mile transmission line that would cut through their farmland and produce devastating environmental and financial effects. When the permit was approved in 1977, a wave of both legal and illegal resistance began, including sabotage of construction infrastructure, human blockades, and, eventually, the toppling of 15 separate transmission towers in four years. (RNC Welcoming Committee, *The Struggle is Our Inheritance*, 41–49).

13   The "Green Scare" is a term used to describe state repression of the radical environmental and animal rights movements in the U.S. The term came into wide usage in 2005 after "Operation Backfire," one of the largest domestic terrorism investigations in U.S. history. Operation Backfire culminated that year in a nationwide, multi-agency sweep of raids and arrests of members of the Earth Liberation Front (ELF). The defendants in Green Scare cases have faced steeply disproportionate sentencing for the political nature of their crimes, as well as terrorism enhancements subjecting them to especially punitive conditions while incarcerated. See: Will Potter, "What is the 'Green Scare'?" Green is the New Red website, http://www.greenisthenewred.com, (accessed February 26, 2012).

14   Ramona Africa is a former political prisoner, member of the MOVE family, and the sole adult survivor of the 1985 Philadelphia Police bombing of a MOVE family house. (See 5).

15   Sara Jane Olson is a former political prisoner who was arrested in 1999, after 23 years living as a fugitive. She was indicted on charges relating to a 1975 bank robbery where a bystander was killed, and several attempted bombings, all committed by the Symbionese Liberation Army (SLA). In 2001, Olson took a plea agreement; she was released to St. Paul, MN, on parole in 2009. The SLA was a controversial armed revolutionary group based in California in the early '70s.

      Chuck Haga, "June 27, 1999: The life and times of Sara Jane Olson," *Minneapolis Star-Tribune*, March 21, 2008; Tim Harlow, "March 23: A return to prison, not St. Paul," *Minneapolis Star-Tribune*, March 23, 2008; John Bryan, *This Soldier Still at War* (Harcourt, Brace, Jovanovich, 1975).

16   Leslie James Pickering was a "Founder and Spokesperson for the North American Earth Liberation Front Press Office, serving with the organization from early 2000 until the summer of 2002. During this period the Press Office sustained two raids by the Federal Bureau of Investigation, the Bureau of Alcohol Tobacco and Firearms and local law enforcement agencies, responded to over a half dozen grand jury subpoenas, conducted public presentations, produced booklets, newspapers, magazines, and a video on the Earth Liberation Front and handled the public release of communiqués for dozens of the most vital Earth Liberation Front actions." Leslie James Pickering, http:// lesliejamespickering.com, (accessed July 15, 2012).

17   The USA PATRIOT Act, whose official title is "Uniting and Strengthening America by Providing Appropriate Tools Required to Intercept and Obstruct Terrorism," was passed in the fall of 2001 following the September 11th attacks on the World Trade Center and Pentagon. The act greatly enhances law enforcement's legal ability to conduct surveillance

and monitor activities of individuals and organizations within the U.S. It also includes a section that considerably broadens what activities can be prosecuted under terrorism statutes. In 2011, President Obama signed a four-year extension for key provisions of the PATRIOT Act. See American Civil Liberties Union, *Reform the Patriot Act,* ACLU website, http://www.aclu.org/reform-patriot-act, (accessed February 28, 2012); and American Civil Liberties Union, *How the USA PATRIOT Act redefines "Domestic Terrorism"* ACLU website, http://www.aclu.org/national-security/how-usa-patriot-act-redefines-domestic-terrorism, (accessed February 28, 2012).

18 Since that time, the state's case against the SF8 has unraveled. In 2009, charges against almost all the defendants were dramatically reduced or dropped. Only one defendant, Francisco Torres, remained—and he had all of his charges dismissed in August of 2011. This success comes in part from the broad base of mass support built by the SF8 and their allies, which included resolutions of support from the San Francisco Central Labor Council, the Berkeley City Council, and several San Francisco Supervisors. See: Committee for the Defense of Human Rights, *Cisco Cleared! Last of the Charges Dismissed,* Free the San Francisco 8 website, http://www.freethesf8.org, (accessed February 29, 2012).

19 The speaker was from the National Boricua Human Rights Network's Philly chapter. The National Boricua Human Rights Network is an organization that works towards the de-contamination, development, and return of the island of Vieques to its people; the release of the remaining Puerto Rican political prisoners; and an end to the continuing political repression and criminalization of progressive sectors of the Puerto Rican community. For more information see: http://boricuahumanrights.org/.

20 Marilyn Buck was a white anti-imperialist revolutionary and poet who spent a total of 29 years in prison for her actions in support of Black liberation movements and against U.S. imperialism. Perhaps most famously, she was accused of helping free Assata Shakur from prison. Buck was released from prison on July 15, 2010, and enjoyed 19 days of freedom before passing away from uterine cancer on August 3, 2010. An audio version of Marilyn Buck reading her poem "Wild Poppies" is available at http://www.freedomarchives.org/wildpoppies/wild_poppies_poem.html For more information see: Friends of Marilyn Buck, *Our Dear Sister and Comrade Marilyn Buck has Joined the Ancestors,* Friend of Marilyn Buck website, http://www.marilynbuck.com, (accessed February 29, 2012).

21 "Racial Disparity Interactive Map," the Sentencing Project, http://www.sentencingpro-ject.org/map/map.cfm, (accessed March 3, 2012).

22 David Gilbert, *Love and Struggle* (Oakland: PM Press, 2012), 84.

23 Brian Glick, "War at Home: Covert action against U.S. activists and what we can do about it," (South End Press Pamphlet Series, 1999).

24 Michelle Alexander, *The New Jim Crow: Mass Incarceration in the Age of Colorblindness* (New York: The New Press, 2010), 5–12.

25 Alexander, *New Jim Crow*, 58–94.

26 "Prisoners at Supermax Ohio Penitentiary Begin Hunger Strike to Protest 17+ Year Solitary Confinement," *Democracy Now! The War and Peace Report,* New York, NY:

January 4, 2011. "Prisoner Advocate Elaine Brown on Georgia Prison Strike: 'Repression Breeds Resistance'," *Democracy Now! The War and Peace Report*, New York, NY: December 14, 2010. More information on Pelican Bay at http://prisonerhungerstrikesolidarity. wordpress.com/.

27 Learn more about Decarcerate PA at http://www.decarceratePA.info.

28 "Investigation Finds US Drones Strike Pakistan Every Four Days, Killing 775 Civilians Since 2004," *Democracy Now! The War and Peace Report*. New York, NY: August 15, 2011; "Let's Admit It: The US Is at War in Yemen, Too," *Wired Magazine*, Wired Magazine website, http://www.wired.com, (accessed June 17, 2012).

29 Stephen Lendman, "Police State America—A Look Back and Ahead," December 17, 2007, http://www.globalresearch.ca, (accessed February 28, 2012).

30 Center for Constitutional Rights, "Communications Management Units: The Federal Prison System's Experiment in Social Isolation," Center for Constitutional Rights website, http://ccrjustice.org, (accessed January 20, 2012); and Margot Williams and Alyson Hurt, "Population Of The Communications Management Units," National Public Radio, NPR website, September 29, 2011, http://www.npr.org.

31 In the year before the RNC, the Welcoming Committee held two national meetings to develop a protest strategy for the convention. The outcome was a pair of goals: to build capacity and crash the convention. The plan for disrupting the RNC was to use a variety of tactics to blockade main points of access to the site of the convention and prevent the RNC delegates from getting there. Different affinity groups and clusters from different areas of the country would "adopt" different segments of downtown St. Paul and blockade them in whatever way they saw fit. The plan was designed to allow for decentralized, autonomous direct action to happen in a coordinated fashion, making space for people to participate in a diverse but unified set of actions while opting for whatever tactics they were most comfortable with.

32 Patrick F. Gillham, "Securitizing America: Strategic Incapacitation and the Policing of Protest Since the 11 September 2001 Terrorist Attacks," *Sociology Compass* 5/7 (2011): 637.

33 All debates about the merits of pacifism and the moral weight of violence aside, we're unaware of any actual organized intent to create violent protest at summits and conventions in recent U.S. history. More often than not, the threat of "violence" some activists worry about is either entirely fabricated by law enforcement and the mainstream media, or else refers to vandalism and property destruction rather than any actual physical harm to people. See Sam Worley, "Fighting in the Streets," *The Chicago Reader*, February 23, 2012.

34 The Animal Liberation Front action under investigation had occurred in southern Iowa while Scott and Carrie were in high school in Minnesota, and the subpoenas were an outlandish attempt by the Assistant U.S. Attorney to close a long-open case. Both Scott and Carrie refused to testify before the grand jury, and were jailed for civil contempt in November of 2009. Two days later, Scott was indicted under the Animal Enterprise Terrorism Act. Carrie was held for four months before being released just as arbitrarily. In a string of highly abusive prosecutorial moves, Scott's indictment was amended several

times, before he was then indicted for an entirely unrelated fur farm raid in Minnesota. In September of 2010, he pled guilty to a single, reduced charge connected to that action, served six months in federal prison, and is now on probation. Scott and Carrie Support Committee, SCSC website, http://davenportgrandjury.wordpress.com, (accessed February 26, 2012).

35   This case comes on the heels of a recent Supreme Court ruling, *Holder v. the Humanitarian Law Project*, which held that activities such as referring lawyers, providing nonviolent conflict resolution training, and even donating food and blankets to humanitarian groups with alleged ties to designated "Foreign Terrorist Organizations" (FTOs), qualify as "material support for terrorism," a federal crime punishable by up to 15 years in prison. The federal government decides what groups to include on its list of FTOs with no real public oversight or recourse. For instance, the African National Congress was on the list as it fought Apartheid in South Africa; in fact, it wasn't removed until 1998. Michael Deutsch, "'Material support' for terrorism: FBI actions, grand jury subpoenas mark ominous expansion of law," *The Rag Blog*, November 16, 2010, http://theragblog.blogspot.com; and Jeremy Gantz, "Terrorist by Association," *In These Times*, December 13, 2010, http://www.inthesetimes.com.

36   The Freedom Road Socialist Organization describes itself as "a revolutionary socialist and Marxist-Leninist organization" whose members are very active "in labor, oppressed nationality, anti-war and anti-imperialist, and student movements." Freedom Road Socialist Organization, About FRSO, FRSO website, http://frso.org, accessed January 28, 2012. There are currently two groups operating under the name "Freedom Road Socialist Organization" as a result of an internal split in 1999. The group to which we refer in this article uses the website http://frso.org. For further documentation on this split, see "Public Statement on the Future of FRSO," http://frso.org, (June 1999), and "Statement on the Split," http://www.freedomroad.org (January 1, 2000).

37   On September 10th, 1999, eleven former members of the FALN (Fuerzas Armadas de Liberación Nacional, or Armed Forces of National Liberation) walked out of prison after spending between 14 and 19 years behind bars. The FALN was a U.S.-based Marxist guerrilla organization that was fighting for the independence of Puerto Rico. They claimed responsibility for over 100 armed actions within the United States in the 1970s and '80s, targeting symbols of U.S. military, police, and corporate power. By the early 1980s many of them had been arrested and charged with seditious conspiracy to overthrow the U.S. government. They received sentences ranging from 35 years to life in prison, and many of them never expected to leave prison at all. However, the independence movement refused to accept what amounted to life sentences for their political prisoners, and many Puerto Ricans and their allies worked for two decades to bring the prisoners home. After many years of hard work on the outside, and the steadfast non-collaboration of the prisoners themselves, the impossible happened: in his final days in office, President Bill Clinton commuted their sentences. A month later they were freed. See: Interfaith Prisoners of Conscience Project, "Proclaim Release: A Call to Conscience and Action for the Release of Puerto Rican Political Prisoners" in *Let Freedom Ring: A Collection of Documents from*

the Movements to Free U.S. Political Prisoners, ed. Matt Meyer. (Oakland: PM Press and Kersplebedeb, 2008), 322–34. And Jan Susler, "More Than 25 Years: Puerto Rican Political Prisoners" in *Let Freedom Ring: A Collection of Documents from the Movements to Free U.S. Political Prisoners*, ed. Matt Meyer. (Oakland: PM Press and Kersplebedeb, 2008), 356–58.

38   At first glance, it might seem contradictory for anarchists to become involved with and committed to a movement centered on a demand for nationhood. While we sometimes wrestle with the particulars of what it means to be involved in a national liberation struggle, we also see that at the core of anarchism is a belief in self-determination, and this belief is also at the core of anti-colonial struggles.

39   Interfaith Prisoners of Conscience Project, "Proclaim Release: A Call to Conscience and Action for the Release of Puerto Rican Political Prisoners" in *Let Freedom Ring: A Collection of Documents from the Movements to Free U.S. Political Prisoners*, ed. Matt Meyer. (Oakland: PM Press and Kersplebedeb, 2008), 322–34.

40   For more information about the alternative institutions that have been built in the Puerto Rican community by The Puerto Rican Cultural Center in the Humboldt Park neighborhood of Chicago, see: http://prcc-chgo.org/.

41   For more information about Oscar López Rivera, go to: http://boricuahumanrights.org/free-oscar-lopez-rivera/.

42   Grand Jury Resistance Project, "Recent Grand Juries" Grand Jury Resistance Project website, http://grandjuryresistance.org/resisting.html, (accessed March 12, 2012).

43   This legacy of resistance began in 1937, when Juan Antonio Corretjer spent a year in prison for refusing to provide the FBI key documents internal to the Puerto Rican Nationalist Party. Jan Susler, "Puerto Rican Independence Movement Under Attack in New York and San Juan," in *Let Freedom Ring: A Collection of Documents from the Movements to Free U.S. Political Prisoners*, ed. Matt Meyer. (Oakland: PM Press and Kersplebedeb, 2008), 359–62. and Grand Jury Resistance Project, "Recent Grand Juries" Grand Jury Resistance Project website, http://grandjuryresistance.org/recent.html#puertorican2, (accessed March 12, 2012).

44   "Recent Grand Juries" Grand Jury Resistance Project website, http://grandjuryresistance.org/recent.html, (accessed April 4, 2012).

45   J. Soffiyah Elijah currently serves as the Executive Director of the Correctional Association of New York, and was previously the Deputy Director of the Criminal Justice Institute at Harvard Law School. She was the attorney for former political prisoner Marilyn Buck, and has represented numerous other political prisoners and social activists. "J. Soffiyah Elijah," Criminal Justice Institute at Harvard Law School website, http://www.law.harvard.edu/academics/clinical/cji/staff/elijah.htm, (accessed April 4, 2012).

46   Laura Whitehorn is a white, anti-imperialist lesbian who was a member of Students for a Democratic Society, the Weather Underground, and the May 19th Communist Organization. She spent 14 years in prison as part of the Resistance Conspiracy case. She is an editor at *POZ*, a magazine for people affected by HIV, and has continued to organize in support of incarcerated people. See: Dan Berger, "The Real Dragons: A Brief

History of Political Militancy and Incarceration, 1960s to 2000s," in *Let Freedom Ring: A Collection of Documents from the Movements to Free U.S. Political Prisoners*, ed. Matt Meyer. (Oakland: PM Press and Kersplebedeb, 2008), 29–30.

47 Ricardo Jiménez was arrested in 1980 for his role in the Puerto Rican Independence movement. He spent almost twenty years in prison on charges of "seditious conspiracy" for his involvement with the FALN, and was one of eleven *independentistas* granted presidential clemency in 1999. Since then, he has been an educator, lecturer, and AIDS activist. See: Dan Berger, "The Real Dragons: A Brief History of Political Militancy and Incarceration, 1960s to 2000s," in *Let Freedom Ring: A Collection of Documents from the Movements to Free U.S. Political Prisoners*, ed. Matt Meyer. (Oakland: PM Press and Kersplebedeb, 2008), 18–21.

48 CrimethInc. Ex-workers' Collective, "Green Scared? Preliminary lessons of the Green Scare," *Rolling Thunder #5* (Spring 2008).

49 The RNC Welcoming Committee was infiltrated by one paid informant working for the FBI as well as one working for the Ramsey County Sheriff's Office, who then became an RCSO corrections officer midway through the investigation. There was another corrections officer who infiltrated the Welcoming Committee for only a brief span of time, as well as an undercover narcotics officer who stuck around through the end. Leslie James Pickering, ed., *Conspiracy to Riot in Furtherance of Terrorism: the Collective Autobiography of the RNC 8* (Arissa, 2011), 218–236.

  See also: Lisa Fithian, "Sexism, egos, and lies: Sometimes you wake up and it is not different," *The Rag Blog*, March 22, 2010, http://theragblog.blogspot.com.

50 North American Earth Liberation Prisoners Support Network, "Cooperating Plea Agreements and Related Court Documents," NA-ELPSN website, http://ecoprisoners. org, (accessed February 28, 2012).

51 Friends and Family of Eric McDavid, "Background," FFEM website, http://supporteric. org, (accessed February 28, 2012).

52 The vouching process meant that attendees to the strategy session were required to provide two known references within the activist community who could attest to their credibility and history with the movement.

53 Fithian, "Sexism, egos, and lies: Sometimes you wake up and it is not different."

54 Pickering, ed., *Conspiracy to Riot in Furtherance of Terrorism: the Collective Autobiography of the RNC 8.*

55 Friends and Family of Eric McDavid, "Background" and "Court Docs," FFEM website, http://supporteric.org, (accessed February 28, 2012); and Cosmo Garvin, "Conspiracy of Dunces," *Sacramento News and Review*, July 27, 2006, http://www.newsreview.com/ sacramento/conspiracy-of-dunce.

56 Vanessa Grigoriadis, "The Rise and Fall of the Eco-Radical Underground," *Rolling Stone Magazine*, August 10, 2006; and CrimethInc. Ex-workers' Collective, "Green Scared? Preliminary lessons of the Green Scare," *Rolling Thunder* #5 (Spring 2008).

57 There are numerous examples of organizations doing transformative justice work. Since 1997, the Audre Lorde Project's Safe Outside the System Collective has been working

to develop community-based anti-violence strategies. The group is led by lesbian, gay, bisexual, two-spirit, transgender, and gender non-conforming people of color and has launched a campaign to teach local businesses how to intervene in violent situations without calling the police. Learn more at: alp.org/community/sos. Philly Stands Up is another example of a group working to build the capacity of communities to address violence, developing transformative justice and community accountability models for responding to sexual assault. For more information, see: www.phillystandsup.wordpress.com.

CONTRIBUTORS

Lydia Bartholow is an educator, psychiatric mental health nurse practitioner, herbalist, writer, and organizer who focuses her practice on mental wellness and radical public health. She lives in Portland, Oregon, with too many animals, and often obsesses about the connections between public health, liberatory healing, and the prison industrial complex.

Chip Berlet, vicepresident of the Defending Dissent Foundation, has been researching, writing about, and organizing against political repression since the early 1970s. He worked as a paralegal investigator on several lawsuits against government surveillance and repression, analyzing over 100,000 pages of federal, state, and private spy files. Berlet authored "Surveillance Abuse" in the *Encyclopedia of Crime and Punishment* and "Encountering and Countering Political Repression" in *The Global Activists Manual;* he was a co-founder of *Police Misconduct and Civil Rights Law Report.* He served as vice president of the National Lawyers Guild, co-chaired the Guild's Civil Liberties Committee, and co-coordinated the original Public Eye Network.

Geoffrey Boyce is a PhD candidate in the School of Geography and Development at the University of Arizona. He is a long time affiliate of the Tucson-based No More Deaths, and he researches and writes on immigration and Homeland Security-related issues.

Elaine Brown is the first and only woman to head the Black Panther Party. She is the author of *A Taste of Power* (Pantheon, 1992) and *The Condemnation of Little B* (Beacon Press, 2002). She is presently co-authoring *For Reasons of Race and Belief, The Trials of Jamil Al-Amin (H. Rap Brown)* with Karima Al-Amin (Lawrence Hill Books, 2014), and she is completing the non-fiction book *Melba and Al, A Story of Black Love in Jim Crow America* (Feminist

Press, 2014). She is the editor of *Messages to Our Brothers and Sisters on the Other Side of the Wall*, a collection of autobiographical essays by black prisoners in New Mexico, published by the New Mexico Department of African American Affairs (2007). And she has recorded two albums of original songs, one for Motown records, *Until We're Free*, and her 1969 album, *Seize the Time*, which includes "The Black Panther Party National Anthem" (*The Meeting*), re-released as a CD by Warner Bros. Elaine remains a social activist, and, among other things, is the Executive Director of the Michael Lewis Legal Defense Committee, supporting the case of Lewis ("Little B"), who, convicted and imprisoned at 13 years old for a murder he did not commit, is still incarcerated after nearly 16 years.

Conor Cash is a PhD student at the School of Geography and Development at the University of Arizona, and thinks that the police are the biggest social problem in the world.

George Ciccariello-Maher teaches political theory from below at Drexel University in Philadelphia. His work has previously appeared in *Theory & Event*, *Historical Materialism*, *Monthly Review*, *Journal of Black Studies*, *Qui Parle*, and *Radical Philosophy Review*, among others, as well as a number of edited volumes. He is the author of *We Created Chávez: A People's History of the Venezuelan Revolution* (Duke, 2013), and is currently completing a book-length project entitled *Decolonizing Dialectics*. George can be reached at gjcm@drexel.edu.

Beriah Empie is engaged in work that focuses on white supremacy, the prison industrial complex, and the intersections thereof. He removed boredom from his life by surrounding himself with high school students, and lives with his incredible partner in Portland, Oregon.

Jenny Esquivel has worked with Sacramento Prisoner Support since 2006. She has gone on tour multiple times speaking about Eric McDavid's case, entrapment, and political prisoners. She is a co-author of the book *Government Repression, Prisoner Support* (P&L Press, 2012).

Luce Guillén-Givens was one of the "RNC 8" defendants; all charges against her were dropped in September 2010. She has been involved in a variety of radical projects, working on issues including prisoner and legal support; border, immigration, labor, and anti-war organizing; and several radical community spaces in the Twin Cities.

Walidah Imarisha is a writer, organizer, educator, and performance poet.

She was one of the founders and first editor of *AWOL Magazine*, a political hip-hop publication, and she served on the editorial collective for *Left Turn Magazine*. She teaches in the Portland State University's Black Studies Department.

Fatima Insolación is an anarchist who lives in Tucson, Arizona.

Claude Marks is a former U.S. political prisoner and is the director of the Freedom Archives, as well as a lifelong activist.

Lara Messersmith-Glavin serves on the board of directors for the Institute for Anarchist Studies, as well as on the editorial collective of *Perspectives on Anarchist Theory*, the journal of the IAS. She is also a member of the Parasol Climate Collective. She is an educator and a writer.

Ricardo Levins Morales is a long-time labor and social justice activist and artist. He helps organizers integrate cultural creativity into their organizing practice. He works out of a studio/storefront in Minneapolis.

Layne Mullett and **Sarah Small** live in Philadelphia and are both members of the Wild Poppies Collective, a Philadelphia-based anti-imperialist group that works to end state repression and the prison industrial complex. They are currently working on a campaign to stop prison expansion in Pennsylvania.

Will Munger is a member of the *Life During Wartime* Editorial Collective and also helped to organize the Counter-Counterinsurgency Convergence in 2011. His recent research was supported by a grant from the Institute for Anarchist Studies.

Vicente L. Rafael is Professor of History at the University of Washington in Seattle. He is the author of several works on the cultural politics and history of the Philippines, including *Contracting Colonialism*, *White Love and other Events in Filipino History*, and *The Promise of the Foreign*, all published by Duke University Press.

Sasha Ross joined the editorial collective of the *Earth First! Journal* in 2009 and co-founded the EF! Newswire in 2010. He works with several organizations, including Bark and Global Justice for Animals and the Environment, while attending the European Graduate School. He is the editor of *Grabbing Back: Against the Global Land Grab* (forthcoming in 2014 from AK Press).

Stop the Injunctions Coalition (STIC) is a diverse group of organizations, families, and concerned community members who have joined together to fight gang injunctions in Oakland.

Evan Tucker has done support work for political prisoners and is a co-author of the book *Government Repression, Prisoner Support* (P & L Press, 2012).

Kevin Van Meter is a member of the Team Colors Collective and has just re-located to Minneapolis, Minnesota, to complete his doctorate in Geography. Van Meter, with Team Colors, co-edited the collection *Uses of a Whirlwind* (AK Press, 2010) and co-authored *Winds from below* (Team Colors / Eberhardt Press, 2010). Van Meter's collaborative and single-authored work has appeared in various radical publications.

Kristian Williams is a member of the Committee Against Political Repression, in Portland, Oregon. He is also the author of *Our Enemies in Blue: Police and Power in America* (Soft Skull, 2004; South End, 2007), *American Methods: Torture and the Logic of Domination* (South End, 2006), and *Hurt: Notes on Torture in a Modern Democracy* (Microcosm, 2012). In 2009 he received a grant from the Institute for Anarchist Studies to support his research on Oscar Wilde's anarchism.

INDEX

ABOUT AK PRESS

AK Press is one of the world's largest and most productive anarchist publishing houses. We're entirely worker-run and democratically managed. We operate without a corporate structure—no boss, no managers, no bullshit. We publish close to twenty books every year, and distribute thousands of other titles published by other like-minded independent presses from around the globe.

The Friends of AK program is a way that you can directly contribute to the continued existence of AK Press, and ensure that we're able to keep publishing great books just like this one! Friends pay $25 a month directly into our publishing account ($30 for Canada, $35 for international), and receive a copy of every book AK Press publishes for the duration of their membership! Friends also receive a discount on anything they order from our website or buy at a table: 50% on AK titles, and 20% on everything else. We've also added a new Friends of AK ebook program: $15 a month gets you an electronic copy of every book we publish for the duration of your membership. Combine it with a print subscription, too!

There's great stuff in the works—so sign up now to become a Friend of AK Press, and let the presses roll!

Email friendsofak@akpress.org for more info, or visit the Friends of AK Press website:
www.akpress.org/programs/friendsofak